INNER MONGOLIA

"THE CHINA FLYER"

KEA

IRAN

NEPAL

LANTAU

GOLDEN TRIANGLE

KUTCH

SOUTHERN THAILAND

GOA

KUMBH MELA

THE BACK of BEYOND

THE BACK
of BEYOND

Angel Falls
Venezuela

THE BACK
of BEYOND

Travels to the Wild Places
of the Earth

written and illustrated by
DAVID YEADON

HarperCollins*Publishers*

FIRST EDITION

LIBRARY OF CONGRESS CATALOG CARD NUMBER 90-55559

ISBN 0-06-016583-9

91 92 93 94 95 FG/MPC 10 9 8 7 6 5 4 3 2 1

for Richard Anderson and
Al Shackelford

—*whose early encouragement
made these adventures possible*

WORDS OF THANKS

Scores—actually hundreds—of individuals showed kindness, encouragement and support during my travels and many others contributed to the completion of this book. In particular I would like to thank:

All my guides: **Angelo, Tin and Pan, Khun, M'stafa, San** and many more who helped me through all the difficult times.

Ali, Abdulali, Ahmed, Fatima, Rahman, Saiid and all my other companions on that memorable if ill-fated Saharan journey.

Amanda and Joel who gave willingly of their time, energy, and love in Kathmandu.

Dick Anderson, President of Lands' End, who provided so much early support and enthusiasm for this project.

Antonio, the little boy in Costa Rica who nursed me back to sweet sanity with bananas, papayas, and Coca-Cola.

Audrey and Lisa whose constant cries of "what's next?" helped me leave the comforts of home in search of even wilder places.

Monica Beliveau-Tobey for all her affection and encouragement (and excellent copy-editing) throughout this long project.

The **Bog-Trotters** of the Pennine Way who taught me to tip-toe the tussocks with the best of them.

Breda from Eire whose bus-bound company for two long days in India made the journey delightfully tolerable.

Marion Campbell of Harris, Scotland, for her explanations of the art of tweed-weaving (and for my enduring yellow finger).

Larry Campbell for insisting I see the wonders of Costa Rica for myself.

Tom Cronin with WGBH of Boston, who gave me the opportunity to ramble on about Haiti and my travels for one of his many TV documentaries.

Sir Arthur Conan Doyle for the pleasures of his book "The Lost World" and for the dreams he made me dream (and **Charles Arkwright Gurnley** for making the dreams reality).

Dick Davies, the Welshman, who learnt his lessons of life through white-water adventures - and passed them on to me.

Dimitrios on Kea island, Greece, for teaching me the true spirit of island life and releasing my Zorba.

John Dixon of Northumberland, who showed me the secrets of the local sheepdog.

Ed Duffy. "King of Cashmere" and raconteur extraordinaire who made the whole Inner Mongolian journey possible (and **Yves and Barney,** our stoic companions).

Joe Foley Sr., Lisa Salerno and all the others for transferring a tattered manuscript into perfect galleys.

Annie Griffiths, the National Geographic photographer who made the Pennine Way adventure much more meaningful.

Stephanie Gunning of HarperCollins who, with gentleness and grace, made the deadlines bearable.

The **Haitian houngan and mamma** who allowed me to sit (and dance) through a night of voodoo, deep in the mountains.

Linda Halsey, of the Washington Post who has been a trusted source of support and encouragement throughout, along with **Renee and Casey.**

George Harrington, who taught me how not to wrestle, Cumberland-style.

Kirk Horton, in Bangkok, for his hospitality and his tolerance at my over-use of his jeep.

Doug Inkster, who took me on an odyssey of flight and helped me discover the wildest places of all.

The **Jain sadhu** in Bombay who explained so much in a single afternoon.

Aubelin Jolicoeur (alias Graham Greene's Petit Pierre) for his perceptions and perspicacity in Haiti.

Julio and his father Thomas for making the few months Anne and I spent on Gran Canaria one of the best times of our lives.

Mike Kaye who welcomed me as a guest to his Tortuga Lodge and **George,** my intrepid guide and fighter of turtle-thieves.

Khusrow in Tehran for guiding me during difficult times and to my friends in Rasht on the Caspian Sea who have all suffered so much in the recent earthquake.

The Maharaj of Jodhpur who entertained me regally during my stay in his city.

The Maharao of Bhuj who gave me new insights about western living.

Hector Macleod in Ullapool, Scotland, for encouraging me to explore the Outer Hebrides.

Mary MacDonald of Harris for her tales, tea, and homebaked shortbread.

Lea Macnally for his guile and guidance in the wilds of Torridon.

Charles McCarry of the National Geographic Magazine for his trust in me and his enthuiasm for the Pennine Way story.

Mike, the Australian, for a long night of learning on Hong Kong's Lantau island.

Richard Morse, owner of Haiti's Grand Hotel Oloffson, for many valuable insights of island life.

My **Mongolian hosts** who let me see the fullness of their lives in that great grassland emptiness.

To my late **Mother** who joined me in Torridon and made the whole journey magic.

Sue Noli of HarperCollins for the fun she had with the book jacket design.

The **officials** of Indian railroads and "special permit" officers who tolerated a true TET in their midst.

The nameless **Pineys** who helped me home safely from the depths of the New Jersey Pine Barrens.

Guillermo Santamaria for his tales of Costa Rica on a hot afternoon in San José.

Maria-Jao Santos and her two lovely daughters for making my brief stay in the Azores so memorable.

Al Shackelford of Lands' End for his careful editing of my "Time Out" pieces, and his humor (and his Morris Minor).

Tom Stephenson and the British Ramblers Association for helping make the Pennine Way and all those other long distance footpaths a reality.

The little saintly **tanka-painter** in Kathmandu with whom I should have spent much more time.

Mike Ventura, a fine photographer, who always gave much-needed encouragement during the dog-days.

And special thanks to:

Hugh Van Dusen, my HarperCollins editor and friend, who often wondered if this feckless wanderer would ever return from his wanderings to tell the tales (and when he did, entertained him royally in the house by the pond).

And finally - to my wife - **Anne**

(once again) for everything.

CONTENTS

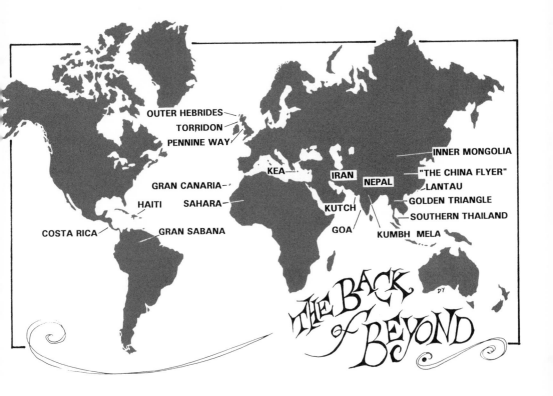

OUTER HEBRIDES
TORRIDON
PENNINE WAY
KEA
IRAN
NEPAL
INNER MONGOLIA
"THE CHINA FLYER"
LANTAU
GRAN CANARIA
GOLDEN TRIANGLE
HAITI
SAHARA
KUTCH
SOUTHERN THAILAND
COSTA RICA
GRAN SABANA
GOA
KUMBH MELA

THE BACK of BEYOND

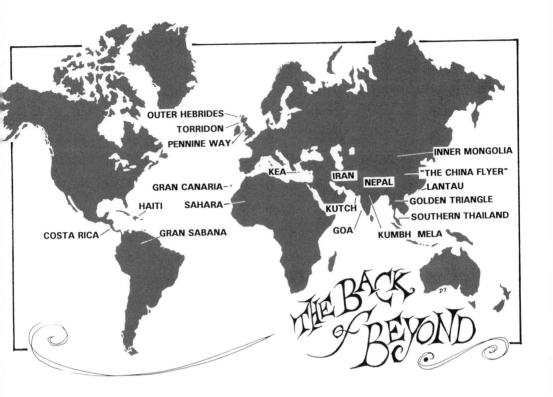

OUTER HEBRIDES
TORRIDON
PENNINE WAY
KEA
IRAN
NEPAL
INNER MONGOLIA
"THE CHINA FLYER"
LANTAU
GRAN CANARIA
GOLDEN TRIANGLE
SOUTHERN THAILAND
HAITI
SAHARA
KUTCH
COSTA RICA
GRAN SABANA
GOA
KUMBH MELA

THE BACK of BEYOND

INTRODUCTION
Adventures Far Too Close to Home

I was ready for my journey around the world.

Every item on the last of my lists had been checked off. Bags plump and polished in the corner of my studio. Even my jeans were pressed—a seemingly ridiculous refinement but it made my wife, Anne, feel better about my going off spouseless this time. "At least you'll look good when you start (tiny tears in the corners of her eyes). . . ." God—I hate leaving. And anyway I wasn't going yet. Three more days before those long sad hugs and last words. Three days to get the mood right. Three days to throw off the shackles and see things fresh again.

The mood had been wrong for far too many weeks. Checklists, bills, letters, tiresome waste-time phone calls, tying up all the loose ends—and more damned checklists. (Even lists of lists. That's crazy.) I measured my days in the number of check marks on my clipboard. (I'd even add stupid piddly items just for the pleasure of checking them off.) I hadn't even left yet and already I was loopy. My friends sensed it too. "For God's sake—go!" they said with various degrees of tact and understanding. They were right. But my mood wasn't.

Just take off for a few hours, I told myself one lovely sunny morning, two days before my flight to Venezuela. Do the old backroading bit—get the "on-the-road" again feel. Let things happen whatever way they will for a day. Get into the flow. (I talk to myself quite a bit. Sometimes I make sense.)

So I did. Off in the car one last time and out from the city on a serendipity jaunt—taking whatever roads appealed. Stopping whenever I felt like it. Chatting with anyone who looked interesting. Going with the flow and all that good stuff.

I found myself nibbling on the edge of the Pine Barrens, an enormous wasteland of sand, swamps, cranberry bogs, ponds, and pines that sprawls over a fifth of the state in southern New Jersey. I'd been there before, years ago in my early days as an "earth gypsy," and written a little on the history and the elusive "Piney people" who inhabit the deeper interior. To some, the Barrens are utter boredom. Mile after mile of javelin-straight highways through the gloom of conifer forests. Hardly anything to see. A brief flurry of activity at the Great Adventure park and then more endless woodland wastes until the Jersey shore resorts.

But to the more adventurous, this area has a special aura of the unknown. There is no silence quite like the silence of the Barrens. On a hot day when the wind dies, the pines stand motionless; ferns droop, ponds and lily-topped swamps lie still without ripples. Nothing moves in the wasteland. Sandy paths gleam bright white in patches and meander into the gloom of the forest. Even the flies—monstrous in size and appearance—retreat into the fissured bark of the pine trees. The aroma of resin hangs heavy. A snake sleeps in a comfortable coil shaded by a rock.

Those who take the time to wander the Barrens find a region bursting with history, legend, and strange tales of even stranger people who live deep in the recesses of the forest. There was once a Robin Hood of the Pines who plagued the region, stealing from the wealthy landowners and giving to the poor. Then there's the story of the "Jersey Devil," a cloven-hoofed enigma whose antics seem to be as varied as the individuals who claim to have seen it. A composite picture of the creature, which seems to spend most of its time in the Barrens region, includes features of a bat, kangaroo, horse, and serpent. Some claim it has a distinct appetite for human flesh, while others endow it with the gentle characteristics of an elderly philosopher whose favorite occupation is the discussion of ethics and politics with learned men of the state.

Tales abound of pirates, smuggling ventures up the Mullica River deep into the Pines, and, during Prohibition, illicit stills down sandy tracks visited by mobsters in long black Cadillacs. But perhaps most curious of all are the tales about the Pineys themselves, the hermitlike inhabitants of the Barrens, who have attracted disproportionate attention.

"The Pineys? I'd use that word careful in these parts if I was you." So I was warned by a bartender in a rundown roadside tavern near Batsto. "Folks don't take too kindly to being called Pineys by outsiders. Too many wrong things bin said about 'em. Too many clever 'fessors snoopin' 'round these woods. Should mind their own damn business."

It's true. Pineys is a much-maligned word for a maligned people who, over the generations, have developed a life-style of self-sufficiency in the forest—living off hunting and harvests from the cranberry bogs around Woodmansie and Possum Trot. Their ancestors may have been early colonists who abandoned the coastal plantations to seek greater personal freedom in the back country. Later they were joined by Tory renegades, deserters from the British army during the Revolution, and members of notorious "banditti" gangs who plagued the area during the 1800s. Other outcasts, criminals, and adventurers from the cities on the fringe of the Barrens gave the forest dwellers a reputation for licentiousness, indulgence, and illegal activities. Marriage was virtually unknown; inbreeding led to an unusual degree of feeblemindedness and Mongoloid characteristics among the young, and hunters brought back tales of abandoned revelries deep in the forest.

Even today, deep down in the narrow backroads, there are those who prefer the silence of the forest to the jingle-jangle world outside. They don't particularly welcome visitors and have a distinct aversion to snoopers, and any stranger using the expression "Piney" might just end up with a backside full of buckshot—or worse. "Best to leave them in peace," I'd been warned more than once.

Such tales of Pineys and bog monsters give these dark woods an overtone of mystery and dread. That day I came the feelings seemed unusually intense. Or maybe it was just me. Liberated at last from lists, I was ready for the joys of "randoming," the wonder of wild places, and the tantalizing tingle of tiny terrors, which gives my unstructured travels the edge that I crave. While the Barrens offer abundant historical and other diversions, including a variety of swimming pools and parks, wineries, and even the restored bog-ore mining village of Batsto, I wasn't in the mood for structured experiences. I sought pure unchecked serendipity.

Somewhere, deep in, I left the main highway. A white sand backroad curled off by an abandoned Baptist church buckling by the roadside. There was no direction sign but it looked an inviting detour. Shafts of sunlight sparkled on the track. Beyond I could see a stream and a small bridge. I'll try it for a mile or two, I thought. See where it goes. If it dead-ends, I'll backtrack. The tingle tingled and my spine loved it.

The first few miles were delightful. The car sped along on the sand. The white surface was dappled with light and moving shadows from the trees. On either side the pine forest grew darker and darker. It had that true backroad feel. I was in my element. I could sense the silly regimens of the daily grind slipping away and something inside soared. I was happy again, rejoicing in freedom—glad to begin the buzz again.

If I ever had doubts about the value and purpose of my life (and I did, often), moments like these removed all my guilt-laden cynicism and questions and reminded me that the decision I'd made years ago to abandon my career as a city planner and become a true earth gypsy all made perfect sense for me now.

I could be nothing else. I had one life to live (so far as I know) and this apparently was the way I was meant to lead it—seeking out the unusual, the unknown, the hidden, the forgotten, and sharing some of these secrets with others in sketches, photography, books—whatever.

I'd had to endure the usual "you're crazy," "you'll never do it," "you'll become a bum" (or more often, "you *are* a bum"), "you'll never make any money doing that," and the inevitable "what're you going to do when you grow up?" But recently, I didn't want to "grow up" and have never been particularly enamored of most of the trappings and trinkets—the materialistic "carrots"—of many Western societies. Life has always seemed too precious and too short to waste it collecting TV sets, cars, and property (even power)—doing things that you know deep down don't satisfy you, don't give you that fleeting but oh-so-invigorating sense of centeredness by responding to the real you (or yous) in you, and not worrying overmuch at the consequences. Just doing it because you know you should be doing it and couldn't really be doing anything else—and hoping that your spiritual overdrive knows where it's going even if you don't.

My car seemed to know exactly where it was going on that lovely warm afternoon, deep in the Barrens. It drove itself on these winding trails through the forest. I just sat there and breathed deeply in resin-scented breezes. I knew there'd be months of travel ahead—all over the world—new people, new experiences, new adventures, wherever I wanted to go. I was on a rolling high. Everything was in synch. This was the moment I'd wanted, I'd needed, before I left on my real journey. Me and life and the beauty of everything around me, all in total harmony. Great!

Damn!

I'm told these moments of truth are fleeting. Very necessary, very satisfying, but short-lived. Well, this one was practically stillborn. One moment I was soaring high as a hawk, gliding in the utter freedom of the moment. Next, the car was leaning at a crazy angle, stuck axle deep in a little black bog at the side of the track. I'd taken—correction—my car, in which I'd placed total trust, had taken one of the wriggles in the track too quickly, had skidded on the loose sand into this pernicious patch of swamp, hardly visible in the gloomy shadows. The driver's side was deep in goo. I peered out the side window and saw the mud bubbling like a slow-boiling cauldron. The passenger's side was still over sand and I managed to squirm out like a snail from its shell.

I had no idea where I was. I had no recall of how long I'd been in my little reverie, but I knew I'd driven miles and miles on that track, taking forks at will, becoming gleefully lost. Walking back to the main road would take hours (if I could ever find it), and it was already late afternoon.

Obviously I had to find a way of getting the car out of the swamp by myself. I'd been in similar situations before. I knew all the tricks—sliding something solid under the stuck wheel, letting the clutch in slow, getting a firm grip, and—zip— you're out. All desert travelers tell you about their experiences in soft sand and suchlike. They always seem to live to tell the tales— with appropriate authorial embellishments. And I felt as cocky as they. Couple of well-placed planks in the goo and I'd be off again.

Unfortunately, I hadn't brought any planks with me—or anything else of use for that matter. So I ambled off into the gloom to find dead pine branches to simulate my plank. Pretty soon I'd managed to shove quite a pile of debris under the offending rear wheel. Seemed nice and firm. Well done, son. (I allowed myself a little complacency.) This guy knows his sticky-situation stuff.

Back in the driver's seat like a snail in rapid reverse. A gentle roll of the engine, into first gear, gently release the clutch until you feel the grip of the wheel . . .

And glop!

The swamp sounded like a ravenous whale about to swallow me, clutch, trunk, and fender. Slurp, goo, and glop. Great lumps of mud flying everywhere and the back end suddenly sinking another foot into the swamp. Not at all the way the desert ramblers do it. A right regal cock-up.

Now I had to climb steeply upward out of the passenger's

side and jump down to solid earth. The front passenger-side wheel stuck a foot in the air. The mud was already over the tailpipe and part of the rear fender. I was well and truly stuck.

And, right on cue, the mosquitoes found me. It was now early evening; the light was getting dusky. And here was this sweet-blooded, muddied human just standing around chomping and cursing and making an ideal happy-hour snack. And did they snack. Far more aggressive than their Alaskan counterparts or the dreaded north woods terrors, buzzing, swooping, plunging their proboscises into every exposed inch of my flesh.

Obviously I would have to find the main road, twelve, maybe twenty, miles back. But I'd taken so many forks . . . and in all that distance I'd not seen any other vehicle or human being. Not even a shack. Nothing but sand, pines, and blood-mad mosquitoes.

The situation had lost all its romance. For the first time in a long long time I felt scared, stuck in the middle of this New Jersey wilderness, awaiting the wail of the dreaded Jersey Devil or, worse still, a visit from the Pineys themselves.

Their sinister reputation is not all myth. People vanish forever in these parts. Only a few weeks prior I'd read of a body discovered deep in the Barrens. It had been there for months and was in six distinct pieces, placed precisely around a fifteen-foot circle. (Have you noticed how your brain loves to bring back useless fragments of data at the worst possible moments?)

The silence deepened. Even the mosquitoes seemed to lose interest in me now (maybe fear gives off a special antimosquito vibration?). No breezes blew and the light was deep gloom, dead gray actually. I was reluctant to leave the car. I had no food or water. What I did have was an enormous forty-pound bag full of my camera lenses and all that professional traveler stuff I was not about to leave behind.

I unloaded as much as I could, locked all the doors, retied my boots, and prepared myself for a long hike. Then Anne suddenly came to mind. She would be worried. I thought of her looking anxiously out from our Philadelphia apartment window (from the twenty-seventh floor of our tower you could almost see the edge of the Pine Barrens, a mere twenty miles east of the city). She would be telling herself that everything was okay. I had to find a phone, I thought, and then managed a bit of a smile—I had to find myself first.

I set off at a good pace, back along the track that possessed none of its previous romance now. Odd rustlings came from the dark forest. Occasional grunts and throaty growls. I started to walk faster. Then something else. Like a growl but different. And getting louder. Way back, down the track near the car. Then flashes through the trees. Very faint at first like glowworms, but getting brighter.

A car, a truck, a real live human being? I could see the lights quite plainly now, flickering through the trees, and hear the welcome roar of an engine. Engines? Yes, definitely more than one engine. Wonderful! See, I admonished myself, all you need is a bit of luck and faith. After all you've always managed to get out of every scrape you've ever been in. Saved again by my guardian angel. Thank you!

I hurried back toward the car, lugging my bag of cameras. Yes, there were lights, lots of them. And they were stopped. Engines were roaring. I had a piece of old rope in the trunk. Bit of a pull and everything would be just fine again. I'd even be home in time for dinner. The cats would be so delighted to see me. Anne would listen enthralled to my tales and we'd drink champagne and have a good laugh. . . .

I could make out three bikes by the car—big Harley Davidson creatures with balloon-type tires for sand travel. People were moving around. Each of the bikes had large containers on the back with metal things sticking out. I came closer, half running, and then slowed down. The metal things sticking out were guns—enormous shotguns and rifles. Also shovels. And pickaxes. And the people didn't look right. In the bright beams from the bikes I could see long hair tied with bandannas, leather jackets trimmed with rivets and spikes, mud-caked jeans, and enormous laced boots with metal toe caps.

Hell's Angels? Or something worse?

"Hi!" I tried to sound nonchalant and cheerful.

No one replied. Not one of the three enormous men even looked at me. A young girl, also encased in black leather, stood off to the side, leg on the upturned wheel of my car. They were laughing. Nasty sly chuckles. One of the men was mumbling something low in a gravelly bass voice and they'd all sniggered again.

"Thought I'd never find anybody 'round here," I said (I could hear my voice rising and cracking).

Still no response. No acknowledgment that I even existed. Then one of the men turned slowly, the apparent leader of the bunch, and looked toward me but not at me. I traced his gaze. He was staring straight at my camera bag. I had so much equipment inside that I hadn't been able to close the zipper. My expensive Nikons with fancy lenses gleamed in the beams of their lights. He growled something to his companions and they all turned and stared at the bag and smiled some of the nastiest smiles I've ever seen. The girl gave a hissing giggle and I didn't like the sound at all. So this is how it happens, I thought (sometimes I wish my brain would just switch off), at night, stuck in the pines, helpless, with a pack of Pineys, armed, eyeballing a couple thousand dollars of easy pickings. And another hapless backroader vanishes forever.

"Can you help me get this thing out?" I asked. "I'm stuck." (Talk about the bleedin' obvious. . . .)

More gravelly sniggers. Still no one looked at me. Then one of the men slowly sauntered over to the car and rocked it. I could hear the bog gurgle. More chuckles. Then, as if they did this kind of thing all the time, two of the men moved to the rear, one moved to the front (the girl still giggling), a quick heave in which they lifted the whole damned machine (half a ton of mulchy muddy metal) and dropped it with a bounce back in the middle of the sand track. All in a second or two. Easy as cutting cake. I stood gaping.

"Thanks. Thanks a lot. Thank you . . ." I chuntered on. Now they all stood, arms in riveted belts and stared—this time right at me—with those sinister smirks.

"Get in." The largest man with the longest hair was speaking.

"Right. Right. I'll see if she's okay. There was plenty of mud around the tailpipe."

I squeezed between them (like passing through a granite wall) and slid into the driver's seat. She started! First go. Ah—

9

what a machine! "Thanks again. I'll just get her turned around and . . ."

"You'll never make it that way." The big one again. But I felt safer now inside my car with the doors locked from the inside.

"Oh, don't worry. I'll find it."

"Follow this guy." He pointed to one of his companions who was already mounting his bike and revving the engine. That girl was still watching and smirking. She really unnerved me. Like a bloodthirsty Madame Defarge with a front seat by the guillotine.

"We'll be right behind." They were already lining up their bikes.

"Where are we going?"

"Faster way out."

Oh yeah. Sure. Right to some broken-down shack in the darkest part of the pines. Bye-bye sweet life.

"Listen . . . ", I began.

"Let's go!"

They literally corralled my car forward, deeper and deeper down the track, which now rapidly became a rutted trail with more swampy patches. It was black. I needed full beams to avoid overhanging branches and rocks half hidden in the sand.

Pretty soon there was hardly any track at all, just snaky patches of flattened earth. How stupid could I be. Like the metaphoric lamb to the slaughter. They were still going fast, not giving me a chance to slow down and think. Then ahead was water, a stretch of shallow swamp. The lead bike spurred through. I skidded and swirled about but somehow made it. Branches were crashing against my windshield. Mud sprayed high on both sides. I couldn't see any signs of trail now.

Okay. Time for action, David, Rambo-style. These guys aren't ever going to let me out of this damned wilderness. At least make a break for it. Put your foot down, get ahead of the front guy and try to blast your own way out. They're going to get you anyway. At least I'll go down fighting. . . .

Waiting . . . waiting for a chance to break. The track is widening again. I can get past. I can see tire ruts ahead. Maybe I've got a real chance after all. . . .

Foot down, fist on horn, lights full beam, and we're off; the car leaps ahead like a leopard missing the front biker by inches, sand hissing on the chassis. A surge of pure beautiful speed, barreling down the track, the bike lights behind me now. Oh boy, I'm going to make it, I'm going to get out alive. . . .

Then the track ends. With no warning. I slam everything on, including the hand brake, and the machine spins in an explosion of flying pebbles and sand. This is it! I thought I'd won but now I've had it. . . .

An enormous eighteen-wheeler roars past, a couple of feet from my front fender. Three cars follow, flashing past in flurries of hot air. There are lights. A lot of them. It's a highway. A real hard-surface, macadam, fast-lane, beautiful, flat, straight, smooth highway. . . .

Someone knocks on my window. It's the big man with the longest hair. His bandanna is halfway down his eyes and he's as mad as hell. "What the mother-f...... hell do you think you're doing you crazy mother-f..... b...... you're out of your f..... mind, you stupid son-of-a-bitch!"

I couldn't think of anything to say or do except smile as nicely as I could. I was safe and that was enough.

The two other bikers strolled up and peered in—dirty, frazzled, old-young faces looking at me as if I'd gone wacko.

Then one of them gave that smile again.

"Bet you thought you'd never make it out."

I still couldn't speak. I just nodded like the crazy man they thought I was. The big man was still mother-f.....g away in the background and I could hear the girl giggling again.

"You're okay now. So—right here and it takes you straight into Philly."

And that was it. They were gone. Bikes revving like a hundred hornets' nests, lights disappearing down the track back into the forest, and then utter silence.

I got out of the car. I was smothered in sweat and my legs wouldn't hold me straight. I leaned against the hood. There were some stars out—beautiful bright stars. The breeze was cool. I put one foot on the hard road. It felt wonderful. Turn right and straight into Philly he said. So I did. And it did. (And much, much later that night I *did* enjoy an expensive bottle of champagne with Anne and the cats.) But I still prefer my adventures a bit further from home. This was altogether too close.

Some very wise writers have defined travel as "the exploration of inner space—the losing of the self in order to find oneself," "a pursuit of rootlessness," "the recurrent human desire to drop our lives and walk out of them," "to leave home where we impersonate ourselves and to become whomever we please." Paul Fussell wrote in *Abroad* about the travels of D. H. Lawrence: "What he really saw in other things and places was the infinite."

Travel indeed has many dimensions. The harassed executive has his needs—to be filled fully, urgently, and with flair, for a relatively short time. Singles often travel to search for the ultimate romance, away from the monotonous mundanity of the daily grind. Many seem to travel merely because it seems to be the way to use up accumulated vacation time. It is often a stress-filled experience (the planning, the schedules, the packing, the itinerary, the flight, the diarrhea, not to mention the inevitable lost travelers checks and absence of good home cooking). One wonders why most people put up with all the grief. Surely a gentle period of country walks close to home, fine dining in local restaurants, visiting nearby sights that would otherwise remain unvisited might be far more relaxing and rewarding.

For me, travel has become a way of life but not just because I happen to write about some of my journeys. The "professional" travel writer seems almost a contradiction in terms anyway. How can one get professional about something as potentially open-ended and intimately personal as travel—the ultimate exploration of self and all its possibilities?

I think I travel because I'm alive. And I don't mean that to sound glib. I mean that I really should be dead. A part of me still thinks that maybe I did die twenty-two years ago when I was an ambitious urban planner working with the Shah of Iran and his wife, the Empress Farah, on the future master plan for the city of Tehran, and that someone else (another me?) took over my body and mind and has been living here happily ever since.

It's a short story, but still a disconcerting one. Even as I write it now I feel the old tremor through my fingers.

Anne and I were high up in the Elburz Mountains of Iran. This dramatic range acts as a fourteen-thousand-foot wall separating the desert of Tehran and the south from the lush jungle hills bordering the Caspian Sea. We'd had a few lazy days of meandering, trying to learn a little more about this anomalous country and its long history. We were returning back over the mountains on the "old road," a narrow unpaved trail that promised more adventure than the carefully graded curves and tunnels of the new road a couple of hundred miles to the west. Everything was going fine. There was no traffic and we felt very much at peace among the peaks and high valleys.

We were descending a steep pass, the road curling and twisting through a broken stretch of country. Around a sharp bend we approached a one-lane bridge with no retaining wall on either side—just a vertical drop of three hundred feet or so into a shadowy ravine. A dramatic place. Then suddenly, with no warning, an enormous Mack truck came barreling across the bridge spewing rocks and dust. He, like us, assumed he had the road to himself and was trying to gain acceleration for the long climb up the pass. By this time we were actually on the bridge, which seemed hardly wide enough for one car, let alone two vehicles heading straight for each other. We realized he couldn't possibly brake without careening off the bridge. We also knew the same applied to us, and there wasn't time to stop anyway. But I did brake. I didn't know what else to do. And—like watching a slow motion film—we could see our car skidding sideways right toward the wall-less edge of the bridge and the ravine. We both closed our eyes and I remembered two silly things quite distinctly: A beautiful color of bright purple inside my closed eyelids, and feeling a strip of torn leather on the steering wheel and wondering why I'd never repaired it. We were still skidding; I could hear the gravel hissing under the sliding tires. We waited, eyes still closed, for the collision with the truck or for the fall into the ravine—or both. We were absolutely calm. No screams. Just acceptance.

What seemed like minutes later, but can only have been a

second or two, we opened our eyes to find ourselves moving slowly forward, down the center of the bridge. The car seemed to be driving itself. We pulled to a stop and looked behind us. There was no truck, no dust. We got out of the car and listened. There was no sound—no indication that the truck had ever been there at all. We were absolutely calm; no fear, no shaking, no aftereffects of shock. We just kept looking around and then looked at each other (we even looked over the bridge to see if the truck had tumbled into the ravine). Nothing.

We got back into the car and drove on. We didn't speak for a long time. Then Anne said: "That did happen, didn't it?" "It happened" was all I could think to say. Though what had actually happened we couldn't understand. All we knew was that something very strange had taken place, and we were still alive. And then we were weeping. Great big sobs. And then laughing and then very quiet for most of the journey back to Tehran.

Many people experience some climactic event that makes a radical change in their lives. Well, this was ours. We still don't know what happened; we don't know how we survived when it was obvious that we were going to die at least in one way if not two. And even now, having written it all down for the first time, I'm none the wiser. Wiser, that is, about the event itself. But we both became much wiser in other ways that completely transformed our lives.

We began to understand with greater clarity the fragility and wonder of life itself; we knew from that moment we would try to live our lives to the full, doing what we felt, deep down, we should be doing, no longer putting things off until we had accumulated enough capital or confidence or security to feel "free." We had found freedom on that bridge. We needed for nothing after that. Even though there were difficult years in material and other ways, we never had any real doubts about what we were doing with our lives. It didn't always make sense, particularly to others. But somehow that singular experience had bored a hole into our souls and certainty flowed out and just kept on flowing.

And we just floated with it as best we could. We found a deeply imbedded love for travel and the open road; we also found a need to give back something to the world (we both work with the blind in developing countries); and we found a need to be alive to life every day through creative endeavors (many of which make no economic sense whatsoever!).

Which brings me finally to this book, a culmination of fifteen years of travel and travel book writing. I've explored a good part of our earth in search of people and places that possess an essential integrity, truth, and centeredness—wild places, secret places, unspoiled nooks and crannies on the backroads, and people who seem to live life as fully as they are able—finding, as Joseph Campbell would say, their own "bliss."

I love travel with a passion, the good days and the bad. And I don't care to analyze the reasons too deeply—running to, running from, inner journeys, outer journeys, fear of commitments, fear of dying, fear of missing out on things—all of the above, or none. Who cares?

My travels are open-eyed experiences of the unknown, the child in the man still romping on from adventure to adventure; trying to learn, to understand, and to share the joys of "earth-gypsying."

May you enjoy all your journeys, too.

CARACAS

VENEZUELA

Canaima

Angel Falls

GUYANA

GRAN SABANA

COLUMBIA

0   100   200

BRAZIL

1. VENEZUELA'S GRAN SABANA

Journey to a Lost World

We'd made it!

The clouds, swirling like wraiths throughout our long climb up the five-thousand-foot-high vertical mountain, suddenly lifted. My two Indian guides hauled me the last few feet through the mud and mossy slime onto a slab of cold black rock. We were utterly exhausted. I had never felt so drained. The ascent had taken two long days, up from the gloom and tangle of the jungle, along slippery ledges hardly wide enough for a toehold, shinnying up wet clefts, and always cursing the constant mists that cut visibility to a few murky feet.

Many times I thought we'd reached the summit only to peer

through fleeting holes in the cloud and see the rock face rising up, endlessly.

I was convinced we'd never arrive but decided to keep going as long as my guides seemed optimistic. It was hard to tell what they thought. I had only the mountain to worry about. They, on the other hand, brought with them an ancient tribal inheritance plagued with terrible legends and fears of *curupuri*, the constant lurking spirit of the forest, and a dozen other demonic entities that kept most of their peers well away from these strange, pillarlike mountains—the mysterious *tepuis* of Venezuela's Gran Sabana.

But this truly was the summit. As the clouds melted, I could see a barren plateau of incised rocks stretching away into the sun. A cold wind tore across the wilderness, screaming and howling in the clefts. There were no trees. Spongy clumps of dripping moss clung to the more sheltered sides of broken strata. The rest of the summit was as arid as a stone desert of scattered black stumps, frost-shattered and worn into shapes like petrified figures.

I was shivering, dazed with fatigue, amazed by the bleakness of the landscape—and elated. After years of dreams and half-baked schemes, I was finally here. One of few, if any, white men ever to stand on this towering tepui in one of the remotest regions on earth, a true lost world, where you could see forever across an infinity of Amazonian jungle.

I blame it all on Sir Arthur Conan Doyle.

Way back in 1912 the world-reknowned creator of Sherlock Holmes released his new novel *The Lost World* to enthusiastic reviews. It was based on a tantalizing premise. Somewhere on the most remote northern edge of the Amazon Basin, an eccentric professor from England had discovered a primeval lost world of flat-topped sheer-sided mountains, thousands of feet high, soaring out of impenetrable jungle. He had seen evidence of prehistoric creatures, been attacked by pterodactyls and returned, after numerous misadventures, to proclaim the existence of land

17

where time had stood still, a bastion of ancient life forms long considered extinct.

Expecting adulation and fame from his discoveries he found himself instead ostracized by skeptical scientists and relegated to the ranks of crankishness. Sir Arthur begins his tale as the professor sets out with a group of fellow explorers to rediscover this lost world and return with tangible evidence that the earth is still a place of great mysteries and secrets. The journalist of his fictional story records the outset of the journey in prose designed to excite the imagination of his readers (and this reader in particular): "So tomorrow we disappear into the unknown. This may be our last word to those who are interested in our fate. I have no doubt that we are really on the eve of some of the most remarkable experiences."

I first read the book as a child and vowed to my ever-patient parents that one day I'd find this place and lead my own expedition to the top of one of those impossible mountains.

Years passed but the idea never faded. I learned that Sir Arthur had indeed traveled in the remotest parts of southern Venezuela and that these strange mountains, hundreds of eight-thousand-foot-high tepuis, did in fact exist on the fringes of the Amazonian basin.

So finally, I went to Venezuela to see them for myself.

Set high above the steamy coastal plain, Caracas overflows the edges of its mountain bowl, bathed in balmy springlike breezes. The temperature rarely exceeds eighty degrees here. The capital of Venezuela is a vigorous place, teeming with traffic on spaghetti strands of freeways, booming (until recently at least) with new oil-cash affluence. Scores of high white towers—real fat-cat architecture—rise above boulevards and formal parks.

On the green foothills, pantile-roofed minipalaces peep out at the city from behind pruned bushes and elaborate gardens. Lower down, hundreds of tiny houses—the ranchitos—cling together with Greek hilltown audacity on craggy cliffs. Venezuelans tend to dismiss these barrios with their tin roofs and lopsided walls as "places for the immigrants" (newcomers drawn to this progressive Latin American nation by its wealth and political stability). They point instead to the abundant riches of the city—proud European-style churches, an immaculate metro, theaters, world-class hotels, enough fine restaurants to keep a discerning epicure busy for a decade, and the material abundance of the Sabana Grande, a two-mile-long traffic-free shopping extravaganza with outdoor cafés and fountains and always filled with immaculately dressed citizens (the fashion consciousness here far exceeds that of New York's Fifth Avenue).

But I hadn't come for city life, no matter how seductive and cosmopolitan. My only concern were the tepui mountains of the far southeast. I was impatient to reach my lost world.

At least in that respect I had much in common with the early explorers of this vast country seeking their fountains of youth and their El Dorado fantasies. Venezuela is wrapped in fantasy. Even its name, which translates as "Little Venice," and is attributed to Alonso de Ojeda, who sailed along the coast in 1499, a year after the discovery of the country's Orinoco River by Columbus, evokes the romance of Indian coastal villages once built on stilts out in the shallow bays of the jungle-covered coast. It was only much later that settlers discovered the reality, and scale, of this wild and broken land with its towering ranges of snow-peaked mountains, deserts, vast plains teeming with wildlife, huge marshy deltas, immeasurable rain forests, fertile valleys—and the unique region of the tepuis.

But in those early days of true exploration, the dream was all. And what dreams! Filling the endless jungles not only in Venezuela but all the way down through Brazil and into Argentina. And the dreamers. What splendid lotus-eating adventurers they were, driven on for years and thousands of miles of deprivation, wasting whole armies in the process, carrying their dreams like glorious banners in their minds, tapping the depths of kingly coffers, and always singing the same refrain, "the next valley, the next mountain, the next time men . . ."

It all really began in the glorious Elizabethan age with a perfect combination of the avaricious Queen Elizabeth I and her power-infatuated courtiers and privateers, particularly Sir Walter Raleigh. Restless Raleigh first arrived at the mouth of the Orinoco in 1595, determined to find the golden city of El Dorado and the mythical "Mountains of Crystal" (he hoped for diamonds) in the southeast. He planned to return to England in his galleons,

GRAN SABANA TEPUIS
— Venezuela

bulging with precious metals and stones, to receive his rewards of power, wealth, and fame from the hand of his beloved Queen. His journal captures his enthusiasm: "Spaniards claim to have seen Manoa, the one they call El Dorado, a place whose magnificence, treasure and excellent location outshine any other in the world."

But alas for poor Sir Walter, royal patronage and patience ran out eventually as El Dorado proved more elusive than expected, and as a result of his excesses in South America, politicking and plundering, he found himself imprisoned "at the pleasure of the Queen" in the Tower of London and ultimately headless for his troubles.

His contemporary, the famous Spaniard de Berrio, sought endlessly for his own city of gold in the green hills of Amazonia, and dozens of other expeditions seeking everything from tribes of female warriors to lost youth-giving fountains, eventually floundered and fizzled out.

Much more recently the notorious explorer Col. Percy Fawcett gained worldwide fame for his Seven Cities expedition deep into the southern jungles. He was convinced he was on the trail of Plato's Lost City of Atlantis (although if you read Plato's admittedly vague geographical hints you may wonder why he chose such a dismal place when it is quite obvious—to me at least—that the Greek philosopher was referring to the Azores, way out in the mid-Atlantic between Portugal and the United States).

But there are still those who believe that Col. Fawcett found his destination. Newspapers carried wild speculations for years following his disappearance in 1925, fantasizing about his transformation into a king over untold Indian multitudes, basking in unbelievable riches, fathering whole tribes of light-skinned descendants. . . .

More recent reports however have suggested his rather messy and inauspicious demise at the hands of irate Indian skull bashers who resented the man's casual intrusion into their territory, certainly a more realistic assumption and not at all the stuff of which legends are made.

My only hope was that skull bashing was a thing of the past.

I had no desire to make this elusive lost world of the Venezuelan tepuis a lost world for me.

You could hear the excitement, even in the pilot's voice over the intercom: "The cloud cover is lifting. We should be able to see the mountains today. I shall be flying as close as possible to the Angel Falls. Please fasten your seat belts. It will be bumpy."

That was nothing new. The whole journey had been bumpy. Five hundred miles from Caracas in a small fifty-seat plane bouncing across the thermals thrown up by the dry red plains and brittle ridges below us. Then up through the clouds, into the blue, peering out of tiny windows, seeking signs of the tepuis.

But he was right about the clouds. We descended through thinning haze, and down below was the jungle. Mile after mile after mile of green sponge in every direction, with occasional flashes of serpentine rivers and streams meandering through this eternity of green.

Then the first tepui. A huge vertical shaft of dark strata cut by creamy clefts rising abruptly out of the jungle. Its profile seemed familiar at first. We edged closer to the towering rock face. A close encounter. Precisely that—*Close Encounters*. The Devil's Tower in Wyoming, that mystical volcanic monolith replicated by Richard Dreyfus in charcoal sketches, then mashed potatoes, then enough wet clay to fill his living room. But not one. A dozen of them here and much larger than the Devil's Tower, separated by scores of square miles of jungle, their flat barren tops, fractured and split, scraping the clouds; the last magnificent stumps of a vast plateau of sandstone and igneous rock, almost two billion years old.

Once a part of the great land mass of Gondwana, the plateau was a notable feature of the earth even before South America and Africa were separated by massive tectonic plate movements over two hundred million years ago. Subsequent cracking of the high plateau led to its gradual disintegration by erosion into individual flat-topped tepuis. Rather like the buttes of Arizona's Monument Valley transplanted into an Amazonian setting.

"Angel Falls approaching on the right."

And there it was. Tumbling in lacy sprays off the summit of

Auyantepuy, an uninterrupted drop of 3,212 feet, the tallest waterfall in the world, billowing in a crochet cascade, sheened by the afternoon sun.

There were more falls. Smaller but no less impressive, spuming off the black cracked top of the tepui and disappearing in a hundred streams far below in the unbroken jungle. And beyond, the hazy silhouettes of other tepuis, stretching out across the green infinity into the 1,500-mile-wide Amazonian basin itself.

Finally, after years of dreaming, I had arrived at the edge of Sir Arthur's lost world.

Base camp at Canaima was more than adequate. A cluster of chalets in a jungle clearing catering to the more adventurous tourists, anxious to catch a glimpse of tepui country and the roaring falls on the Carrao River. For most visitors this was the beginning and end of their journey, a lovely interlude of meals and cocktails on a shady terrace overlooking the falls, maybe a river excursion to the base of Angel Falls for the explorer types, and then back to the hectic hedonism of Caracas and the coastal resorts.

For me it was just the beginning, or at least I thought it was, but having bored several guests with my plans to travel deep into tepui country, I found myself no closer to leaving after three days of negotiation with local guides.

I had almost given up hope. Everyone seemed to consider climbing the outer tepuis to be a ridiculous idea anyway, especially for this rather overweight traveler who sweated like an ox at the first thwack of morning sun.

Then I met Charles Arkright Gurnley.

So often in adventures of this kind, something comes up that transforms an apparently hopeless situation. You need to keep your mind focused on your goal and to sidestep setbacks with agile optimism.

I was at the local airstrip, a hop, skip, and a bump down the rutted track from my cabin, exploring the possibilities of leaving Canaima early. There seemed little point hanging around only to be told "no" all the time. A few yards from the airline office was a ramshackle place that doubled as a café and souvenir stall selling hammocks, masks, blow pipes, all authentic stuff produced by the local Pémon Indians.

Mr. Gurnley suddenly appeared, a gaunt figure, tall and jangle-limbed, with thick-rimmed spectacles, neatly trimmed moustache and beard, balding head and jungle-stained shorts and shirt. He was hardly a Hemingway but there was something in the way he carried himself, erect, like one of those Buckingham Palace guardsmen, and with the same distant focus in his dark brown eyes.

We almost bumped into each other. I apologized and his focus shifted to the tip of my sun-scorched nose. He had a haughty, stiff-upper-lip glance, and my first impression was that of a Britisher, ex–public school (which in Brit-lingo means private fee-paying), almost a caricature of the type. His face was a smother of incised lines, and I couldn't tell if he was scowling or in pain, the kind of look you get when you take a bite out of a lemon (although why would anyone ever take a bite out of a lemon?). He reminded me of my old school headmaster—acetic, furrowed, stoic.

"My fault, my fault," he murmured, and then he smiled, and his smile was remarkably angelic, turning all the furrows into instant laugh lines. I liked him immediately.

"I'm trying to find a bit of shade," I said rather uselessly.

"Yes—it's hot today. Bit much for this early."

"You're British?"

"Yes. You are too?"

"Yes."

"Like it here?"

"I'd like it a lot better if I could find a way up into the tepuis."

"Beyond Auyantepuy?" he asked with an incredulous glint.

"Yes."

"They're difficult to climb y'know."

"You've been?"

"Oh yes. Once or twice."

"How do I get up them?"

He laughed and exposed a keyboard of ivory-white teeth.

"You ask me."

"You?"

"Well you could ask the boys here, but they won't be very interested."

"Why?"

"They don't like climbing."

"Why?" (I was feeling like a kid with his dad.)

"They don't trust it very much."

"Frightened?"

"Yes."

"Of what?"

"Aha!" Another toothy grin. "It's best you don't know."

"Seriously?"

"Oh it's all a lot of guff." But the way he spoke made me feel I wasn't getting to the whole truth.

"So how do I get up?"

He stopped smiling and looked at me, a little quizzically, with his head on one side.

"It's very difficult."

"You've told me that."

"Yes. Yes, I did." More piercing looks.

"So?"

"You really want to go?"

"Yes."

"Why?"

(You're always tempted to give the standard Edmund Hillary "because it's there" response, but I didn't.)

"Because I've never seen anywhere in the world like this place, and I don't want to leave."

"Yes, it can affect you that way."

"Do many people climb?"

"No."

"Can I do it?"

"Perhaps."

"So how do I go about doing it?"

Another long pause.

"Meet me here tomorrow. About nine A.M., after breakfast. I'll see what I can do."

"All right?"

"Right then."

And he was off, like a giraffe, stiff-backed and long-necked, with a final "Say nine-thirty! That'll be better for me."

"Okay."

A quick smile and he vanished.

I was back at our meeting place promptly the following day, but Mr. Gurnley wasn't. Instead I was met by two of the most unlikely looking Indians, solemn faced, slightly bowlegged, and very small. Both were wearing old torn shirts, grease-stained shorts, and broad straw hats that kept their faces in perpetual shade. One stepped forward and handed me a note. It was from Mr. Gurnley.

"I think you will find these two gentlemen adequate for your purposes. They are Pémon Indians. The taller one is named Tin, at least by me, and I call the other fellow Pan. (Their tribal names are unpronounceable.) Tin can speak some English. He will explain about the cost of their hire and the boat. I shall be away for a few days but hope to see you on your return. Bon voyage. CAG."

Tin and Pan! How could I refuse such a combination even though I was a little doubtful about their ability to lead me deep into the unknown. I had no choice anyway. We agreed terms, their terms, and I asked when they could be ready. They turned to each other and smiled. Tin held up a small canvas bag, Pan shrugged. Apparently they were ready right now. Well—so was I. The comforts of Canaima were beginning to pall.

The river is placid and oily-surfaced. The ripples made by our wooden dugout canoe or *curiara* powered by a modest outboard motor, hardly ripple at all; the water moves reluctantly in thick undulations toward the jungle shore. The sun hammers its surface into submission. Even at full acceleration (not particularly fast in our case, especially against the current) there's hardly a breeze to cool my pumping pores. I'm biting off lumps of limpid air and trying to swallow them, and trailing my hand in the river. It's as warm as a hot tub. Then I remove my hand remembering all those tales of subsurface creatures awaiting the unsuspecting novice—the giant Cayman alligator whose bite will snap off an arm fast as a die-cutter; the notorious anaconda, a huge river-dwelling boa said to reach fifty feet in length and more; the piranhas, with a hundred teeth of honed glass set in bulldog jaws, driven into communal frenzy by blood and capable of shredding a fifty-pound capybara to the skeleton in a few frantic minutes.

Worst of all is the candiru, like a bit of broken string, said to have a fondness for man's lower orifices, whence inserted, it spreads its body spikes into flesh to prevent extraction. A barbed arrow of destruction that blocks passages and bursts bowels and bladders with insidious ease. And overhead, the ever-watchful, ever-ravenous black vultures, circling silently, waiting vigilantly for rich pickings. All the jungle contradictions: peace disguising panic; order in the midst of chaos; horror hovering over the happiest of moments, mellowed by complacency. I keep my fingers to myself, gripping the side of the canoe.

The jungle eased by, a solid exuberant mass of green, edged in parasol-topped palms. Taken in small sections it was a senseless tangle of vines, dead limbs out of which soared new limbs, fallen trees still standing half straight in the gloom, fresh perky foliage striving for the sun, masses of dun-colored leaves, ferns, and palm fronds sinking back into the pulpy floor of the forest. Taken in larger sections, you could see the calm, changeless form and structure of the jungle, the striated tiers defined by the varied species of trees, ferns, and bushes, peaking in hundred-foot treetops where breezes made the branches frisky in the freedom of space and air and endless sunlight.

It was at once dull and full of endless variety. It tantalized with the partial transparency of its riveredge fringes and threatened with the impenetrable gloom a few yards in. It invited and repelled. Its scale was impossible to imagine. Hundreds of miles of the same stuff in every direction, an infinity of contradictions, a complete and separate living entity needing nothing save itself —discouraging all but the most cursory of explorations, keeping all its mysteries well hidden, safe in those endless sanctuaries.

And yet vulnerable—as the rape of the Brazilian Amazon is now showing us. An elephant being destroyed by a mouse. Easily decimated forever, leaving behind weak soils incapable of protracted cultivation. The "green hell" of white man's legend or the last true earth lung? A graveyard for the uninitiated, rife with malaria, yellow fever, beriberi, dysentery, or a lost world in need of safekeeping? A humid, fetid hot pot of mosquitoes, chigoes, jejenes that turns even the best-sprayed white torso into an overnight battleground of whelts, bites, and festering sores, or a place of magic and mystery where the body can learn to develop unimagined immunities, find salve in its natural medicines, and discover the secrets of the stars from its potent hallucinogens. A place to end terribly in the whirligig flailings of a Cayman's body, locked in locked jaws, being beaten to a pulp on river rocks as the alligator does its ritual somersaults of death in the muddy depths—or a place to touch the harmony of Gaia herself and sense the great slow rhythms of the earth, eternally beating, eternally steady, and, with our understanding and participation, eternally strong.

We wriggled on up the river, avoiding the stronger currents in the center, keeping to the calmer water near the bank. For such a small outboard motor, it seemed to be making a surprising amount of noise. Conversation was almost impossible. The sun was hammering in spite of the breeze made by our zigzagging movements; I found it hard to think, and my brain kept whirling off into half dream states.

My companions looked dreamy too, almost drugged.

The jungle is full of plants, barks, and fungi with hallucinogenic properties, much more powerful than the initially benevolent cocaine and those other concoctions found in the "designer drugs" of western cities. Someone back at Canaima had warned me about the pernicious *yopo*, which even the Indians use with great caution.

"You should see what happens when one of these little guys gets a nose job from one of his buddies," a young world wanderer told me in Canaima. "He sits down and his buddy pushes a yard-long bamboo tube up his nostril and blows in a load of this yellow powder and poof—he's gone in a flash. Throwing up, coughing, sneezing, spitting out black stuff, weaving about, shouting, moaning, prancing like a bird, and then charging around like a stuck pig. They can't stay still. They'll go on for hours. . . ."

My guides seemed reluctant to talk about yopo. They explained in hesitant English that only selected individuals were permitted to take the drug-induced journey to meet the tribes' "spirit-guides" and return with wisdom, insights, and even predictions for the benefit of their fellows.

"Very strong," said Tin.

"Very bad," said Pan.

Neither had ever tried yopo and neither seemed at all tempted by the possibility.

After two long days of relatively calm riding, the peat-brown river suddenly narrowed to swirling rapids, and our tiny canoe bounced like a bottle on the frothy current. The jungle closed in, tangled foliage on either bank almost meeting overhead. It was a forbidding stretch of angry water; I felt we were unwanted, like so much useless flotsam, enveloped in shadows, waiting for something unpleasant to happen, something to pounce, some disaster that would sweep us all away, unnoticed, irrelevant, in the great scale of the place.

Rocks rose up, black and pyramidal, topped with green mosses and forest slime. Pan had eyes for nothing but the river, watching every eddy, steering the boat with his long guitarist's fingers, avoiding the approaching calm sections, which slowly whirlpooled away into the shadows. We were drenched. The canoe was taking in water. Sometimes there were only a couple of inches between the sides of the craft and the snarling torrent. Tin scooped out the water with his hands. I helped, but it didn't seem to make much difference. One kamikaze wave, and we'd be as waterlogged as before. The noise was deafening, ferocious. The river would forgive nothing. One mistake and we'd be somersaulting back down the rapids, back into those rocks. I watched Pan's mouth. He was either chanting or talking to the river. His body was still except for that outstretched hand on the rudder; part of something that could end our lives in an eye-blink. He and the water were one, not exactly on friendly terms, but certainly role-matched. My fears turned to trusting admiration as I watched his eyes. I knew we would make it.

And we did. Half an hour or so later we were through the rapids and into a wider, calmer stream. The jungle pulled back and sparkled in the afternoon heat. The first trial was over and we eased toward a small rocky beach. Both men were smiling. I took Pan's hand and held it. I could have hugged him but the gesture may have been unfamiliar to him.

"Thank you," I said.

He squeezed my fingers, placed them on my stomach—and grinned a rare grin before leaping out and pulling the front of the canoe out of the water.

We'd chosen a lousy place to land. Not only was the bank collapsing and root-riven but if you put one foot wrong you were up to your thighs in a putrid black goo that stuck like molasses.

A few minutes later though I wished I was covered head-to-toe with the stuff. At least it would have been some protection against the unbelievable onslaught of mosquitoes and a million other blood-sucking bombardiers. They settled on every inch of exposed flesh and without so much as an exploratory jab, thrust their evil little proboscises into each available blood vessel, willy-nilly. For every dozen I smashed, two dozen more took their place, with ever-increasing frenzy. And what made me so mad was that, as I was thrashing and cursing through the under-growth, dear Tin and Pan were sauntering on, virtually naked and unmolested. The more I exhausted my vocabulary of exple-tives, the more they smiled and nodded benignly. I slapped, sprayed three different kinds of expensive repellent, leaped about, threw water over myself, even rubbed mud on my arms and neck. But they were utterly unassailable. Where the hell did they feed when I wasn't around? They must have been waiting for years for this precise moment!

Nowhere in the world have I been so plagued. My limbs were visibly swelling with scores of white lumps that began to itch immediately.

Some serious so-called explorer once advised: "Spread your spit around—and never—but never—scratch them." Spit! I didn't have a drop. My mouth was desert dry from all the jump-ing about, and how could I not scratch? The itching was driving me crazy and—the hell with it—I scratched.

In retrospect I suppose I can take comfort in the accounts of early explorers who faced similar torment. Here's Baron von Humbolt describing his travels up the Orinoco in 1802.

Persons who have not navigated the great rivers of equinoctial America can scarcely conceive how, at every instant, without intermission, you may be tormented by the insects of the air and how the multitude of these little animals may render vast regions almost uninhabitable. Whatever fortitude may be exercised to endure pain without complaint, whatever interest may be felt in the objects of scientific research, it is impossible not to be constantly disturbed by the mosquitoes, zancudos, jejenes, and tempraneros that cover the face and hands, pierce the clothes with their long needle-formed suckers, and getting into the mouth and nostrils, occasion coughing and sneezing whenever any attempt is made to speak in the open air. . . . At Esmeralda, to make use of an hyperbolical expression of the monks, "There are more mosquitoes than air."

The monks certainly got it right—"more mosquitoes than air"! And I admire Humbolt's measured prose against my maniacal protestations. Maybe he followed the Wordsworthian code of "emotion recollected in tranquility." My problem was that as soon as I began to write this section, I could feel that unbearable itching again, and the sense of hopelessness at my plight. Usually I can find at least a temporary solution to the most overwhelming of problems. But not in this godforsaken place.

And then there were the other irritating fears—the feeling that something alive may have got inside you—some evil little worm, or nasty little chigoe flea that lays eggs deep in the flesh of your arms or feet. You wonder at the utter vulnerability of the body with all its orifices and pores and soft skin and secret places that you'd never think of looking at back home. You fear becoming part of the slow jungle rhythm of growth and decay, filled with the seeds of imminent destruction and demise, your limbs mere repositories of uninvited life that one day will unexpectedly and painfully eat its way through those cozy inner passages and emerge as a ghastly slug or beetle or something larger with teeth and slime, threshing and gnashing, a horrific creature out of *The Thing* or *Alien*. Your body no longer seems the sacrosanct castle of the softer life, rather an apartment complex for free-loading tenants, an all too vulnerable victim of probers, nibblers, biters, burrowers, and borrowers of fleshly spaces.

That's what the jungle can do to you. Make a raving paranoiac out of a perfectly well-adjusted world wanderer.

For all the animal clamor of the jungle you don't actually get to see much. You know there are monkeys out there, their howling and screeching follows you as you climb higher through the sticky brush, but all I caught were shadowy glimpses and shaking branches where they had been seconds before. Parrots are less shy—but you expect exhibitionism from parrots.

Perhaps one of the most alarming occurrences was a casual aside by Tin in the morning after a particularly sweaty night. He pointed to a set of paw marks near our camp and said quietly, "*Tigre.*"

"Tiger! You gotta be joking!"

But apparently, *tigre* doesn't mean tiger. It's usually applied to the jaguar, black creature of the dark shadows, and other smaller members of the cat family that run free through the Venezuelan rain forests. The marks told an obvious story. The creature had come down during the night to drink at a nearby stream and possibly to wait for a prey or two. And there we lay, around our smoldering fire, fitfully sleeping, oblivious of the animal and its threatening presence a few feet away.

Sometimes I'd rather not know about these things. But then, at other times, I can sit transfixed as kingfishers flash like blue diamonds, skimming the surface of streams with their wings. And hummingbirds. No matter how many times I see them I am still entranced by their speed and the way they hover over blossoms, tiny wings beating invisibly, dipping their thin beaks into the soft hearts of each flower. Their colors change constantly like shot silk, and their eyes are big and black. Tiny two-inch-long birds, bee-humming their way through the promiscuous petals, never seeming to tire. How do they rest—and where? I've never seen one sleeping or even stilled. People in medieval Europe used to marvel at the devil bird, the swift, which was said to take brief naps on the wing and never landed (later to be found untrue). I get a similar feel with the hummingbird—there's something mystical in its constant movement. I'd feel a lot better if I could catch one nodding off.

And then there were the butterflies. What a paradise for the serious collector. Some as big as bats, others with harp-shaped wings, some mere shards of electric shimmer—scarlet, indigo, gold, silver-edged, vermillion—swirling like colored snowflakes, catching the shafts of sunlight, turning the dank jungle into a canvas of Klee colors. In moments such as these the ever-present mosquitoes were forgotten. Even Tin and Pan seemed moved as we passed pools where butterflies fluttered in the hundreds over the water and damp pebbles. And it took a lot to move these two.

In fact it was hard to tell what they were thinking while guiding this odd white man through territory that was once entirely their own.

I have no desire to add to all the diatribes and pious monographs about Western man's tendency to eliminate rather than assimilate. The latter requires empathy, a tolerance for entirely different perspectives on life; agreement to disagree without violence. The former is far easier and, during the early colonial days of emerging white domination, it was inevitable. The old phrase "One sneeze from the conquistador and a village dies" was so often true. Of course, for a while, there was something of a balance; the white man was no match for malaria, yellow fever, beriberi, and a dozen other fatal ailments until the discovery of immunity drugs. The Indians' resistance to such afflictions had grown over thousands of years, years of timelessness when change was unwelcome and the old ways tightly bound the forest-dwelling societies. But soon the balance was lost; the white invaders multiplied and the tribes disintegrated or were systematically destroyed by the newcomers. The remnants of once vast tribal cultures were offered "salvation by Jesus" as their ticket to the new world, along with hand-me-down clothes from well-intentioned charities and hand-me-down ideas that bore little or no relationship to the mega-century mysteries of their own indigenous cultures.

Occasionally I saw something sad and lost in Pan's eyes. He was possibly considered by the local missionaries to be a fine example of paternal assimilation, a pliable first- or second-generation unnative. But a glance at his face would suggest that the indoctrination had taken only shallow root and deeper down lay all the genetic and cultural structurings of his ancient society, the society of his forest-roaming ancestors. At least he was still in his habitat, unlike many of his counterparts, high in their Caracas hilltop barrios or ranchitos. He was free, or free enough, among the soaring tepuis, tolerating the novice antics of this strange man struggling to keep pace with him on these slimy slopes.

It was not hatred or even dislike I saw in his eyes. It was the wary glance of the jaguar, tinged with perhaps a little mirth, and ultimately, I suppose, indifference.

I wish I'd brought a hammock. They're cheap—especially the authentic Indian ones knotted out of coarse fiber and tough enough to hold a lolling hippo (not that I bear any immediate resemblance to same). My companions always had theirs handy, rolled tight and strapped around their waists. At regular intervals, once every couple of hours or so, we'd pause for a rest and out they'd come, a quick flick to unravel, tied onto a couple of handy trees, and voilà, an instant airy bed on which they lay diagonally, safe from scorpions and ants and snakes, while I dozed off half upright against a tree, my backside only partially protected from nipping predators by a rubber groundsheet. Next time—if there ever is a next time—I'll know better.

On the third day we woke to a world of gray. Utterly seamless slate gray—the sky, jungle, us. Even the riotous cacophony of howls, screeches, and whistles seemed subdued in the dun dawn. There was none of the normal wet heat of morning. I ate a breakfast of roasted plantains with hardly a bubble of sweat on my face, a most unusual and welcome occurrence. Tin and Pan looked cold. They huddled together like the Indians of the high Andes with hammocks and shirts pulled over their shoulders, sitting close to the fire. For the first time since we'd left Canaima my body felt comfortable. Of course it didn't last for long. By the time we'd packed up camp the sun had broken through in patches and the heat rose by the minute. But it was a pleasant

35

interlude, and I treasured its memory all through the grinding day.

Tin didn't seem to want to talk about the Pémon Indians' poison darts, blown from bamboo blowguns at speeds of up to 120 mph and amazingly accurate, even for the novice. He carried two guns with him and half a dozen arrows stuck in each tube. Each arrow was tapered to a needle-sharp point; the other end was encased in a cottonlike wad that protruded slightly from the blowing end, a sort of primitive packing, not too loose, not too tight, which acted as a flight pad for the blower's blast and kept the arrow centered down the bore of the tube. The outer casing of each blowgun was decorated in brown dye patterns and tightly woven bamboo strips. One looked like an ancient instrument, chipped, scratched, and darkened with years of use. "B'long father," Tin explained.

In a pouch he carried, a small leather calabash dark blue in color, was a thick gooey ball of curare paste. Instantly lethal to animal and human alike, it is produced in conditions of great secrecy from the pounded and roasted stems of two specific jungle creepers. All Tin would tell me was that his father made one of the most potent concoctions in the upper Orinoco region, and people from other tribes would travel great distances between the tepuis to barter for his tiny leather pouches. The weaker varieties merely disoriented the prey, leaving it vulnerable to clubs and knives for a few minutes. Tin's left nothing to chance.

We were by a stream one night. He had developed a liking for my Venezuelan cigars and took delight in sucking the pungent smoke deep into his lungs while I merely puffed and dispelled it like a first-time indulgee. It was cool (anything below eighty degrees in that jungle would justify that adjective), and the air was strangely still. Nothing moved; leaves of every size and shape drooped over the chuckling water—big rhubarby ferns, elephant ears, fat succulents, thin mean spindly leaves like stilettos, vivid purple explosions of shamrock-shaped leaves, high palms, and dense ground-clutching clusters of olive-green shoots. A melting pot of leafy variants, each one perfect in itself . . . but that's another long diversion.

Tin nudged me and pointed with his head to a large black

bird with a huge multicolored beak. A macaw! We heard them all the time and often saw them high against the sky like gliders. I never realized they were so big close up. With slow flowing movements Tin pulled the blowpipe from his waist belt and slid one of the curare-tipped arrows into the tube. At first I didn't realize what he was doing until the tube was at his mouth. The bird was motionless, unaware of our presence. He was going to kill it.

"Tin. No!"

He paused and looked at me.

I shook my head again. "No. Please don't."

On a couple of occasions I've been at the firing end of rifles and know the power you feel at that moment before squeezing the trigger. But this seemed too easy, too unnecessary. We didn't need meat; we were doing fine on fruit and the staples carried with us. Grilled macaw just didn't appeal anyway. Keeping the pipe at his lips, he picked a pebble from the earth and threw it at the stream. It splashed about two feet from the macaw, which turned, extended its wings, and flung itself frantically into the air.

Almost simultaneously, a huge brown frog that had been sitting on a rock not far from the macaw croaked in alarm and leaped for the stream.

A quick rush of air. The arrow sped out of the pipe like a silver bullet and, impaled in midleap, the frog turned gracefully and landed with a flatulent sound in the shallows. It never moved again. The stream eased past, shaking the arrow's cotton top. The frog must have died instantly, not just from the curare but from the amazing accuracy of the shot.

Tin turned to me and smiled. I couldn't believe what I'd seen. Much later that night the two of them introduced me to the finer points of the frog-barbecuing. I won't belabor the details but as a Yorkshire friend of mine used to say, "It weren't arf s'bad."

The next day was hard going through the jungle. My guides were way ahead of me as usual. Then Pan turned suddenly with a raised hand and beckoned. We peered together through the sticky gloom at the path ahead (path, of course, being a euphemism for the almost invisible indentations in the rampant foliage). At first I saw nothing unusual but, as my eyes focused, the whole jungle floor became a mass of movement, like a rippling green pond. Tens of thousands, who knows, maybe millions, of leaf fragments with neatly clipped edges were moving upright through the low ferns, each one carried by a tiny brown ant.

"The ants who carry the leaves," Tin explained.

"Leaf ants?"

He nodded and smiled. We watched the procession, like a New York harbor regatta of little green spinnakers tacking in unison. A magnificent display of precision, endlessly parading in front of us, with the participants totally oblivious of our intrusion. Once again that sensation of absolute order-in-chaos, finite patterns in the green infinity. A single-mindedness of purpose that at once amazed and alarmed.

What a shambles we humans seem to make of our pathetic efforts at coordinated action and social harmony. Ah, you say, but we are given the freedom of choice, liberation from pure unquestioning instinct. We find our higher meanings through trial and error, in freedom. True, to some extent, I suppose, certainly the error bit, but many of the great religions would have us believe that our ultimate destiny is a similar single-mindedness, a similar harmony of "living as one" in mutual tolerance and support. Transferring the great unifying concepts of God into our collective daily lives. Well, if these leaf ants have a god, he must be delighted by their unity. As for me, I'm still well and truly in the error stage of the trial and for the moment at least, that'll have to suffice. But thank you, little leaf ants, for your reminder of what we all could become one day (one day in the far, far distant future, I hope).

As we approached our isolated tepui, the view became more elusive. Occasionally it would rear up like a vast totem over the trees. But most times it was hidden behind jungle curtains or thick cloud cover with only its dark base exposed.

While climbing the lower flanks we lost sight of it altogether. The jungle closed in around us. Tin and Pan improvised a trail through the scratching palm scrub and dangling vines. We were ascending, so at least we were headed in the right direction. But the tepui gave us no clues. Having beckoned us from afar it now ignored us as we flailed around its muddy slopes.

Then we had our first real moment of contact. Tin was leading us up along a streambed full of tiny waterfalls and still, black pools. It was a wet, tiring slog with no rhythm to it at all—slime-coated rocks, unreliable handholds, and a couple of dousings. I was getting rather fed up with the whole idea of this journey until the jungle drew back, light tumbled into a clearing, and a filigree of waterfalls, like floating gossamer, rained down on us.

We looked up and there she was, all three thousand feet of her, rising straight into a clear evening sky. There seemed to be no way up. The walls were too sheer. It was a beautiful and very depressing sight. My legs decided they'd had enough and buckled. I just wanted to sleep.

Then the rock face vanished again, and the dainty waterfalls floated down out of thick clouds. Maybe it was better that we couldn't see the impossibility of the climb otherwise I might have given up and set off back to the camp. Tin and Pan seemed to have no such reactions. They claimed to have made the journey once before and only failed to reach the top because one of the two elderly Germans they were guiding broke his arm and had to be half carried back to the river.

Sometimes at night I wake in a cold sweat, remembering that climb. First of all I am not a mountaineer. Ropes and pitons and fancy claw-soled boots hold no appeal whatsoever. I'm a scrambler. Give me boulders and bits of root to cling to and I'll improvise a way to the top in no time. And, to be honest, most of the climb was precisely that. Edging and squeezing our way up deep clefts in the tepui, cursing the black mossy slime that seemed to coat everything—rocks, trees, bushes, and most of our bodies.

But there were three occasions when I thought my nerve would snap, and I'd have to admit ignominious defeat. I won't bother with the details except to mention that you've never experienced the essence of helplessness until you begin sliding slowly, horribly slowly, downhill on a slime-coated rock, with no handholds around and no way of stopping yourself, toward the edge of a thousand-foot drop into total oblivion. It was the slowness of it all that still sends tingles to my toes, and the absolute predictability of my fate. I'm still not exactly sure how I escaped except that by rolling slightly to my left I found a pocket of rock uncoated by the slime and used that as a brake. By the time my slide had stopped I could feel the updraught of air on the vertical side of the tepui rushing past my face. . . .

I decided not to dwell on the possibilities. If my confidence went, then the whole little expedition would have been a wasted effort. So I concentrated on the climb; one more cleft, a narrow ledge swirled in mist, then an easier stretch up a forty-five-degree incline, then a cleft again. On and on and on. I never knew that three thousand feet could seem so far. . . .

The summit was all I had hoped for and more—a barren black wilderness of worn rocks, as remote and bleak a landscape as you can imagine. Another world, another planet.

We floated in limbo. Above, nothing but blue in all directions; below, a cotton-ball landscape of low clouds, cutting out views of the jungle. And rising like fantasy castles in the distance, the great tepuis themselves, enormous islands in the sky, all flat topped, each one unique in bulk and profile, ancient keeps of ancient life forms, untouched and unexplored since the beginning of time. I thanked Sir Arthur Conan Doyle again for bringing me here, to the solitude and majesty of this amazing lost world.

According to my map, the summit of our tepui was roughly circular and only a couple of miles across from one rim to the other, a relatively modest island compared to many of the others we could see. I'd hoped to spend a couple of days up here but hadn't realized how cold it would be. In spite of the open skies and brilliant midday sun, it was hard to keep warm in the biting wind that screeched across the rocks.

Tin and Pan showed little interest in exploring. They found a small hollow behind one of the eroded pillars and, using their hammocks as blankets, huddled together, looking frozen and forlorn.

I was too excited to sit and told them I'd be back shortly

after a little alfresco exploring among the black clefts. They nodded glumly and huddled closer together.

Based on cursory studies of this virtually unexplored region, botanists estimate there may be as many as four thousand plant forms unique to these summits. No dinosaurs, no pterodactyls, no wild tribes of missing-link apemen such as Conan Doyle fantasized, but at least he was right in principle. The isolation of the tepuis has given us a living laboratory of hitherto unknown species.

At first I saw few signs of life anywhere. The clefts between the eroded pillars were damp, puddled, and bare. At one point I had to squeeze sideways to pass between the monoliths only to find myself peering straight down a deep fissure that seemed to have no bottom. A small stream trickled off a ledge and disappeared, doubtless reappearing as a lacy waterfall out of the side of the tepui hundreds of feet below. Here I found a rich little grouping of lichen and minisucculents and a cluster of brilliant red flowers, only an inch or so across, with yellow-edged petals. Although I've never taken much interest in botanical matters, the idea of being the first human ever to see a new plant species filled me with awe. And there were more. Fifty yards on from the murky pit I almost crushed a group of green and pink flycatchers, only a few inches high and coated with sticky residue on the uppermost leaves. An ant was stuck in the top of one of them, very dead, but apparently undigested by the plant. Obviously it had larger prey in mind and in a strange way that was reassuring. At least that meant I wasn't completely alone up here. And there were miniature orchids, tiny purple and lemon extravaganzas, nurtured by clumps of dark green moss.

Moving on deeper into the labyrinth I lost track of time. Carelessly I'd left my watch back in my rucksack with the guides and was so enamored with the possibility of being the first explorer of this unknown world that I'd failed to notice a change in the weather. It became much darker. The blue sky had been replaced by clouds, not the happy puffball variety, but that cloying mist again, wrapping its chilly tentacles around the tops of the black pillars and sinewing through the clefts.

I'd mentally registered a series of distinct rocky landmarks into the labyrinth, but suddenly it all seemed very different. I decided to go back to the starting point on the rim of the tepui and see how bad the cloud cover really was. The idea of having my explorations cut short by a bit of mist was ridiculous.

I found the flycatchers without any problem but couldn't see far enough ahead to the next reference point. Somewhere in the gloom was a protrusion shaped like an ape's head. At least that's what it looked like from the other side, but from here . . .

One cleft on my right seemed familiar so I edged my way between the rock walls for a hundred feet or so until it ended abruptly. There were enough handholds to scale the wall. Maybe I'd be able to see my starting point from the top.

Covered in moss and mud I eased myself up into a world of whirling mist and nothing else. I retreated into the cleft and back to the reassuring clump of flycatchers. Only they weren't my flycatchers. There were only three of them and they were the wrong color.

Okay. Hold on. No reason to panic. Just a slight error of orientation. If only I could find the ape's head. I can't be more than a hundred yards from the rim.

Then came the thunder. It began as a gentle stomach rumble way off among the tepuis, then headed straight for the labyrinth with ground-cracking fury, and climaxed in a shattering roar right over my head.

Enough! Time to panic.

I matched the thunder blow for blow. Between the booms I roared out the names of my guides into the mist. (Tin and Pan. How ridiculous can you get?) Nothing. Another boom. More name calling. Boom! Tin! Pan! More nothing.

I was angry with me, with my guides, with the thunder, with this stupid maze of rocks. I was so angry I almost stepped into the fissure with the little disappearing stream.

What a wonderful fissure! What a lovely little stream! Now at least I knew where I was.

The guides were just where I'd left them, fast asleep, oblivious of all the din and the cold mist swirling about them.

"Tin, where's my bag?"

I was a bit rough in waking him but was peeved he'd been peacefully dozing while I was losing my marbles in the labyrinth. He'd been using the bag as a cushion and handed it to me sheepishly. I decided not to tell him about my lousy sense of direction and fumbled instead for my watch. It was 2:00 P.M. We had five maybe six hours of light left. I wanted to stay on the summit but felt decidedly unwelcome now.

"Can we get back down to the trees in five hours?"

Two sleepy heads nodded enthusiastically. Their hammocks were rolled in seconds, stuffed into their bags, and they were ready. Eager. If it had been a cultural norm, I think they might even have kissed me.

One last look. The mist still swirling around the black rocks. So much to learn up here. So much to discover. These islands in the sky don't relinquish their secrets easily. The careless will be punished, and I'd been too careless by half already. I prayed for a safe descent and an uneventful return to the comforts of Canaima camp.

A soft bed, a decent meal, and a few cold beers with Charles Arkright Gurnley suddenly seemed very appealing. . . .

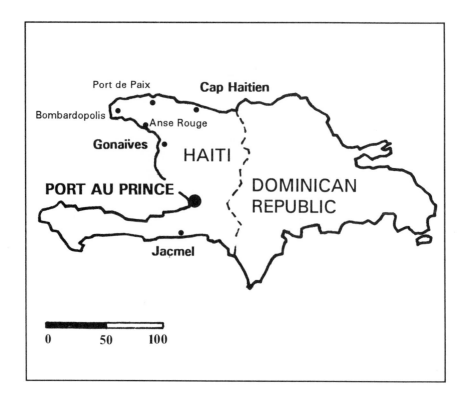

Port de Paix

Cap Haitien

Bombardopolis

Anse Rouge

Gonaïves

HAITI

PORT AU PRINCE

DOMINICAN
REPUBLIC

Jacmel

0   50   100

2. HAITI

"Behind the Mountains, There are Mountains"

It's Africa, Arizona, and the Caribbean all rolled into one.

I was way out on Haiti's wild northwest peninsula, a place unknown to most Haitians and, except for a brief visit by Columbus in 1492, rarely seen by whites (or as Haitians say in their Creole version of French, *blans*).

A high scrub desert of rolling hills, dry and parchment-colored, with occasional flurries of cacti, some almost tree height, clustered in gullies. To the north and east the land seems to go on forever, purpling with distance, receding into the evening haze.

Immediately below, the gentle undulations end abruptly as eroded cliffs and rain-gorged gashes which flatten into rocky

44

washes and then become a sudden oasis of palms and mangoes and bananas. The vegetation, so sparse on the high open slopes, is transformed into a tumult of greens and bronzes; clusters of bright fruit sparkle in the evening light; you can see the outline of every leaf defined in an orange halo. It's a Rousseau painting —an orgy of color and form, full of deep shadows, suggesting something almost too rich, too mysterious, to be real.

And then the tiny huts. African-style daub and wattle "kays" with palm thatch roofs and smooth mud walls, all a delicate peach shade in the setting sun. Smoke curls slowly from half a dozen fires. Little children, naked and black as lava, play among the trees at the edge of the clearing. A fat pig wallows in a sandy pit watched by a couple of scrawny brown goats. A dog barks for no reason, then rolls over and goes back to sleep.

A stream eases past the huts; two old women are washing clothes there with a slow rhythmic pounding on flat rocks while a young girl, naked from the waist up, gathers water in a large gourd shell. The stream flows on, hidden for a moment by palms and fruit trees and tight patchwork gardens of manioc and millet, then emerges in a small blue lagoon edged by more tall dry cliffs, and beyond those, the ocean itself, wide and shimmering.

There's a beach, pink-silver, and a pool of Caribbean turquoise-blue water before the reef, then a vast expanse of the richest purple-blue water I've ever seen anywhere. A color so deep, so intense, so translucent, it makes my eyes ache.

All this I see in a few seconds. The silent high desert, the hidden oasis, and the village and the ocean, stretching south six hundred miles to the coast of Columbia.

It certainly isn't what I thought Haiti would be like when I decided to come here a few days ago.

But then that's the problem with Haiti, a tiny nation, the world's first declared "Black Republic," tingling with contradictory images, plagued by vociferously opposed opinions about its nature and condition. AIDS, violence, political unrest, rampant poverty—you name it, Haiti's either got it or had it or very soon will, according to conventional wisdom. Haiti's horror stories are popular press fodder.

What amazes me, even after a few brief days on the Caribbean island of Hispaniola (Haiti occupies the western third; the

A VOODOO PERISTYLE
HAITI

rest belongs to the Dominican Republic), is the resilience and the *bamboche* (partying) vitality of the people themselves in the face of strident poverty and political uncertainty. I read an abbreviated history of this nation of 6.5 million people in Amy Willentz's book *The Rainy Season* and was left punch drunk at the tales of shattered dreams, conniving schemes, the duplicity of major world powers, the gory demise of most of its leaders, the terrible era of the Papa Doc and Baby Doc Duvalier dictatorships, and the chaos of its most recent series of takeovers by frustrated generals and their still-existent supporters, the Tontons Macoute (Papa Doc Duvalier's notorious secret police force).

My decision to explore this beautiful and battered little nation generated an unusual amount of ridicule.

"You're joking!" My friends were not at all supportive.

But I wasn't joking.

"Why not Jamaica, St. Barts, Saba—anywhere?!"

No. My mind was made up.

"You'd better not walk around after dark. And what about AIDS?"

I'd checked out the latter. Far less danger here than a ramble through Greenwich Village, and I had no intention of doing drugs or developing illicit relationships. As for all the walking at night guff, I do it everywhere I go and had no plans to change my habits now.

"You're crazy!"

True. Crazy for a Caribbean island that's not cheek-to-cheek tourists (both sets of cheeks), rum-punched to terminal catatonia and priced in the stratosphere for gullible "we'll take anything 'cause it's a vacation" visitors. How often do you read of "Real Caribbean" promises in the glossy brochures? In an age of mass migrating to "unspoiled beaches" I wanted truly unspoiled beaches, honest local culture, and a sense of adventure-travel well away from the pablumed pleasure pits.

So, Haiti it was to be. Poor, rejected, ridiculed Haiti? No—proud, resilient, untrammeled, inexpensive Haiti. Or, maybe something else . . .

The plane was half empty but, then, it was off-season. My fellow passengers were almost all Haitian, with a handful of New Jersey

Baptists off to some global gathering there, well stocked with guitars, songbooks, and bottles of purified water.

The mood was quietly festive. Many of the Haitians were returning home after years of diaspora during the chaotic era of Papa Doc and Baby Doc. "Things," they assured me, "are much better now. Not perfect—but much better." They were willing to trust Haiti again and give their homeland another chance.

I smiled. I suppose, in a way, I was doing the same thing. Ignoring all the negative imagery and giving Haiti a chance.

The images piled up fast.

For a country notorious for its poverty, I was amazed by the amount of traffic in the capital, Port-au-Prince. It took me an hour just to get through town and up to my hotel in the mountainside village of Pétionville. Enormous battered trucks piled high with green bananas competed for narrow road space with a public transport system made up of hundreds of gaily painted Nissan trucklets—the appropriately named "tap-taps"—crammed with passengers inside, on the roof, and dangling off the back. Mercedeses, BMWs, and Accords swooshed past, treating the road as their own private racetrack. (Auto prices here are triple U.S. prices but new dealerships open up all the time.) Mix all the traffic with impromptu street markets (everything from daily staples to concrete blocks and second-hand TVs to bamboo furniture and fried pork *grillots*, fried plantain *péses*, and fried blood sausage stands), free-roaming pigs, mangy dogs playing bite-a-truck, groups of neatly uniformed schoolchildren returning home along the muddy edge of the road, and gracefully gliding women carrying ridiculously large loads of laundry or plastic water containers or straw shopping baskets on their heads.

Mix all this with the ear-maiming racket of traffic horns, the din of the markets, the thump and clatter of tap-taps bouncing through the potholes, and the brayings of half mad donkeys (plus the heat, the molasses-thick fumes of trucks, burning charcoal, and stagnant mud pools) and you begin to understand how driving through Port-au-Prince can be one of the world's most exhausting experiences.

After the chaos, utter comfort. Almost like a dream. A burnished bronze evening, sun setting over the bay, and, far below my vantage point, the twinkling lights of the city. A purple-black night closing in over the mountain-bound valley; palms creaking in a warm breeze and the dry rattle of fronds over the two swimming pools. The chink of ice cubes in a glass of five-star Haitian rum.

"Y'know, this is such a beautiful country." The rheumy eyes of a middle-aged American businessman suddenly lit with fire. He slid a tanned hand with finely manicured nails across the table and squeezed my wrist.

"Been here fifteen years. I tell you, there's no place like it!"

Wonderful, I thought. Someone who knows the country. Most of the other guests at the hotel seemed to be fly-by-night, would-be Trumpies, gripping Naugahyde briefcases and mumbling to one another about sky-high-profit deals, great percentages, hot tips, and the latest inside info from "my guy at the ministry." I remember one little fragment of overheard conversation by the poolside bougainvillea bushes:

"Great workers, these Haitians. Six bucks a day."

"What time's the plant open?"

"On the nose, six-fifteen A.M."

"And they're there on time? I get the feeling time's not that important out here."

"Sure they're there on time. Gates are locked at six-thirty."

"What happens if they're late?"

The first man smiled at the naïveté of the question.

"They go back home. Lose a day's pay."

Silence and complacent grins.

"Yeah. Not much absenteeism here. Great workers."

Anyway. Back to my rheumy informant at the bar. I was ready with my list of questions about places to go.

"They say Jacmel is worth driving to. Over the mountains."

"Oh yes. Definitely."

"You've been recently?"

"Well I planned to go a couple of years ago but I had to fly to Chicago that week."

"What about Cap Haitien?"

"Yeah, great place."

"A lot to see there?"

"Hell of a lot. Hell of a lot. I'm going this summer. Sometime."

"You haven't been to Cap Haitien?"

"Road was pretty bad till last year. It's better now, though."

"So, where have you been? What have you really enjoyed?"

"Hell—the whole country's great. Everywhere you go."

"I'm thinking of driving up to Lake Saumâtre. I heard there are pink flamingoes."

"Lake what?"

"Saumâtre."

"Where's that?"

"About forty miles northeast of town."

"Oh yeah?"

"You haven't been there?"

"You sure that's the right name?"

"Yes—it's here on the map."

"Oh yeah. Well—it'll be great."

We sipped our cocktails silently. He was still glowing. The fifteen-year veteran of Haiti who hadn't been anywhere.

"No place like Haiti. I tell you—you're gonna love it."

Nobody at the hotel could tell me much about Lake Saumâtre but I decided to go anyway. Sort of break in slowly before the big adventure.

The drive back down the mountain the following day and through Port-au-Prince was as colorful and chaotic as before. But then, suddenly, it was all over. The city sank into its haze and I found myself slowly climbing cactus-studded slopes toward the Chaîne des Matheux mountains. Even the potholes were gone; the air was fresh and full of desert perfumes, the sky was a brilliant cloudless blue, and big yellow butterflies bobbed and bounced in the heat shimmers. Way out to the west I could see the misty outline of Ile de la Gonâve, once the bastion of an American marine proclaimed king of the island during the U.S. occupation of Haiti from 1915 to 1935.

As my journeys in Haiti continued, I became more accustomed to these sudden changes of mood. This little nation is full of such surprises and contradictions. Just when you're reaching

51

the point of total exasperation there's a sudden shift of atmosphere—it doesn't take much—the bright wide-eyed smile of a young mulatto girl; the offer of a banana or mango (with no follow-up request of "dollar blan"); a flush of flamboyants in full bloom; the wave and grin of an old man on a donkey, face as black as a silhouette; the soaring vistas of valleys and jungled ranges after a drive up impossible mountain roads. "Land of Contrasts" is a terribly overworked travel brochure cliché, but in Haiti it takes on fresh meaning.

My brief euphoria was soon replaced by bone-crunching reality as I turned off the main highway over the mountains to Mirebalais and floundered through mud pools on the road to Thomazeau. After ten miles or so I began to understand why my nontraveling businessman preferred the idea rather than the actuality of exploration in Haiti.

I passed through small villages of tiny houses painted bright turquoise and salmon pink, with intense little clusters of people and pigs and goats wearing strange wooden frames around their necks to stop them from entering doors or breaking through fences in their incessant search for the next snack.

I was tempted to turn back. The road had become little more than a mud and dust path playing hopscotch with an abandoned narrow-gauge railroad track, a remnant of the old days when this vast fertile valley was one huge sugar plantation. But occasional tantalizing flashes of sparkling water between the palms kept me going and going until, without any warning, the track ended in green salt marshes and I had arrived.

After all the banging and crashing over ruts, railway lines, and boulders, the silence buzzed in my ears. The air was limpid, and it was hot. Very hot.

I heard voices, chattering and singing. A path meandered through clumps of succulent bushes, and I followed it into a broad open meadow below a line of towering mountains and crags. The voices stopped. Ahead, scores of naked and half-naked women stood staring at me. The water of the lake glinted and rippled gently behind them. The ground was a patchwork quilt of sheets and clothes, sparkling like splashed paint in the afternoon sun. The women showed no sign of confusion or embarrassment. Their bodies glowed amber and they stood proudly, hands on hips, waiting for my next move. There were no other men about. I had obviously trespassed on their private laundering and bathing turf. I decided to withdraw as gracefully as I could, waving and mumbling inanities, until the bushes once more hid them from view.

I found the perfect private spot a little while later after skirting the marshes. Three large palms cast a pool of shade on clusters of pond apple and buttonwood and I sat down to enjoy the lake.

The challenge of reaching many of Haiti's most beautiful places doubles the reward of their beauty. Lake Saumâtre stretched out before me, purple-blue against the sage-green mountains enclosing the northern edge. Along the southern shore, rolling foothills rose slowly to the Massif de la Selle. Its surface was still now; the mountains were mirrored flawlessly. Way at the far end were the hills and ranges of the Dominican Republic, shimmering in the heat. At my end of the lake, only a few yards from where I sat, a tricolored heron stood stick still, gauging just the right moment to select his later afternoon tidbits. Two white egrets posed coyly on the back of a horse, let out to pasture on the salt marshes; grebe, teals, and terns flurried through the shallows, restless, lacking the grace and patience of the statuesque heron.

I'd heard the lake was a favorite haunt of Cayman crocodiles but today there was no sign of them.

But the pink flamingoes were there for me. Hundreds of them, scattered about in rosy clusters, heads down, endlessly scooping through the shallows. Only when alarmed would they raise their heads in orchestrated formation and walk slowly in single file on those ridiculously skinny legs, all their necks and bills pointing in the same direction, until they had selected a safer grazing place. They made no sound as the line of bodies passed me like a funeral procession.

They were comical and regal at the same time, mesmerizing in their measured movements. A delicate horizontal of pink and white against the purple lake and the soaring silver-gray crags.

From way in the distance the chatter and singing of the bathing women were carried toward me in soft waves by the breeze. Smoke from charcoal fires in the village, hidden behind a hazy line of bushes and palms, curlicued into the evening sky. Children laughing; three women gliding between the trees carrying bundles of clean laundry home on their heads to a tiny kays among mango and banana trees.

And the feeling that came so often to me in Haiti, when I saw the simple, enduring, self-sustaining rhythms of these secluded villages far from the clamor and flash point frenzy of the cities, was a feeling of wholeness and completeness. Ancient patterns. Still strong, still sound. Still Africa.

"You won't believe our history."

"I won't?" I was back in Port-au-Prince, sitting on the verandah of Haiti's most famous hostelry, The Grand Hotel Oloffson, talking to a thick-set, middle-aged Haitian who claimed to have once been "a pretty well-known opponent to the Jean-Claude Duvalier government." He introduced himself obliquely—"They call me Jacques"—so I left it at that. In the ghostly gingerbread fantasy of the Oloffson, mystery and intrigue seem appropriate. Graham Greene captured it perfectly in his book *The Comedians*: "It had the air at night of a Charles Addams house in a number of *The New Yorker*. You expected a witch to open the door to you or a maniac butler with a bat dangling from the chandelier behind him."

The hotel has recently been saved from terminal decay by Richard Morse, a descendant of President Sam (ruler of Haiti for five months in 1915), whose brother built the place around the turn of the century. Now it sits in all its restored Victorian glory on a rocky hill shaded by a junglelike profusion of royal palms, banana trees, and flowering magnolias. Suites named after Mick Jagger, Sir John Gielgud, Marlon Brando (one of the largest beds I've ever seen), and Graham Greene reflect its celebrated clientele, and you can still sense its reputation as a center for whispered rumor mongering and revolutionary intrigue.

"No—you won't believe this little country," Jacques continued. "You know how big we are? We're about...we got about six million people. M'be more now. They coming back again. They coming back because things got quieter a bit—not much— never gets real quiet in Haiti. Not for las' twenty years anyway.

"We had everyt'ing—massacre, revolutions, more revolutions, dictators, generals, civil wars—thirty-five rulers since we got free in 1804, and almost every one of them executed, blown up, assassinated or kicked out in revolutions. Ev'n the Americans took us over once for thirty years, till 1934! We had starvation, corruption like nobody's business, bankruptcy—I mean, the whole country's been bankrupt since I was a kid and longer —every time the top guy gets kicked out—if he's not dead—he takes all the cash he can grab. One guy—this minister—tried to carry off his own computer system—the whole thing, one hundred computers! Don't know why he bothered, they never worked!"

The mood at the Oloffson seems to encourage this kind of exchange. You feel safe here, even though you're only a mortar shot away from the enormous Presidential Palace. Couched in this pretty neighborhood of old delicate gingerbread mansions, you sense neutral territory. Rare for a city that has had its fill of *pèzé-sucé* ("squeeze and suck" tactics of governments, a popular phrase named after a frozen stick of sweet-flavored ice) and when *brigandes de vigilance* still patrol the slum *bidonvilles* of La Saline and Cité Carton, seeking out informers and the resilient remnants of Papa Doc's Tontons Macoute.

"It's a crazy place. We battled them all to get out of slavery and colonization—French, British, Dutch, Americans, Dominicans. Then when we beat 'em, we start in on ourselves—blacks against mulatto, poor against rich, bureaucrat against peasant, voodoo against priests, and now general against general. Jean Claude [Duvalier] even sold off thousands of our peasants as slaves to work sugar plantations over in the Dominican Republic. Most never came back. They died there."

Two rum cocktails arrived courtesy of Richard Morse. He's always hovering around with his baby-face smile, a lanky catalyst, making introductions, easing the exchange of whispered gossip, an indispensable resource for journalists, with his fingers deep in Haiti's multiflavored (and very sticky) pies.

"The Duvaliers were a mess," Jacques continued. "You wouldn't believe. But they held the country together for a while —terror, voodoo, torture, execution, massacre—old Papa Doc playing Black Baron Samedi, the voodoo loa of the graveyard.

'I'm an immaterial being,' he said, and they believed him. When we finally got 'em out we didn't know what would happen. There's been some nasty stuff but...I don't know, maybe it's coming together. May not seem like much of a free place to you but it's our freedom—and it's all we've got. And when you get that close to nothin', you give a lot to keep the bit you got...."

The recent film *The Serpent and the Rainbow* (a very free and spirited adaptation of the rather scholarly book of the same name by Wade Davis) began as follows:

> The Serpent is the Symbol of the Earth
> The Rainbow is the Symbol of Heaven
> But because he has a soul
> Man can be trapped in a terrible place
> Where death is only the beginning...

The film deals with the much-publicized (and much misunderstood) cult of voodoo zombiism in Haiti (on which more later). But the words also seem, in an ironic way, to suggest the dilemma of Haiti herself—"trapped in a terrible place"—bound by the tentacles of a savage, grotesque history, voodoo mysteries and magic, the power of the *bogons* (witch doctors), and a grindingly hopeless economy crushed by markets way beyond the control, or even comprehension, of Haitian politicians and bureaucrats.

Some pundits wonder aloud whether Haiti can ever break loose from its tangled web of chaos. The cynical fringe even claim that Haiti has got so used to being the Western Hemisphere's whipping boy and socioeconomic basket case that it has come to rather enjoy the game playing, particularly with the United States, and the benevolent cash and technical assistance handouts of international institutions and agencies.

One CARE worker suggested to me it's the *Mouse That Roared* syndrome—make a lot of noise and threats and wait for peace-at-any-price loans and grants. His ultimate scenario was another U.S. "benevolent takeover" (less repressive than the 1915 escapade—more like the Panama debacle instead), during which much of the physical infrastructure would be refurbished once again (Haitian minor roads are unbelievably bad) and the economic system put on something of a solid footing. At the opposite end of the scale there are those who believe that one more bloody rebellion, accompanied by all the familiar gory reprisals (plus one or two "accidentally involved" tourists, Peace Corps workers, or priests), and the world will fling up its collective hands in exasperation and turn its back, once and for all, on this hapless horror story of a nation.

"There are indeed those, sir, who delight in poking fun at Haiti as an example of the hopelessness of blacks trying to run their own country. Not only here, but virtually anywhere on the face of this troubled globe."

Aubelin Jolicoeur sat in his customary position on a high barstool at the Oloffson bar, immaculate as always in a crisp, cream linen suit, silk tie, and gold-handled cane, carefully placed on his lap. You have to love the man. He's the epitome of postcolonial pomposity but with a sly self-deprecating humor; his manicured pose matches his meticulous fingernails and carefully primped moustache on his honey-skinned face. He is a slice of history, a real-life *Comedians* character, still as frisky and gossip hungry as he was as Petit Pierre in Greene's put-down of the notorious Duvalier era.

Beyond the Oloffson's shady gingerbread tracery, the streets were a tumult of shouting, laughing people. It was the first day of a two-day strike by the populace to protest the illegal imprisonment and torture of three electoral candidates by the current government of General Prosper Avril.

Aubelin Jolicoeur continued. "You see, my dear sir—and I say 'dear' in all sincerity, for I feel that anyone who travels as freely as you do about our beautiful country either has the most nefarious of purposes or the dearest, most optimistic outlook on life. And you, sir," he rubs the handle of his walking stick with long fingers and leans forward, smiling, "you undoubtedly fall into the latter category from the sparkle in your eyes and your enthusiasm as we discuss my unfortunate country."

All this slides out as smoothly as soft skin on a satin pillow. Aubelin pauses to sip his rum cocktail. (They're still pretty good here. César, the barman, has been making them for over thirty years at the Oloffson and hasn't lost his touch.) He pats his moustache with a neatly pressed handkerchief and begins again in his conspiratorial tone. "We have a Creole saying here in Haiti: 'Deye mon, gen mon'—'Behind the mountains, there are mountains.'" Another dramatic pause and flourish of the handkerchief. "One can interpret this on so many levels. Topographically—geographically—it is certainly true. Emotionally it suggests a somewhat pessimistic outlook, an expectation of disaster on the part of my countrymen. But most important—spiritually, philosophically—that is where the significance of this phrase becomes most pronounced. Everything here is so complicated." He sighs a long sigh and gives a sad smile. "You see— the lines go back so far. When you think you've found the right answers you realize that you've merely been asking the wrong questions. Remember sir: Nothing in Haiti is what it appears to be!"

For a moment Aubelin became utterly serious. I had heard of his reputation as the ears and eyes of whichever ruler happens to be in power and wondered if I was receiving some kind of subtle warning. But then his self-parody returned and he laughed—an infectious laugh. A man who tempered his truths with a finely honed blade of irony and humor. I couldn't help chuckling with him, even as he ordered himself another rum punch and charged it to my bill.

"Nothing is what it appears to be." I'd heard a similar phrase from my friend Ed Duffy as we traveled the wilds of Inner Mongolia. But Aubelin Jolicoeur was right. It seemed to apply in Haiti as well, and there were two events in particular that revealed the contradictory spirit of this unusual country.

The first occurred on my third or fourth day. I had driven into a small town, attracted by its rather prominent church. On closer inspection I realized the prominence was due more to its sheer size than any semblance of architectural refinement. Rusty tin roof, broken stucco and brick exterior, and gloomy mold-blue interior with a few sad plaster sculptures of saints and madonnas. Bit of a letdown.

I had seen all I needed to see in a few minutes and was preparing to move on when I noticed a long line of people approaching down the street. They were all dressed smartly in gray-and-black suits and were walking very slowly to the beat of a drum. At the front of the line was a covered casket on wheels. Obviously it was a funeral.

Great, I thought. Bits of local color in this otherwise dull place, and I pulled off to the side in the shadow of the church to watch.

The procession moved closer, very somber, very stately, very silent, very Catholic. The drum droned on. It was hot even in the shade, and the flies were beginning to irritate. I thought I might move on. I'd seen plenty of funerals in my travels and this seemed to be pretty standard fare.

Then, without any warning, all hell broke loose. A rather large woman who had been walking well behind the casket, head bowed beneath a broad black hat, suddenly let out a horrifying scream, followed by a howling screech that stiffened the hairs on the nape of my neck. It was an inhuman sound, far too loud and full of sorrow for one person. She hurled herself sideways from the procession, flung her arms high, and began swirling and yelling and kicking wildly in the air. Others joined her. An elderly man, dignified and starch-stiff, suddenly collapsed in the street as if he'd been shot, then rose immediately in a leap that sent him skidding back into the mourners behind him, then half-cartwheeling into the line in front. At the same time three women were seized with convulsions, shaking and shrieking and throwing their fists furiously in the air. Some of the mourners tried to hold them but their strength seemed—again —inhuman. Bodies fell, others rushed in. It took eight people to hold down the woman who'd started it all and who was carried off to a patch of scrubby ground and sat on until her spasms began to subside.

The procession had halted, but not in disarray. Those at the front near the casket never turned, never moved. They just waited as they might for a sudden violent storm to pass, while the screaming and shrieking continued and bodies tumbled all around them.

Onlookers also stood silently in doorways, showing no shock or surprise. Gradually, the cries grew fainter, becoming garbled mumbles and quivers. People picked themselves up and dusted off each other, replaced hats and, in one case, shoes. Jackets were rebuttoned. The line re-formed slowly. The drum-

59

mer began his mournful drone again and gradually the procession moved on, closer and closer to the church door. By the time they arrived at the steps where the priest waited for them, it seemed as though nothing had happened. Heads were bowed, nods exchanged with the priest, and the mourners entered the church with the same dignified and quiet grief one would expect at a traditional funeral back home.

I seemed to be the only one still shocked and stunned. People in the street had resumed their conversations as if nothing had occurred; as I drove off, I could hear the first Catholic psalm being sung slowly and reverently from inside the church with the mold-blue walls and rusty tin roof. I was left with the heat and the flies and a sense of wonder at what lay below the seemingly placid Haitian exterior.

The second event was equally curious and alarming. I was driving over the magnificent mountain road from Gonaïves to Cap Haitien, one of the scenic wonders of Haiti. On all sides were vistas of mountain ranges, layer upon layer, cut by deep shadowy valleys. Clusters of African-looking villages perched on steep green slopes surrounded by tiny fields of corn and millet and brimming gardens of mangoes, bananas, and palms. In the far distance the ranges turned purple and disappeared into their own cloud caps. The breeze was cool and refreshing after the heat of the plains. I sat for a long time by the side of the road, lost in the richness and beauty of it all.

At the next roadside village, near the head of the pass, I noticed a crowd gathered around a lopsided cockpit about twenty feet square with a palm frond roof and two tiers of very wobbly-looking benches. Almost every community in Haiti, no matter how small, has its own cockpit, and Sunday cockfights are one of the most popular recreations for the men (the women stay well away or sit at the side selling plantain fritters and pork strips fried to stringy, but actually very tasty, crisps).

The fight had been going on for quite a while by the look of the two tired cocks, leaping half-heartedly at one another with extended talons (they don't use all the spurs and fancy accoutrements of European cockfights in Haiti). They were bloodied and half blind but gamely hacking away at each other for the delight of the noisy but good-natured crowd. Someone told me the fight had been going on for twenty minutes, and it could take another half hour before it was over, either by a kill or by one of the cocks making a run for it over the foot-high boards surrounding the square patch of earth.

But then something went wrong. The two cocks seemed to lose all interest in fighting and began nuzzling one another in an almost affectionate manner, cheek to bloodied cheek, like a couple of over-the-hill boxers. The mood of the crowd changed fast as a switchblade knife. Fifty or so smiling village males, out for a bit of Sunday afternoon fun, suddenly became a maddened wild-eyed mob, shrieking at the cocks, at the cocks' owners, at each other, and even at me (I was trying to be very inconspicuous, standing in the shadows, nibbling my pork crisps). The two owners stormed into the pit, each grabbing his bird and smashing their broken beaks and featherless faces together to rekindle the fighting spirit. The crowd had turned crazy for blood—and death. Money—lots of it—had been bet on this fight. Pride and reputations were at stake. The fight had to go on—and now!

Spitting and cursing, their faces the epitome of crazed anger, the owners hurled their birds at each other. I stepped back. I couldn't watch them anymore. My stomach churned. I wanted to get away, but the crowd had sealed me in, pressing me from behind in a furious need to witness the final death agonies.

I saw their faces—the incredible anger, the frustration, the lines of weariness and sorrow from soul-tearing work, day after day in a blistering sun, the tedium of life, all the petty squabbles and vendettas of close-knit family and village life—it was all there, tangible as knives and spears, aimed purportedly at the poor cocks but, if the cocks gave up, at themselves and one another. And I was in the middle of it all, and the cocks still showed no interest in fighting and the whole damned cockpit was about to explode in a whelter of blood, guts, and fury. . . . I had to get out of it.

I lashed out and felt my elbow hit soft flesh. The line behind me gave a little, and I pushed backward, hearing screams and curses in my ears. I pushed some more and finally tumbled out into the dust as the crowd closed in again to fill the place where I'd stood.

The woman cooking fritters gave me a long look and then smiled. I stood up shakily and dusted myself. Some children were laughing.

The woman brought a hot fritter over from her pan of boiling oil. She looked very closely at me—into me. Then she nodded, smiled, gave me the fritter, and went back to her cooking.

The din never ceased. It seemed even louder now that I was out of it. I felt less nervous, and part of me wanted to stay to see the outcome. But another part—the part I must learn to listen to more—told me it was time to leave. I'd peered partway into the soul of Haiti, and it was very different from the pleasantly mellow rhythms and pace of life I'd seen so often on the surface.

But that was only the beginning. The soul of the Haitian is ancient and deep and full of mystery. "Nothing is what it appears to be." Aubelin Jolicoeur's words still floated around in the back of my head, and as I was to see later on in my journeys, he was more right than I could have ever imagined.

But enough of the lazy ramblings. It was time for the big adventure.

"The northwest peninsula! Now why in the world would you go there when there's Jacmel, Cap Haitien, La Citadelle, Sant d'Eau—that's the waterfall where you get all those Catholic-voodoo ceremonies. Then all those beaches down south. It's fabulous down there! You're missing all the best spots."

The American owner of one of the largest Pétionville hotels seemed quite confused by my plans. He sprawled in his swivel chair behind a desk littered with my maps, whirling a cocktail stick between his fingers like a miniature baton.

I tried to explain my decision. "Everyone who comes to Haiti visits those places—it's the national 'grand tour.' I want to go where the blans don't go."

"Well—you've picked the right part. Definitely! I'll bet you the northwest hasn't seen more than a hundred blans in the last century. I haven't even been there! And I've covered most of Haiti. That's wild country, David—I mean, it's really wild."

"That's what I've been told."

"Well—best of luck. You're going to need it. Better get your-

self a tough truck." Then there was hesitation. "Y'know...
Shoot. I wish I was going with you."

Bingo! I'd made the right decision.

About thirty miles out of Gonaïves, heading west on the coast
road to Anse-Rouge, I knew this journey would be special.

To the north the ranges rise abruptly out of the scrub and
cactus forests—the Chaine de St. Nicolas, the Chaine des Trois
Pitons, the Montagnes de Terre. Buckling ridges above the
creamy whiteness of the coastal hills and beaches that would
excite the most demanding connoisseurs of world-class suntan-
ning locales. A sense of exhilarating emptiness. It's unlike the
rest of Haiti where, even in the most rugged places, you're
always aware of the presence of people and villages. Here on the
northwest peninsula you find a different kind of Haiti. A place
that belongs to you and you alone. Beaches that are yours to
roam alone all day. Of course there's nowhere to stay unless
you bring your own equipment—but that's why the adventure-
travelers still love Haiti. Adventure is guaranteed.

And fantasy too. Imagine a string of bamboo and palm-
frond shanties sprinkled along a perfect white-sand strand and
separated by mini-mountains of pearly pink conch shells, millions and millions of them. The people were friendly. I was invited to join two families (highly extended families, everyone
from nipple-sucking newborns to great grandparents) and share
a lunch of *djon-djon* (a rich rice dish cooked with dried mushrooms, which turn the whole concoction an alluring shade of
black) and a wonderful seafood stew thick with strips of marin-
ated conch or *lambi*, as they call it. I'd discovered the lambi capital of Haiti.

Although Haitians are not great lovers of the ocean, and
fishing is still undertaken in primitive boats, sometimes little
more than hollowed logs, they often seem to possess a French-
like sensitivity when it comes to cooking the fruits of the ocean.
The conch sauce prepared by these villagers and liberally served
with black rice, was the purest essence of sea and seafood. One
of the older women told me in singsong Creole how she would
pound the bones and heads of fish and all the leftover bits and
broken shells from the cleaned conch and then simmer them

slowly for hours in charcoal embers with brine, lemon, pepper, nutmeg, and cumin until the mixture was reduced to creamy stock. As the stock was needed for soups and sauces she would ladle it out and then add more ingredients and brine to keep the pot slowly bubbling for the next meal.

The aroma of that superb stock, the flavor of the djon-djon, the warmth of the people, the pink mountains of conch shells, the brilliant blue of the ocean, and the headiness of Haiti's excellent Prestige beer...I was soon dozing in the shade with the other men while the women washed and played with the children and chatted quietly, using the gentle patois of the countryside. It was hard to leave this lovely place and move on.

Half an hour later I was convinced I should have stayed where I was. Beyond the great salt pans of Anse Rouge and the straggly shacks of the salt gatherers, the previously benign dust road suddenly decided to get nasty. My lunchtime euphoria was replaced by wide-eyed vigilance as I bounced over boulders, sank into eroded gulleys, and generally gave my four-wheel-drive Jeep the road trial of its life.

Ironically the worse the road became (I use the term "road" euphemistically. I called it many other names during the next few hours), the more magnificent was the scenery. Petit Paradis was as lovely as its name—a tiny clustered village shaded by palms on an arc of white sand, and a few fishing boats (one with a graceful *dhow* sail), all against a backdrop of soaring mountains. The only things spoiling the picture were the vultures following me since Anse Rouge. They knew what was ahead....

A few miles on I saw what this road could do to even the toughest of vehicles. A long-wheelbase Land-Rover lay partially on its side at the edge of a deep gulley. Its front passenger-side wheel sat in the dust a few feet away. Four black women were huddled in the shade of thorn bushes; a tall scraggly white man with an Abraham Lincoln beard stood off to the side, shaded only by his broad straw hat.

"What a place to get stuck!" I smiled to disguise my surprise. I hadn't expected to meet anyone on this road, least of all someone white. After all, I'd been told, I was only "one of a hundred in the last hundred years" to venture into the northwest. I was rather proud of that image. Now I had to share the honor with this strange-looking character resembling a combination of Amish farmer and eccentric professor out of some Agatha Christie mystery.

"Good day, sir." No smile and no extended hand. The accent was hard to place.

Maybe Dutch or German.

"Can I help at all?"

"No. The boy has gone for help, thank-you."

"I didn't see anyone on the road."

"No. He has gone another way."

Another way, to where? According to my map there wasn't any other place around except Petit Paradis, and that was ten miles back. And what could anyone in a tiny fishing village like Petit Paradis do with a wrecked wheel ripped off an axle? I mean Haitians are fabulous innovators in a "make-do" culture but fixing a Land-Rover out here in this condition...

"Look, can I take you somewhere—to the nearest village? Anywhere?"

"No. I must stay with the machine."

"What about the ladies?"

"They must stay with me. We are fine, thank-you."

"Why don't you stay in the shade? You could be here quite a while. It's very hot."

"No. I am used to this."

All very odd. I walked around the Land-Rover to look at the wheel. A painted insignia on the door was still visible beneath a thick coating of dust: MISSION OF GOD, FIRST CONGREGATION COLLEGIATE UNIT.

"Oh, you're with a mission? I wondered why you were out in this wilderness."

"Yes, a mission."

"I'm just traveling. Thought it may be interesting down this way."

"And is it?"

"Interesting? Well—so far it's been different. Fascinating."

"Ah."

I began to get the feeling that he would be happier left alone. There was something otherworldly in the way he kept looking over my head, turning his neck like a cockerel about to crow, staring at things beyond the thornbushes and the hills.

"Look. I really feel I could be doing something to help. I've got a jack in the Jeep. Maybe we could use yours and mine together and get the wheel—"

"All will be well, sir. Help is coming. Please don't worry about us."

"I'm going to Bombardopolis. I'll see if anyone's coming down this way. . ."

"Thank-you, but that really will not be necessary."

He reminded me of another of Graham Greene's characters in *The Comedians*—the evangelistic vegetarian determined to transform the eating habits of all Haitians. Along with regular infusions of fast-buck buccaneers that have plagued this little country, there have always been the "higher agenda" exponents seeking to bring enlightenment, either religious or communistic, to a nation still shrouded in the ancient African mysteries of voodoo.

Just before my meeting with the missionary I'd been dialing my way through the static on the Jeep radio and had found only two intelligible stations. One was wall-to-wall proselytizing programs beamed in from Grand Cayman island, mainly featuring Billy Graham's crusade messages. The other was Radio Cuba (Cuba is only fifty miles to the west of Haiti), which combined Latin pop music with regular dousings of Castro himself, pounding out his philosophy of social equality with a never-flagging fervor. Not a flicker of good old rock n' roll anywhere on the dial. No wonder most rural Haitians seem to prefer their own companionship and quiet conversation in the shade of their kays to all this endless rhetoric. The country's had its fill of rhetoric, no matter how well-intentioned. Everyone seems to know what's best for the Haitians but the Haitians themselves. . . .

The missionary had walked off down the road to look for his "help." The four women had not said one word or shown the slightest interest in their predicament or my presence. They were now asleep under the thornbush. Four Henry Moore figures in the shade.

"God is good," say the voodoo *houngans* (priests). "He provides all your needs." In a nation that seems to have so little left to give to itself, maybe that's the only remaining dream—leaving God to work it all out.

The road rolled on, sometimes over high dry desert plateaus, sometimes down into luxuriant oasislike clefts, occupied by little villages with their verdant gardens of maize, millet, sweet potatoes, mangoes, custard apples, bananas, and breadfruit.

There were no other vehicles around. I had the land all to myself again and was enjoying the solitude and sense of self-containment. And then, in the early evening and with no warning, came Bombardopolis. A huge cemetery appeared out of the bushes, hundreds of hefty stone sarcophagi (the heftier the better, according to Haitian beliefs, to keep the deceased well and truly in the ground and prevent the emergence of the dreaded "living dead"—the zombies), crammed together over four acres of bare land at the edge of town.

As towns go in Haiti, this was quite small, but after all those wide-open spaces it felt like a teeming metropolis. A long main street, lined with a mix of concrete block and mud-and-thatch houses was dominated at the far end by a dainty, pastel-painted church. The weekly market was still in full swing on the main plaza in front of the church. Scores of women in brightly colored dresses and scarves sat cross-legged by blankets and plastic sheets on which were displayed all the traditional wares of country markets—from staple foods, fruits, and dried fish to long bars of domestic soap purchased by the inch, little piles of sun-dried coffee beans, hairpins and combs, round brown paper packages of unrefined brown sugar, tiny packages of sea salt, even tinier twists of wrapped tobacco and clay pipes, Marlboro and Kent cigarettes sold singly, piles of boxed matches, and bottles of cheap and potent crude rum known as *clairon*.

I bought some small straw-woven baskets, beautifully crafted by two young men who sat weaving together near the water fountain as the women came to fill their plastic containers for the evening meal.

"Kouman ou yeh?" ("How are you?") was my attempt at a greeting to the curious faces, which broke into smiles and giggles at my hesitant Creole. Children scampered up, stared in disbelief at my beard and cameras, and rushed off to bring more children.

Old men approached gracefully and offered a handshake in welcome. For a while I became the feature attraction of the afternoon. "We do not see many blans," explained one young man in hesitant English. "I hope you like my town, thank-you-very-much."

I nodded enthusiastically. I did like his town. It had life, vigor, and color. I wandered around as the evening sun turned the whole place orange and gold. By the time I returned to the square in twilight, the market was gone, but the little pink, green, and white church still glowed. A full moon rose up behind the belltower.

As for a place to stay, I was in luck. CARE had a modest guest house near the cemetery, and for a few dollars I was given a bed and an evening meal of saltfish, plantain fritters, sweet potatoes, rice, and beans—a regal repast for a rather weary traveler.

I couldn't resist a last stroll before turning in to the cemetery, of course, spiritual center of the Haitian psyche. The stone coffins, silvered by the moon, seemed larger than they did during the day. They were set in apparently haphazard fashion, wherever a bit of spare land existed, some even encroaching on the road itself. I was the only person around and, in spite of the bright moonlight, I felt uneasy. All those voodoo tales of zombies and the crushing of old bones for spiritual potions...I didn't hang around long.

After a breakfast of superb French-roasted Haitian coffee, fried eggs with more plantain fritters, a huge flat round of cassava bread, and orange juice fresh squeezed from oranges grown in the guest house garden, I was ready for the road again.

And the road was ready for me too. A mile or so out of Bombardopolis I had my first puncture on a particularly rocky stretch in the middle of a wilderness of thornbushes. I thought I'd have to go through the whole arduous business of tire changing all by myself, but hardly had I climbed out of the Jeep when I was surrounded by helping hands—children, young strapping men, and old pipe-smoking grandfathers, full of advice and encouragement. They seemed to appear from nowhere (an experience I later got used to in Haiti). The job was done in no time. I had to drive back to the town to fix the punctured tire (crossing this country without a reliable spare is a guaranteed catastrophe). I sat bemused for half an hour as the inner tube was pried out, patched, and then heat-sealed using a "make-do" device of metal clamp and iron pot in which kerosene was burned to create the heat to heat the clamp to seal the patch. Ingenious innovations everywhere in Haiti.

The first two hours or so after dawn in Haiti are idyllic—early-morning perfumes, dewy blossoms on corn tassels, the haloed tops of tall millet plants, the curling smoke of new fires, the sounds of cocks, donkeys, sleepy dogs. After that the heat increases by the minute, and by 8:30 A.M., I'm usually a pathetically dripping wretch seeking shade wherever I can find it. I drove with the windows wide open, choking in the dust but finding some relief in the humid breeze. Usually there are trees around or buildings, but in the desert northwest cactus and thornbush provide little relief from the hammering heat.

It was hard to believe here that Haiti was once almost covered in rain forest. Although deforestation is not a new phenomenon, it was a problem even at the end of the nineteenth century, when the peasants, liberated from the old French plantation system (the island was one of the richest colonies on earth under its European occupiers), began clearing their own land in the mountain foothills for small-farm cultivation. This, coupled with the still extensive use of charcoal for cooking, has resulted in a situation today where less than four hundred square miles (about three percent of the country) still have viable tree cover. Elsewhere erosion, abandoned farms, and lost irrigation potential have led to a semidesert transformation of much of the island. Later in my journey I passed through one of the last remaining rain forests, a powerful reminder of how this poor nation has wasted one of its greatest natural resources.

Beyond a remarkably large church, the remnants of a stone fort and magnificent white sand beaches, Môle St. Nicolas seems to have little else to boast about. Vacant lots, abandoned buildings, a small harbor whose main source of income is the transport of charcoal (one wonders how charcoal is made from the stumpy vegetation on the dry hills all around)—the town has certainly seen better days.

"But we are famous, M'sieur. Very famous." A rotund middle-aged storeowner, trying to sell me beer at twice the going rate, became adamant about his home town.

"The famous Christopher Columbus came here, M'sieur, in December 1492. This was the first place he saw in the New World after leaving Spain. We are very proud."

"Did he stay long?"

"Oh well. Not so very long. Just a few hours maybe. But he liked it very much."

"Where did he go?"

"Oh, off down the coast towards Cap Haitien. And then he got stuck at Limonade. They were all drinking with the Arawak Indians. He let a young boy steer his ship, the *Santa Maria*, and he smashed it into a reef!"

"And then?"

"Well..." his voice became conspiratorial. "Very strange. No one really knows. Columbus left thirty-nine of his men behind to build a fort and get gold from the Indians and he went off in the *Niña* for about a year. When he came back he found the fort and houses burnt down and all his men gone..."

"Where were they?"

"Ah, no one knows.... They were never found.... The Indians had gone too.... Very strange, M'sieur."

I gave him a cigar. He paused to light it with exacting care.

"Haiti has so many stories like this, M'sieur," he said. "And where are you going now?"

"East. Through Jean Rabel and Port-de-Paix. Hopefully to Cap Haitien."

"It's a bad road, M'sieur."

"I've got a good Jeep."

He paused again, undecided about something. Then he leaned across the counter, pushing the bottles of beer aside.

"What do you know about Haiti voodoo?"

"Not very much. No one talks about it—except for foreigners!"

"Yes, that is so true. Those who know least always talk the most. Isn't that true about so many things?"

We chuckled together and his face disappeared in a cloud of cigar smoke.

70

"This is an excellent cigar. I have not had one for over two years now. I thank you."

He became serious and conspiratorial again. "Today is Saturday. When you get to Anse à Foleur—it's a small village about halfway between Port-de-Paix and Cap Haitien—ask for Jean-Claude."

"Okay. Why?"

"Tell him Jules at Môle sent you and give him one of your cigars. Maybe give him two."

"And then?"

"Who knows? Maybe he'll show you a few things..."

A wink, followed by more billows of smoke. "Haiti is a very strange country, M'sieur. Full of surprises...."

I thanked Jules and loaded the beer into the Jeep.

"M'sieur," he seemed a little embarrassed, "Is it possible that you have just one more cigar for me?"

There were times when I really questioned the sanity of this journey. True the scenery was magnificent, the beaches, the sky, that purple-blue ocean, but the track along which my poor Jeep bounced and crashed was idiotic. It seemed that an army of workers had carefully cleared all the adjoining land of boulders and rocks and then thrown them, higgledy-piggledy, across my road.

It was a barren brittle terrain of limestone crags and broken strata, holed like Swiss cheese, gleaming white under a searing sun. At first glance it seemed utterly devoid of people and vegetation. But then, peering through the heat shimmers, I began to see mud and straw kays among the boulders, and tiny patches of tilled earth. Something was being grown here. Four-foot high plants surrounded by piles of rocks. They looked like fledgling trees. I'd heard that CARE had forestation projects in the northwest but surely not here, not in this wilderness?

There were patches of millet, too, and other staples. And women out in the hellish heat, clearing more land. The endurance and perseverance of the Haitian hardscrabble farmers hit home that day. Their instinct for freedom, independence, and land to call their own drives them to the most herculean efforts just to keep alive—to grow enough to eat, to sell a little at market, to buy seed to grow again . . . the eternal cycle. Yet no matter how hopeless their situation seems to outsiders, you see pride and life and determination in their eyes. Somehow they make it work. Year after year after year. As governments tumble in Port-au-Prince and millions of treasury dollars disappear into political pockets, and the Pétionville princes and princesses drive around in shining and ever-larger sedans and the world throws up its hands at the horrors of hapless Haiti, the peasants keep on clearing their fields, planting their crops, and living lives whose rhythms and patterns have ancient origins in their original West Africa homeland, long before the slave traders and the colonialists and the kingly dictators and the never-ending chaos. . . .

Somehow in spite of the boulders, I reached Jean Rabel. A pretty little blue-and-white church, perched on a bluff at the end of a long line of palms, acted as a beacon. The track then promptly became a riverbed—not a ford—but the actual bed of a river for a few miles. A novel way of traveling.

At a riverside market, I bought bags of mangoes, oranges, and bananas for pennies, and gorged my way across the fertile foothills of the Chaine de St. Nicolas to Port-de-Paix. Here at the docks I sat overlooking the famous Tortue Island, once a cave-laced haven for pirates and buccaneers in the days of gold-filled Spanish galleons.

Soup seemed to be the only dish available at the dockside restaurant in spite of its wall painted with every kind of fish and seafood and a sign in Creole boasting "We got everything!" The soup looked tolerable at first, big chunks of chicken and potatoes and carrots. But I'd missed the chilies, whole green chunks of those nefariously lethal, lip-searing, stomach-scorching creatures, obliviously slurped down with the rest of the broth and now sending me into somersaults of agony as I swallowed beer after beer, trying to douse their fires.

Fortunately the coast road after Port-de-Paix was tolerable. The fords were not very deep, the boulders smoothed, and the ruts flattened. My inflamed stomach could at least travel unknotted as I passed lovely beaches and little fishing villages and arrived in Anse à Foleur feeling almost recovered. I even found Jean-Claude without any difficulty, although I still wasn't sure why Jules had recommended I seek him out. He was very black, very short, and by the wrinkled skin of his face and arms, very old.

One cigar got me a smile, two a handshake, and three a gush of information given at great speed in a raspy half-whisper (the whispers seemed unnecessarily melodramatic as we were sitting in the Jeep), all about voodoo ceremonies, back in the hills, tonight, special celebrations, a houngan called Alisio, and a *mamma* (female voodoo priest), Theral.

I didn't believe a word of it. He was so theatrical he was ridiculous. Voodoo, I'd been told by people who claimed to know, had virtually disappeared since the ouster of Papa Doc. I was being treated as a tourist and a sucker. I told Jean-Claude that I had to leave to reach Cap Haitien by evening. He looked surprised and hurt. I gave him two more cigars. I didn't mean to offend him, but Haiti gets too much of a bad rap with all this voodoo stuff. . . . (Looking back it's hard to believe I could have been so arrogant—and so dumb.)

From Anse à Foleur the track took a sudden turn inland. My map showed an alternative route along the coast but I was told it had been washed out by recent storms.

"The only way is over the mountains."

So—over the mountains it was, back to the boulders and gulleys. I had no choice, so I sang songs, ate my mangoes and generally tried to ignore the thrashing and crashing of the poor Jeep as we edged up into the clouds, further and further from the coast.

At the crest of the climb the clouds melted away and I looked down into a magic land. Range upon range of jungle-clad hills rolling away into a violet haze; rivers like bronze snakes winding through the shadowy valleys, thin veils of waterfalls between the canopied tiers of trees. No sign of people or villages.

This was virgin country. All Haiti must have looked like this once, way back before the days of slaves and plantations and colonial empires. I sat by the roadside watching the clouds play tag across the green peaks. The wind was so cool and fresh you could almost drink it. I had been lucky on this journey. I had seen a part of the island few whites had ever seen and this was the climax, this glimpse of ancient Haiti. A moment to treasure.

But Haiti can be mean with its moments. The wind became stronger and colder, the clouds moved in, covering the ranges and the forest. It was suddenly dark, really dark. Leaves and branches began to blow across the track. Time to move on, down the mountainside, into the shelter of the valley. Only the track was even worse on this side, great diagonal gashes of gouged earth littered with loose rocks. I turned the beams on full and drove down slowly through the cloud. Thunder pounded the hills. I tried to whistle to myself as the Jeep creaked and skidded. It could be worse, I thought. We could be having one of those notorious Haitian rainstorms . . .

And—guess what. A notorious Haitian rainstorm. Wonderful. Just what I needed to end a day that began with a puncture, followed by a morning of the worst desert roads imaginable, followed by a river for a road, a stomach seared by chilies, some phony voodoo peddlers, and now, just when there might be a chance of a nice fluffy bed in Cap Haitien, an evening of skidding down mountainsides, mud slides, and the distinct possibility of being drowned in some raging river crossing. Not my idea of a perfect day.

The rain was like a band of rum-crazed drummers on my roof. I could hardly see anything in front of me. The windshield wipers were useless.

At the first village I knew it was hopeless to go on. The last stream I'd crossed had gone mad, tearing at its own bank, tossing huge branches like twigs, almost toppling the Jeep as I eased her through the surge of syrupy brown water, frothing furiously at the doors.

I'm not sure the village even had a name, it was such a small ramshackle kind of place, looking utterly forlorn in the sheeting rain. I stayed in the Jeep and saw people peeping at me through the narrow doorways of their kays. They probably thought I was mad; they were probably right.

After about half an hour, things eased off. No, that's completely the wrong image. Someone switched off the storm like a spigot. One moment it was a gray miasma outside, then the pounding on my roof ceased, to be replaced by a pleasant dewy dripping. Color eased back into the picture as if someone was playing with the controls of a TV set. The village actually began to look quite pretty with its little gardens and cottages crouched in the shade of palms. Well—time to move on. Who knows—I might still reach that fluffy bed in Cap Haitien.

A boy came running up, waving his hands.

"Non, blan."

I pointed ahead.

"Non." He was adamant.

A few of his friends joined him. I opened the window.

"M'sieur. Rain very strong. No good."

The other boys all nodded their heads.

"The river. Much water. Very danger."

They were right. The streams would be full and, according to my map, I had quite a few fords ahead of me. Cap Haitien would have to wait.

And then the strangeness began.

It wasn't frightening, at least not in the usual way. It was just that things got out of control—out of my control at least. Everyone else seemed to know what was going on except me. I had apparently arrived in the middle of some celebration. The rain had been merely an amusing diversion. Now it was over, I saw all the movement, the lights of candles, the murmurs of songs; I heard drums, not in the village but somewhere back in the hills. There was a sense of festival in the air. . . .

An old man dressed in a torn shirt and baggy black pants came over to me carrying two candles, skinny things, strips of rope dipped once in tallow. He looked at my eyes and laughed, revealing a black maw of a mouth with three enormous teeth. Then he handed me a candle and pointed to where other villagers were walking, up through the forest, beyond the mango trees. Well—why not?

The path was muddy. My boots were soon caked in the stuff and I skidded like a drunk. What am I doing now? Part of me wondered if I should be here. The other part knew I really had no choice. Everyone else walked in bare feet, huge splayed feet, hard as rock on the sole with pink-edged toes. I was tempted to imitate them.

The next few hours were utter confusion to me. Subsequently I've learned more about what I actually saw and experienced, but at the time, I was ignorant, cynical and, occasionally, scared stiff. At the Oloffson in Port-au-Prince I'd seen an evening folk dance show that purported to have voodoo elements in it, but, while being colorful and energetic, it felt harmless, sanitized. A safe entertainment for the amusement of blans.

But this night was all fire and power and magic. The spirit I sensed went far beyond any showbiz extravaganza: the villagers were tapping into vast reservoirs of energy, energy that in no way correlated with their thin and often prematurely aged bodies. It was as though the quiet, smiling, candle-carrying inhabitants of this lonely mountain valley had become transformed, possessed by primeval forces that hurled them into dances and spasms and gyrations that, in their everyday world, would have left them drained and gasping after even a few minutes, but which here flung them into higher states of being, made them superhuman, with seemingly boundless energy.

Yet it all began so quietly, almost boring, with three drummers beating out ragtag rhythms and people chatting outside a small mud hut, eating fritters and pork gigots, and placing candles in the trees and around the door of a hut.

It became obvious that this modest building, a peristyle, not much larger than a family kay, was to be the center for the evening's event. Somehow fifty or so people managed to cram themselves inside around the walls, which were painted in violent purple-blues, lemons, and reds, with primitive figures representing the loas of voodoo but with amusing Catholic overtones—Erzulie, the god-spirit of the heart and love with overtones of the Virgin Mary; Damballah Ouedo (the Snake) with the staff of St. Patrick, and St. Peter as Papa Legba, a sort of master of ceremonies at voodoo rites.

Worshippers believe in the "great God"—Gran Mèt—but see him as too aloof, too concerned with universal challenges to worry about the day-to-day problems of his earthly supplicants. So that's where the loas come in—the lesser spirits of the plants, the streams, fire, death, and love, and the fierce Guédé, voodoo lord of the crossroads to the underworld. These are the forces that must be recognized and kept in balance and harmony. These are the spirits that are "called" and dominate the fiery ceremonies. Said to enter through the roof of the peristyle down the painted pole, the *poteau-mitoo* in the center of the room, they possess worshippers, seemingly at random, and fling men and women, whirling like dervishes, around and around the cramped space, sending them into paroxysms, reaching out to touch the forces that felt so tangible in that tiny room.

As a novice I understood nothing of the careful sequencing of the ceremony led by the houngan. The incredible noise, the dancing, the sweat, the elaborate drawings of *vévé* patterns in cornmeal in the earth floor, the trembling bodies possessed by the loas, the whirling of machetes, the frantic clapping and chanting in the ancient languages of Benin and Western Africa, the constant boom of the *maman* (the largest drum) behind the sharper sound of the *seconde* drum and the *bula*, the ritual exchanges of sweat, the violent sacrifice of two chickens, the offerings of food at the central post, the strangeness of the interludes when the sounds ceased but continued on in my head... then the crash of the maman and the whole rhythm beginning again, on and on, hour after hour.

It was too much; I couldn't think. I wasn't even sure what I was seeing was real. All I could do was let go and feel, remembering the words of one of the CARE workers in Port-au-Prince: "Voodoo is everything—it fills every part of the life of believers —it's faith, it's medicine and very necessary medicine in a countryside with hardly any doctors; it's justice; it's the ultimate faith and yet it's tangible—if you ever get to see one of the ceremonies you'll feel those loas are real—real flesh and blood and with a power you won't believe. . . ."

Much later on there were more rituals around an altar in a side room, the *houmfor*, filled with sealed urns (said to contain the spirits of the loas), tied bundles of dusty sticks and leaves, plates of flour that had been used for drawing the vévés, and a stone bath set in the floor for sacred washings, rattles made out of gourds, and, most strange of all, neatly framed prints of Christ (with a glowing pink heart), the Virgin, and statuettes of Catholic saints, all under a low ceiling decorated with paper streamers like leftover Christmas decorations.

Sometime just before dawn the ceremonies ended and the people began drifting down out of the forest and back to their homes in the village below. For a while I walked behind a frail elderly man with bowed shoulders and a limp. He turned to me and smiled a wrinkled smile, and I knew I'd seen him before, only then he'd been Papa Legba and he'd been dancing like a disco-crazed youth around the post, crashing into bodies, his face filled with sweat, his eyes bursting with fire and life. . . .

The rest of the drive back through the mountains was uneventful. The fords had become mere trickles again, the sky was aqua blue, and the rain-washed trees sparkled. Eventually I arrived on the coastal plain, passing more world-class beaches, all pristine and all empty.

At last—Cap Haitien. An active and colorful port city of narrow streets lined with Spanish-style stucco buildings, all couched in a bowl of jungly hills. A large white cathedral with a prominent dome sat at one side of a shady plaza.

Here I played the hedonistic tourist for a while, splashing in my hotel pool set on a steep bluff overlooking the town and harbor, eating elegant five-course dinners while a Haitian band played out-of-tune folksongs.

King Henri Christophe, one of the first rulers of Haiti after its fiery independence in 1804, chose this area for his regal headquarters and had an enormous Versailles-style palace built at Milot, about twenty miles east of Cap Haitien, where he entertained his court and foreign admirers with all the elegance and extravagance of French royalty.

He had great dreams for his new nation and formed a fitting model for Eugene O'Neill's *Emperor Jones.* "Haiti and the Haitians were born to glory," he reputedly stated, "to greatness, to life, to immortality." He forgot to emphasize though that such glory would only be won by keeping the poor Haitians working as virtual slaves in the old colonial plantations and sacrificing the lives of twenty thousand of his countrymen in building one of the largest fortresses in the world—Citadelle La Ferrière—on a mountain peak, high above his palace, as a bastion against any neocolonial invasions by Napoleon or others.

His suicide in 1820, at a time of peasant rebellions, began Haiti's long tradition of errant leaders, most of whom have been violently disposed of by a populace still seeking its own "glory and immortality."

Standing among the crumbling rooms and terraces of Christophe's palace ruins and looking down on the tiny shanties and patchwork of gardens and sugarcane fields far below, I let the contrasting images of this strange little country flash by: a nation of artists in love with vibrant color and form; a nation of enormous inequities between the peasant farmers and the "mountain monarchs" in their mansions and walled compounds high above Port-au-Prince; the explosions of flamboyants, bougainvillea, and hibiscus against deforested and eroding hills; the power and energy of country voodoo ceremonies against the slovenliness and sloth of city "bidonville" slums; the fiery souls of peasants, haunted for generations by the "specter of the master," hidden under a surface patina of smiles, laughter, and laissez-faire lethargy.

"Deye mon, gen mon"—"Behind the mountains, there are mountains"—goes the saying. And it's true. The enigmas endure. Haiti is still mystery, complexity—and pure adventure.

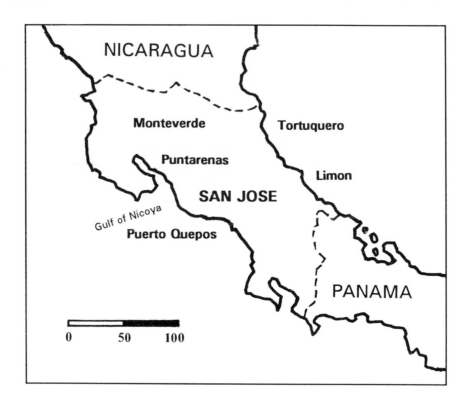

3. COSTA RICA

Misadventures in an Oasis of Peace

Iceland—ah, Iceland!

A vast, treeless terrain filled with all the teeming folklore figments of the wild Viking imagination—a place of boyhood fantasies—a place to roam across wind-scoured wastes, scaling glaciers, wandering the great ice dome of Vatnajökull.

"Sorry, sir. Iceland is closed."

Two days before departure and the nice lady from the national tourist office calls to tell me that there's been a general strike. All flights are canceled.

So here I am with a free week between Major Commitments and nowhere to go.

I trust my travel agent implicitly. He and I have worked our way through many sticky schedules, and when he suggested Costa Rica I thought, what the heck, it'll be fun to go somewhere I know nothing about.

"Central America? You gotta be out of your mind. That whole place is nothing but bananas, guerilla wars, and loony drug-dealing dictators!" Friends can be like that—very bigoted in a protective kind of way.

My travel agent held fast. "Costa Rica is different from any-where you've ever been—it's one of the most peaceful and lovely places on earth. Trust me."

Florida flashed by from thirty-six thousand feet—miles of empty sunburned scrub with occasional rococo swirlings of subdivisions scratched in the dry earth and no houses on them (I bet the fancy brochures make them look like bits of paradise). Mexico was much the same color without the subdivisions; occasional wrigglings of mountain ranges gave the martini-mellowed passengers some startling landscapes to look at. Guatemala was on fire. Thousands of tiny slash-and-burn *milpas* were clearing virgin jungle for peasant farmers (deforestation chomping through the mountains like King Kong at a wedding breakfast).

Honduras came as a surrealist pause in the middle of endless plains of banana trees; a ramshackle airport littered with sinister, slouching police; snoozing staff who forgot to fuel the plane, and one terrified native who tried to make a dash for somewhere across the runway and was dragged off by soldiers in green fatigues bristling with grenades and automatic weapons. Nicaragua was invisible—not an acre of that war-torn place could be seen through the gray haze.

Then came Costa Rica, sparkling-clear with vistas of open-mouthed volcanoes along the cordilleras and a marshmallow-soft landing at San José in the middle of the cool central valley. I felt like a kid with a Christmas stocking full of unopened presents.

The presents came brightly wrapped, intense little moments on my first day in the capital of a million or so inhabitants. Comfortably settled in the delightfully old-fashioned Gran Hotel (with casino!), in a room overlooking the main square, I flung back the tall windows and found a miniature version of the Paris Opera House facing me, the Teatro Nacional. A Verdi opera was advertised for that night to be followed in a couple of days by a group of Central American folksingers notorious for their left-wing views on everything from bananas to bombs. It was my first introduction to the democratic verve of this tiny nation of 2.5 million people.

Directly below me, street vendors sold replicas of black-clay Indian whistles, flowers, string hammocks, and mini-mountains of fresh fruit to couples strolling by hand-in-hand. Cicadas buzzed furiously in the shade trees. There were lovers every-where—smooching, hugging, whispering and swooning into each other's eyes. ("Making love is the number one pastime in Costa Rica," I had read somewhere.)

It was the evening rush hour. Traffic snarled and honked all the way down Avenida Central; elegantly coiffured ladies jay-walked, jiggling slim hips in tight skirts, a neon temperature sign flashed 75° (it's always 75° in San José); inelegant tower blocks rose into the brilliant blue sky behind a jumble of smaller stucco buildings adorned with shutters and pantile roofs. And beyond all this were the soaring cones of the great volcanoes, Irazú, Poas, and Barva, whose occasional irritable shrugs and burps are a reminder to the Costa Ricans, better known as "Ticos," of the tenacity of life in their capital.

"Our volcanoes give one a distinctly existential perspective." Ticos can be very eloquent, at least around San José, and in Guillermo Santamaria I had obviously met one of the more loqua-cious examples at the hotel café on the square. "When Irazú blew in 1963 she covered most of the city and our valley with *ceniza* [ash] day after day for months. It was terrible. Thick fog all the time."

Guillermo drank his tiny cup of black coffee with three fingers extended like porcupine quills. When he first introduced himself I expected some sell-job of a touristy nature. Now it was obvious he merely wanted to talk.

He continued. "And poor Cartago [a colonial city ten miles east of San José], almost completely destroyed in 1841, then again in 1910, then half-buried in ceniza in 1963." He sighed a long Latin sigh. "So sad. It was such a beautiful city."

A policeman walked by with dark glasses and a big revolver,

high on his hip. I made some inane remark about Central American dictators and their impressive armies.

"Army!" Guillermo spluttered over his coffee, sprinkling a little on his crisp white shirt. "We have no army in Costa Rica. You, my friend, are ensconced in an oasis of peace here. Truly. Our colleagues to the north and south have their problems, many problems—El Salvador, Nicaragua, Guatemala, Panama— but we've had peace here since 1948. That's forty years with no revolutions, no dictators, and no army, thanks to "Don Pepe" Figueres Ferrer. He brought us democracy, free elections, and free education and medicine. He helped peasants to own their own land, he even established a 'University of Peace,' which is still here today. And you know about Oscar Arias Sanchez..." He couldn't resist a little jab, "You have heard of our president, Arias? Well, he is now *trying* to bring peace to all of Central America. He is a good man, a brilliant man, but—such a task! Our country is surrounded by..." He thought better of explicit epithets. "Momentico."

He raised his three spiny fingers again and a waiter appeared immediately.

"Dos quaros."

The drinks arrived in tiny glasses. We toasted Arias with the harsh clear liquor, distilled from sugarcane. Two more arrived.

"I welcome you to Costa Rica," he said slowly, "and I trust you will discover and enjoy our very special and very real peace."

After a third round of quaros, peace was taking on a very tangible quality on my first evening in Tico-land.

Costa Rica really is a tiny country, about half the size of Virginia, but that in no way detracts from the amazing diversity of topography and nature. From the "land of eternal spring" at four thousand feet in the high central valley, the topography falls steeply on both sides, fifty miles to the humid Pacific Coast and sixty miles to the even more moist Caribbean. Toward the northern border with Nicaragua, beyond Lake Arenal, is the arid Guanacaste, a mysterious empty region with ancient ties to the Maya and Olmec cultures; in the south, toward the Panama border, are the still-unexplored ranges of the Cordillera de Talamanca and the torrid tropics of Golfo Dulce and the Peninsula de Osa.

There are over eight hundred species of birds here (more than all of the United States and Canada combined); eight thousand plant species (with over twelve hundred different types of orchids); twenty national parks and reserves covering almost ten percent of the nation; the world's finest "high-acid" coffee and sweetest bananas; three symphony orchestras; twice as many teachers as policemen.

Columbus was right when he sailed along the Caribbean side of the country in 1502 and named it Costa Rica, "the rich coast." Typically, of course, his idea of riches referred more to the possibilities inherent in the gold ornaments worn by the coastal Indians than the natural fecundity of the country. King Ferdinand's early Spanish colonizers were sadly disappointed by the lack of significant gold sources and the aggressiveness of the natives. Settlement was sparse and half-hearted even after the establishment of Cartago as the capital in 1563. The Spanish felt abandoned and adopted native lifeways (while still managing to decimate the native population); Costa Rica was too poor and too far from the center of Spain's Central American empire in Guatemala to be of lasting interest.

Following independence in 1821, the undeveloped country was ripe for domination by avaricious visionaries. On my second night in San José I attended a powerfully satirical production in one of the city's many underground theaters. The young cast presented a musical synopsis of the nation's history, highlighted by the theme song "Quien Soy?" ("Who Am I?"). The tight-packed audience constantly broke into spasms of laughter, tears, and jeers (how the Ticos *love* their theater!) as the troupe of eight acted out the arrogance of the nineteenth-century coffee barons, the empire-building antics of the American pirate, William Walker, and the machinations of Boston's Minor Keith who supervised the construction of the incredible 104-mile-long San José–to–Limón coffee railroad in the 1880s (a most unusual jungle ride experience for adventurous travelers).

Keith went on to found the notorious United Fruit Company (La Yunai) on 800,000 acres of free banana land in the eastern coastal plain. Even the gradual emergence of democracy here, following the demise of those larger-than-life intruders, was marred by occasional oppressive dictatorships, and it was only (as Guillermo had proudly told me) the unifying gift of Pepe Figueres that ultimately brought social reform and peace to this battered land. When the final chorus of "Quien Soy?" came, the audience rose as one and surged to the stage, embracing the players, some openly weeping, shouting slogans of pride for the peace and democracy of their little nation. That night they knew exactly who they were.

After two days of museums and remarkably active nightlife in San José, I was ready for sun, sand, and the simple life. So I rented a car and drove the winding road down from the high central valley, through mile after mile of coffee plantations, to the languorous seaside town of Puntarenas on the Pacific Ocean.

Doe-eyed Brahma cattle lolled about in the moist green fields of the coastal plain, attended by their retinues of white egrets. Most of the peasant homes were simple, colorful clapboard structures with tin roofs, hidden in profusions of palms and banana trees.

At Puntarenas I left the land behind and sailed off on a small launch across the Gulf of Nicoya, into a hazy blue-on-blue limbo. Pelicans perched on quano-coated islets, occasionally dive-bombing the waves for snacks. Cormorants skimmed like shadows, low over the swell.

The mainland was soon lost in warm mists and we eased among islands, dozens of them, into hideaway-heaven. Most of them had a few fishermen's homes on them, simple driftwood shacks shaded by coconut palms, looking out over strips of pure white sand. The boats were often nothing more than hollowed-out tree trunks; nut-colored children splashed in the surf, waving. Behind the beaches the jungle rose up in a tangle of vines, covering high rocky hills.

A few islands were free of inhabitants, lovely lonely places where you could live out beachcomber fantasies among the butterflies and orchids, eating the always-abundant wild fruits, fishing whenever the mood was right, and generally bidding farewell to the fripperies of the high-tech life for as long as it took to touch and know again the things that really matter.

You lose track of time out here. The haze, the moist heat, and the gentle rolling of the boat move you into a different reality; the endless yammer of the mind ceases as you drift from one island to the next and the next, watching the greens move back into the blues, and on through shimmering silver to a gold so soft and translucent you feel you're disappearing into a Turner landscape of pure light. . . .

The next day I drove south from Puntarenas down the Pacific coast, through the hot and funky little town of Puerto Quepos, deep into the jungle wonderland of the Manuel Antonio National Park.

I stayed in a small cabin high on a hillside overlooking arcs of white beach and turquoise ocean. While the park was not as remote as the Nicoya islands, I still managed to find my own stretch of pristine sand here, snorkeling the day away, climbing up through the dense clammy jungle on Cathedral Point for even more spectacular vistas of cliffs and ocean. I shared the walk with hundreds of scarlet-and-black land crabs who live in little burrows among the roots and have a frustrating disdain for photographers.

Closer to the beach, I was joined by statuesque iguanas who exhibited just the opposite reaction and spent most of their time posturing their prehistoric profiles like movie star has-beens. One rather large three-foot-long male became incensed when I took portraits of his female companions but ignored him. So he followed me fifty yards along the beach until I finally succumbed to his persistence, then swaggered back to his harem, brandishing his sharp spines pompously.

Around eight o'clock the following morning I knew something had gone decidedly wrong. My mouth was dry and then full of saliva, then dry again. My body sweated like a bilge pump, streams of it, and the day's heat hadn't really hit yet. My simple cabin was still cool.

I had to get to the bathroom—fast. And then again. And again. By midday I'd spent most of my time there and, so far as I could tell, I had nothing more in my body to expunge. But still I sat. Waves of nausea flowed over me, sending hot and cold ripples up my spine. The mirror on the wall showed a deathly face edged in a moldy-green sheen and eyes so tired and egglike that I began to wonder if survival was in the cards at all.

Hour after hour passed. Time twisted in cobra coils; my brain wandered around its confines like an inebriated slug. Crazy thoughts kept popping up—utter free association. I was definitely in the throes of some emerging fever. All energy had long since been dissipated.

I moved to the bed and twisted and turmoiled. Occasional shards of sound came from outside: the surf, gulls, someone passing my cabin. The sounds became a series of symphonic variations, sometimes so distorted that I couldn't recollect what the original sound was as my brain now became a freewheeling bagatelle. The voices of passing children reverberated like Buddhist bells and gongs—booming, peeling, cymbaling into switchbacking roller coasters of sound.

By evening I was far out of the realms of reality. The fading colors played kaleidoscope forms on the walls; shadows became ogreous and then stretched out into landscapes with giant cacti, stunted trees, and shattered mountain ranges.

A butterfly fluttering through my open window became a kite, then a jeweled bracelet freely floating, then a silhouetted hawk, and finally a sinister shadowy presence lurking high in the upper corner of my room. I think a lizard came in for a while or a dragon or just another dream.

I stopped trying to make sense of anything. There was no me left in me—I was no longer fighting back, no longer interpreting and filtering—just letting the tides of images and sounds and smells and colors roll over me in this place where time had long since lost any meaning and I was free of everything.

On the second day—it seemed like the second day anyway —I had a vision. Something so clearly outlined and tangible that I reached out a long sweaty arm to touch . . . a basket of ripe bananas. Bananas? Something in the recesses of my battered brain was sending a message. Bananas. I had to get some bananas!

Someone was passing the window. I could hear voices. But I couldn't get off the bed. I could hardly lift my head. So I reached out for something hard and found a book I'd been reading before my world collapsed. Gripping a corner as hard as I could I flung it at the window. The noise of the impact was wonderful, the first recognizable noise in almost two days. Swish, thunk, keer-plop. Welcome real-world sounds.

The voices stopped and I heard a slither of feet in sand. A face appeared at the window and a young boy peered into my shadowy room. Big black eyes, pink lips, bright teeth.

"Bananas, please. And Coca-Cola." It didn't sound like my voice talking. The boy didn't seem sure what to do. I repeated my request slowly and pointed to my mouth.

A sudden smile and nods. "Si—bananas—si, si, Coca-Cola." And the face was gone.

More time passed, frozen shapes of time, each one distinct, glowing with different colors. An utterly new experience. And bananas were in there too. Curved scimitars, gleaming, linking blocks of time like golden chains.

A knock.

I said something, but it came out a grunt.

The door opened slowly. I thought I'd locked it, but it opened anyway and in came my little saviour with an old battered tin bucket.

He stood by the bed and smiled.

"Bananas."

He reached into the bucket and pulled out a stem of bananas—a dozen or more beautiful ripe fruits.

"Coca-Cola. And papaya."

There it was—sliced, wet, peach pink. The best papaya I had ever seen!

I pointed to a pile of my usual traveling detritus on the dressing table—pens, notebooks, knife, film, and scrunched-up paper money.

"Take money," I thought I said, but it was another grunt.

"No, I come back—later," he said shyly and left with a smile, closing the door quietly behind him.

The next hour (I think it was an hour. Time was still slithering around) was pure joy. Just the sight of the bottle and the fruit made me feel better. And never has Coke tasted so magnificent, that first fizzing gush, listening to it going down, down, filling all the oh-so empty spaces in this useless lump of wet flesh I assumed was my body.

And the bananas! Such sweetness and softness. I could feel my digestive system eagerly sucking in every molecule of nutrition, every protein, mineral, vitamin, and whatever else that miracle fruit contains. Then the soft sensuality of the pink papaya—if there is such a thing as a fruit orgasm I had one as the sloppy pulp ran down my throat, my chin, my chest. . . .

I slept a sleep of utter peace.

Much, much later, deep into the evening, I awoke to find a plate of rice and plantains, some rum, and another full bottle of Coke. The boy must have been back—all the banana and papaya skins had been cleared away. A clean moist cloth covered my forehead.

I was safe. I'd come through the uninvited torment and turned up whole and alive on the other side, hog-happy in banana-papaya-Coke and boiled rice heaven. Who cares about yesterdays and tomorrows? I was here right now and being pampered like a prince in my modest palace, and the sunset was blasting through the window and those wonderful buzzing things outside in the trees were buzzing away again and doubtless more bananas were on the way. . . .

A few days later I could—maybe should—have taken Minor Keith's famous railroad to the Caribbean coast (eight hours minimum and fifty-two stops) but chose a three-hour car ride instead to Puerto Limón, down the long slopes of the Cordillera Central, through endless miles of banana plantations.

Limón at night is three parts Graham Greene, two parts Gabriel Garcia Marquez, a hot dash of Vonnegut and a flash of *Apocalypse Now*. It's funky, greasy, sweaty; lopsided turquoise-blue buildings grow mold as thick as ivy creepers; raunchy bars burst onto the street in flurries of reggae and florid-faced punchups; the eyes of young girls in bright, tight dresses seem old before their time; deals of a distinctly illicit nature are made by huddled Caribbean men in broad straw hats shadowed under the fluorescent glow of tamale and empanada stands.

Everywhere there's music; thick, mushy back-beat rhythms in the mildewy air. The banyan trees in Parque Vargas, roots exposed like mountain ridges and sheened in green moss, drip with vines and dead strips of bark like creatures in a *Dark Crystal* movie. The air is stagnant with old sea smells; no breeze blows in the dankness. It's hard to believe you're in the same country —this could be some dockside corner of Kingston, Jamaica. Is Verdi really playing tonight to primped patrons in San José's Teatro Nacional, only a few hours away by car?

But in the morning everything changes. An easterly wind blows out all the flotsam of the night and Limón adopts the hustle-bustle "hey, what-happen', mon" flavor of a commercial port with a lively market, street vendors, everyone seemingly employed in loading and unloading huge cartons from overburdened trucks. A dozen witch-black vultures snack from the garbage pile outside the market. The owner of the café offers me aquadiente (sugarcane brandy); I gasp at its sharp potency, take his photograph, then head south along the coast, past endless banana fields and cocoa plantations, my stomach and face glowing.

Mile after mile of empty beaches look out over the green-blue ocean. At Cahuita National Park I searched for sloths in the untouched rain forest and snorkeled among the coral reefs, playing catcher-man with the parrot fish and 120 other colorful varieties. No one seems overanxious to develop this part of the country; it's a sleepy backwater livened by the young San José crowd at weekends, but most of the time it's just the local fishermen in their tree-trunk canoes still lobstering the same old way.

"Don' use traps too much and only one guy uses tanks in Cahuita. Mos' of us got good lungs, 'nuff for a fifty-foot dive and a long stick with a loop on the end."

I was talking with Vernon Barber, a young black fisherman I met after a lunch of fresh crabs and *casados* (the traditional platter of rice, beans, plantains, meat, and tortillas) at Stanford's beach front place in Puerto Viejo.

"You put the lease end over the lobster and pull it on up. And that's about it. Only once I got a little problem down there. My ears went all wrong and it had me goofy. I was jus' floatin' around lookin' at the fish . . . you feel nice jus' looking at the fish . . . then I said hey, Vernon, something's going on here and I went to get out but I couldn't. I didn't know which way was up.

I went this way, I went that way... I was real gone... They hauled me up and pulled me in the boat and my ears was bad—real bad—they was bleedin'. They hurt for a long while. Some say I ain't never been right in the head since then! But I still go down—not deep though, not for lobster—I jus' go down for fun, I like the fishes—red, green, blue... some with gold and black stripes..."

They say the beaches further south around Puerto Uva and south to the Panama border get better and better. I wouldn't know. I drove for miles on a rutted track until it finally disappeared in a still yellow pool. A truck was stuck right in the middle ahead of me, mud halfway up its doors. It looked as if it had been there a long time. I suddenly missed my pleasant room in the Gran Hotel overlooking San José's Plaza de la Cultura. The urge to play beach bum for a few days had obviously been satiated by my time in the Gulf of Nicoya.

But I was to be given no choice. Although I managed to extricate the car from the pool, the rain that had been forecast for the last couple of days began to fall. Actually *fall* isn't the word at all. It just tumbled in pummeling sheets, turning the track into a quagmire within minutes. Somehow I made it back to a beachside village I'd passed twenty minutes before and managed to find shelter in a rundown bar to wait out the storm. Only it never ended. The rain just kept coming. So I rented a small room and decided to leave traveling until tomorrow.

The rain became my jail.

Solid white bars of the stuff, so many and so thick that they blocked out the view across the road—correction—river. There was no road in evidence. From building to building, a molasses-brown snake of mud, water, and floating debris roared past the verandahs, buffeting a badly carved monument to Simon Bolivar, playing hide-and-seek around the palm trunks, to disappear out of sight around the bend by the beer shop.

For a while the sight intrigues. You wonder at the power of the clouds capable of holding such vast amounts of water. The patterns in the street-river fascinate, from the gouging surf of the central flow that rolled palm branches, tin cans, and even a dead dog with the skill and dexterity of a circus performer, to the swirling eddies at the edge of the flow, froth-topped and fragrant with the blossoms of bougainvillea and frangipani, patterning in ever-changing colors.

But then after a while all you see are the white bars of the rain itself, a portcullis, locking you into yourself. The sound of water is everywhere, never changing. The boom on the metal roof above your head; the wind-whipped whine as sudden gusts send the rain prattling and rattling on windows and doors; the slower, solemn drip, drop, drip from a roof leak somewhere in another room (and then in my room), and the hiss, swish, and gurgle as it nudges ever closer up the roadside to your door.

Rain makes me think of English summer Sundays as a child when more often than not, a planned fun-run into the country or backyard game of cricket had to be abandoned as the gray closed in and drizzling overtures commenced. And you ended up with a house full of people, expectations dashed, wondering what to do next. (You'd think that this regular occurrence in rainy England would have led to an array of interesting alternatives, but it rarely did.) Instead it was back to the newspapers for the men, back to the kitchen or the "lounge" (only used on Sundays, even in the smallest homes) for the ladies, and a sulky search on the part of the kids for some diversion that invariably met with the usual remonstrance of "too much noise," "go and play up-stairs," or—horrors of horrors—"why not have a nice little nap?"

"Napping," a traditional English pastime after an humon-gous Sunday lunch (always called "dinner"), seemed to me to be one of the most disgusting wastes of time. My sister and I would wait impatiently, horrified, as the mahogany clock ticked away good outdoor time and the air rumbled with tremulous snores and grunts from the grown-ups who had promised faithfully "just forty winks" before collapsing into a comatose state for what seemed like an eternity.

It all came back to me in this doused Costa Rican village— the aroma of overcooked beef, the cloying aftertaste of treacle sponge pudding. The heat of the fire (when I was young fires were needed all through summer in many English homes to heat the water), the grayness of the wet light, the emptiness of the road outside (no cars to spot), the strange malty smell of stale beer from the dinner glasses, and a sense of doom and boredom as another Sunday afternoon trickled away down the blurred windowpane.

Rain. I loathe it.

Ah, but thunder I love. And the thunder came, booming over the barrage of coastal mountains, crashing over my tin roof, rattling the windows and sending satisfying tremors across the plank floor. Suddenly I felt alive and invigorated—the stuffy, claustrophobic little room became a warm cave, a safe haven to watch the jagged spines of lightning bleach the jungle outside and to feel the surge of nature's fickle power, boom-boxing and blasting overhead—a bombardment of solid sound. But, it's never enough. I want it louder, thicker, continuous—I want a climax of clamor and vibration. I want eardrums ringing and teeth jiggling. I want all the pent-up power of the storm to be loosed in one enormous gut-blasting crack and thwack and tumble. . . .

And then it was gone.

Skittering and echoing off across the hills, the storm dragged the dungeon bars of rain with it and the last tatters of gray soggy cloud. The blue is back, a clean, fresh, purified blue sky and a haloed sun. And the familiar sounds, which strike up like a record just switched on, the cocks and hens, the cicadas, the doves, people laughing and whistling, a car or two, someone hacking wood, the swish of bicycle tires, doors being flung open. Figures stepping out into the new air, saturated with scents and the smell of opened earth and the sparkle of leaves, freshly sheened. A day begins again—a bit muddy perhaps, but in an hour or two it'll all be dry and the prisony pall of the storm forgotten.

And so it goes, each day renewing itself, in this little forgotten corner of Costa Rica.

The final part of the drive back to San José on the new highway through the Cordillera Central must be one of the most spectacular scenic routes in Central America. Soaring up from the interminable pineapple plantations of the Santa Clara lowlands, I arced through the green-on-green mountains, cloaked in dense virgin rain forest and wrapped in whisps of mists. The road is so well constructed you forget it's there at all and just float up through the jungle with fleeting glimpses of the great gray-topped volcanoes peeping through the lower ranges. Green-and-red-winged parrots swoop out over the hazy hills; you may spot monkeys and sloths—even one of the rare jaguars (I didn't).

Far below, silvery threads of rivers wriggle around the ridges, fed by feathery waterfalls. I peered into a primeval land, unchanged for thousands of years. Once most of Costa Rica looked like this, before the aggressive deforestation, spurred by easy wealth from coffee plantations. You touch a little of the earth here in pristine form and feel a surge of empathy for the ancient Indian cultures once spiritually centered in these silent ranges, before being wiped out by the Spaniards.

And then, just as the jungle has entered your soul, you vanish into a long tunnel and emerge into the bright light of the central valley and the San José sprawl far below. The transition is far too rapid. I wasn't ready for neat fields, farmhouses, frilly suburbs, and concrete towers. I wanted to go back to the purity at the other side of the mountains.

Monteverde! That's a long hard drive, they said, you've got thirty miles on really hard backroads—all uphill, they said, and all for what?

"For the golden toads," I said. And that quieted them.

Ever since Carol and David Hughes's photographic forays for *National Geographic* into this remote part of northwestern Costa Rica, Monteverde and its profusion of wildlife have become world reknown. Naturalists and botanists flock to lose themselves in the six-thousand-foot ranges of virgin cloud forest in the Cordillera de Tilaran. They come to study the mating habits of the rare quetzal and the Bell birds, to photograph the more than two thousand plant species native to Monteverde (an orchid-lover's paradise), and even to spend weeks high in the jungle canopy examining the world of epiphytes—miniature jungles in themselves of plants living on other plants. But it's really the elusive golden toad that has captured everyone's imagination—tiny creatures that can be found only in one small pool here where they come to mate. I decided I'd like to see them for myself.

The doomsayers were right about the journey. It *was* long,

and the last thirty miles indeed pummeled my backside to pulp in the somewhat spartan automobile. I arrived at dusk to find the dining room of my alpine-looking hotel filled with eager-faced young hikers from Scandinavia singing Swedish folk songs which took me back to my hearty, healthy camping days in the mid-sixties. Suddenly I felt rather old and decided to have an early night.

At dawn, mists filled the lower valleys thousands of feet below, but the cloud forest on these high ranges was cloud free, today, basking in fresh light. I'd been told this was the best time to set off so, clutching cameras and a lunch pack, I left the soft morning sun behind and entered the dark forest.

Within minutes I realized that finding the golden toads would not be as easy as I'd assumed. Recent storms had made a mire of the narrow trail, which wound around fallen trees and thigh-high tangles of roots. Flies were out even so early in the morning and seemed to relish the streams of sweat pouring down my face and arms. The air was stagnant, smelling of decayed leaves and mossy rot. Occasional views out of the jungle showed steamy ridges of virgin forest; the mists were creeping higher now up the valley sides; there were strange rustlings all around me and every once in a while came the eerie echoing scream of howler monkeys—one of the most unpleasant "natural" sounds I have ever heard.

After another hour I was a mud-caked wreck, flailing up almost vertical hillsides, tumbling down again into swampy patches buzzing with cicadas. And then the mists moved in, making everything indistinct and blurry in the half-light. No one else was around. I lost the trail briefly and felt utterly helpless. From the air the jungle seems so ordered, a Teddy-bear textured coating of deep green over rolling hills. But below, that deceivingly benign canopy is total chaos, with only the thin thread of a trail to maintain an intruder's sanity.

Somehow, much later on, I found the pools where the golden toads were said to congregate and mate and was not at all surprised to find them empty—just inky black puddles in the gloom. I was too tired to walk so I sat among the mossy roots of a fallen tree and let the flies have their way with me.

I may have dozed because when I next looked the pools were rippling. I looked closer and there they were, a dozen or so golden toads no more than four inches long, frolicking about in the blackness, totally oblivious to me, seeking out the females who seemed to be successfully eluding them. In that setting of riotous vegetation and otherworldly confusion, they seemed utterly perfect, unblemished, sparkling little creatures doing what comes naturally in these lonely pools high in the Monteverde cloud forest.

The experience was worth all the discomfort of that day.

Much (much) later I finally staggered back into civilization to be greeted by an elderly gentleman in a straw hat carrying two aluminum milk cans. We met by chance near the dairy and small cheese-making plant for which Monteverde is nationally famous. He introduced himself as Osborne Cresson and invited me to his home for "homemade lemonade and a fresh-up!"

There I met his wife Betsy and son, Oz, who told me the fascinating story of Monteverde's founding by a group of world-weary Quakers from Alabama who purchased six thousand acres in these high hills in the 1950s for a farming community and biological reserve. Their struggles to reach their elusive eyrie in oxcarts on almost nonexistent trails, build their own homes, and establish an economically viable colony would make a wonderful film. The three of them, and their talking parrot, exuded such a sense of peace and calm that I knew I had found yet one more shangri-la in this land of hidden shangri-las.

Inspired by the enthusiasm of the early Quaker settlers, this cloud forest region has attracted worldwide scientific and conservationist attention and is one more example of Costa Rica's "peace-in-action" philosophy. A portion of the Quakers' original manifesto states: "In contrast to increasing militarism we hope to discover a way of life which will seek the good of each member of the community and to live in a way that will naturally lead to peace in the world rather than war."

Outside the wide windows of the Cressons' simple wooden house, flowers and orchids bobbed in the mountain breezes; off to the side were orange trees, macadamia bushes, banana and breadfruit trees, blackberries galore, and even a small cluster of coffee bushes.

Betsy spoke for the family. "This is paradise—truly. Every year I'm here I get a year younger." Osborne and Oz smiled and nodded. Even the parrot seemed to agree.

After Monteverde I became a frustrated monkey seeker. I was tired of hearing their chattering high in the cloud forest canopy and seeing nothing. Then I got an opportunity to visit Mike Kaye's Tortuga Lodge in the Tortuguero National Park on the Caribbean coast. So I postponed departure for a few days and found myself, very early one morning, flying eastward at ten thousand feet through a torrential thunderstorm in a creaky twin-engine Piper and wondering if monkeys were really all that important after all.

We eventually broke cloud cover at about treetop height and landed on a grass strip, with dark jungle on one side and long empty strands of beach on the other. The rain continued to pour as we crossed a narrow channel to the bamboo and thatch lodge set in fifty acres of tamed jungle.

Breakfast was waiting for us at a long table in a room adorned with photos of guests standing beside catches of enormous sharks (a 232-pound bull shark caught by an A. Grassi seemed to be the most prominent), tarpon, and snook. The talk was all sport fishing. First-timers ogled at the enormous jaws of shark trophies on the wall; the more experienced fishermen discussed the finer points of battling 150-pound tarpon whose strike and aerial acrobatics exhilarate the initiated and usually terrify novices.

In spite of the teeming rain there was an atmosphere of excited expectation in the room, and Mike Kaye, plumply regal in spite of his baggy shorts and green Tortuga T-shirt, watched over his guests benignly. Some of them were avid turtle watchers, come to observe the nocturnal egg laying of over five thousand green turtles and enormous seven-hundred-pound leatherbacks along the nearby beaches. "It's a very touching experience to see these creatures laboring for hours in the sand, digging their holes, laying their eggs, covering them up, and dragging themselves back into the ocean. You never forget it." Mike is still a romantic.

As the fishermen prepared to leave I joined my guide,

George, in a small shallow-draught boat. We were off to look for monkeys and chugged slowly up the river, past a small village of palm-thatch cottages, watching the jungle slowly close in around us. The rain eventually stopped, the sun emerged, and it became steam-heat hot. The river narrowed to a creek and the jungle canopy formed a one-hundred-foot-high nave overhead. The banks were a riot of vines, broad-leaved heliconia, philodendron, and anthurium. A white heron eased itself langorously into the wet air; two macaws watched us slip by, and a flurry of green parrots thrashed through the trees and vines, their screeches echoing in the gloom. A "Jesus" lizard (basilisk) ran upright like a jogger across the water from one bank to the other on wide webbed feet; a Morphos butterfly with an eight-inch wingspan enjoyed a free ride on our boat for a while before fluttering off in flashes of bright blue.

Screams came from deep in the rain forest. "Howler monkeys," said George. I nodded. I'd heard them before. Now I'd like to *see* them—just one would do. George pointed to a clump of elephant ear leaves above a patch of water lilies by the bank. At first nothing, then very slowly an enormous gray iguana with a four-foot long tail emerged from a tangle of vines and gave me his spiny profile to photograph at leisure.

Between brief bouts of jungle noises, utter silence. The boat drifted by itself and we sweated and listened and watched. The jungle on the west side of the creek stretched unbroken for one hundred miles to the high cordilleras; we could peer in about ten feet. After that it was just a tangled mystery.

We floated on, dazed by the heat. In the stillness I was struck by the total aliveness of the forest; an incredible green machine of endless self-perpetuation, dripping with seeds, berries, pods, nuts, blossoms, pollen-coated stamens, all bursting with perfect blueprints for the next growth and the next ad infinitum—eternally re-creating itself, unseen, unhurried, and unchecked.

In that tiny boat I felt like an openmouthed intruder, hardly understanding anything of what I saw, irrelevant to the place, almost envious of the jungle as an unquestioning participant in the enormous rhythms of life, responsive to a far deeper purpose. The little tribulations of our conscious lives and the apparent inability of us human beings to find a common harmony with all the myriad life systems around us seem to leave us spinning on the surface like flotsam, so tangled in our petty patterns that we fail to comprehend the larger whole of which we are a part. And while we're trying to understand what we dimly sense unconsciously, we slowly destroy ourselves and the earth too. . . .

And then I saw the monkey.

It was a whiteface, sitting in a banyan tree on the opposite side of the creek watching us with dark unblinking eyes. We stopped the boat and just sat looking back; I had an odd feeling he knew exactly what I'd been thinking. What struck me most was the humanness of the face: he seemed like a very old, wise man, wrinkled and balding, a little sad at what he saw below him. I tried to take a few photographs but my heart wasn't in it. He just sat there, never shifting his gaze. George was smiling and nodding. "I seen him before," he said quietly. "I know him." The jungle was utterly still; nothing moved.

And then he was gone. A few waving leaves, a quick shadow in the gloom, and then nothing.

George was still smiling. Even he knew what was on my mind. "Bet he could teach you a few things," he said.

I nodded.

I bet he could too.

It was all George's idea to camp out on Tortuguero beach and wait for the turtles to come in. I would have preferred a comfortable bed at the lodge but George said we should do it "Archie Carr's way." Dr. Carr was founder of the Green Turtle Research Station here in 1957. He and his followers over the years managed to save this largest known nesting ground from the massacres of native poachers, who made small fortunes from the flesh, leather, and shells of this endangered species. But it's a hard job—never-ending vigilance during the egg-laying season. And we were about to become part of the ritual.

"Arribada! They're here!"

One eye opens. It's dark but not too dark. A moon makes the beach gleam like burnished armor. Phosphorescence sparkles

MY
TORTUGUERO
IGUANA
—Costa Rica

along the surf. It's cool, too, with a breeze—a welcome change from endless days of one hundred-degree sticky heat.

George shakes my shoulder.

"Said they'd be here round two. On the button, man."

It is two-ten in the morning on a twenty-mile stretch of beach along the Caribbean shore of Costa Rica's Tortuguero. Behind us, across the river, is the jungle, black and silent now, stretching back a hundred unbroken miles and more to the Nicaraguan border. Fifty yards in and you could lose yourself forever in that tangled chaos of vines and vegetation. Scary place.

"Counted four—an' there's more comin'."

I peer out into the surf as it froths and skitters across the sand. Gradually black domed shapes, edged in moonlight, are wallowing up the beach.

They've arrived! Just like clockwork—some primordial pre-time clockwork—the green turtles of Tortuguero are coming home again to lay their eggs in the warm sand here as they have been doing every year for millions on millions of years. The eternal life-death-life cycle. And tonight we're their only witnesses.

George is a native of this part of Costa Rica, one of Central America's wildest regions. He's seen it all before but seems as excited as I am.

"Just look at them!"

More are moving in now.

"This is going to be a night."

George nods his grinning black face.

But we had no idea just what a night it would turn out to be....

Earlier in the day my monkey had moved me to introspection. Now it is the turtle's turn. I'm fully awake. As they crawl laboriously up the long, moonlit beach I feel part of some eternal ritual, something that predates man's appearance on earth by eons. A sensing of those ancient rhythms again.

"No flash, no lights," warns George. "They git scared n' go back."

We don't need them, the moon is full and everything is clear as daylight.

Slowly—unbelievably slowly—the great dome-backed creatures pull themselves up the sloping sand. One is enormous, almost five feet in length ("'bout eighty pounds a foot," says George). She is only a few yards from our camp and has reached the nadir of the beach, near the sand-grass. Using her back flippers one at a time she begins to dig out her nest. We move closer slowly so as not to disturb her. Other turtles further down the slope see us and hesitate but the big one seems indifferent now, her eyes glazed and tearful.

"She cryin'. She'll cry all the time till she finished. Keeps sand outa her eyes. An' she don't care 'bout us—she's nestin'."

As she digs deeper, well over a foot in now, her body becomes more steeply angled. Then she stops and just lies still, her eyes streaming. Suddenly her neck tightens, the leathery skin stretches like sinews and she opens her mouth wide. I expect a sound, she seems to be in pain, but nothing comes out except a gentle hiss. And then it happens. One by one, the tiny white eggs begin to drop into the sandy hollow. They're like oversize golfballs glistening and leathery; you can see them dint a little as each one falls. Four or five and she pauses, lowering her head. Another straining heave and three more appear.

Within twenty minutes I count at least sixty eggs.

"Still got a ways to go," says George. "She'll drop 'bout a hundred. They comes back every two weeks 'bout three times— m'be five times, till they got no more left."

George reaches out and pats her enormous shell but there's no reaction from those crying eyes.

"Real gone."

Before the coming of Archie Carr and the creation of the Tortugero National Park, the beach here, known locally as Turtle Bogue, was a gory killing field during the nesting season. Green turtles by the hundred were turned on their backs by *veladores* and were either slaughtered on the spot for their meat and gelatinous *calipee* (the essential ingredient of true turtle soup) or floated out to offshore boats with driftwood tied to their flippers. In addition, dozens of *hueveros* (egg stealers) and offshore *har-*

poneros (harpoonists) added to the carnage. By the 1950s the species was almost extinct.

"Was real bad," George had told me. "Shells, bones—all the way up. Twenty miles. They didn't even let 'em lay. If they did, they'd take all the eggs n' sell 'em.'"

Even Columbus himself noted the excellence of the turtles captured by his men when he explored this rich coast in 1502. Later, the eighteenth-century British Navy used these beaches regularly for supplies of turtles, which were kept alive for months in the holds of their ships.

We walk slowly across what seems like miles of beach. We're a long way now from Archie Carr's place and our kayuka (George's canoe hacked out from a single tree trunk). The phosphorus in the surf is like a silver brush fire; the breeze is cool. The egg holes are filling. One smaller female (a mere two hundred pounds or so) has ended her laying and looks around as if emerging from some trance. She waves her back flippers and begins raking the sand over the eggs. She seems agitated and speeds up, using all four flippers at once; she lifts and drops her body on the sand to compact it.

"Sixty days there'll be a hundred baby turtles runnin' for the sea."

George watches the mother.

"She's gotta get back. Tide's going out. S'long crawl."

Slowly she turns to face the ocean. It's hard to tell where her nest is now. She looks worn out, her flippers hardly move her at all. I feel like giving a push. Her route is erratic, zigzaggy tracks across the soft sand; she's disoriented.

"Lights do that," says George.

"What lights?"

He points up the beach. Those *are* lights. I thought they were fireflies.

"Who is it?" I'd expected to see more travelers here to witness this unique spectacle. Maybe that's who they are.

"Veladores."

"Poachers! You've got to be kidding. They stopped that years ago."

George smiles.

"Are they armed?"

"They'll have machetes. M'be more."

"What have we got?"

He reaches under his loose T-shirt and slowly pulls out an eighteen-inch-long knife with a flat broad blade from a scabbard inside his trousers. We start walking toward the lights. At the top of the beach where the sand is harder we move faster. I can see a boat in the swell beyond the surf. There are two men ahead. They see us coming and turn their lights toward us. George raises his machete; sweat is dripping off his chin, his eyes are as hard as granite. They raise theirs and start toward us. This is starting to get a little frisky. George shouts and moves faster. They stop (thank God). There's commotion, a lot of kicking sand; one of the men drops his light, then I see them scampering off down to the surf. George shouts again in the local dialect. The men keep running, tumbling into the waves, swimming to the boat. The motor roars, the men are dragged aboard, and it surges off through the choppy waves.

We reached the dropped lamp, pick it up and shine it across the beach. Ahead we can see at least six turtles on their backs. We expect the worst—turtles stripped of their valuable calipee and left to die. Luckily we'd come in time. The veladores had only turned them and possibly intended to float them alive to the boat for later dismemberment.

We stand looking at them, out of breath. We've got no energy left.

Righting overturned three-hundred-pound turtles is no easy matter. We work together grasping one flipper each, prying over the shell with our lower legs and leaping back out of the way of the four flailing flippers equipped with knife-edged claws that could quite easily slice off a finger. We watch the creatures crawl back down to the waves.

George strolls into the jungle behind the beach and brings back four small coconuts. He slashes the tops off with the machete and we pour the sweet liquid inside down our sand-raspy throats. We're drenched in sweat; my head feels as light as a balloon. We lie down and sleep the sleep of the dead till dawn.

Come to think of it, I suppose the seventy-mile flight back to San José was quite an adventure, too, in a single-engine plane that rattled, bounced, and plummeted through another torrential thunderstorm with nil visibility all the way. Somehow we missed the ten-thousand-foot peaks of Volcan Barva and Volcan Irazú. The young pilot cringed with every metallic creak and kept fingering his rosary every time we lost radio contact with the airport. But I was obviously adventured-out and grinned like a baby all the way back. After all it's not every day you're given a chance to save a few endangered turtles with a friend like George.

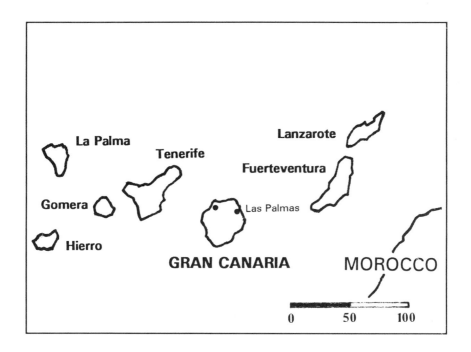

4. GRAN CANARIA

On Becoming a Native

Luck and I were on very amicable terms.

I couldn't put a step wrong. Everything I did seemed to be turning out right. And what made it all so ironic was that a few days previously my situation, at best, had been desperate: funds at an all-time low, weather in southern Spain cold and lousy, ridiculously expensive ferries to North Africa, and border closings all along the North African coast, making a disaster out of plans for my journey. Oh yes. And some very old noises were coming out of my VW camper's engine!

On the worst day of all I almost gave up and was about to dump the camper, hitch a ride to the airport and use up my return ticket home—home to wife and cats and warm baths. But

107

I couldn't. Go home early? What an admission of defeat. What a letdown. Crawling back like a drenched dog in the middle of January (and I was definitely drenched—it was the worst winter on record in Algeciras, that miserable little pimple of a place immediately to the west of Gibraltar, on the rump of Spain).

And then I saw them. Tanned as taco shells, in shorts and T-shirts, slim, fit, bright-eyed, giggling like kids at the muddy puddles, the rain-pummeled umbrellas, and miserable faces of the locals who were too depressed even to douse their sorrows in the ritual café-y-cognac tipples.

"Where the heck have you been?" I sounded like a drowning man crying out for rescue.

"The Canary Islands," they said and smiled so happily that I hugged them, ran them out of the rain to a waterfront bar, and used up my day's budget on cognacs for all of us, eliciting every detail and nuance about those magic isles that take poor, jaded, downtrodden, burnt-out cases from the gray climes of a North Europe winter and turn them into perky little paradise dwellers, who giggle at the rain and whose faces radiate pure sunshine.

Obviously I decided to go there. The next day.

For pennies I loaded my camper and me on board the enormous linerlike Canary Islands ferry. I looked forward to two days of oceanbound hedonism, feasting on tapas and splashing in the pool with all the pretty Spanish ladies. What I actually got was two days strapped to my bunk, foodless, as the ship lurched and plunged southward through Atlantic storms, to those remote volcanic blips off the Saharan coast of Africa. The only bonus: I finally read *War and Peace*, cover to cover, something I'd been promising myself since high school.

A few hours before arrival in Gran Canaria, the largest island of the seven Canaries, the storm ceased and we skimmed through mirror-glass waters, gleaming gold in a hot sun. Around six in the evening we saw the green and purple volcanoes of Gran Canaria rising out of the evening haze. Everyone congregated on deck and there was a communal silence, cathedral-like in its reverence.

Although referred to briefly by Pliny the Elder as the "Fortunate Isles," little was known about these remote volcanic outposts until the arrival of Jean de Béthencourt in 1402, who came with plans for establishing embryo colonies for the Spanish crown. The randomly scattered Guanche and other Indians, the islands' only inhabitants, were quickly rousted out of their cave-dwelling languor and eliminated long before Columbus's brief but famous stopover here on the way to discover the New World.

Gran Canaria and Tenerife, whose 12,188-foot-high peak of Pico de Teide acts as a focal beacon for all the islands, experienced the first great surges of tourist-resort development in the 1960s. Little Lanzarote followed later and now boasts a handful of world-class beach resorts below that tiny island's moonscape hinterland of still-active volcanoes, sinister lava fields, and "black deserts" of sand and ash. More remote and undiscovered are the tiny islets of Gomera and Hierro where dense rain forests and terraced mountains mingle with high sheep pastures (watched over by burly Castilian shepherds famous for their mountain-to-mountain "yodeling" language), towering volcanoes, and hidden lava-sand beaches—real earth-gypsy territory. Nobody could tell me much about them or the other two outer islands of La Palma and Fuerteventura. I planned to visit them all once I had gained my shore legs after a few days in Las Palmas. But things didn't quite work out that way. . . .

As we drew closer to Las Palmas harbor I heard music. Lots and lots of music. "Fiesta!" The word spread around the ship. Fiesta! Of course. It was New Year's Eve. I'd lost track of the days in my fusty little cabin. It was celebration time and the capital city of Gran Canaria was full of people dancing, singing, shouting, waving crazy hats, letting off firecrackers. What a way to be welcomed!

I was one of the first off, scampering down the gangplank and sinking into soft sand (the sinking bit was involuntary; my legs didn't adjust well to firm land at first). An enormous conga line of bodies snaked by, past the customs house, across the city park, and down through the narrow streets of pastel-colored houses to the main beach. I left my camper at the quay and joined in all the skipping and tripping like a lopsided lamb, losing myself in the frisky folk songs of the Canaries, laughing and hugging like everybody else, splashing myself with local rum from a leather *bota* flask, and finally collapsing in a sweaty heap on the soft sand, silvered by moonlight.

The beach was full of bodies—singing, kissing, dancing, and swimming in the slapping surf. Someone gave me a cigar "made in my island, senor, and may God be with you for the next year." I offered all I had in return, some chocolate and nuts (meager remains of my oceanic staples), and I received more rum, a bottle of pungent red wine, half a pack of Gauloise cigarettes, three kisses, an invitation to breakfast, a bunch of grapes, another kiss, a song sung specially for me by a young man with a face like an angel, half a chorizo sausage, and still more Canary Island rum.

I danced again, joined in the choruses of those catchy local folksongs, swam, and finally as dawn began to creep up over the still ocean, curled up in the sand and slept the sleep of the gods for a few hours.

"Senor."

Someone was touching my shoulder. I could feel the heat of the morning sun.

"Senor, some coffee."

I woke up to find a tiny cup of espresso being pushed into my hand by a waiter from one of the beach-front cafés.

"You not dead, eh?" He was an elderly man dressed in a crisp white jacket. His wrinkled face spoke of vines and olive trees and years under the sun—and kindness.

"I see you sleep and I bring you something for wake up."

I grinned a thank-you and swallowed the strong brew in two gulps.

"Ah—you forget." He pointed to a glass of amber liquid on the tray. "Drink with coffee." It was brandy, the strong Canary Island type, hardly distinguishable from the local rum and with the same kick. My first introduction to the ritual morning "café-y-cognac." And it worked. I was suddenly wide awake, with a healthy flush on my cheeks. The old man was laughing.

"I think you like, eh?"

"I know I like," I told him.

"Come to the café. One more is good for you."

So I did, and it was. I left my bags with the old man and walked into the morning sea, surfless and still. There were bodies all over the beach, still sleeping. Someone was playing a timpale, the Canary version of the ukelele, with soft plunky notes that can be made to sound so sad when played close to the bridge and so alive when strummed in the rapid island manner, using thumb and all four fingers outstretched.

I lay back in the warm ocean and just floated, looking up at a cloudless gold-blue sky. . . .

This was perfection. I had found my paradise. But it all seemed a little crazy. I had little in the way of cash. I hardly had enough to return the six hundred or so ocean miles to mainland Spain. I had no real idea why I'd come except for the warmth. I knew no one. I had no place to stay except for my faithful camper. I didn't know how long I planned to stay or where to go next, and yet, the island spoke to me. Gently but firmly. "Stay," it said. "Just stay and see what happens." For a person who's always on the move and loves to be on the move, it seemed an odd proposition. But the voice inside sounded so certain, so totally clear. "Stay. Stay and let things happen."

And so that's what I did. And that's when I began to realize that luck and I were on very amicable terms. Once I allowed myself to let go, things literally arranged themselves, and I stood around watching like a delightful spectator as my life on Gran Canaria was fashioned gently before my eyes.

First a place to stay.

Well I obviously couldn't afford the hotels, and I didn't want to be near the crowded beach resorts and the winter tourists, many from the dark dank climes of Scandinavia, on a protracted two- or three-month winter sojourn. I wanted somewhere quiet, honest, basic. Somewhere near the ocean, hidden away. A place to think and paint and write. . . .

My camper seemed to know where she was going. We left Las Palmas that afternoon in a rummy haze. The map of the island was open on the passenger seat but ignored. I let her just take the narrow island roads at whim. We climbed high up the slopes of the largest volcano, Valcequello, pausing in a pretty

111

EL ROCOVE
Gran Canaria
Spain

mountain village for tapas in a tiny blue-painted bar with a vine-shaded patio overlooking the whole island.

Here? I wondered. But we kept on moving.

More villages with lovely little churches and tiny plazas enclosed by neat white-and-lemon stucco buildings. Huge sprays of bougainvillea burst from roadside hedges. The scent of wild herbs rose from the tiny fields sloping down to the ocean. Banana plantations galore on terraced hillsides. Vast fields of tomatoes. Small vineyards. Cactus windbreakers protecting the huddled houses, white against the purpled green of the hills.

A tiny cottage with a stone roof appeared in a cleft between two church-high rocks. It had everything: vines, bananas, a small cornfield, two donkeys, two flagons of wine against a bright red door, blue shutters, and a view over cliffs and black volcanic soil beaches and ceaseless lines of surfing ocean.

Here? I wondered. But I still kept on moving and at dusk parked on a patch of grass below the volcanoes. Some bread, cheese, and chorizo sausage, a glass of brandy, and bed. I felt utterly at peace. Someone else was orchestrating this trip and that was just fine.

Very early the next morning it was all settled. I strolled away from the camper and sat on a rock, watching the sun come up. The black lava-crusted crest of Valcequello sparkled in the crimson-gold light. Then I looked down and saw something I'd not noticed the night before. A tiny white village, huddled, Greek island–fashion on top of a rocky promontory that jutted like an ocean liner straight out into the Atlantic. It was different from anything else I'd seen on the island. Most of the villages were straggly affairs, scattered over hillsides like blown confetti. But this place looked bright and strong and enduring on one-hundred-foot cliffs. A long flight of steps climbed up to it from a track. There was no road through the village, just a sinewy path with Cubist houses packed together on either side and ending in an area of level rock at the end of the promontory. I could see laundry blowing in the morning breezes; the hillsides below rose steeply from the rocky beach and were smothered in banana trees. It looked completely cut off from the rest of the island. A true hidden haven. Mine!

Somehow the camper groped her way down from the volcano, bouncing and wriggling on cart tracks cut through the brush. It was wild here. Not at all like the softer eastern side where the tourists congregated. I saw no one around as we descended. But my camper knew where she was going and I was happy to play along.

Around midmorning I arrived. The village looked even more dramatic close up. Scores of white-painted steps rose up the rock to the houses that peered down from their cliff edge niches. Some children were playing in the dust at the base of the steps. They stopped and slowly approached, smiling shyly. A rough hand-painted sign nailed to a tree read *El Roque*.

"Ola!"

The children grinned. "Si, si, Ola. Ola!"

One of the larger boys came over and shook my hand. And he wouldn't let go. He tugged and pointed to the steps.

"Mi casa—my house. You come."

It was an invitation and I accepted.

We all climbed together. The smaller children straggled in a line behind me; I felt like the pied piper, and even my wheezing at the end of the 130-step climb had a pipe-ish sound to it.

I've never seen a place quite like El Roque before or since. The lime-white cottages clustered tight in medieval fashion on either side of a six-foot-wide stone path that twisted and roller-coasted up and down, following the idiosyncracies of the promontory's rocky top. I passed a couple of shops the size of broom closets that doubled as rum bars for the men. Crusty bronzed faces peered out curiously from shadowy doorways. Old women, shrouded in black, scurried by. One very ancient woman, her face a mass of deeply etched folds, cackled wildly as we passed, exposing an enormous toothless mouth. The older boy smiled at me and did a loopy sign at the side of his head to indicate she was a little mad. The young boys touched her upraised hand gently with a sign of respect—or fear?

About halfway down the wriggling street we paused outside one of the larger houses and faced a ten-foot-high carved wood door decorated with etched brass medallions. The older boy, obviously one of the leaders of my pack of frisky followers, pushed at the door and a panel squeaked open. The rest of the door remained solidly in place.

We entered a dark lobby with bare blue walls and a richly tiled floor. I could hardly see in front of me and bumped into a low iron table. The boy took my hand and gestured to his followers to stay back at the main door. We moved deeper into the house where it was even darker. Then he opened a smaller door and the sunshine rushed in, blinding me.

We were in the living room, simply decorated with small tapestries and a broad oak table on bulbous legs topped with two fat brass candlesticks encased in wax drippings. Eight dining chairs were placed around the table; their backs and sides carved in high Baroque style with vine leaves and grape bunches. Straight ahead were three large windows looking out over a bay of black sand edged by banana plantations and, high beyond that, the great cone of Valcequello. The room was filled with light. The windows were open and I could hear birds, canaries I think, by their flighty chattering, and mourning doves, issuing soft cooing sounds.

The boy's name was Julio. He called out and I could hear someone coming, the swish of sandals on tiles. I was still mesmerized by the view until a figure stepped in front of me and gave a slight curtsy. At first the face was in silhouette against the light. Then it turned to smile at Julio, and my heart (I know this sounds corny but it really does happen) skipped at least two beats. She was utterly beautiful. Devastating.

"My sister," said Julio in slow English. "She is named Maria."

"Maria, this is Senor David." Now my wife, Anne, tells me I have a "soft spot" for the beauty of youth, particularly female beauty, and although I think she exaggerates, I can occasionally be touched by open-eyed innocence and the unlined face. Nothing insidious you understand, just fascination of things unspoiled. But this amazing creature . . .

I couldn't speak. Literally. My mouth sagged and stayed sagged. My smile must have seemed a terrible grimace. A gurgly sound was meant to be "Buenos dias" but was just that, a gurgle. Julio pulled my hand.

"Please sit. Sit here," he gestured to an elephantine armchair by the window, and I made a lot of motion getting in, trying to regain composure.

"Maria. Cognac, por favor."

He was the young master of the house even though much younger than his sister.

She smiled, proud of her brother's performance. Then she smiled at me and was gone.

"This is a beautiful house—your casa." I tried a bit of light conversation to see if my tongue was working.

"Oh yes," said Julio, sitting in another equally enormous chair beside me.

"Yes—beautiful." Well I got those words out. I was recovering fast.

"And my sister?" He looked very directly at me. (So he had noticed my reaction. A perceptive boy.)

"Your sister?"

"She is beautiful?"

"Oh, yes. Yes. Beautiful also."

"Yes. All people says so." Well I was relieved to hear that. At least I was among like-minded company. Maybe she had this effect on everyone. Quite the princess no doubt. Smiling and blinking those long black eyelashes at anyone who comes around. Spoiled too, I suppose. Maybe devious—innocence is rarely as innocent as it seems. A real little Lolita. Oh yes. I've seen it before. People all googly-eyed over a pretty girl. And they look so stupid, gibbering inanities and falling head over heels in instant infatuation. Well I'm wise to all that, Julio m'boy. Just let her come with the brandy and I'll show you how to handle that kind of nonsense.

"Please, Mr. David."

She was back, offering me a glass of brandy on a small silver tray and, damn it, I was doing it again. One look at that utterly perfect porcelain face framed in long black hair and those big black eyes and that aquiline nose and I was lockjawed again, trying desperately to shape a sensible smile that said "thank you for your courtesy" and nothing more....

The door opened and the room suddenly became much smaller. A great bear of a man entered, hands as big as frying pans and fingers like thick bananas. A bushy moustache covered most of his mouth and curved down, walruslike, at either side. His hair was as black and bushy as his moustache. A long scar, reaching from forehead to jawbone, gave him a dangerous look, but his eyes were the gentlest blue, shining, exuding welcome without words. Julio stood up, rake straight, Maria gave one of her curtsies and vanished again, and I rose to meet the man.

"Papa, this is Senor David."

Somewhere under the moustache a grin grew. A gold tooth flashed in the sunlight, and one of his enormous hands engulfed mine completely. He stood for a long time boring into me with those eyes, then he released me and gestured me to sit. He lifted one of those gigantic carved chairs at the table with two fingers, twisted it around, and sat down facing us both with his arms folded.

Tomas Feraldes could speak no English (his words rumbled from deep in his chest, like boulders tumbling down a ridge) but during the next half hour or so I enjoyed one of the richest conversations I have ever had with a stranger. His son acted as interpreter, and we talked in baby language of everything—the village, the banana plantation upon which all the villagers depended for their livelihood, the ocean, the wonderful variety of fish you could catch by a simple hook from the promontory cliffs, the history of Gran Canaria, and the great pride of the islanders in their little green paradise. I remember one of Julio's translations: "We are of Spain but we are not of Spain. We are Canary people. This is our land. This is our country."

The brandy flowed. Little dishes came—calamari in lemon and garlic, big fat fava beans that we squeezed to pop out of the soft flesh, spicy mixes of tomatoes and garlic with chunks of lime-marinated fish, sardines, island cheese, and more brandy.

Then Tomas motioned to Julio and spoke softly and firmly. Julio looked very intense and then smiled. He turned to me.

"My father says you will stay here if you wish."

"Here? Where? In this house?"

"No—in another place. My brother's home. He is away in Madrid."

"Where is this house?"

"It is very close."

Tomas spoke softly to Julio again.

"My father says you will come to see your house now. If you wish."

"My house!?"

"Yes. Come now. I will take you. You will stay, I think."

I now knew I had no control over anything. I'd followed my inner voice and let things happen and they were happening so fast and so perfectly I had no wish to impede the flow.

We were outside again in the narrow street. The children were still there, waiting patiently as if they knew what would happen long before I did. And off we all went, pied-piper fashion again, wriggling between the houses, right to the end of the promontory, where we all stood on the edge of the cliffs watching huge waves explode fifty feet in the air and feeling the vibrations through the rock.

Julio nudged me.

"This is your house."

I turned. He was pointing to a small square building, the last house on the rock, white and blue, with a staircase leading up to a red door. On the flat roof I could see plants waving. There were windows everywhere overlooking the beach, the volcano, the broad Atlantic.

Grinning like an idiot again, I followed him up the stairs. He unlocked the door with a key big enough for a castle dungeon, and we walked into one of the most beautiful rooms I have ever seen. Light filled every niche. On the left was a small propane stove, a sink, a big working table, and four chairs, Van Gogh chairs with straw seats and big unpolished wood uprights.

The living area was simply furnished—a few scattered rugs, armchairs, low table, lamps, empty shelves hungry for books (my books!). I could see the bathroom, tiled in blue Spanish tiles, and then another staircase leading up and out onto the roof, with views over everything—the whole village, ocean, mountains, bays. . . .

It was a dream.

"You like your home?" Julio was watching my face.

"Julio, this is the best house I have ever seen." I meant it too. "Yes," he said simply, "I know. My brother was happy here, but he is away now for a long time."

"Your brother has a lovely home."

"My brother's house—now your home."

I didn't know what to do or say. I felt like giggling, weeping, even praying a prayer of thanks (something I do far too infrequently). I shook Julio's hand and then I hugged him. At first he pulled back, and then he was hugging me as hard as I hugged him.

Moving in was splendid chaos. Every child in the village came to help me carry my belongings from the camper (she looked so tiny from the top of those 130 steps) to the house at the end of the village—clothes, sleeping bag, books (far too many books), cameras, food (far too many useless cans), fishing rod, cushions, towels—and my guitar. When the children saw that they went wild. Compared to the island *timpales*, this was a brute of an instrument, a battered Gibson with a deep tone. They were all shouting something at me. Indispensable Julio stepped in again.

"They say play, Senor David. Please."

But what? Which of my English and American folk songs could make any sense—Baez, Dylan, Guthrie, Paxton, Hank Williams, Pete Seeger, Donovan? Pete Seeger! Good old Pete always had a knack with kids. He could get them to sing in the middle of a tornado. I'd never sung much with kids before, but what the heck, everything on this island was new to me anyway and all I had to do was flow with the flow. . . .

"Skip, skip, skip to m'Lou . . ." I'd used the same song before on one of my journeys, and it had worked wonders. The chorus is simple, the melody obvious, and even if you couldn't get the words straight you could hum and la-la all the way through it. Which is precisely what they did.

Twenty-three little voices "Skip to m'Lou-ing" it up at the bottom of El Roque's steps, bouncing around in the hot afternoon sun, making the dust rise in golden haloes, singing faster and faster, "Skip, skip, skip to m'Lou." High above, a crowd of villagers gathered by the wall at the top of the rock, began clapping, and then the kids started clapping—"skip, skip"—and the whole bay rang to the sound of this crazy ditty that was utterly meaningless to them and perfect for this impromptu getting-to-know-you celebration on this, my first day in El Roque.

I thought—maybe a week or two here and then off to new places. But it didn't happen that way. It was four months before I left that island. I even managed to tempt Anne to put aside her work for a while and join me in my island home. The villagers were delighted. Once they realized I was married, all attempts had been abandoned to match me up with one of the many eligible females in El Roque. (No, Julio's sister, Maria, was already spoken for.) And on the day Anne arrived I invited the whole village to the house for a celebration. I had no idea what a Pandora's box I'd opened with this innocent little gesture.

Very casually I'd asked everyone to come over in the evening after their long workday in the banana plantation. Come anytime after six, I said. Anne and I had prepared some platters of bread and cheese and opened bottles of island wine and rum. Then at 6:30 P.M. precisely, there was a knock on the door. It was Julio (he'd long since appointed himself as my social secretary and general factotum).

"Please. Come. We are all welcoming your Mrs. David."

Anne and I walked out on the platform at the top of our steps and looked down. Faces! Scores of laughing, smiling Canary faces staring up at us, clapping, singing. And everyone was carrying something—we could see cakes, pans of broiled fish, a bucket of live crabs, banana branches, straw baskets of tomatoes, bottles of wine, more cakes . . .

"Everyone who comes to the house must bring present," Julio told us. "It is our custom." I have no idea how we got the whole village of El Roque into our tiny house, but we did. The kitchen, the living room, even the roof was jammed with villagers—many of them we'd never met. Anne and I were buoyed like froth ahead of the surge onto the roof, and we never made it back to the kitchen to serve the simple dishes we'd prepared. At one point Julio went to check for us.

"They've gone. They've eaten them. I've told them to bring the cakes for you to cut."

One by one, six brightly iced cakes made the journey over the heads of guests from kitchen to rooftop where we ceremoniously sliced them and sent them back downstairs for instant consumption. Then someone carried up the timpales and the guitar and off we went into a spree of folk songs that set the whole house bouncing long into the night. . . .

What had been intended as a one-time "Welcome to Anne" occasion became a regular weekly event for the rest of our stay. Every Thursday evening there'd be a "folk-fest" gathering at the house, which would leave our voices hoarse and our kitchen table bowed with food. The problem was actually getting rid of all the fish, sausages, tomatoes, bananas, cakes, and wine before the next session on the following Thursday. The most difficult items were the bananas. They'd bring whole branches with as many as 150 firm green bananas hanging from them. We tried every way we could think of to use them—banana bread, banana cake, banana crêpes, banana omelet, banana purée, banana souffle, fried bananas, banana with garlic (interesting experiment there), and even fish with baked whole bananas. And we still ended up with huge surpluses, which we invariably had to heave over the roof wall into the surfing Atlantic, one hundred sheer feet below.

We were living a virtually cash-free life. We insisted on giving Julio's father something for the house he'd so generously provided. He refused to take more than $20 a month, including all the electricity and even two bottles of Canary rum, which he left outside our door on the first Monday of each month.

We were utterly happy in our village and had no real desire to go anywhere else on the island. I found great satisfaction in painting again, something I'd let slide for months, and Anne discovered a previously unknown gift for knitting enormous shawls in bright wool colors with one-inch-diameter needles!

Every couple of weeks we'd pack a box of these new creations, leap into the camper, and drive thirty or so bumpy miles back into Las Palmas to sell our work to bored tourists with lots of money and very little to spend it on. Not that we needed the money, but it was rewarding to see people willing to pay real cash for our rooftop creations. And it somehow justified our return to the village for another two quiet weeks.

The residents of El Roque were a hard-working bunch. Up by five o'clock every morning, the men moved off quietly to tend the banana plantations on the surrounding hillsides, while the women cleaned every part of their houses (even the outdoor steps and the cobblestones on the main path through the village) before baking, washing, cooking, buying from the peddlers and fish vendors who passed through the village every day. No soap operas or siestas here. No meeting at the mall for a brioche and a bitch. Just the solid, daily, dawn-to-dusk ritual that should have left everyone worn out, but in fact seemed to have just the opposite effect. Our village had dignity, pride, and constant pep. If there were family problems, we never saw them. If there was malicious gossip or backbiting it must have been taking place well off the main path that we walked every day. If there was infidelity or illicit romance, it was done with such craft and guile as to be unnoticeable.

I know I'm a naïve romantic at heart and maybe I wanted my village to be a little too perfect, but, at least for the two of us, it brought a peace and a pace of creative energy that we had never experienced before and only rarely since. El Roque was a true home and we became as close to the villagers as our natures could allow. We went fishing and crab hunting with the men (the latter at night with huge torches of reeds dipped in tar that drew the crabs from the rocks like magnets). We worked in the banana plantations, we picked minimountains of tomatoes, we painted portraits of the villagers and gave them as gifts, we learned how to prepare the aromatic sauces for Canary Island fish dishes, and we even learned to love bananas in all their culinary variations!

El Roque is still a touchstone for us both—a place we have vowed to return to one day, a place that will remain with us forever and a place, in hindsight, where we perhaps should have stayed longer...

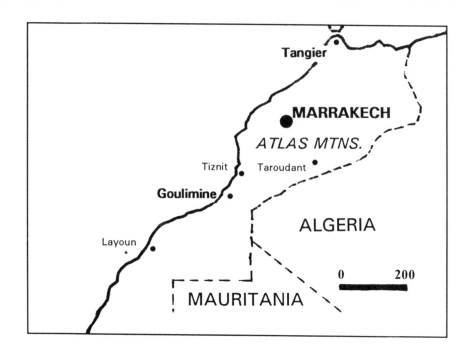

5. MOROCCO—
THE LAST
CARAVAN

Travels with the Blue People

I lie wrapped in blankets on the warm sand, looking up at the star-filled sky. I can't sleep. The moon is full and throws silver-edged shadows across the desert. The camels are restless too. They know their days of lazy grazing in the hills outside Gouli-mine are at an end. They have been watching our long preparations—filling the goatskins with water, packing the rugs and boxes of silver jewelry and all the other trading items, sorting the sacks of flour and sugar, cleaning the saddles and harnesses. They know today is departure day. We are finally off across the Sahara with the "Blue People" nomads.

I smile under those stars and the camels burp and fart in sympathy.

* * *

Say *Sahara* slowly and it's the hot *sergi* that blows for days on end across the deserts of Western Africa. Say it fast and loud and it's the sharp, knife-blade ridges that rise from endless gravel plains. Whisper it and you've got the vast nothingness of wind-skimmed sand stretching fifteen hundred miles south from Morocco's Atlas Mountains to the steamy tropics of Nigeria, Senegal, and the Ivory Coast.

Sahara. A vast empty world as big as the United States and hardly known at all. It's the epitome of desertness; a place everyone has dreamed of exploring with the nomads and their camel caravans—to go wherever they go and see the infinities through their eyes.

So, after years of musings and procrastinations I finally come to Marrakech, Morocco's northern gateway to the High Atlas and the desert. I expect Saharan overtures here but instead find a lovely rose-red city of minarets, broad boulevards, and a mazelike older quarter, the medina, couched in a bowl of palm groves and orange orchards. No sign here of any "Blue People" nomads.

Founded as a tent city way back in 1062 by Yusef ibn-Tashtin, a ferocious leader of Saharan nomads, the city has experienced the inevitable periods of invasion, cultural demise, and dramatic renaissance, most recently following the proclamation of Moulay Hassan as king here in 1873. At that time the country was known as the Kingdom of Marrakech, and the city, with its ornate palaces and shaded gardens, was reestablished as the great cultural crossroads of this powerful nation. Today, under King Hassan II, it retains that role.

"So where's the desert?" I ask.

"Far away, behind the Atlas," I am told by the locals who point proudly at the snow-capped peak of J'bel Toubkal (12,720 feet), the highest mountain in Northern Africa. "First enjoy our city, then go to your desert."

I am restless, impatient for the Sahara. But then I find the Djemaa el Fna, the nation's tribal meeting place and market, right in the middle of Marrakech. To many Moroccans the Djemaa is still the center of the world, and after two days held in its hullabaloo, I begin to understand why. It's a tumultuous prelude to my desert journey.

Surrounded by a scrabble of seedy hotels, arcaded tea-houses, and lean-to stores piled high with Moroccan trinkets, the Djemaa is a raggedy space as big as three football fields and about as charmless. The name translates as "Place of the Dead" (the severed heads of rebels and traitors were once proudly displayed here), and for a few hours a day it feels that way. But shortly after dawn the magic comes—even as early as 5:00 A.M., life begins to leech into the space from the dozens of little alleys that feed in from the *souks* (markets) and medina. The eerie cry of the muezzin echoes from the minaret of the Koutoubia mosque, which rises over the Djemaa like Allah's warning finger.

A couple of hours later you begin to see this place for what it really is and has been for almost eight hundred years—a magnificent daily melting pot of Moroccan cultures, a teeming urban oasis for the Berber tribespeople from the mountains, the nomads from the Sahara, the Bedouins, the Tuareg, the diminutive Chleuh and black-skinned traders from Senegal and Mauritania.

They flock in by the hundreds, turning this amorphous space into an amphitheater of activity: wily merchants from Fes and Casablanca spreading their silver bracelets and necklaces on worn shards of carpet; loquacious medicine men extolling the virtues of syrupy potions in brown glass vials, promising potency and "power of the limbs" to the gathering crowds; turbaned counselors offering advice for the lovelorn; astrologers with elaborate charts; jugglers; men with monkeys; men with snakes swirling out of baskets and around their necks to rasping tunes played on tin flutes; men who pull scorpions from their mouths; a pyramid of acrobats in scarlet tights featuring a tiny tot of a boy who bends in the most unusual places; a holy man, shadowy and aloof under his umbrella; veiled and cloaked women selling hard-boiled eggs served with a pungent dipping sauce, and the exotic bell-ringing, trinket-adorned water vendors offering refreshments of questionable quality from brass cups dangling from their bright red costumes. I was captivated by the beauty of blue-robed Berber dancing girls adorned in silver and jewels, their teeth and eyes flashing in the bright morning sun.

The crowd increases with the heat. Outsiders like me retire to the sidelines at regular intervals to sip sweet mint tea in the shady cafés. By 10:00 A.M. the orange sellers are out in force, squeezing those wonderfully aromatic Moroccan fruits for the juice addicts. A young man who has been offering his services as guide for the last hour nudges my arm and laughs at the old men gathered at the stalls, drinking the juice devotedly as if it were the very nectar of life.

"They can't drink alcohol. It is forbidden," the young man explains. "So they get drunk on oranges!" And they do seem a little tipsy as they wobble away, tripping over their long striped *djellabas* (thick, hooded kaftans). Does the juice ferment in the heat? Does Allah know about this?

Over on the south side of the Djemaa are the storytellers surrounded by circles of enthralled listeners—a hundred or more in each circle, silent and still as the raconteur swirls, leaps, crouches, shouts, whispers, weeps, and wails in a mesmerizing one-man theater, acting out every nuance of some ancient drama that they all know by heart and yet hear fresh again every time.

Then comes the rich aroma of cinnamon from the trays of sweet cakes carried by artful youngsters, almost Dickensian with their sly eyes and "pick-a-pocket-or-two" demeanor. Everyone eats them—even the black-shrouded figure of an aged scribe pauses in the middle of a letter he is composing for a distraught veiled woman and licks his sticky fingers, one by one. Next to him a magic-man sells predictions on little pieces of folded paper while a young apprentice snake charmer milks the venom from a squirming black cobra and dodges the lightning strikes of a second, which rears (four feet of flared anger) from a battered cardboard box. Even the shoeshine boys, who've seen this kind of thing every day for years, watch with awe and nod knowingly as the boy snatches the cobra in midstrike and bundles it back into the box.

And the smells! By midday the whole place shimmers with the aromas of the mini–spice mountains displayed by merchants on the edge of the square and the broiling lamb *mechoui* from open-air kitchens set up by Berber cooks who left their high mountain villages before dawn to spend the day here sweating,

127

swatting flies, and serving up some of the tastiest meat in the world.

Less pleasant are the smells from the leather tanneries hidden way back in the murky depths of the medina where scores of half-naked laborers toil in mud-walled vats pounding, stretching, and drying the ragged skins in a hellhole of noxiousness.

My guide (he has now proclaimed himself my "friend-for-life") suggests a change of scene—a stroll through the bazaar "just to see what's there" and swearing that spending my money is the last thing on his mind. "It's much cooler there, not so noisy. And if you don't like, we come back. No problem, okay?"

So I prepare myself for battle, girding my loins with guile. We enter the shadowy labyrinths of the souks, a place of endless twists and turns and suffocating cul-de-sacs ending against impenetrable wooden doors big enough for elephants to pass through; a place of secretive dealings and sideways glances from eyes lurking under the hoods of muttony djellabas; a place from which you wonder if you'll ever emerge.

The din is unbelievable, particularly in the souks of the blacksmiths, wood carvers, leather embossers, silversmiths, copper pounders, and rice-pot cleaners. Donkeys bearing enormous loads are driven through the milling throngs by irascible boys barking out the watch-your-back cries of *"balek-balek!"* We seek relief in the quieter souks of the rug weavers, the wool dyers, and the makers of those lovely pointed slippers known as *babooshe*.

There is no middle ground. I leave my guide behind in the souks and abruptly enter even more mazelike alleys bound by high mud walls with the beetle figures of widow-women, cloaked entirely in black and scurrying in the shadows, on errands of apparent life-or-death import. I know that behind the high walls are gracious courtyards with little gardens and splashing fountains and all the intense domesticity of Moroccan family life, but I see nothing of this. The ancient wooden doors are sealed tight. There are no windows. There is no apparent logic to the endless meanderings, laid out centuries ago to baffle enemies. The outsider is alienated, threatened, and very quickly lost. You try to return to the comforting din of the markets but every way you twist only seems to lead you deeper into the endless maze. A hand touches your arm and body and heart leap together. "Sir, you should not be here. Not good place at all, sir. Come with me."

You'll clutch at any straw and follow any stranger who shows the semblance of a smile, hoping that a few words of thanks will be gratitude enough when you regain your bearings.

Except you never do.

Your newfound guide knows your confusion and leads you ever deeper into the mysteries, asking endless questions about your ancestry, your education, your vacation plans, and your current level of affluence. He claims to know everything—the places for the finest carpets, the cheapest turquoise, the best silver bracelets, the softest leather, and you go along with it because you have no choice.

Finally as you turn the last corner and reenter the market throng you are reminded by your wily guide that he has saved you from the terrible perils of the dark alleys and that his only purpose in life now is to ensure your safety, your happiness, and your pecuniary well-being. (Another friend-for-life.)

And so begin the real rituals of the souk—the time-honored tradition of bargaining for objects you're not really sure you want but can't resist, because the longer you spend talking the cheaper they get. Who can refuse an ornate silver-handled Berber knife in a bejewelled scabbard that starts at $100 and ends at the giveaway price of $12? Of course you know it's not genuine silver and you know the blue and red stones cannot possibly be real turquoise and amber for that price, but where else can you have so much fun, with complimentary mint tea and sweet cake snacks too? Here in the comforting hustle and bustle of the souk time can be forgotten and the slow subtle rhythms of Islamic life can be enjoyed from your seat on a camel saddle, burnishing your bargaining skills with patience, eloquence, and endurance.

How dull and unimaginative seem the sterile price tags, cash registers, and retail regimentation back home. Here the ritualized process of negotiation becomes a little lesson of life you'll remember forever. You learn to resist without insult, to reject without rancor, to reconsider with grace and benevolence. You offer wonderfully esoteric arguments to justify your offered price, supported by anecdotes, clever analogies, and stimulating similes. You permit the process to encompass a discussion of the weather, world politics, the sweetness of Moroccan oranges, the excellence of the tea, and the honeyed richness of the little pastries that are brought specially for you by the young son of the merchant. You imply interest in other objects, digress for a while, then return to the price of the original item. You flirt, you cajole; he praises, he sighs (he may even weep a little if the item is more than a mere trinket). You hold hands, you toast, you laugh at the pathetic antics of other foreigners who appear too impatient or too embarrassed to bargain; you share little secrets with shrugs, you exchange little wisdoms with your eyes.

In short, it becomes a wonderful exercise in mental shadow-boxing, where every twist and turn only seeks to bind the two of you together in mutual admiration and anticipation of the outcome. A voice in your head, becoming smaller and smaller, tries to remind you that you already bought two of these knives somewhere else yesterday and that Customs may confiscate them all anyhow, but it's too late. You're in too deep. The bond is too strong. The game is already won by the merchant, who bows again, proclaims your negotiating prowess to an assemblage of admiring onlookers, pours you another glass of sweet mint tea, and explains how his love for you is such that he is almost willing to give you the invaluable knife just to maintain your new-found friendship. The result is inevitable, the memory indelible!

The sun is setting. Shards of brilliant scarlet flash on the rough mud walls. It's time to return to the Djemaa to find fresh diversions in that vast space, full of hype and hullabaloo.

Night comes and crowds cluster around even more bizarre antics than those offered during the day. Five little boys with powdered faces, dressed in effeminate costumes, dance strangely sensual dances in the glow of a dozen kerosene lamps. The men in the crowd stand silently, mesmerized by the delicacy of their movements; the women refuse to watch. There are unusual smells in the air—scents of an illicit nature. Perfumed young girls parade together, unveiled, yet untouchable. Young men stroll hand-in-hand (a familiar custom between male friends) watching the girls' flouncings or collect in conspiratorial huddles on the café terraces. Two men box each other in a carefully orchestrated warm-up as a crowd builds and wagers are exchanged; a group gathers to watch as an old man in a huge turban seems to keep a tray with two glasses on it, suspended by itself in midair. . . .

My head is spinning with the oddness of it all. Over at the top end of the Djemaa, lines of instant kitchens complete with tables and chairs have appeared, as if by magic. Here you have a choice of a dozen aromatic *tagines* (slow-cooked stews featuring an array of vegetables with chicken, beef, or lamb and olives galore) poured over golden pyramids of couscous, followed by deliciously crisp fried fish, lamb and kofte kebabs served with large ovals of sweetish bread, superb little *b'stila* pies (a rich mix of chopped pigeon breast, more usually chicken, and eggs wrapped in layers of wafer-thin pastry sprinkled with sugar and cinnamon).

It's hard to leave the Djemaa. I'm foot weary and mind weary, but I don't want to go. I've run the range of my emotions in a single day—delight, revulsion, intrigue, rejection, love, distaste, understanding, and utter confusion. An old Berber tribesman told me, "The Djemaa is the world and the world is Djemaa," and you begin to believe it if you allow yourself to become part of this unique place.

But it's time to move on to fresh adventures. The Sahara is calling again, so early the following morning I leave Marrakech behind and head due south into the foothills of the High Atlas. Serpentine curlings take me deeper into the green gorges terraced with tiny fields. Berber villages huddle on hilltops, tight-knit and earth-colored. Groups of women in bright costumes are washing clothes in the mountain streams. The Roman geographer, Pliny the Elder (not known for his exuberant hyperbole) was awed by the grandeur of "these most fabulous mountains in all of Africa."

My little Renault 4 seems to drive itself, switchbacking higher and higher toward the Tizi N'Tichka pass (7,415 feet). The villages become *kasbahs*, fortresslike and bounded by crenellated walls and towers. I am entering the wild domain of the "Lords of Atlas," fierce Berber chieftains who once ruled these lofty realms and repelled all invaders well into this century. It still feels like a land apart, a place where traditions die hard and the old ways are very much in place among the snow-clad peaks. Part of me wants to stop, to abandon the car and take off with a backpack into the remote valleys. But I keep on moving.

Ahmed accosted me at a roadside café. He asked for a lift to his family village over the pass (everyone seems to hitchhike in Morocco) and presented me a section of Atlas geode as a good-will gesture. He spoke passable English and made a lively companion as we zigzagged down the southern slopes of the mountains, passing tiny brown boys holding ferocious-looking lizards by horny tails and rickety roadside stands selling chunks of sparkling Atlas quartzite.

The pause at Ahmed's house was welcome. The simple setting in which he and his family lived seemed a reflection of the land itself—powerful, even majestic, in its lack of superfluous detail. Outside the mountains soared abruptly from shadowy canyons; a plateau ended in sudden eroded bluffs and beyond that, blue haze and nothing else. Inside, the walls were the same color as the earth, built of earth. There were few trimmings beyond the layered carpets on which we sat, cushions, and the ornate tray used for the tea; no pictures, no tables, chairs, sofas, TV sets, china cabinets—none of the usual paraphernalia with which we fill our Western homes. Ahmed told me that when the family was ready to sleep they rolled out thin camel-hair mattresses and covered them with wool rugs they had woven themselves. When they ate they shared a large communal dish and served themselves with their fingers; when they wanted distraction they talked together or sang or asked the old man of the family (a rambunctious character with a face as crinkled as old parchment and a mischievous glint in his eye) to tell them the long ancient tales they knew so well yet heard fresh every time.

"Bismallah."

For a moment there is total silence.

Inside the mud house we pause and whisper the ritual grace before mint tea is served from a battered tin teapot with a conical lid. The room is black; my eyes are still blinded by the brilliance of the desert outside. Then comes the splatter of tea in small glasses, the aroma of steeped mint, the sheepy smell of babouche slippers and djellabas, the purr of a tabby cat close by,

132

and the soft chatter of the women outside the room in the high-walled courtyard.

This is the way to do it, I told myself.

I could—maybe should—have stayed. But I was impatient for the Sahara. I wanted to see and sense the infinities—the thrill of a space that sweeps for two thousand miles deep into the heart of Africa. I had hoped Morocco would let me experience Africa, but Africa is too big, too grand a scale, for the mind to encompass all at once. Like trying to think of the universe.

After the pass the descent is rapid and the scene change sudden. There is little green now, no terraced hillsides. The mountains are baked brittle in the hot sun; shattered ridges rise from purple shadow canyons; buzzards circle seeking infrequent flickers of life among the rocks. Villages are rare and look hard, pounded-down places, scratching an existence from little patches of earth among the soaring scarps. I see few people except one young boy ploughing a hardscrabble piece of ground with two mules.

Gradually the mountains ease themselves into vast sandy plains. A hot wind is blowing, the Saharan sergi, and my eyes sting. I pass twisted argan trees with barks like reptile skins; high in their branches goats nibble the tiny leaves. I pause at the picture-book hilltop kasbah of Tifoultout, once a stately palace of El Glaoui, Pasha of Marrakech, and now an impressive pile of towering adobe walls and labyrinthine alleys skittering down to a dry riverbed, bronzed in a setting sun and wrapped in wispy silences. A couple of dogs barking and nothing else.

After Agdz, a hectic hilltop town with a main square full of Moroccan carpets and "antique" Berber jewelry, I slipped down into the linear oases of the Draa Valley. All around were dry shattered crags and buttes, but alongside the meandering river was a veritable jungle of date palms and almond and orange orchards set on green carpets of wheat. The Drawa are different from the mountain Berber tribes; many are black, descendents of slaves brought north generations ago by Saharan nomads. The men have shaved heads bound by white turbans. The women shroud themselves in black dresses and shawls trimmed with thin strips of brightly colored ribbon and silver trinkets. The veil is an imperative here; this is no "cool" Casablanca scene with

133

tight T-shirts and jeans. Here the women fold up like bats if they suspect the presence of an outsider (they have an almost telepathic sensitivity and hate being photographed).

The villages or *ksour* are straight out of the Arabian Nights —high square towers and turreted mud walls, slits for windows, six-inch-thick slabs of wood for doors—a sturdy massing of Cubist forms softened by feathery palm tops. The women gather around the communal well, always chattering; the men discuss affairs of state in the dust by the main gate; children scamper everywhere.

Inside their high ochre walls are the same labyrinthine alleys and shadowy passages as in Marrakech. I had learned my lesson and keep close to the main gates.

An old man, wrinkled as an oyster shell, sits by the outer wall selling oranges.

"Salaam alaikum." ("Peace be with you.") I'm learning the language slowly.

"Alaikum as salaam," ("On you be peace") he replies.

I ask the price and he raises one finger, so I give him a single dirham (about ten cents), expecting one orange. Instead he carefully selects fifteen of the finest fruits I've ever seen and places them gently in my arms.

"Shoukran," I thank him sincerely and give him another dirham.

He obviously thinks I'm crazy.

For the next two days of driving I live on oranges.

I marvel at the power and variety of this sub-Saharan landscape —the soaring strata behind the ancient palace of Taliouine, the peculiar village of Tafraout hidden among barn-sized boulders, and the exotic pink-walled city of Tiznit on the flat coastal plain. I could have dallied for days in each place as I meandered around the southern Atlas foothills but Goulimine is my goal, end point of the ancient camel caravans, where I was assured I would find the elusive Tuareg nomads, the famous "Blue People" of the Sahara. So, reluctantly, I keep moving on.

I can sense the Sahara now. Horizons flatten and sand devils swirl across the plains. But I want dunes. That's my idea of the Sahara. So I'm told to go further south to M'Hamid where I'll find camels and the "Blue People" and all the dunes I need. Only no one mentioned the road was closed after sixty miles due to some border conflicts with the Algerians!

Back in Zagora a young guide senses my despondency and leads me through a ksar south of town, along half a mile of sandy lanes enclosed by high bamboo fences and, finally, into my dunes! Miles and miles of them stretching in golden glory to hazy mountain horizons. I thank him and set off to exorcise my Lawrence of Arabia fantasies under a still-burning sun. Two camels sleep nearby making odd snoring noises. A flock of white sheep and black goats nibble incessantly on stubble at the edge of the sands. Then after that, nothing but those endless undulations of silver-beige waves.

At last I felt I had arrived somewhere—or more precisely—nowhere. For it was the nowhereness, the Saharan infinity, that had brought me all this way in my rattle-trap Renault. I walked for what seemed like hours across the dunes, floundering in *fêche-fêche* (talcum powder–textured sand) and amazed by the range of colors—rich blendings of orange with beige, gold with brilliant silver, brick red against white, sienna with primrose, burnished gold streaked with amber—always changing as I wandered across this silver landscape, swimming in light.

A sense of timelessness began to creep in. I saw spectacular mirages where the whole landscape became a lake-studded panorama of blue and gold. But after a while I got used to that, I almost expected it, and my mind became totally divorced from my body in the heat-stunned stillness. It focused on little details, childhood memories, conjuring up brilliant kaleidoscopes of fantasies, all rolling together under the blazing sun.

I found shade in the lee of a dune and watched the day slowly fade into a fireball. For a few magic minutes everything became a brilliant scarlet—the sand, the sky, and me—and then just as quickly the color leached away, leaving a strange dead grayness and a chill evening breeze.

By the time I retraced my steps to the ksar it was dark and the stars were out by the billion, strewn across a velvet-black dome. I felt invigorated; I had touched a little of the desert and it had touched me back in return.

* * *

135

Poring over my sand-scarred maps the next day I found a tempting alternate route to Goulimine across the desert on *piste* roads of hard-packed sand. I boasted to the French-speaking manager of the Hotel Tinsouline (English is rare in these parts) of my intention to take the desert road to the tent town of Foum Zquid.

"I don't think so," was his wry reply.

After fifteen miles of chassis-shattering corrugations I had to admit that I didn't think so either, and retraced my route up the Draa Valley. I gave a lift to two fully costumed Berber women, who smiled wonderfully with their eyes (all I ever saw of their faces) and left behind an enticing aroma of barbecued lamb and cumin that lasted all day.

Then came hills of solid iron ore, rusted, gleaming like anvils under that pounding sun. No oases here, just more endless horizons of rocky plains broken by abrupt ranges, which, after sixty or so miles, begin to swirl in hypnotic curlicues. Tight square ksour huddled under the writhing strata.

I was entertained—way out in the desert—at the tent of a lonely nomad who had been left behind by his camel caravan. (I never found out why.) He was so delighted by unexpected company that he insisted on killing a goat to honor the occasion. Fortunately, I managed to dissuade him.

We sat together by his tent for a long time and in the stillness I could smell the desert. Just over the next low ridge of hills, or maybe the one after, I knew I would soon find the *real* Sahara.

On the third day, I arrive in Goulimine smothered in dust and weary of driving across eye-burning half desert. I had expected something of a climax, a high point of Moroccan architecture, a ksar supreme. Instead I enter a rather bedraggled city of nondescript cement-block buildings set on boring boulevards, with no hotel worthy of the name and few features of any interest to anyone.

"There are no more Blue People, no camel caravans," I am told with bureaucratic bombast by a fat little customs officer in Goulimine. "You can see the nice camel market on Saturday... very nice pictures there."

I don't believe him. Officials have a tendency to discourage travelers seeking the unusual. But I go to the market anyway and get some "very nice pictures" as scores of turbaned desert farmers, herdsmen, and nomads come to pinch, poke, and haggle over livestock. But I also find something much more valuable; I find M'stafa, a bright-eyed boy with a quick smile and a knack for solving problems. "I can help," he whispers and pulls his seat close to mine at the teahouse in the market. "There are some Tuareg in the hills. They will be leaving for the south very soon. Perhaps you can go with them." I am delighted with the prospect. "Of course," M'stafa whispers again, "it is not permitted for you to do this. . . ."

The Tuareg, a proudly independent subrace of Berbers, have been Saharan traders par excellence for centuries. From the north their long caravans of one hundred or more camels carried rugs, blankets, swords and daggers, leather goods, prayer mats, and silver jewelry and returned from Timbuktu and cities farther south, weeks or sometimes months later, laden with ivory, spices, gold, exotic plumage, even live monkeys and parrots. Their main possessions were their camels, their heavy tents of brown tightly woven camel hair, their layered djellabas and cloaks of indigo-dyed cloth. They call themselves "the people of the veil" and are particularly proud of their twenty-foot-long headdresses which cover most of their faces while traveling.

In the intense heat of the Sahara the indigo dyes of their robes would gradually seep into their skin turning it a distinct shade of blue. Not surprisingly they became known as the "Blue People" and their mysterious lifeways, their freedom to roam at will, and their ferocity when threatened gave the name a romantic ring, intriguing to Western travelers. (Blue bodies are now a rarity. Modern dying methods have virtually eliminated the transference of color even in temperatures as high as 130 degrees.)

The Tuareg detest cities, even relatively small ones such as Goulimine and Tan-Tan, which are the endpoints of their Saharan camel caravans. They come to trade, to buy supplies and then leave as quickly as possible to return to their ancient tracks across the Sahara, their only home. But again, modern ways have brought change to their apparently ageless traditions. Roads, trucks, and planes have made Saharan trade a brisker business, and the slow caravans are becoming an anomaly. Their

137

demise has been quickened by constant border bickerings among Morocco, Algeria, and Mauritania, which make desert travel hazardous.

M'stafa and I drive miles from Goulimine on rough sand tracks to find the Tuareg traders. We eventually locate their camp by a lovely oasis set against a line of low hills. At first their reception is muted, if not hostile. No mint tea is offered (a bad sign) and Ali, the small, wiry leader of the group, reeled off a string of reasons why this foreigner (bristling with cameras and possessing a very limited Arabic vocabulary) is crazy even to consider a trans-Saharan journey. He begins by emphasizing the terrible heat, the discomfort and lack of privacy, the backside-blistering bounce of camel riding for eight hours at a stretch. Then he emphasizes the length of the journey, maybe up to a month across twelve hundred miles of the wildest country imaginable (M'stafa translates his horrific descriptions with relish), and, pointing straight at my well-fed frame, the atrocious diet of sour camel milk and old goat. Finally, as a grand denouement, he adds the fact that he will not allow any photograpy of the three women who are part of the caravan.

Now I've always believed in little miracles—the kind that seem to come when you want something so badly that you don't (or won't) see the obstacles. The more I'm told something is impossible, the more I know that little miracles will occur if I keep my mind fixed on the endpoint.

And M'stafa is my miracle worker. In a stroke of genius he bows graciously to Ali, leads me inside one of the dark camel-hair tents, and carefully fits me out in the djellaba, robes, dagger, and headdress of the Blue People. Then he proudly strides with me back to Ali's perch on a rock in the shade of a palm tree.

There is utter silence. Ali looks me up and down very slowly. Some of the other Tuareg emerge from their tents and stand staring at me. At first I feel rather stupid. Then I realize that the robes are in fact most comfortable; the headdress seems almost like a crown, and the heavy dagger on my right side makes me feel like some kind of warrior (memories of my childhood battles against the infidels in the hayfields behind my house). I seem to be taller and filled with a strange energy.

Next thing I know Ali leaps up and begins hugging me, and laughing and hugging me again. Then everyone is smiling; even the camels begin burping and braying. M'stafa gives me one big wink and that is it—the deal is done. I am part of the caravan; I've been accepted in spite of all the objections. The little miracle has happened, and the adventure I've waited for most of my life is finally about to begin. I am going to cross the Sahara.

Ali, the leader of our small caravan of twenty camels, a few goats, twelve men, and three women, is the first up. It is still dark. He adds wood to the smoldering fire, and the women begin to heat the cauldron of harira soup, a rich mixture of lentils, chick-peas, and meat, and bake the morning farina bread in the sand under the fire. Everyone except me seems to know exactly what to do. I help lower and pack the men's heavy camel-hair tent (the women have already folded their own flimsy cotton tent), then I make a final trip to the little oasis pond to fill two remaining goatskins with the cold sweet water.

As I kneel by the spring the first gash of scarlet appears across the flat horizon and the brilliant star dome under which I've slept for two nights now begins to fade. I watch the shadowy figures scurry about on the bluff, loading the camels and tightening the ropes. The animals are now fully awake and irascible, bellowing, screaming, and spitting.

Before leaving, we all walk together (chewing on the sweet dried dates we eat with every meal) to a quiet valley below the campsite. Here small piles of desert rocks are marked by vertical slabs of stone. Ali kneels on the hard ground and the others follow. Fatima and her two granddaughters, teachers of the sensual *guedra* dance; Abdulali, the old man of the group, bearded and veteran of seventy years of desert travel; Saiid, the foxy-faced humorist, always making us laugh; Rahman, hardly more than a boy, and his stern-faced father, Ahmed, and seven other men who had joined us the previous day.

They have come to say their farewells to members of their tribe who have been buried in this quiet place for generations. The smallest pile of rocks marks the grave of Ali's youngest boy who died almost exactly a year ago. He prays quietly as the sun eases over the horizon, spraying the desert with color.

A few minutes later we are off, swaying together across the red plateau, leather saddles creaking, the camels still protesting with wide-open mouths, exposing sets of dangerous-looking yellow incisors. A breeze blows, rattling the desert bushes, all tinged with green following a series of fall rainshowers. During the summer months we would have traveled mainly at night, guided by the constellations, and rested during the heat of the day, but Ali decides to risk day travel during this "cooler" season (a euphemism for temperatures under 100 degrees).

By midmorning it is hot (at least by my standards). The flat landscape dances with color. Far to our left are a string of dunes, their knife-edged summits dark against creamy hollows. I am amazed by the range of hues—always changing as we move slowly across an enormous plain, swimming in light.

Around midday we climb a low ridge, the camels sweating profusely now and their mouths dripping with frothy saliva. Ahead of us, a vast bowl of shimmering dunes stretches away into the haze. There is no sign that anyone has ever been here before us. Ali is trying a new route to reach a string of oases near the Mauritanian border. The whole enormous vista seems like another planet—a lost world where nothing has ever changed.

A sense of timelessness begins to creep in. The camels are linked together by ropes but we are all far apart and conversation is rare. Wrapped in a turban and floating ten feet high in the air, I vanish into the cooler spaces of my mind, lulled by the lolloping animals into exploring netherworlds where thoughts take on the tangibility of form and illusions become realities. There are spectacular mirages where the whole landscape is a lake-studded panorama of blue and gold. But after a while you get used to that—you almost expect it—and your mind becomes totally divorced from your body in the heat-stunned stillness. It focuses on little details and childhood memories for what seems like hours at a time—the brain conjures up brilliant fantasies, all teeming together under the blazing sun.

Whatever you notice, a brittle needle of eroded rock, a sudden shattered scarp, a few bones in the scrub, your mind plays with like a kitten and its ball. And then you begin to fly! I remember so well, skimming high over the dunes in a state of utter weightlessness; all I had to do was tip my arms one way or the other and my body would cut through the air clean as a knife until reaching equilibrium as I turned my shoulders. I was so alive! I felt I could fly forever in this soft silence under the bluest of blue skys, circling the globe effortlessly. . . .

Something grabs my djellaba and I'm aware of Ahmed's angry face a few inches from mine. He is babbling away, shaking me furiously. I can't understand a word he is saying. Then Ali comes up on the lead camel and explains in guttural English that I must never allow myself to fall asleep on my high perch as a tumble would quickly end my journey and jeopardize the whole caravan.

Ahmed's wrath is nothing compared to my own self-anger when I realize how stupid I've been. No more floating fantasies I promise myself, and vow to learn the desert ways as quickly as possible.

In the late afternoon we pause for prayers and the preparation of mint tea, one of the most soothing rituals of desert travel. We all sit in a circle in the sand watching the water come to a boil, waiting for just the right amount of frothing in the pan. Then Fatima pours a precisely measured amount onto the mixture of tea and dry mint in the silver pot with the conical lid, an ancient battered utensil treated with great reverence by everyone. We wait again, this time for the slow infusion. Then she adds pieces of sugar broken from a solid block and begins the pouring ritual by picking up the first of the small glasses lined up on a richly decorated silver tray. She lifts the teapot high in the air and, without spilling a drop, pours a stream of green-brown liquid into the glass. We can smell the tea, fresh and spicy, in our dried-up noses, but we don't drink yet. Instead we watch as Fatima pours it back into the pot and repeats the process with a second glass; like an alchemist, she checks for just the right amount of aeration and bubble count. Four times she repeats the process until finally offering the glasses, one by one, to the salivating circle. And it's so good, sweet and perfumed, trickling over parched tongues and down our throats, warming as it goes, bringing smiles to dried lips. Conversation begins again and we drink the customary three glasses before eating dates, bread

141

AHMED (in lighthearted mood)
& son RAHMAN
in the Moroccan Sahara

dipped in honey, and scoops of camel milk from a communal bowl. Ah! Life seems so good.

Ali had warned us that on this new route it might be a few days before our first oasis. He had decided to travel into the night as the camels seemed fit and frisky. When we finally reach a resting place in a sheltered hollow on the edge of yet one more gravel plain, the moon is high and we are all too weary to pitch the tents or even eat. We unload the camels, hobble their legs to prevent them from straying too far when grazing (another euphemism for their desperate search for anything worth nibbling in that empty land!). Then after lighting a fire we wrap ourselves up in blankets and vanish into a long deep sleep.

For the next three days there are no more dunes. My assumption that the Sahara consists mainly of a sand sea rolling on forever is badly mistaken. Much of our route lies across interminable gray gravelly plains where my romantic enthusiasm for infinity begins to pall. The animals are becoming weary now, bodies jerking in protest as they tear their padded soles on sharp-edged rocks. It's a long time since we've had fresh water and drinking the sour dregs from the goatskins has become a necessary but unpleasant ritual.

In the early evening, when we halt again for mint tea, I sit with Ali and we watch the camels in their endless search for food. "They are so patient. So strong." He smiles and tugs at his djellaba. "We learn from them how to be strong ourselves. They teach us again and again."

Ali doesn't talk much. In fact the whole group is rather silent, as if everything that needs to be said has been said long ago, and they exist as a single entity, bound together by years of common experiences. Ali's commands are mere nods and single gestures; everyone has a role and fulfills it without question. I wait to be given mine.

The sudden reality of an oasis is hard to grasp at first. Abruptly you are shunted out of your mental fantasyland into the actuality of other humans, the smell of unfamiliar dishes being cooked, the pleasure of deep palm shade, and the utter delight at the sound of splashing water.

You experience a kind of desert jet lag. It can take hours to

recover from the long days of riding. I would talk and not remember what I said. I would look and not remember what I saw.
But gradually the peace of the oasis seeps in. I sit with the others
in the sand as they meet old friends and listen to tales of desert
troubles, the fortunes of other families, the lucrative trading
deals they have done in the south.

As the sun sinks (there's no dusk here; the sun just vanishes
in a brilliant fireball and it's dark), a goat is killed and we smell
the grilling meat, the bubbling soups, the tagine sauces, and wait
restlessly for dinner.

And then the real stories begin, long rambling folktales like
those told by the storytellers in the Djemaa of Marrakech. And
although I have little idea of the themes, I watch as entranced as
the others in the flickering firelight while the water splashes
nearby and the camels moan to themselves out in the chilly desert. I now feel part of the caravan and I think they're learning to
accept me.

Later on something beautiful happens. Fatima and her two
granddaughters disappear into their small tent and adorn each
other in elaborate headdresses, robes, and jewels. Then they
enter the circle by the fire and begin, very slowly, the famous
Saharan guedra dance. Rahman and Ahmed play the small
earthenware drums, and Fatima sings the long sad phrases with
a strong guttural rhythm. They all sway together on their knees,
blue robes waving, silver necklaces sparkling, using their arms,
shoulders, and heads in movements that are somehow both
erotic and yet the epitome of modest femininity. No one moves
or makes a sound. We are all wrapped in this ancient rite, bound
together in a tight circle of humanity against the vast infinities of
stars and desert. We need no more.

Abdulali, the quietest member of the group, is treated with a
respect verging on awe by everyone, particularly Fatima.

"He has been with the caravans for almost eighty years,"
she explains. "He knows everything."

Most of the time he sleeps. He even (sin of sins) had found a
way to sleep on his camel as we travel. He also acts as our doctor, applying mixes of powders and lotions to wounds and burns
and making fever remedies from dried bark and herbs he carries

in a small leather pouch. One of Fatima's girls received a scorpion bite on her ankle and he eased the pain in minutes with one of his secret rubbing compounds.

About the only time I saw him really animated was when he discussed dates with Ali. His face suddenly lost its wrinkled, half-asleep look as he described with elaborate gestures the sweet wonders of the *deglet nour* ("fingers of light") dates, the smaller and firmer *deglet beida* ("white fingers"), and half a dozen other prime varieties. But when Ali asked his opinion of our daily ration of "ghar" dates, the syrupy pressed "bread of the caravan" we ate with every meal, his face went grumpy and he returned to his silent state.

Slowly I began to learn the codes of desert travel: share everything, accept the trials of each day with humor and a fatalistic sense of "this too shall pass," don't worry about regular bathing because all the sweating seems to keep your body remarkably clean, never get into an argument because in the heat of the day it can burst into a firestorm, enjoy it when a goat decides it wants to lick the salt off your face in the middle of the night, and laugh with the others when a camel walks all over your newly washed djellaba. I also learned that while "everything is in the hands of Allah" there are usually a few things you can do to help him along.

Quietly the old man, Abdulali, watched my apprenticeship and would nod encouragement when he saw me struggling to load my camel or trying to mount up with the same fluid movements as Ali and Rahman. After one particularly grueling day, when we'd had to walk the animals for a good ten miles, he sat by me in the cool of the evening and pressed into my hand a shard of quartz crystal with something engraved on it in Arabic. It was obviously an important gift.

Later I showed it to Saiid who stared in surprise.

"He gave you this?"

I nodded.

"This is very precious. This was given to him by his father when he became a man, when he was not a boy anymore."

I asked what the inscription said.

"I'm not a good translator."

"Try."

Saiid paused. "I think it means this: 'The strength you need already is inside you'."

Gradually I begin to get used to the heat and become more aware of the light itself—a cleansing, almost transcendental energy that seems to penetrate directly to the soul, opening up the pores of the heart. I feel stripped naked of all pretensions and unnecessary trappings; everything around—my companions, the landscape, the colors—seem elements of a much larger whole that is almost tangible. I look at the others and know that they sense the same feelings except that these have been a part of their lives since they were born. They live in dual realities, the material and the spiritual, constantly and comfortably. My mind at first rebels, seeking distractions—something to occupy the vast silences of the daily experience. Then somehow the light itself seems to take over, the mind yammer ceases, and I become an integral part of the whole continuum. By surrendering I begin to understand the ways of the desert nomads—to sense new realities in their ancient world.

About a week or so after leaving Goulimine one of our camels died. Again we had been walking them across a difficult stretch of fêche-fêche dunes for hours and they were all exhausted. There was a sudden commotion at the back of the caravan; Saiid shouted and we all stopped and turned. One of the old she-camels lay on her side, her load scattered across the sand. The old man, Abdulali, rushed to her and poured long draughts of precious water down her nostrils. She coughed violently but it was too late. She gave a long sigh, shuddered twice, and lay still under the burning sun.

Rahman burst into tears. He had seen her limping the previous day and had lightened her load and spent the night sleeping by her side. Saiid continued washing her face with water refusing to believe she was dead. We were all stunned by the suddenness of the calamity and I began to realize just how precious these animals were. Without their endurance and their daily milk we were all helpless. I had learned a lesson deeply ingrained in all the others—that the camels are the lifeblood of the caravan. You sacrifice everything for their safety and well-being, willingly.

147

Ali knelt down in the sand, rested his forehead against the camel's ear, and very gently stroked her neck. We stood for a long time before redistributing the fallen load and moving on.

The rituals of each day vary somewhat depending on whether or not we pitch camp. If we reach an oasis there is little point in unpacking the heavy leather and camel-hair tent for the men. We usually curl up by the fire or near the water. Ali tells one of the men to fix the cotton tent for the women, but they often sleep in the open air anyway, using the tent merely for modesty after washing.

Our diet is just as mundane as I'd been warned; round farina bread (*tagella*) cooked in the sand under the embers of the fire, endless cauldrons of harira soup (essentially a bottomless repository for leftovers), tough old goat (how I longed for that melt-in-your-mouth *mechoui* lamb sold in the Marrakech's Dje-maa), sour camel milk, big communal platters of couscous mea-gerly spiced with peppers and meat juices and, of course, endless sticky slabs of dried dates.

If there were complaints about the food (the men could be finicky after a hard day's riding) Fatima would remind us all that she had once crossed fifteen hundred miles of desert alone on a she-camel, living on nothing but wild grass seeds and camel milk. And she would add, with searing pride, there were many days when the camel had no milk at all to give so she existed entirely on dew collected at dawn from scrub bush! This tirade was usually enough to silence the most picky eater.

Something is not right. For days since we left the first oasis we have been following trail markers in the form of small piles of desert rocks, hardly visible to the uninitiated. But there are none now and Ali seems hesitant. We all feel the change. The flowing hypnotic swaying of the camels has become jerky and uncoor-dinated. A restlessness ripples down the caravan; we wait for someone to speak, but no one does. Ali is a stubborn man; that is part of his power of leadership. People mistake his stubborn-ness for certainty, but this time we all know that we have lost the trail and we're heading into strange territory.

Two hours later Ali turns and announces that he had taken a

shortcut and has missed an expected oasis. With grace he apologizes to us all and asks if we prefer to camp or to travel on to the next oasis further to the southeast. We decide to keep moving. The stars are spectacular—billions of tiny bright pinpricks in the great black dome. What better than a moonlight ride with the expectation of a whole day's rest up by a pool of cool water shaded by palms? I manage to move my camel abreast of Ali and, when he turns, his face is one huge grin. I must look quizzical so he just stretches out his arms as if to enfold the whole universe. And I suddenly realize that after years of traveling across these endless spaces, he's just as much affected by it all as I am.

It is already well after dawn when we reach the ridge overlooking a thin green oasis. The water glints like liquid gold and looks inviting after days of hard traveling. Ali grins at us as if to say, "See—look what I've found for you." Everyone is smiling, everyone except the ever-sceptical Ahmad, who seems uneasy.

"Is something wrong?" I ask.

"No one is here. There are no tents."

"Is that unusual?"

"Maybe."

We ease our camels down to the flats around the oasis. A gentle breeze is blowing; the camels can smell the water and give little snorts of anticipation. The palms are laden with bunches of golden dates and I make plans to stay here forever. . . .

Then everything changes.

First comes a gunshot. Then out of the thick scrub at the base of the palms come two battered jeeps, each with three men, heading straight for us. The camels are alarmed at the sudden commotion and begin to weave violently. Ali calls out to us to rein them in but they resist. Fatima is thrown off and almost trampled by their elephantine feet. She is obviously hurt and can't get up. Ali jumps down quickly and pulls her away from the frightened animals.

The jeeps keep on roaring toward us throwing up spumes of sand. There is another shot and one of the freight camels rears, scattering its load of rugs over the rocks. The men bound from the jeeps pointing their guns and shouting at us to jump down. It is a long drop but it is obvious that the intruders are not interested in the niceties of dismounting. Two camels begin running back up the ridge; one falls and is pinned to the ground by its load. Its strangled cries and flailing hooves send the rest of the caravan into total confusion. Sand and dust billow around us but the attackers ignore it all and begin herding us toward the palms. I looked at Ali and the others but they have their eyes fixed firmly on the ground. The two young women are carrying Fatima and weeping as we are pushed into the shade of the palm trees.

We see a line of one-room mud huts. They look like the remnants of a long-abandoned caravansary (the traditional form of desert resting place); their walls are deeply eroded and their once-solid wood doors are cracked and pierced by bullet holes. The windows are mere gaps in the mud, crudely boarded up.

We are taken to separate huts. At first they intend to put me with Saiid, but one of them rips off my litham, points to my red beard and hair, and becomes very angry. A short, stocky man with a huge black mustache and carrying a submachine gun runs up and peers fiercely into my face. Ali begins some long explanation but is quickly silenced with a gun pointed directly at his throat. I am obviously regarded as some kind of dangerous alien and am taken off to the furthermost hut, the only one with iron bars on the window! The stocky man with mustache, apparently the leader, pushes me through the doorway, shouts something very abusive, spits violently at the wall, and orders someone to guard the door.

I won't dwell on the details, but the next twenty-four hours are some of the most unpleasant I can remember. I have no idea what is happening; I can hear nothing of the others, only the occasional braying of the camels. Sometime before sunset there is a shattering burst of machine-gun fire way down at the end of the oasis and then silence again until someone sticks a greasy plate of couscous under my door after dark and vanishes.

It is amazingly cold at night. I shiver for hours in a half-sleep full of violent images and sudden awakenings. I call out to the guard for something to wrap around me but there is never any reply. I can hear my voice bouncing off the rocks and hills around the oasis. I feel utterly alone and deserted. I am also scared—why have we been attacked, who are these people, how long will they keep us here . . . ?

By the following morning I've had enough. I hear raised voices nearby and begin kicking the door and shouting as loud as I can. I am ready for anything now, machine guns or not. I am cold, hungry, and very angry. The voices get louder so I kick harder. Then who should appear at the window but Ali and Saiid, leaping about and calling the others. They unbar the door, pull me out, and we hug and dance and hug again, tumbling about in the sunshine.

Bit by bit, between the hugs and the ferocious devouring of dates, the story emerges—or at least as much as we can piece together. Who our captors were is never clear. At first Ahmed thought they were Algerian guerrillas, the Polisarios, who had been a constant irritant for years along Morocco's eastern border. But that makes no sense. We are deep in the nation's "new" territory of Western Sahara, which King Hassan II had claimed following Spain's relinquishment of the region in 1975. Disputes with neighboring Mauritania over ownership of the thousand-mile-long territory had supposedly been settled, but Rahman says two of the captors had claimed to be Mauritanian rebels out to establish revived land claims.

But then Ali tells us sadly that they were far more interested in desert piracy than land-grabbing and had made off silently during the night with our best camels, all the trading goods, and every single item of value they could find, including my cameras and precious films of the journey. All they left us were a few older camels and a couple of half-dead goats. We would now never be able to complete the original journey to Senegal, nor had we enough supplies to return the way we had come.

"We have to go west, to the coast," Ali finally decides. "There is no other way."

Fatima and the girls, who seem to have come through the chaos safely, nod sadly. Their plans for teaching the ancient Saharan dances to nomads at the oases to the south will have to be abandoned. The others also begin to calculate their enormous losses, their rugs, their silver daggers, their boxes of Berber jewelry. . . . We are becoming a thoroughly miserable lot until Saiid leaps up and begins shouting:

"This is stupid. We should be thanking Allah for our lives. We are alive! They could have taken all the camels. They could have killed us! We could all be dead! But—we are still here!"

He is right! We are alive—and it feels very good.

The next few hours are some of the happiest of the whole journey. We frolic like kids in the sparkling oasis pools. We wash our bodies over and over again. We eat dates from the trees, drink endless glasses of mint tea, and doze in the shade of the palms, breathing the dry desert air and rejoicing in our freedom to enjoy another day. We were indeed alive!

The journey to the coast takes four days. It is an unfamiliar route for Ali, but as we cross the dry riverbed of the Oued al Khatt we can see the coastal plain ahead of us and the sun glinting on white villages and the distant Atlantic Ocean.

At a small oasis we all dismount and sit together in the sand for a final time. We are tired and silent. We all know we have experienced the end of an era. Border wars and guerrilla piracy are anathema to the old-fashioned ways of desert trading. Ali says very softly what we are all thinking: "There can be no more. This is our last caravan."

We are slipping into melancholy again. Even the chirpy Saiid is looking glum. Then Abdulali, who has hardly said a word since our imprisonment, begins giggling like a little girl. We all turn and watch. In his lap is a bunch of delicate light-colored dates he'd knocked from one of the palm trees by the spring and he's eating them with unchecked abandon.

"Deglet nour!" (his beloved "fingers of light" dates), he says and smiles at each one of us in turn. "Allah always provides."

He pops two more dates into his mouth to emphasize his point.

"Always!"

And somehow, in spite of everything that's happened, we just can't stop laughing.

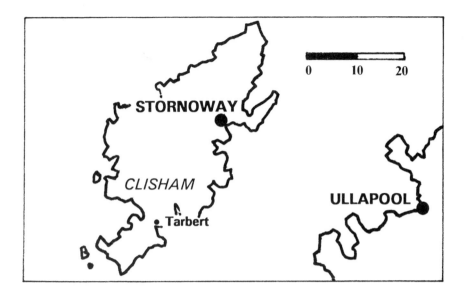

STORNOWAY

0   10   20

CLISHAM

ULLAPOOL

• Tarbert

B.

6. SCOTLAND— THE OUTER HEBRIDES

Among the Crofters and the Weavers of Tweed

The storm was sharp and violent. Winds shrieked like banshees across the brown-gray wilderness of dead heather and bare boulders. The normally still, almost sinister, surfaces of the black lochans among the bogs were whipped into froth by the gale; the brittle marsh grass lay broken below the eroded edges of ancient peat banks.

A primeval scene—no signs of habitation anywhere, no welcoming curls of smoke, no walls, no trees, no dainty patches of moorland flora here among the eroded stumps of Archean gneiss, breaking through the peat like old bones on an almost fleshless torso. On the wild moors of the Outer Hebrides island of Harris, forty miles out in the Atlantic off the northwestern highlands of Scotland, I sheltered in a hollow among Europe's oldest rocks, formed more than three billion years ago, gouged and rounded in three ice ages and sturdy enough to withstand three more.

There's a Hebridean Gaelic saying: "When God made time, he made plenty of it," and here, on the desolate slopes of Bleaval mountain, you sense the infinitely slow passage of time. This is a fine place to know the insignificance of man and wonder if this is how the earth may have looked at the very beginning.

And then—an abrupt transformation! The storm passes on, whirling out over the Sound of Shiant, heading for the dagger-tipped peaks of the black Cuillins on the Isle of Skye, crouched on the eastern horizon. The sky is suddenly a sparkling blue, the sun warm, and far below is a scene that would seduce the most ardent admirer of Caribbean islands: great arcs of creamy shell-sand beaches, fringed by high dunes, and a turquoise-green ocean gently deepening to dark blue, lazily lapping on a shore-line unmarked by footprints for mile after mile. . . .

"Aye—it's a magic place you're going to," said Hector Macleod at the Ceilidh Place pub in Ullapool, a small port town of tiny whitewashed cottages overlooking Loch Broom on Scotland's west coast. "Some of the kindest people you'll ever meet—not pushy mind . . ." Hector paused and then winked. "Well— they've a bit of the magic too." The barman laughed. "They're Gaelic and Celtic—what can y'expect?—they've all got the touch of Irish in 'em!"

For years I've been promising myself a journey to these mys-terious islands where the Scottish crofting families still weave the famous Harris tweed in their own homes. "There's over two hundred different islands out there," Hector continued, "and there was a time—not so very long ago—when every one had its crofters and its own kirks. But then came the terrible famines —the potato famines—and all these great 'clearances' in the middle of the last century when the big lairds got together, kicked many of the people off the land—sent them to Canada and suchlike places—and moved the sheep in. Now I think there's only thirteen islands with any people at all. Maybe less. Crofting's a hard life."

A frisky three-hour ferry journey from Ullapool brought me, a little shaken, to Stornoway, capital of the 130-mile-long Outer Hebrides chain. This small town of 6,000 people is the hub of life on the main island of Lewis and Harris, and the epitome of all the best and worst of island life. Fine churches, big Victorian houses, lively industries, new hotels, even a mock castle and a colorful fishing fleet mingle with bars, pool halls, fish and chip shops, and, according to one local church newspaper, "palaces of illicit pleasures whose value to the community is highly questionable," referring to the town's two rather modest discos.

Stornoway's stern Calvinistic appearance was no great inducement to dallying so I was soon off across the bleak moors and peat bogs looking for the tweed makers in the heart of Harris. And that's how I got stuck in the storm.

But as the weather cleared, I came down slowly from the wind-blasted tops and could see, far below, the thin crofting strips on the fertile *machair* land fringing the coastal cliffs and dunes.

They say the milk of cows grazed on the machair in the spring and summer is scented by the abundance of its wildflowers—primroses, sea spurrey, campion, milkwort, sea-pink, sorrel, and centaury. Each strip, usually no more than six acres in all, had its own steep-gabled crofter's cottage set close to the narrow road, which wound around boulders and burns. Behind each of the cottages lurked the sturdy remnants of older homes, the notorious "black houses" or *tigh dubh*. Some were mere walls of crudely shaped bedrock, six feet thick in places; others were still intact, as if the family had only recently moved out. They were roofed in thick thatch made from barley stalks, held in place by a grid of ropes, weighted down with large rocks. Windows were tiny, set deep in the walls, and door openings were supported by lintel stones often over a foot thick. Nearby were dark brown piles of peats, the *cruachs*, enough to heat a house for a whole year.

Looking at these black houses, which until recently formed the communal living space for families and their livestock, you feel pulled back in time to the prehistoric origins of island life, long before the invasions of the Icelandic tribes and the Norsemen from Scandinavia, long before the emergence of the Celtic clans of the MacLeods, the MacAulays and the MacRaes.

All around the islands are remnants of ancient cultures in the form of *brochs* (lookout towers), Bronze Age burial mounds, stone circles, and the famous standing stones of Callanish on Lewis, thought to have been a key ceremonial center for island tribes since 2000 B.C. The ponderous tigh dubh houses seem very much of this heritage, and I experienced a strange sense of "coming home" again to something half remembered, deep, deep down, far below the fripperies and façades of everyday modern life. Something that sent shivers to my toes.

Lord Seaforth, one of the islands' numerous wealthy "utopian benefactors" during the last century, was anxious to improve "the miserable conditions under which these poor scraps of humanity live" and ordered that "at the very least a chimney should be present and a partition erected between man and beast in these dark hovels." But apparently the crofters were quite content to share their living space with their own livestock. They also considered the quality of peat soot vastly superior as fertilizer for their tiny "lazybed" potato plots. The smoke was allowed to find its own way through the thatch from the open hearthstone fire in the center of the earthen floor.

And in spite of such conditions, the crofters were known for their longevity and prolific families. Dr. Samuel Johnson, accompanied on an island tour by the ever-faithful Boswell in 1773, put it down to island breakfasts! "If an epicure could remove himself by a wish," Dr. Johnson remarked, "he would surely breakfast in Scotland." I concur wholeheartedly. My first real Scottish breakfast came at the Scarista House hotel overlooking the Sound of Taransay on Harris and included such traditional delights as fresh oatmeal porridge, smoked herring kippers, peat-smoked bacon, black pudding, white pudding, just-picked mushrooms and tomatoes, free-range eggs, oatcakes, bannock cakes, scones, honey, crowdie cream, home-churned butter—everything in fact except the once customary tumbler of island whiskey, "to kindle the fire for the day."

"Och, the breakfasts are still very fine," agreed Mary MacDonald, postmistress of Scarista village. I had made the long descent from Bleaval and sat by her blazing peat fire drinking tea and nibbling her homemade buttery shortbread. "The world's getting smaller everywhere," she told me. "Things are changing here too—we talk in Gaelic about *an saoghal a dh'fhalbh*—'the world we have lost'—but you can always find a good breakfast!"

I wondered about the changes.

"Well we're losing a lot of the young ones, that's always a big problem. But those that stay still work at the crofting and keep up the Gaelic." She paused. "I miss the old ceilidhing most I think. We used to gather at the ceilidh house to talk about local things and listen to the old tales by the *seannaicheadh*—an elder village storyteller. Now they're a bit more organized, more of a show at the pubs with poems and songs and such. Not quite the same."

I asked about the famous Harris tweed makers of the islands. "Och, you'll find plenty of them—more than six hundred still I think—making it the old way in their own homes on the Hattersley looms. You can usually hear the shuttles clacking way back up the road."

Mary was right. I went looking for Marion Campbell, one of Harris's most renowned weavers, who lived in the tiny village of Plocrapool on the wild eastern side of the island, where the moors end dramatically in torn cliffs and little ragged coves. And I heard the urgent clatter of the loom echoing against the bare rocks long before I found her house, nestled in a hollow overlooking an islet-dotted bay.

Through a dusty window of the weaving shed I saw an elderly woman with white hair working at an enormous wooden contraption.

"Aye, come in now and mind the bucket."

The bucket was on the earth floor crammed in between a full-size fishing dinghy, lobster pots, a black iron cauldron, cans of paint, and a pile of old clothes over the prow of the boat, just by a crackling peat fire, which gave off a wonderful "peat-reek" aroma.

"You can always tell a real Harris tweed," Marion told me. "There's always a bit of the peat-reek about it."

She worked her loom at an alarming pace and the shed shook as she whipped the shuttle backward and forward between the warp yarns with bobbins of blue weft. I watched the blue tweed cloth, precisely thirty-one inches wide with "good

157

straight edges and a tight weave" grow visibly in length as her feet danced across the pedals of the loom and her left hand "beat up" the weft yarns, compacting them with her thick wooden "weavers beam." Then her sharp eyes, always watching, spotted a broken warp yarn. "Och! I've been doing this for fifty-nine years and I still get broken ones!" She laughed and bounced off her bench, which was nothing more than a plank of wood wrapped in a bit of tartan cloth. "And mind that bucket."

I looked down and saw it brimming with bits of vegetation, the color of dead skin and about as attractive. "That's crotal. Lichen—from the rocks. For my dyes." In the days before chemical dyes most spinners and weavers made their own from moorland plants and flowers—heather, bracken, irises, ragwort, marigolds—whatever was available.

"I'm the last one doing it now," Marion told me. "By law all Harris tweed has to be handwoven in the weaver's own home on the islands here from Scottish virgin wool, but I'm the last person doing it the really old way—dyeing my own fleeces, carding, making my own yarn, weaving—I even do my own 'waulking' to clean the tweed and shrink it a bit. That takes a lot of stamping about in Wellington boots!"

I pointed to a pile of tan-colored fleece and asked if it had been dyed with the lichen. Marion giggled. "Ooh—no, no that's the peat—the peat soot. Makes a lovely shade." I suppose I looked sceptical. "Wet your finger," she told me, so I did and she plunged it into a pot of soot by the boat. "Now rub it off." I obeyed again and—surprise—a yellow finger! Her laughing made the shed shake. "Aye, you'll be stuck with that now for a while." Three days actually.

Later I sat by her house overlooking the Sound of Shiant as Marion spun new yarn for her bobbins. On an average day she weaves a good ten yards of tweed. "I do all the main patterns— herringbone, bird's-eye, houndstooth, two-by-two. I like the herringbone. It always looks very smart." On the hillside above the house I could see a crofter walking among his new lambs in the heather; out on the sound another crofter was lifting his lobster pots.

"You're a bit of everything as a crofter," Marion told me as her spinning wheel hummed. "You're a shepherd, a fisherman, a gardener, you collect your seaweed for fertilizer, you weave, build your walls, cut and dry your peats, shear your sheep at the fank, cut hay, dig ditches—a bit of everything. In the past you'd leave the croft and go to your *shieling* in the summer to graze the cows, and each night the girls would carry the milk back to make butter. I remember that so well."

And I remember my walks on Harris, particularly around the peaks of Clisham and West Loch Tarbert.

I picked a clear day for one of my rambles here and lay back on a soft hillside basking in a warm sun. A curlew flung out its dismal warning somewhere behind me and meadow pipits and greenshanks chirped. Among the rocks, dappled with lichen and puffy with tufts of heather, were scatterings of starry saxifrages, butterwort, and roseroot. Breezes off the ocean shook their leaves and bowed the brittle nardus grass. I thought of nothing really important. At one point I may even have been thinking of nothing at all, which is a rather difficult thing to do for any measurable length of time, for me at least.

Some obscure guru with a name longer than his beard once offered the thought to an impatient world that "in nothing is everything." The world as usual ignored him, and the guru eventually disappeared into his own nothingness, claiming as he departed that he was now everything. I didn't quite understand at the time and I'm not sure I do now. It sounded like one of those Zen wordplays, infinitely complex and infinitely obvious, and a little too obscure for most Western minds to grasp.

And yet there are moments—tiny capsules of nontime— when the incessant chatterings of the mind cease. One is touched and exposed, and a link is made with something beyond the body. Most people are fortunate if they experience this kind of sensation a dozen times in a life. But each occasion can never be forgotten. Names have been given to the experience—spiritual awakening, a sense of the infinite, universal harmony. I had that sensation, a little shiver of awareness, on that hillside, and it more than made up for the ankle-busting climbs up Clisham.

And I too remember my other moments on these islands— some sad, all revealing. I remember the shepherd, Allistair Gillis, recently returned after years of adventure in the merchant navy, only to lose a third of his ewes in a long cold winter and spring.

MARION CAMPBELL
— Harris Scotland

"You can't win in a place like this," he told me with Gaelic melancholy. "All you can do is pass your time here. Just pass your time as best you can."

And then I remember Andrew and Alison Johnson's honest island cuisine at their Scarista House hotel, where you dine on Harris crayfish, lobster, venison, salmon, or grouse (whatever is fresh that day) as the sun goes down in a blaze of scarlet and gold over the white sands of Taransay Sound. And then the two Johnnys—the brothers MacLeod—on "the first good day at the peats in nine months," slicing the soft chocolaty peat with their irons into even-sized squares for drying. I talked with them at dusk as they moved rhythmically together along their family peat bank (their piece of "skinned earth"). "Another eight days like this should see enough for the year," the elder Johnny remarked, still slicing. The younger Johnny nodded and eyed the whisky bottle half hidden in a nearby sack. "Not jus' yet," said the first Johnny. The second Johnny grunted and lifted his fifteen hundredth peat of the day.

Not far away, Dougie MacDonald was working his own peat patch, alone. His grandfather and his father had both been crofters but Dougie found little appealing in the life. "I tried it but the land was sour—there wasn't enough anyway. Two ridiculous acres! When I was a lad it didn't seem so bad. Don't suppose it ever does. We always had a fine fire of thick peats. My dad would cut 'em with the others over in the bog—he was a dab hand with a tuskar, once cut a thousand peats in four hours and kept on going all day. I used to help him a bit. We'd come on back around five o'clock and tackle my mother's 'pieces' (flour scones with butter) before supper. Not much meat, maybe once a week on Sunday. Breakfast was *brose*—a scooping of oatmeal with salt and milk. Salt herrings were good, though. It was mainly our own stuff—tatties, turnips, oatmeal—same as now."

He nodded toward a pan boiling on the stove. It was full of potatoes. In the sink were more unpeeled potatoes and on the table, salt, pepper, and margarine. I saw no meat or eggs, and no refrigerator. On the wall above the table was a faded color print in a frame of a stern-faced man.

"William Edward Gladstone," Dougie told me. "My dad called him 'the crofter's hero.' Didn't make much difference, though, in the end. Most of them had to do what I did—work for somebody else. You couldn't do much else."

His surly attitude reminded me of an incident that had occurred a few days previously. I'd been wandering through the Lochinver Peninsula, a wild area of Scotland forty or so miles to the east across The Minch, which separates the mainland from Lewis and Harris. I had paused for a dram of Skye malt whisky at Lochinver's Culag bar, and someone was talking about recent discoveries in the Allt nan Vamh caves where eight-thousand-year-old human bones had been discovered. Apparently the remains of lemmings were also found, which led to the remark by a thickly bearded student, accompanied by his dog, that lemmings and crofters "had much in common."

It had been a boisterous evening with Gaelic songs by the locals and free-flowing beer. The spirit of the Highlands was an almost tangible presence. But abruptly the mood was broken and an ominous silence spread over the room. The barman paused in the middle of pulling a pint. Someone coughed nervously. The barmaid went pale.

"I wonder," began one of the singers, a burly man in a navy blue fisherman's sweater, "I wonder if you'd care to repeat what you just said now."

No one moved. The student took the bait, apparently oblivious of the mood, and began to explain his thesis that Highland crofters brought about their own destruction by refusing to cooperate with the landowners in modernizing the marginal economy of the region.

"They were stubborn—bloody minded," he said. "They wanted their own patch of land and that was all. They didn't consider changing, most of them. They wouldn't listen, even when it was proved they'd never last another generation—they'd all starve. They just went ahead and destroyed themselves."

A moment's silence was followed by a thunderous uproar as a dozen men bellowed out rebuttals, and the student began to realize what was happening. The barmaid had vanished. Even the dog began to look uncertainly at his master. People began moving for the door, and an old man passed me chuckling. He paused and whispered, "I'd be getting back a bit, laddie, if I were you. You're a wee touch too close sitting there."

He was right, and much as I would have liked to record the ensuing discussion, I decided I had a lot more traveling to do, and discretion, in this instance, was certainly the better part of valor.

"He's opened up a real wound wi' that one," the old man remarked as we strolled alongside the fishing pier. He was still chuckling. "M'be there's something in what he says. We're sticklers for tradition in these parts, and I'm not sure that it's got us very far really. There's a few that carries on, but the old places are pretty much dead nowadays—it's all holiday cottages and outsiders trying to preserve everything like it was theirs. S'not bad here yet, but south of Torridon it's hard to find anyone who's lived there for more'n a few years. Some only come for a few weeks a year. Rest of the time their houses are empty. Applecross is the same. They opened a road but it was too late. Most of them had gone. Now the houses are falling in or they've been snapped up by outsiders. Captain Wills (of the Wills tobacco family) is tryin' some new ideas, so I've heard, but he'll have a job on. Even 'round here"—he gestured at the village of Lochinver straggled along the bay in the moonlight and the fishing boats nestling against the harbor wall—"the trawlermen aren't local, most of them come by bus from the east coast every week. They say property's too expensive. City folk have been buying it all."

The picture he painted sounded very bleak. I asked him how he thought it might all end and he chuckled again.

"Maybe with a few more cheeky bastards like that one," he nodded over at the bar where the hubbub still continued. "At least it makes 'em think a bit." His face tightened. "They've all got families that've lived 'round here for God knows how long— forever, more'n likely. If they want to stay they'll stay. Some go off for a while and come back. Some you'll never see again. But it goes on y'know—and they're still around to argue about it."

We stood on the edge of the quay. A chilly breeze blew in off the loch and wavelets clicked against the seawall. "You staying long?" he asked. I said I had no plans.

"Best way," he murmured. "Best way." And then, "If you're

around tomorrow I'll show you a few places, if you'd like." So I stayed and delayed my next journey.

It's the only way to travel.

The Outer Hebrides left many more memories: the Sunday silences on Lewis when no buses run and everyone is "at the stones" (at church); the colors of Calum Macaulay's tweeds produced in his weaving shed—all the tones of the lochans and the rocks and the moors captured in his sturdy cloth; Catherine Macdonald knitting her woolen cardigans and jumpers from hand-dyed island wool; the stooping winkle pickers of Leverburgh whose sacks of tiny shellfish leave the island by ferry for the tables of famous Paris restaurants; that first taste of fresh-boiled island crayfish; ninty-three-year-old Donald Macleod carving sheep horns into elegant handles for shepherds' crooks; the sight of a single palm tree against the enormous lunar wilderness of Harris (the offshore Gulf Stream keeps the climate mild here).

Then I remember Derek Murray at Macleod's tweed mill in Shawbost eyeing with pride the tweeds collected from the homes of his crofter-weavers; the strange conversations in "Ganglish"—an odd mix of Gaelic and English; the lovely lilting names of tiny islets in the Sound of Harris—Shillay, Boreray, Coppay, Berneray, Tahay, Ensay, Pabbay; the huge Blackface rams on the machair land with their triple-curl horns; the gritty and occasionally grim Calvinist protestantism of Lewis compared with the Catholic-Celtic levity of the Uist and Barra islanders in the southern part of the chain.

Finally I remember that Hebridean light—sparkling off the turquoise bays, crisping the edges of the ancient standing stones of Callanish on a lonely plateau overlooking Loch Roag, making all the colors vibrant with its intensity and luminosity, making the place just the way I knew it would be. . . .

Magic.

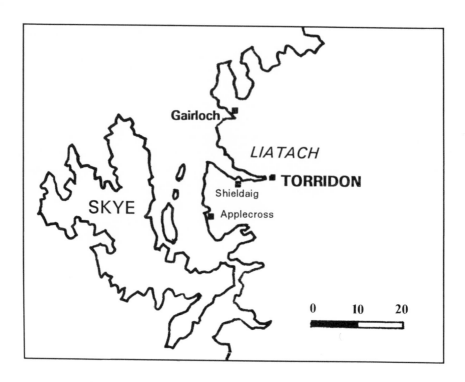

7. SCOTLAND—
TORRIDON
Learning with Lea

A peat fire glowed in the hearth and my cup of tea steamed. "He'll be back in a while." Mrs. MacNally adjusted the crochet cover on the little afternoon tea table and eyed the plate of short-cake. "Now go on, help yourself to another. He won't be long at all."

It was warm and cozy in the study of the old farmhouse. There were books everywhere, piled on the chairs by the door, on the desk, spilling out of Heinz Beans cartons in the corner by the potted plants.

"He loves his books," she whispered.

Outside the wind howled through the pines, a broody hud-dle of trees in this treeless place. Clouds were moving fast; the surface of the Loch Torridon was leaden gray most of the way across to the crofts of Annat. Sudden shafts of sunlight struck the water and burst into silver shards, shimmering for a moment, then disappearing. Seagulls were silhouetted black and moving inland.

"It'll be a storm tonight. Look at the sheep."

Across the salt marshes I could see them snuggled together in the hollows of old grass-covered dunes.

"They always know. Much better than barometers."

A mahogany clock ticked on the mantelpiece. My wet boots steamed along with the tea in the reassuring warmth of the peats. I felt utterly comfortable in the small room surrounded by all these books and framed photographs of eagles, foxes, and badgers. I reached for another piece of shortcake.

"He's coming."

There was just the sound of the wind. I followed Mrs. Mac-Nally through the hall and outside to the gravelly track that linked the farm to the valley road. Way in the distance I saw the Land-Rover, splashing through puddles and banging over the ruts with the single-mindedness of a tank.

Suddenly I felt tiny. The tight human scale of the house where I'd arrived after hours of boggy hiking was gone, and I was staring once again into one of the wildest landscapes of Scotland—the high "empty lands" of Torridon. Straight ahead the seven summits of Liathach rose almost vertically from the cleft of Glen Torridon to shiny quartzite domes that gave them the appearance of perpetual ice cover. Behind Liathach was the gray bulk of Beinn Eighe, the razor ridge of Creag Dhubh and, far beyond, the solitary giant of Slioch towering over Loch Maree.

Few outsiders come to this part of the country. It's far too remote and difficult a region for the casual traveler. The weather is notoriously fickle; the great peaks often vanish for days on end in sluggardly sea frets; infrequent "blue days" quickly turn black in sudden mountain storms. Walkers have vanished forever in the peat bogs behind the mountains, out beyond the Pass of the Winds.

Here are some of the world's oldest rocks displayed in clear Grand Canyon sequence from the six-hundred-million-year-old

THE WILDS OF
TORRIDON
—Scotland

quartzite caps through the pink sandstone strata to the more than two-billion-year-old-Lewisian gneiss bedrock. One wonders at the original height and bulk of these monoliths, but millions of years of earth movements, erosion, and glaciation have failed to erase their impact as you emerge from the lower peaks of Glen Shieldaig Forest, turn east at Shieldaig village, and come face to face with them across Loch Torridon. You feel you've entered some secret world here. As a child I remember catching a glimpse of their white summits on a ferryboat from Skye. They appeared briefly through sea mists, flashed in the sun, and vanished again. No one else on the boat saw them, and I later wondered if I'd imagined the moment. But now finally I'd come back and found that they were just as real and magnificent as I'd hoped.

"He's here." The mud-splattered Land-Rover came to a halt near the windbreak of pines, and Mrs. MacNally grinned like a young girl. "Late as usual."

It's hard to think of Lea MacNally doing anything "usual."

I first heard his name by chance as I chatted with Donald MacDonald at the general store in Fasag village on the north side of Loch Torridon.

"Lea's a real man of the land. He's the National Trust warden here and knows every nook and crevice and every bit of bog around Beinn Eighe. He's a very canny man, keeps to himself—a pretty wild one too in his younger days. They say he'd outfox any keeper they put out there. He knows all the tricks of the red deer. He thinks like a deer—knows where to find them and what they'll do next. If you're walking up around here, talk to Lea first. And listen to what he tells you. If it wasn't for Lea there'd be no more reds left in Torridon now. He's the one that keeps them alive—an old poacher fighting off the poachers! He's the Deerman. That's what we call him."

So now there were two cups of tea and two pairs of steaming feet in front of the peat fire. Lea gazed quietly at the glow. He'd been out on the moors for more than twelve hours, and his small wiry frame was almost lost in the cushions and folds of the big armchair.

"Y'see," he began slowly, "the one thing you've got to understand is that these creatures—all the mountain animals—everything's against them. It's not just your poachers and such-like. It's the little things you don't even think about—wire fences, plastic bottles, broken glass, even a backpack thrown away. Deer comes up, gets the straps tangled round its antlers and mouth—starves to death. Sometimes the things I see—the way they've died—it makes you want to weep."

He paused. "Come and look at this."

We left the cozy room and walked down the hall to the old dairy. "I'm making this into a museum of sorts. It'll not be finished yet awhile."

Lea turned on the light and I gasped. The place was a charnel house of skulls, bones, and antlers, scores of them, all carefully labeled.

"Most of these creatures died because of someone's carelessness." Stark photographs told the stories: a huge stag choked to death on an iron tent peg; another tangled in barbed wire; two "knobbers" (young deer) torn apart by an unleashed dog, another whose jaw had been smashed by a weekend-hunter's bullet, leaving it unable to eat or drink. . . .

"These hills teach—or at least they should teach—respect. First of all respect for yourself because this is some of the toughest walking-climbing country in Britain. But respect too for the creatures who live here—the deer, foxes, badgers, eagles, wildcats. This is one of the last places you'll find them. Most other habitats have been wiped out long ago. By the time everyone starts to get all upset it's too late—they've gone. And they'll never come back. All we've got left are photographs and cranks like me prattling on about preservation and suchlike. . . ."

Our conversation carried on well into the night and over the long slow days that followed as I roamed the high hills here and began to see life in a new, quieter way. I put aside plans for my great hike across the Torridon wilderness for a while and instead sat quietly among the great golden surges of gorse and broom, watching and listening.

"A deer can smell you half a mile away even on a calm day," Lea had told me. "But we've got senses we never use. We can smell animals too. Its hard at first but if you give yourself time . . ."

I saw rare ptarmigan in the lower rubbly hills, among the glacial boulders, suddenly rise up like a snow squall. I watched a fox "mousing" on tiptoes with its back arched like a cat, trailing a rabbit. I saw skeins of geese and whooper swans heading south in great fall migrations across the tundra landscapes of Mulcach. One warm evening I watched a young buzzard practicing dive-bomb attacks on clumps of tufted grass. Grasping its "prey" it soared a hundred feet, dropped it, and then caught it again before it hit the ground.

I saw woodcocks and grouse so well camouflaged in the burned browns of autumn bracken that you could almost step on them without noticing. I watched the cruel ways of the hoodie-bird, a pernicious scavenger and attacker of weak creatures, always going for the eyes of its victim first and then slaughtering slowly with cool dispassion.

I heard but never saw the lonely wildcat. She was out one night hunting near my tent; something alarmed her and the dark was cracked open by her terrifying scream and hiss. The following morning I saw paw marks leading to a narrow gap in a scree pile and the remains of the two tiny voles outside her den.

It was the height of the red deer rutting season, but they were far too cunning and elusive for me. They stayed well back in the wilderness, beyond the waterfalls of Allt a Bhealaich; occasionally I would spot a small herd moving like wispy shadows across the umber grasses of the bogs. In the evenings the clack of horns in the ritual male duels and the bellows of the stags would echo down the high valley of Coire Dubh Mor.

Eagles were always around. At first they were wary of me, but after a while they ignored my flailings among the heather. One actually saved my life. It was a misty day high on the quartz flanks of Laithach. The morning had been clear and bright and I set off climbing the steep sides of the mountain with every intent of being back in Annat for afternoon tea at the Earl of Lovelace's Torridon House Hotel. But I'd forgotten the fickleness of the Scottish climate. With no warning at all, a sea fret moved in off Loch Torridon, wrapping the mountains in a clammy gray fog.

I decided to sit it out, but after half an hour or so I was wet and impatient. So I began the descent as best I could, trying to memorize my route around the eastern flank of the mountain.

The fog became thicker and colder. My inner voice warned me to find a hollow and wait till it passed, but stupidly I kept on going. Then out of nowhere came a shriek, a cracking of twigs, and a flurry of brown wings. Ahead of me a huge golden eagle reared up from its eyrie, its hard eyes staring right at me, its crooked beak open and tallons outstretched. I slipped and fell hard on the quartzite; the eagle shrieked again and soared off into the fog. I could feel the rush of air from its wings.

My legs were useless, they'd gone to putty. I felt nauseous and pulled myself into a crack in the rock as far from the nest as I could. I stayed there for what seemed like hours until the fog finally lifted. Then I could see the eyrie quite plainly, a three-foot-high pile of twigs and bark perched among rocks on the edge of a vertical drop that ended four hundred feet below in a splay of dark scree. If the nest hadn't been occupied, if the eagle hadn't shrieked, I'd have walked right off the edge into foggy oblivion.

After that little escapade Lea joined me on some of my rambles. "You're not really ready yet," he told me when I described my planned hike across Torridon. "Wait a few days. Watch the creatures with me." And how he loved the creatures of Beinn Eighe —*his* territory, *his* creatures, *his* lifework to protect them as best he could and yet to respect their wild, spontaneous spirits.

We wandered over the low rubbly hills littered with glacial boulders. "Can you imagine the ice," he said, pointing to the ancient gouged valleys, "hundreds—thousands—of feet thick, great white ice cliffs high as Beinn Eighe?"

He told me hard, cruel tales of the old days when the hills were the home of wild rustlers. "Way back of Liathach there's the Pass of the Dividing—a cold place, that—they once killed one of their women there. She stole an ox liver before they divided the meat, tried to hide it under her shawl. That's one of the best bits of an ox. They chased her, stripped her, sliced her head off, and struck it on a pole in the pass. They say it was there for a good quarter century or so—screaming in the nights. Gory stuff. Hills are full of these tales. Amazing anyone goes out after dark!"

Lea is responsible for organizing the annual culls of deer to keep the herds from becoming overpopulated and underfed in the long winter months. "I do it because I know they'd starve if I didn't. Twelve stags and thirty-five hinds—sixteen percent of the herds. But I don't enjoy it. And I don't always like the people we get on the culls either." He described the art of "still-stalking," where you have to crawl on your belly sometimes for miles through marsh and nettles and spiky gorse. He used a polite phrase: "On a cull you're very much at the mercy of the capabilities of the guests."

"Which means?" I said.

"Well—some are not as fit as you'd like them to be."

We laughed.

"In other words," he said, "you get fed up of fat, rich, city wiz kids and would-be great white hunters messing up a good day's stalking. Can drive you barmy!"

"You talk like a poaching man."

Lea laughed. "A reformed poacher—very much reformed."

From stories he told me, his past life had been as checkered as a chessboard, but he'd finally found his calling one day years ago on the moors of northern Scotland. "I'd seen it all before. Deer killed by stupidity—our stupidity, not theirs. But this one time it got to me—it really got to me. A pregnant hind wounded by some jackass idiot with a gun he couldn't use, her bottom jaw blown off—can you imagine the agony... the deer calf dying inside her... starving to death in a pain she can't even begin to understand... and for no reason, no purpose at all... I wept like a kid that day. I really did. Then I decided—well Lea, somebody's got to do something about all this so it might as well be you...."

The day before my hike I lay in tufted grass by the side of a peaty stream. The brown waters frothed over rocks, curling in the shallow places, swirling into still, dark pools. I could see trout in the shadows, their tails moving just enough to hold them stationary in the current. I did something that I'd always wanted to do as a boy but never had the chance. I slid my hand gently into the water, allowed it to drift under one of the trout, and let it rise until the fish rested in my palm. Then very gently I stroked its belly, backward and forward. I expected it to dart away immediately but it just lay there. As I continued stroking I could feel the fish settling its weight into my hand. It seemed to sense no danger. Only an inch or so from the surface of the stream I could have easily flipped it right out and enjoyed a delicious dinner that night. But I couldn't do it. I'd make a hopeless backwoodsman. I just continued stroking until it eventually eased downstream and vanished into the shadows.

Finally I had gathered energy and know-how for the trek across the heart of the Torridon wilderness—the vast emptiness of Mulcach from Annat to Shieldaig Lodge overlooking Loch Gairloch. After careful coaching from Lea on the best route, the notorious bogs to avoid, and the fickle wiles of highland weather (I scoured the great skyscapes for warning signs like a lost mariner), I felt more than well equipped for what was, after all, only a twenty-mile hike, at least, as the crow flies. Had I realized what lay ahead I would have stayed in my cozy bed at the Loch Torridon Hotel or at least prayed for the abilities of that mythical crow and flown the distance.

It all began so idylically—big breakfast of juice, kippers, and soft Bannoch buns at the hotel and out into an early dawn light with bags full of sausage sandwiches (special request) and slabs of whisky cake tucked into my rucksack. The black highland cattle by the loch gave me curious, bleary-eyed looks; the sheep hardly noticed me at all as I bounced across the springy sea pastures past the curves of golden sand to the village. I'd planned originally to do it the hard way by scaling 3,456-foot-high Liathach and then heading northwest by Beinn Dearg to Loch a Bhealaich.

"Don't be a madman, man," Lea had warned and laughed. "Liathach's enough for anyone in a day—and going down the backside'll finish you. That mountain—don't play around with her. She's a killer."

So much for Liathach. Instead I followed a narrow trail up through a small pine forest west of Fasag and past the lovely waterfalls of Coire Mhic Nobuil (yes, I know all these odd names make it sound like a Tolkienesque Hobbit-land—and I love them).

As I climbed higher, the great broken bowl of Sgurr Mhor rose up on my left, looking like the fractured crater of some ancient volcano. No more trees now, just the occasional eagles and some distant movement on the flanks of Beinn Dearg, which I took to be a small herd of deer. More lovely waterfalls too, skittering icy cascades; stick your head under and fatigue vanishes like magic.

I crossed over the watershed, left behind the dry rocky landscape, and entered a strange world indeed—silent and very still. The narrow path vanished (obviously a warning I should have heeded) and ahead of me was a sodden infinity of bogs, mud pits, peat hags, and dozens of sinister black pools edged with brittle marsh grass, stretching as far as I could see. A series of equally black lochans followed the broad valley to the west. My map told me I was entering Shieldaig Forest, but not a single tree could I spot anywhere. This is definitely some of the bleakest scenery in Britain—or almost anywhere else in the world, come to think of it.

Two sausage sandwiches, a slab of whisky cake, and I was ready to move on—right into my first bog. Then a second. Followed almost rhythmically by a third. (Which turned out to be particularly deep and enveloping and anxious to devour both my boots.) Lea had given me good advice for situations like this—"head for higher, drier ground." The problem was that these were rather pernicious little bogs, hardly apparent to the novice eye, and unless you had developed Olympian standards of "bog trotting" (leaping from grassy tussock to tussock with syncopated grace), you could hardly avoid them. I must have struggled through every one of them on my scramble for steeper ground and eventually ended up half crawling (and caked in black ooze) along the rocky protuberances of Beinn Bhreac.

And just when I felt firmer ground under my elephantine mud-caked boots, a whirling tidal wave of wind swept up the valley without warning, followed minutes later by a torrential rainstorm, then thunder, than hail, which hit me with horizontal machine-gun impact. . . .

At first everything seemed manageable. After all, this was Scotland, not some balmy Caribbean hotspot, and the weather came with the territory, certainly with this territory. And I'd had good luck too. My life had been saved by an eagle a few days back so I could hardly complain when the greater powers were protecting me. Laughter was the only response, so I laughed into the hail and got mouthfuls of ice cubes, and I laughed even louder, like some deranged wild man of the mountains.

I think the greater powers had other things to think about that day. At least they seemed to forget about me. I could see a stream ahead, swirling and grumbling through black rock crevices, but not too wide. Surely no more than six feet. A quick leap should do it. No problem. So I leaped. But at that moment my rucksack decided it needed a spot of liberation; the shoulder strap gave way and the weight of my pack went sideways as I tried to fly forward. Result—a sort of semitangential course right into the middle of the stream. For a moment I thought I could make it. My feet landed on a sloping rock and I floundered like a badly balanced ballerina, pirouetting on its uneven surface. But the rock was no friend. It was covered in slick moss; I lost my footing completely, my legs shot out from under me (I've seen it happen slower to lassoed calves in roping rodeos), and I was down, rucksack, maps, hat, boots, the lot, shoulder deep in tumbling waters, struggling to keep my head aloft, cursing the surging stream.

When I finally clawed up the heathery bank at the other side, I was a very sorry sight to behold. There wasn't a dry patch anywhere on my body, and I was freezing. As the adrenaline rush faded I began to realize just how cold I really was. My lower jaw began an insistent chatter, and my legs and feet were without feeling. To make matters worse, the hail had increased its pummeling and the mist was down again. I was mad, with myself, the weather, the stream, the maps that made no sense, the whole stupid idea of trying to cross this treacherous no-man's-land.

I found a cave, well more like a crack, that widened behind two boulders into a hollowed-out niche hardly bigger than a two-man tent. But at least it was dry. Not warm, warm would be unthinkable up here, but with a flat earth floor and a ceiling that allowed me to stand to shoulder height. I removed my trousers and anorak and used them as a screen across the entrance. At least that kept out the wind and hail. Fortunately the inside of the waterproof rucksack had remained dry and I dragged out a towel, some fresh clothes, and my small butane stove. I'd almost left this behind as camp cooking was the last of my intentions. After all, this wasn't supposed to be a long hike; cake and sandwiches were more than adequate. But, with some rationalization or another, I'd packed it, and now it was a key survival item, heating up the tiny cave so effectively that after a few minutes it all began to feel rather cozy.

But something happened. Maybe it was the aftereffect of all these adventures, maybe I was just tired of making mistakes, trying to do things that I really wasn't prepared for. Maybe . . . who knows? It happens. All wanderers know the feeling. A sort of deadening melancholic emptiness.

Travel has odd rhythms. Most days you're up, bright-eyed and brimming with the rush of new tastes, smells, people, situations. And then, for no apparent reason, the mind closes up, the eyes glaze over, and the feet no longer have that natural inclination to wander off in search of random experiences. Maybe it's the weather, particularly this weather; maybe a touch of intestinal, or even intellectual, revolt; maybe just a case of sensory overload—the constant barrage of the unexpected and the unusual. Whatever. When it comes there's not too much you can do about it. Fighting it doesn't work for long. "Give it a rest," says the tired brain. And that's what I usually do. There's nothing worse than a traveler trying to squeeze excitement out of something that's suddenly lost its zing.

So it's snail-shell time. Back into the quietude of small tight spaces; a modest hotel room, a tiny hidden beach with no intruders, a mountain hideaway with a pup tent. Anywhere the mind can make its own peace. No writing. No sketching. No interviews. Just mindless mind meanderings for as long as it takes to see the dawn again with fresh eyes.

It's hard to break the rhythm of constant movement, but it's worth it. You forget the schedule, no matter how loosely structured, and just flow with the flow. Time becomes elastic again and the sweet numbing of nothingness soothes away all the petty problems of the journey. The mysterious inner journey runs its course for a while, digesting, compiling, perceiving new patterns, rearranging the images, seeing previously unseen truths. The thrill returns, given time. It always does.

So I curled up and dozed. The cave was warm. I was tolerably dry. The howling tumult outside seemed to make my little hibernation hole even more appealing. I'd move on later. Or maybe I wouldn't. There was nothing I needed for the moment.

I dreamed of home. Anne by the fire. The two cats. The view across the lake. The sound of breezes rattling the leaves outside the living-room window. The prospect of an evening of reading.

Ah, reading. At home I'm always promising myself more time to read. We have a small library there, bulging with untouched volumes and always increasing in size as dear friends and relatives, who correctly assume writers should be avid readers, add to our collection. But it always seems that something else takes precedent—cooking for friends, entertaining house guests, general home maintenance, keeping up with the newspapers and magazines that flood in daily, and if I'm lucky, some watercolor or oil doodling. Reading, alas, always seems to be pushed way down the scale of priorities and only becomes a real option if I've hit a momentary period of blockage and want to enjoy the sweet guilt of doing something I really shouldn't be doing because I should be doing something else (a sort of principled procrastination).

But when I'm traveling, reading takes on an entirely fresh significance. I'll forgo a week of decent dinners to purchase a handful of tattered, hand-me-down paperbacks, and invariably they'll be travel-related works. Talk about a bus driver's holiday. I can think of nothing more delightful than sprawling on a deserted beach with a couple of Theroux's earlier works (yes, I know he can get a little cranky and, in some of the later books, downright depressing, but he's still hard to put down).

I can't remember how many times I've read *The Great Railroad Bazaar* and his *Riding the Iron Rooster* and every time, as if I were listening to a fine symphony, I discover whole new segments either missed or read in that half conscious fuzzy time just before sleep. And Jonathan Raban. His *Old Glory* is a masterpiece of cameos and caricatures threaded together by an ever present fear of riding the fickle Mississippi. Then, of course, there's Peter Matthiessen's *The Snow Leopard*, the epitome of the inner journey wrapped in rich externalities. I've found his book in stores from Kingston, Jamaica, to Kathmandu, invariably in the used section and well marked by previous readers, along with many of my other favorites: Jan Morris's *Journeys* and *Spain*; Peter Jenkins's *A Walk Across America*; Andrew Harvey's enticingly mystical *A Journey in Ladakh*; Bruce Chatwin's *In Patagonia*; John Hillaby's ascetic and ascerbic *Journey Through Britain*; Durell's *Sense of Place* and his close friend Henry Miller's masterpiece *The Colossus of Maroussi*; Somerset Maugham's *The Gentleman in the Parlour*; and Robert Bryon's *The Road to Oxiana*.

I usually keep a copy of Jack Kerouac's *On the Road* somewhere handy (always good for a refresher course in earth gypsying), and Ted Simon's free-spirited tale of his round-the-world motorbike odyssey, *Jupiter's Travels*. And then of course there are Laurie Lee's little gems (my tattered copy of *As I Walked Out One Midsummer Morning* is one of the most lyrical travel books ever published). Finally, lying around somewhere close at hand are John McPhee's *Coming into the Country* and his earlier *The Pine Barrens*, as reminders of what real writing is all about.

If I'm in a reading mood I'll seek out the longest, least interrupted way of reaching my next destination (night trains in India justify a caseload of reading material), cocoon myself in a corner, and devour words, rhythms, images, textures, emotions, even little wisdoms, with the appetite of an aardvark.

By the time I arrive home, travel wearied and ready for days in the tub, half my baggage is books. Shirts, socks, and underwear rarely seem to make it back but my beloved books do, torn, covers rubbed raw from jiggling about on buses with no shock absorbers, buckled from dousings in streams and monsoon storms, scribbled on (blank pages at the back teeming with "notes to myself" of varying degrees of lunacy). But they're home with me, safe and loved.

So I dozed and I read John Krich's "bad mood" travel odyssey *Music in Every Room* (my latest find) and dozed again. There was no point moving on any further. The storm gave no signs of easing and it was getting dark anyway. Another sandwich, a sip or two of whisky . . . I'd feel fine tomorrow.

Oozing into morning wakefulness. A slow, crisp dawn; strips of scarlet and gold on the gray walls of my cave. Lighting the stove again and feeling the heat rise. Pulling down my "door" of frosted trousers and shirt and looking out across the lochans and bogs bathed in a soft amber glow. No wind. No hail. A few flecks of ice on the ground outside, nothing worse . . . and no melancholia. The night had done its repair work. I felt fresh again (a little stiff maybe but that would pass). The storm had long since bansheed up the valley, over the towering cliffs and screes of Sgorr Dubh. Everything was at rest now. My traveler's lethargy had disappeared. It would be a good day today.

And it was. I took my time repacking the rucksack and fixing the broken shoulder strap. My boots were dry enough for walking. The rest was easy.

Leaving my cave I found firm ground, a dry sheep track, and, after another hour or two, at tiny Loch Gaineamhach, the semblance of a footpath heading slowly downhill for miles to Shieldaig. Much, much later came the most wonderful sight of all—rose-colored Shieldaig Lodge and all the Victorian comforts of home in this restored hunting lodge overlooking Loch Gairloch.

Later that evening a weary, but very happy (and well-bathed) wanderer sat down at a window table watching the stars twinkle over the water, feasting on home-smoked salmon, venison pie, and summer-pudding. What more could a bruised bog trotter ask for? I had paid the first installment of my dues to this wild country, and I was content to rest for a while on a laurel or two (albeit rather small ones).

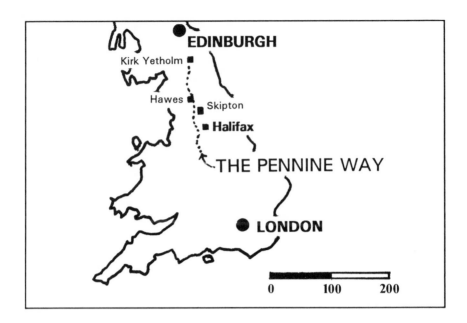

EDINBURGH

Kirk Yetholm

Hawes
Skipton

Halifax

THE PENNINE WAY

LONDON

0   100   200

8. ENGLAND— THE PENNINE WAY

Along the Backbone of England

The subtle art of bog trotting still eluded me.

For the eighth time in as many minutes I was calf-deep in a slurping black goo that clung gleefully to my walking boots. After five hours of my journey I was seriously questioning the sanity of my attempt to conquer the Pennine Way, a 270-mile footpath across some of Britian's wildest country, up the spine of England.

"Oh it's an easy two or three weeks' walk," I'd been assured by experienced members of the Ramblers' Association. Inspired in the 1930s by journalist Tom Stephenson's idea for a national equivalent to the Appalachian Trail, the Ramblers made him their leader and finally achieved such a route after years of "mass trespasses" across privately owned moorlands. In 1965 the Pennine Way was declared the first of Britain's nine official long-distance footpaths, which now total over 1,650 miles.

Today, the ninety-one-year-old Stephenson is amazed by all the recent enthusiasm for walking: "I did my little bit, but I had no idea it would ever be the way it is now. Quite marvelous!"

"It's a big, wet, soggy mattress for the first twenty-odd miles," said Gordon Danks in the information center at the start of the footpath at Edale, in Derbyshire's Peak District National Park. Andy Barnard of the National Trust warned: "People don't believe you when you explain how bad it can get. They get lost, they don't trust their compasses, they panic, and they end up in the oddest places way off course and waist-deep in bogs, or," he added somberly, "worse." He advised me to leave the name and address of my next-of-kin.

Wild desolation is characteristic of much of the route, which meanders like an inebriated snail along northern England's mountainous "backbone" from Edale to Kirk Yetholm, a few miles over the Scottish border. This is not the picture-postcard England of thatched cottages and downy woods. Much is treeless terrain especially in the boggy moors of the south.

After the first fifty miles of this kind of soul-grinding terrain many contenders retire. Tom Stephenson estimates that only around six thousand manage the whole distance annually: "It takes a heck of a lot of stamina, determination, and real spunk to finish."

Those who persevere after the first boggy stretch still have a long way to go among the limestone mountains of North Yorkshire, cut by glaciated "dales," across the bold intrusions of hard dolerite "sills," over the Northumberland fells and the grumpy stumps of old volcanoes in the Cheviot Hills.

"Oh, but it's such fine country," said Arthur Gemmell, member of the Open Spaces Society and creator of a series of footpath maps for the Pennines. "You can see just about every phase of history here—Iron Age hill forts, Roman roads and Hadrian's Wall, farms and villages started by Anglo-Saxons and the Norsemen, remnants of the Norman feudal system—particularly those superb abbeys—Fountains, Bolton, Jervaulx, and the others. The church was all-powerful in those days—the monks ran huge sheep farms in the Yorkshire Dales. But the Scots kept coming down and stealing the livestock and the women, so the barons built those castles in the main market towns—Richmond, Barnard Castle, Middleham, Penrith. You slice right through the last two and a half thousand years of English heritage when you walk up here. There's a tremendous sense of endurance and permanence. But," he added, like the others, "watch your step. It's hard going."

Yet after all the warnings, demure Edale (starting point of the Pennine Way) throbs to the thud of walking boots for much of the year. While villagers hide behind peek-a-boo curtains, hundreds of hikers from tiny Cub Scouts to gritty bog trotters, with formidable boots and enormous framed rucksacks, gather on summer weekends around the Old Nag's Head pub to prepare for their individual odysseys.

I joined them in the quieter fall, sketchbook in hand, looking for adventures and fresh understandings of regions I had roamed as a youth. I prayed for fair weather but knew the Pennines are no respecter of seasonal fripperies. They'll turn a balmy day into a rollicking thunderstorm at the twist of a thermal. Equally obtusely, while the distant plains lie sniffling under blankets of fog and drizzle, the air up on the tops can be as crisp as the crust on a well-baked Yorkshire pudding.

After all the initial wallowing, walkers are delighted to find a neat footpath of chestnut pailings tied together and packed down by sandy gravel. "This used to be terrible here," said Geoff Truelove, a hiking enthusiast. He was out looking for remnants of old aircraft wrecks on Bleaklow and Featherbed Moss and had found seven so far, including a World War II Lancaster and a Boeing Fortress with engines still intact.

"People were coming across the moor in all directions so they put this path in to keep them on course." He forgot to mention that it finished half a mile away in a dip, reverting promptly to molasses. Peaty streams burst like frothing ale from the soggy hills all around. A haze of heather flowers floated over the moor like a mauve mist.

* * *

By Black Hill, though, I was taking the tussocks with the best of them, and in a surge of complacency, made errors that could have been fatal. I had joined a morose bunch of hikers protesting some proposal for yet another reservoir in these overburdened hills. A turnout of thousands had been hoped for but there were eleven in all. We climbed up Laddow Rocks to an undulating ocean of mud and jollied along swapping tall tales of hiking exploits, until one of the girls fell and twisted her ankle, and they all decided to go back.

"Clouds are comin' down. It'll mist up, sithee," said one of the group. With a knowing scowl and a warning of, "Think on na'," he left, taking my compass by mistake. I didn't miss it until an hour later when his prediction proved all too accurate and the mist came down, thick and chill.

Following other people's tracks was useless. The Pennine Way name suggests a clarity of route that rarely manifests itself on the ground. It is invariably tenuous and, in a mist, invisible. I was quickly lost, wandering in bad-tempered circles with all sense of orientation gone. There was nothing to do but sit it out in a sheltered spot, munching on such legendary hiker's energy snacks as Kendal Mint Cake and other sugary delights, bought more for effect than use the previous day.

It darkened and the mist thickened, swirling wraithlike around hags of worn peat in the gloom. I experienced a gray surge of blind, unreasoning fear and felt enormously alone. Things seemed to be moving out there, and strange gurgling sounds came from the bogs. I gave up all hope of leaving the moor that night, cocooned myself in an enormous plastic survival bag (a joke gift from my sister), thought of Caribbean beaches and Christmas dinners, and half slept through a fitful frosty night.

By dawn the mist had lifted into ponderous low cloud and I felt to be the only survivor in a dead world. Then two silly sheep popped up suddenly from a grough and looked so startled to see me that I bellowed with laughter, and the day became promising again except for a head cold, souvenir of my carelessness.

At the A62, another trans-Pennine route, walkers find "Rambler's Relief" in the form of five pubs, all within two miles of the crossing. A couple relegate hikers to rather spartan rooms well away from the red velvet plush and horse brass decor. Further down the Colne valley at Linthwaite I discovered a haven for beer connoisseurs at the Sair Inn where Ron Crabtree, an ex-schoolteacher, is one of a handful of British landlords to brew his own ale. Five Linfit beers range from a gentle dark mild all the way up to Enoch's Hammer, a rich barley wine named after the hammers made by a local blacksmith. These were used in 1812 by Luddite gangs of cloth croppers who resisted the installation of automated shearing frames in the wool mills by smashing them.

"Wool from the hill sheep was the whole way of life on this Yorkshire side of the Pennines, just like cotton on the other side," Ron told me as we sipped pints of Old Eli (named after his pet spaniel). "Machines meant less jobs and there was no dole in those days. So it was like a real revolution. Government was fighting Napoleon and America at the same time, and they got really nervous about troubles at home. So—they hanged all the ringleaders in York."

Two young men sitting near the fire overheard the conversation. "Should 'appen be some Luddites round here nowadays. There's seventy-six of us got laid off last week for't same reason —automation. Same bloody story all over again."

Not far from the pub came an unexpected surprise.

A stubby-spired church rose up from a clustering of houses set in fields against a backdrop of stumpy hills and a sky filled with topsy-turvy clouds. Next to the church was a well-dressed field, a level rectangle of velvety grass on which white figures pranced in summer sunlight. Ah!—a cricket pitch—with a Sunday afternoon cricket match in progress. Just the kind of diversion my aching bones needed.

"Owzatsir!"

The umpire in white coat and flat cap standing behind the stumps (three twenty-eight-inch-high sticks topped by two "bails") agreed that the batsman had indeed been "bowled out" and raised his finger in solemn day-of-judgment fashion. The crestfallen cricketer tucked his beechwood bat under his arm, adjusted his cap, and walked, tall but despondent, to the wooden pavilion. A polite sprinkling of doughy-handed applause greeted him; he'd scored twenty-seven runs in just over half an hour. "Not bad for a young 'un"; "Tha's Tommy Thwaite's son tha' knows"; "He were daft—he should've seen that one comin' "; "In't he t'one as got Sally Atherton into trouble?" . . .

A young freckle-faced girl in a pretty pink dress ran up to him before he reached the pavilion steps. "Lovely game, darling. Honestly. You were super." The warrior-batsman smiled wearily . . .

I love cricket! (Don't worry, I'm not going to explain it. That's far too mighty a task for this writer.) I just enjoy the moods of this odd summer institution whose nuances have shaped the great leaders of Britain's institutions and Empire. That old chestnut "The Battle of Waterloo was won on the playing fields of Eton" gives a clue to the importance of the sport in shaping and strengthening the British character.

"It's not so much a game," I was once informed by a bristling colonel type at Lords (England's mecca of cricket in London). "It's more a way of life, y'might say. It teaches you patience, courage, a little gamesmanship—not too much of that though—fair play, gentlemanly conduct, with a touch of real aggression now and then to assure a win."

We were watching the fourth day on an interminable five-day "Test Match" between England and Australia. "Patience is perhaps the most important," he mumbled petulantly as England lost another "wicket" for no additional score.

Back at my own cricket pitch a new batsman emerges to another sprinkling of polite applause from spectators and team (even the opposing side applauds) and the crowd settles down to watch the game again in canvas deck chairs and on old backside-polished benches. It's a typical village setting—pub, church, pond with random ducks, a cluster of hoary oaks for shade, the clink of teacups in saucers, straw hats, and kids playing tag in the weeds at the edge of the mowed "oval" (I can smell the just-cut grass). A setting untouched by time; a place for manly games and rituals in the warm Sunday afternoon doldrums.

The men in white—white sweaters, shirts, trousers, boots, leg pads—even invisible white groin "boxes" for protection—are trying to bowl, stump, catch, run-out, or otherwise decimate the eleven members of the opposing team for as few "runs" as possible before the end of this one-day match (from 2:00 to 7:00 P.M. which, by happy coincidence, are precisely the hours during which pubs traditionally close on Sundays!).

It's a typical country game. Long pauses, then the fast run up by the bowler (balls can exceed ninety mph), the quick click of red ball on blonde bat, the flurry of white flannels as the batsmen scamper to opposite ends of the pitch and score a "single."

"Good show!" says the vicar, clapping vigorously.

"Nice one that," says the village bobby, resting on his bike.

"Better start the kettle," says the vicar's wife. "Did we get the Eccles cakes from Mrs. Harris? She promised."

"Go on, Charlie—show 'em, lad," from the old men in the shade.

The game has hardly begun, following lunch, but the village ladies are already fussing around the table inside the pavilion preparing a gargantuan tea of sandwiches, pork pies, sausage rolls, Scotch eggs, hot crumpets, and cakes with pink icing, all for the men in white.

The casual commentaries from the spectators are a fascinating sublanguage. "Should shift his silly mid-on"; "That were a real googlie-ball"; "Leg-before-wicket—he's out!"; "Worst third man I've ever seen—send him t'long stop"; "Move your bloody gully, Charlie!" . . .

And the game goes on—a duel of enduring dullness with moments of deft marksmanship and cries of "Oh, well played sir!" Spectators doze in the sun. The players all break for tea and then return. One batsman is hit on the shoulder by a high-speed bouncer, and there's great concern shown by both teams. "C'mon now, lads, play the game right," mumbles the vicar, upset by such ungentlemanly bowling. Looks like a draw is in the offing; there's no way the opposing team will be annihilated by 7:00 P.M.. Plus there's rain coming. The wind is up and a brief sprinkle dampens the pitch. The umpires agree to "play on," but a sodden downpour wipes out the match entirely.

"Nice playing lads," says the vicar, wondering how he could use the vagaries of this afternoon's game as a telling metaphor in his evening sermon.

"Some pork pies left, love," offers one of the tea ladies.

"Same time next week then," says the umpire.

After the storm, I climbed back up the hill out of the tiny village in the middle of nowhere. The path was muddy, my boots were caked in the stuff, and I was hoping for a warm place to stay in that desolate country. It was a shame the match ended so soon, I was just getting into the rhythm of it, dozing, then cheering with the crowd, then dozing again . . . all in all not a bad way to spend a warm Sunday afternoon in England's wild heartland.

On the wide open fells you own the earth. In all directions are rolling waves of purple heather cut by chittering streams, belly-high thickets of bracken in the hollows, bubbly little springheads where waters bounce out of the ground, sparkling like ice-cold champagne.

At Blackstone Edge more thin streams slipped through the grasses and over rocks in the shadows. Peewits whirled overhead like thrown confetti, and a haze of heather flowers floated over the moors. I peered out over the county of Lancashire where Manchester and its satellite cities sprawled across the plain far below.

To the north the somber bulk of Pendle Hill huddled on the horizon.

I've always been curious about Pendle. It's a strange, little-explored part of northern England, full of tales of witches and pagan worship. Now was a chance for a slight diversion—a short ride on a local bus, a walk across tiny fields bound by dry stone walls, and what looked like a relatively steep but easy climb.

Mists smothered the high moor and the sleeves of my anorak were sheened with moisture. The sweet smell of heather hung about me as I groped up the rocky path to the high flat summit.

"Tha'll happen have a bit of weather." I should have listened to the warning of the shepherd in Newchurch. The village was a tiny place, a peppering of thick stone cottages along a steep dip in the road below the bulk of Pendle. I almost missed the church, hidden behind hedges. On the west wall of the bell tower was the "eye of God," an oval protruding stone with a distinct pupil peering out over the surrounding moors. "Tha's for witches." The shepherd's face imploded with wrinkles and he laughed. "Tha's what they says, anyroad. They says it were a charm again them witches." He nodded his head toward the isolated farms and cottages straggled around the base of the hill as if the infamous Pendle witches were still in residence.

As a young boy I had heard the stories. For generations Lancashire children trembled in early beds, fearful that their errant mischievousness would bring parental dispatch "to't Pendle folk" and terrible torment on those misty moors. Today many of the local legends are regarded with disdain, dismissed as the feudings of miscreant families whose hysterical accusations and counteraccusations resulted in their mutual destruction. But that was not the way the superstitious country folk around Pendle interpreted the gory incidents in 1612.

Old Chattox ("a very old withered spent and decrepit creature"), one of her contemporaries, Mother Demdike ("the rankest hag that ever troubled daylight"), and her wild and "fearsome ugly" daughter, Bessie, had long been regarded with trepidation by the residents of these lonely hills. In March 1612, Mother Demdike's granddaughter, Alizon, was refused a handful of pins by the peddler John Law and, being a creature of high passion, hurled a violent curse at the terrified man, which instantaneously caused him a stroke. He survived the ordeal, "with his head drawne awrie, his eyes and face deformed, his legges starcke lame," long enough to testify at her trial in Lancaster.

His tale and the indictments of a local magistrate, Roger Nowell, led to the imprisonment not only of Alizon Demdike but of eighteen other local witches accused of such scurrilous crimes as communing with imps and the Devil himself (Bessie Demdike was said to possess a third nipple for suckling the Lord of the Underworld), desecrations of graves, at least sixteen murders, and even a plan to destroy Lancaster castle by incantation (witches were wonderful suspects for unsolved crimes). Panic gripped the region. One of Nowell's assistants wrote in his journal, "Is every person a witch in these hills? I have a list in excess of a hundred. Every day I receive more names. Where will these things end?"

No one was safe. Alice Nutter, a gentlewoman of fine reputation, whose large house still stands at nearby Roughlee, was somehow assembled with the accused and hanged with eight of the others in August 1612. Mother Demdike escaped by dying of "natural causes" in her cell (a most inauspicious demise for a witch).

"Most of it's jus' plain rot," the Newchurch shepherd had told me. He was not at all impressed by all the pen scratching inspired by Pendle. "It's just a gert bloody hill. My dad wouldn't have none of it. Folk were daft, he said, and he were right. They'd lie brooms across doorways to stop witches gettin' in and throw salt in t'fire when they felt scared. They carved them special witch-posts. And my grandma, when she were making her own butter, she'd shove a great poker, red hot, int t' cream to burn t'devil out and stop butter being 'bynged.' I thought it were a bit daft then but I didn't say nowt. She'd clout me." His face crinkled again. "She'd have scared all of them witches off, given arf a chance. She were a terror."

But up here in this silver world of moist mists and silence, the sceptical shepherd's humor was less reassuring. I remembered a phrase in Harrison Ainsworth's book *The Lancashire Witches*: "Pendle Forest swarms with witches. They burrow into the hillsides like rabbits in a warren." Before leaving Newchurch I'd browsed through the village shop brimming with witch lore. A life-size tableau of cauldron-scraping cackling hags was accompanied by a corny taped commentary, which no longer seemed quite so corny. "On wild and stormy nights when the clouds are scurrying across the moon you may hear their fiendish laughter..."

I was lucky. The mist cleared as quickly as it had descended and sun filled the hill, the browning bracken, and the purple deeps of the heather. Damp stalks gleamed. A curlew whirled against the clouds, hurling its hollow cry at a world invaded by me and a flock of soggy wandering sheep, Roman noses sniffing warily at the sudden brightness. The wind rattled the sharp-bladed nardus grass and brought the smell of cut hay scooping up the flanks of the hill and across the high summit. I could see the fields below Sabden and Barley bound by a spiderweb of lanes and paths. The chimney-crusted skylines of Nelson and

Burnley stretched along the Calder. Invisible from the foothill villages, they seemed overclose from up here. To the north stretched the domed loneliness of Bowland, the empty gray hills of Lee Fell, Calder Fell, Mallowdale Fell, and Burn Moor, receding into a hazy nothingness.

I walked on to the "Big End" of Pendle near the gurgling spring where the first Quaker, an impoverished shoemaker, George Fox, refreshed himself in 1652, after his momentous vision of a new faith. As he wrote in his journal, "We came near a very great and high hill, called Pendle Hill—I was moved of the Lord to go up to the top of it. I saw the sea bordering upon Lancashire; and from the top of this hill the Lord let me see in what places He had a great people to be gathered." His ideas were greeted with interest in the nonconformist hill country, but the authorities were distressed and imprisoned him at Lancaster Castle in 1664.

Pendle is the kind of place where one expects to have great thoughts. It was also a place for lighting bonfires either as warning beacons against regular raids from the ancient Viking stronghold on the Isle of Man or as celebrations of coronations and great victories. In a less dramatic context it provided an ideal base for the farmer-sponsored "flagman" to wave his large black flag during the harvest season at the first sign of inclement weather from the west or noisy little "chipping-duster" storms from the north. Also, according to a farmer friend, the hill and the loneliness of the surrounding countryside have created a froth of odd customs and eccentricities. Particularly bizarre are the activities of the Nick o' Thungs, an all-male club whose activities include annual meetings on the first Sunday of each May in a secluded clough between Barley and Rimington and the regular recitation of such doggerels as: "Thimbering Thistelthwaite thievishly thought to thrive through thick and thin by throwing his thimbles about, but he was thwarted and thwacked, thumped and thrashed by thirty thousand thistles and thorns for thievishly thinking to thrive through thick and thin by throwing his thimbles about." Well, I suppose they have to pass the time some way or another in this lonely region.

Reluctantly leaving my mountain eyrie for the softer foothills and woods of the Ribble valley, I set off walking the wriggling roads to Slaidburn, a village of great charm with its cobbled courts, tight twisting streets, riverside meadows, and the Hark to Bounty Inn, where one of the rooms is preserved as an ancient "forest court." The church was usually quiet. A sign on the door read: "Visitors may photograph any aspect of this ancient church they desire." A welcome change—and subjects abounded, including a pillared Jacobean chancel screen and squire's pew, a collection of dog whips for the farmers' unruly hounds (the locals liked to bring their dogs to church), and a splendid three-decker pulpit with canopy.

"Excuse me."

I was admiring the fine screen carving and failed to notice a small, elderly lady in a long green coat standing by my side.

"Would you wish a dog?" She stared at me very intently as I tried to make sense of the question.

"Do you mean do I want a dog?" I asked.

She continued to study me. "He's only little but he barks too much."

I made some joking reference to the dog whips, which left her totally unamused.

"Would you wish a dog?" she repeated.

I hardly thought my faithful feline companion Fred would welcome a canine intruder back at home but was curious and asked her where the creature was. She gave me a puzzled look and pointed over my shoulder to a spot halfway up the nave. "He's only little but he's harmless."

I turned and I saw nothing. I thought maybe he'd vanished into one of the pews. The little lady was under no such illusion. "He always sits there," she said, quietly, looking at the empty floor.

I mumbled some excuse and moved rather hastily toward the door.

"It's a shame about his ear, isn't it?" she called after me.

When I was half out of the door I heard what sounded like one very shrill bark and stepped back inside. The lady was smiling at the still empty floor. It must have been the door hinges. An odd place, this Pendle country.

* * *

A couple of days later I was back on the Pennine Way again and crossed over the remnants of a stone-paved "packhorse" trail, thought to be of Roman origin. It was such routes as these that carried the trains of tough packhorses from town to town and formed the trans-Pennine trade networks before the nineteenth-century Industrial Revolution roared into these quiet valleys, leeching the people from the land and cramming them into the new mill towns.

On the long descent into the Calder cleft near Hebden Bridge, the whole profile of that rapid transformation can be seen in a single glance. High on the fells are the ancient Norse-styled farms, long low meldings of house and barn, sunk heavily into hillsides and almost windowless. Then the dry stone walls begin, wriggling down past black stone weavers' cottages with long sets of upper-story windows, which once let in the daylight for the weavers of Pennine wool.

"Everything was nice and orderly until the early 1800s," said Roland Wright, who, with his wife, Jean, runs Sutcliffe's Inn on the moors high above the Calder valley. "Then it all happened— new spinning and weaving machinery, coal-fired steam power, turnpikes, canals, railroads. These tranquil valleys became long strips of mill towns feeding down into the rapidly expanding cities on either side of the Pennines. And all in less than fifty years!"

For almost a century the valley economies flourished on worldwide monopolies in the cotton and wool trade. Then at the end of World War II the economic doldrums came, characterized by empty mills, unused canals, and a dwindling population. Only recently has pride returned to the valleys. The powerful beauty of the setting coupled with low rents and property values attracted artists, writers, and craftspeople. Row houses were gutted, refurbished, and the blackened stone washed back to its original golden color.

In a flurry of fresh enthusiasm, small museums of valley life were opened and people like Bill Breakell and his Pennine Heritage organization began restoring abandoned mills for craft workshops and small businesses. Old valley customs and festivals were revived with a vigor that astounded many of the locals.

John Taylor, secretary of the Calder Valley Driving Club, a

newly formed society for lovers of horse-and-trap travel, is amazed by all the recent activity: "It's come back fast in the last ten years. There's so much going on now—the pigeon racers, mice fanciers, clog makers, and clog morris dancers, the Bradshaw Mummers, dock-pudding competitions in Mytholmroyd, faith healers, the medieval Pace Egg Play, and the Rushbearing festival—they even brought back the old game of "knur and spell"—sort of a poor man's golf. And there's that group, Mikron, traveling the canals in a 'narrowboat,' giving theatrical histories at pubs all round here."

According to Susan Booth, who recently opened her Wheat Croft whole-food store in the Holme Valley, the South Pennines has become "one of Britain's most unlikely tourist areas."

I arrived just in time for the late August procession of the Sowerby Bridge Rushbearing, a recently revived seventeenth-century festival celebrating the distribution of fresh rushes for the earth floors of churches. The fourteen-foot-high thatched "ark" containing the rushes was pulled by forty men in morris dance costume, led by women in gold-and-brown dresses carrying hoops of flowers. A nervous "queen" sat on top of the ark clutching at anything secure as it wobbled along narrow country lanes, pausing at pubs and churches for dancing and "largesse, beer, and spirits."

Ron Pickles, sweating profusely, removed a huge cow skull and black cloak from his head. "I'm supposed to be a kind of fertility symbol or something. There's a horn in here for blowin' but it's all bunged up and the eyes are supposed to light up an' all but battery's gone flat!"

When the weary caravan finally eased into the town of Ripponden at the end of the journey, the local junior brass band played, the morris men danced again, the people gorged themselves on pork pies and ice cream, and festivities frolicked on into the evening. The dance at the local village hall was attended by the young girls from the band, who had exchanged formal caps and uniforms for frilly dresses, setting the young men blushing at so much loveliness in that lively night.

The Pennine Way climbs steeply through Heptonstall, a black, tight-knit weaver's village huddled on a hilltop. This is one of the most memorable villages in the South Pennines, a cramped cluster of tiny houses edged by crags.

There are two parish churches here. The first, built between 1256 and 1260 and dedicated to St. Thomas à Becket, is now a dramatic remnant set in a cemetery of ponderous headstones said to contain the remains of 100,000 bodies. John Wesley was not impressed by the ruins on a visit here in 1772 and described them as "the ugliest I know." The "new" church, located only a few yards away, was built in the mid-1800s but lacks the somber power of the original.

I moved on, peering over drystone walls at old manors and ornate seventeenth-century "clothiers" mansions and pausing at moorland pubs to listen to the endless anecdotes of the older regulars. As I walked I could smell cow dung over old broken walls; the dark rim of woods rose up against pool-table-green fields and flurries of fern and bracken; clouds floated across the breasty hills like fat fleecy sheep. I was free-falling through my mind again.

A few miles east of the Pennine Way the valley roads converge on Halifax, one of the most visually dramatic of all Yorkshire cities, clustered in a rocky, cliff-edged bowl, with the black grime from long-dead mills still stuck in the pores of its sand-blasted towers. In the sixteenth century, beggars and vagrants were terrified of the city. "From Hell and Halifax, may the good Lord deliver us," they prayed, alarmed by the city's strict theft laws whereby anyone stealing cloth valued at more than one shilling was punished by beheading at the gibbet. This gruesome implement was last used in 1650, and a replica stands today on Gibbet Street, above the town center.

I found a city in the process of rediscovering itself. The Victorian town hall now rises glowing golden like a Mayan temple. Even such structures as the castlelike Dean Clough Mill, epitome of the "dark satanic mills," has retired with grace, like a monster transformed with a kiss into a (somewhat aged) princess. On the outskirts the fifteenth-century Shibden Hall sits in rolling parkland, a rich repository of Pennine crafts and industry.

196

Most notable of all, though, is the rebirth of the famous Piece Hall, once one of Europe's most renowned cloth markets. Opened with great ceremony in January 1779, the market consists of a series of balustraded galleries surrounding a large central courtyard. More than three hundred salesrooms provided a barter space for buyers from as far afield as London and Belgium. What a turbulent scene this must have presented on market days. The cloth halls of Leeds, Bradford, and Huddersfield were minuscule by comparison. Today it is a little more serene, full of tiny craft shops and known for its Saturday market, which brings visitors from all over western Yorkshire.

But always, when wandering these valley towns, climbing steep steps between tight terraces or admiring the work of skilled stonemasons so evident on the town halls and churches, always there's the moor, the sweeping flanks leading upward to the great, empty, Pennine Plateau, those vast wastes, browned by sun and storm, ravaged by gales, torn by tumbling streams. It's a part of England that should be explored, but explored with respect and care. There's a power in these hills and these villages that is truly Yorkshire—truly Brontë.

I resumed my 270-mile hike and entered this famous land of literary associations by the roofless walls of Tops Withins farm, said to be the setting for the Earnshaw house in Emily Brontë's *Wuthering Heights*.

The wild country for miles around is littered with Brontë associations. Lovers of their books instantly recognize the landscape as the haunt of Heathcliffe, Jane Eyre, and a host of other memorable characters whose fictitious lives were lived around the village of Haworth. The bleak moors were treated almost as if human, lurking ominously behind the tragic tales of fractured human relationships in this wild high country.

There are few trees and no walls here, just the constant rushing of wind across the cotton grass and the occasional cry of a curlew. Lower down, long terraces of stone cottages are packed together tightly; Haworth hides itself like a nervous snail in its shell, on the edge of a steep drop into the valley. The village possesses a somber beauty, even though the steep main street has now become a line of twee shops selling the typical range of

197

tourist goods from overpriced Shetland shawls to "Souvenir of the Brontë Country" ashtrays (from Hong Kong).

Tucked away behind St. Michael's Church and the grave-yard brimming with mossy memorials is the parsonage where Patrick Brontë resided as the village priest from 1820. Now it is the Brontë museum, and a cobbled lane leads to the rear entrance where you leave the twentieth century behind and wander through Victorian rooms graced with memoribilia of the three sisters. Creativity flourished in these decorous surroundings. As children, the sisters lived here in their fantasy kingdom of Gondal and produced an array of tiny magazines, history books, songs, and illustrations describing in minute detail the life and times in "Great Glass Town" and "The World Below."

Their father was a little concerned at all this imaginative volatility; his housekeeper Tabitha Aykroyd ignored it, and Branwell, ever popular for his learned discourse at the local pubs (particularly in the adjacent Black Bull), gradually wasted his talents as the sisters refined theirs. Under the pseudonyms of Currer, Ellis, and Acton Bell, a selection of their poems was published in 1846, followed quickly by Emily's *Wuthering Heights*, Charlotte's *Jane Eyre*, and Anne's *Agnes Grey*.

Halfway down the steep path from Top Withins, I met a girl "doing literary England" with a group from a Washington State College. She was sitting alone in the heather by the tiny Brontë Falls, her long red hair hanging in tresses over her bowed head, and weeping.

"This is where Charlotte died," she sobbed. "She'd just got married. After years and years of looking after her cranky father she finally married Arthur Nichols, and they walked up here together, she caught a chill, and she died—just like that."

The story sounded more Brontë than a Brontë novel.

"Can you believe it? Emily, Anne, Branwell—all of them died in their twenties! It's all so sad."

She looked lonely and forlorn, so I stayed to chat. At least that was my intention but Angela (she introduced herself and asked my name) was a compulsive monologuer so that conversation became distinctly one-sided. I merely happened to point out the strangely erratic flight of grouse that leaped squalling from

198

the heather as we strolled down the moor toward Haworth, and her amazingly agile brain butterflied out a string of associations that included references to Prince Charles, the Pope, Mozart, Einstein, the atrocious quality of English coffee and public toilets, the current miners' strike, hairpins, and the problems of removing dried egg yolk from fine porcelain.

After a string of these remarkable streams-of-consciousness I was exhausted and tried desperately to dream up a way of regaining my solitude. I slowed my pace, complaining of an irritating blister, and she slowed with me. I paused with the pretense of finding my notebook, and she paused too. I said I might break off to sunbathe, and she said she would too. Unfortunately the sun never came out so I had her company all the way down the long path. When we finally rejoined her group of literature-loving companions she said good-bye and then turned to me for what was our first real contact.

"By the way, what do you do?"

I smiled and said it would take too long to explain. A bit rude I suppose but I was looking forward to being alone again.

In subdued mood I slipped and skidded my way into Haworth and bed-and-breakfast in the sixteenth-century Haworth Old Hall set at the bottom of the steep cobbled main street. I had dinner here too at a baronial table in front of a blazing log fire, and then stood outside under a star-filled sky listening to the local brass band race through their Thursday night rehearsal before joining in choruses of old English sea shanties at the folk club next door. Angela was there with some of her tour group. She didn't see me.

An elderly lady stood in blue woolly slippers on the doorstep of her nearby rowhouse. "Oh, I love to listen to that band. They sound so manly, don't they? They've been playin' up in that room for as long as I can remember," she sighed. "There was a time y'know when every village and every factory and pit in Yorkshire had a brass band, but you don't see so many nowadays." She smiled and closed the door.

An easy alternative to long and often boggy moorland walks is a trip on the Worth Valley Railroad. I followed the steep main street down past the Haworth Old Hall, through Central Park

199

with its summer brass band concerts, and onto the station platform where a steam locomotive waited to puff its way along five miles of clanking nostalgia. The bar on board serves some of Yorkshire's finest "real" ales as you wobble along past mill villages set in rolling green hills. All in all—a delightful diversion for this weary bog trotter.

But some experiences were not so delightful.

On the edge of town was a junkyard of some kind, a muddy maze of old windows, scores of scratched doors with rusty hinges, cracked sinks and tubs, piles of bent plumbing pipes, and garden ornaments, half hidden in a jungly patch of elderberry bushes and wild lupins. A wonderful subject for photographs of "accidental esthetics."

A thin man, with nervous eyes and a face full of middle-age furrows, came out of a hut and, with hardly a greeting, began this amazing monologue (my second in twenty four hours), as if we'd known each other for years:

"Honest. I mean it. If it weren't for her...she's bloody eighty-five, no she's bloody eighty-six now...she don't live in this world anymore. I mean she's old. If it wasn't...look at this ...it costs a hell of a lot nowadays to run this place...four thousand pounds for a car park it's gonna cost me...just to park bloody cars in...council says they'll close me down if I don't put it in. I cleaned this out here—it were all steel and ovens and windows. I had two hundred eighty doors here—what I've got left I'm selling for five pounds a pop—look at 'em. Whatever you want. Five pounds flat!"

I explained that I wasn't looking to buy doors and had only stopped to photograph one of his barns now being used as a storehouse for every kind of plumbing fixture imaginable. But he continued on, oblivious, "persistent as a donkey's fart," with the facile lachrymosity of a lonely alcoholic.

"If it wasn't for her, I could clean all this place up. It's solid. Nice beams. Bit o'country charm, so to speak...I could rent it out to some craftspeople, y'know, little stalls with pottery and all that. She won't even listen to sense. I could sell the whole bloody place. There's some fancy poofters from London gonna build in't back. Course they've got so much bloody cash down there. They built a fence, closed all this in. Said they didn't want

200

people to see into my yard. So I'm going to clean it all out. The hell with it. I'm selling it. All of it. Now look, see what I can do. I'm going to get people on weekends. For crafts and that. Look at t' traffic. This is where they all come by. It's a bad corner but I'll smooth it out. Make it biggest damn antiques and crafts place in Yorkshire. Antique people don't always like crafts—so I'll put 'em in different parts."

"Sounds like you've got quite a plan," I said.

"Aye, it would be if it weren't for her . . . I do crafts myself y'know. Dolls' houses. Victorian. Keeps me busy in't winter. I don't design 'em—not yet—I put 'em together from kits. Bad winters round 'ere. Keeps me going y'know. But I mean—jus' look at this place. Worth a bloody fortune . . . I got land—and all this stuff. But she just doesn't see it. She just keeps saying sell the stuff, sell the bloody stuff. She's bloody mean is what she is. Sets a price and that's it. She's got no idea. She doesn't see it. She doesn't see what it could be, I could rent out all this—I could rent it tomorrow but she still owns it all and she won't do bloody nothin'. Just watches me, all around the place—hey look, she's there! Behind t' windows—watch that bloody curtain move back. Somebody should just talk to her. Tell her. This could be bloody fantastic. All I need is a bit of cash . . . but she just won't . . .

I wondered if he talked to every visitor like this. I felt I'd walked into a Samuel Beckett monologue, an *Endgame* litany of woes and tarnished dreams that will always be tarnished; a *Waiting for Godot* stalemate with this strange presence of his mother lurking offstage and ruling his destiny. Although, after five minutes more of this, I seriously began to wonder if there really was a mother there at all or whether I'd strolled into some *Psycho* scenario.

The next day, with no regrets, I crossed the boggy fringes, sang farewell to the soggy tops, and descended through gentle valleys and little rounded hills of glacial debris (drumlins). Clouds as dainty as duck down floated over the fells. Trees were bathed in heavy-honeyed sunlight seething with sappy juices; fields were flushed bright green after recent rains.

Tiny villages like Lothersdale still possess active mills. For five generations, since 1792, the Wilson family has been spinning and weaving here but according to Alec Wilson their silk production ceased fifteen years ago: "We had to go into more specialized areas of rayon production to stay alive. Running a small mill like this isn't easy today."

Oh, but the walking was. I slipped down into the broad gap of the Aire valley graced with velvet meadows, winding streams, and a canal lined with vacation boats and barges. Nearby Skipton has become a popular center for this recent form of summer recreation but somehow it keeps its market-town charm for all the bustle.

Malham does too in spite of coachloads of tourists, and I approached the tiny village after an arcadian walk alongside the youthful river Aire, moving deeper into white limestone country with white dry stone walls, white farms, and the towering white crags.

This is a magic land. Starting at the rock wall of Malham Cove and the waterfalls of the Gordale Scar canyon, I soared up through dry valleys where the water runs underground and hopscotched across strange limestone "pavements" of broken wobbly blocks (clints) separated by deep fissures (grykes), onto the lonely plateaus where silence seems to go on forever, cut only by the cries of curlews. Fragments of rainbows (glints) floated in high cirrus clouds above the still surface of Malham Tarn. This anomalous lake in limestone country rests on a bed of Silurian slates and is held in place by a glacial moraine left by the ice sheets that gouged and rounded the region in the Pleistocene era.

The moor was all mine again and I felt fat with time, a born-again walker, striding across the limitless tops easing away to hazy horizons in a procession of purple domes. Far below were tiny tight-walled fields, huddled farms, and sheep shining like scattered salt on emerald pastures. Then—quite unexpectedly—came another bout with bogs on Fountains Fell. I'd forgotten that most mountains in the limestone country have a spongy cap of millstone grit and peat, which gives them distinguished "stepped" profiles but does little for the spirits of a walker whose boots have just dried. Peaty pools lay still and hidden in malicious anticipation, and I squished into every one across those claggy brown summits.

A final teeth-gritting haul up the long slope of Pen-y-Ghent and then down into cave and pothole country known to the world over as the best in Britain. I spent a good part of a night trapped down one of these sinister shafts.

It was an event I intend to forget one day.

"Fancy a bit of potholing then?" they said—they being a burly bunch of spelunkers I met by chance, bathing in the buff in a Pennine stream. "Maybe," I said. "It's a new one," they said. "Just found it a couple of weeks back. Simple stuff." "Fine," I said, pretending I went potholing and caving every weekend like a regular Dales troglodyte.

We met next day at the local pub, then trekked four miles of open fell east of Pen-y-Ghent mountain. Lovely bright afternoon, no one about. Easy entry too, through a crack in the limestone. Utter blackness for a while until our eyes got used to the helmet lamps, then a bit of squeeze down a narrow shaft until we made it to the first tiny cramped cave in twenty minutes or so. Lovely sinuous stalactites, white against a blue-gray roof. "Wait till we get to the next," one said. "Oh, oh!" another said. "What?" said I. "Must be raining up top," he said. "So it is," the other said as a trickle of water turned into a stream and then into a raging torrent of mud pouring down the shaft we had descended. "Won't last," they agreed.

Half an hour later the little cave was half full of water, and we were up on sections of old fallen roof, sitting among the stalactites. "Won't last," they said a bit less certainly. "Can't!" But it did. Another three feet of swirling water. Our helmet lamps were running low. We were all quiet now. The songs and the sandwiches were long gone, and the brandy too. (I won't describe the thoughts that go through a mind about to be doused out forever in a black cellar hole of a cave three hundred feet under the limestone cap of Ribblesdale, but they're not pleasant.)

Hours later, when the water finally seeped away into deeper caves, we managed to haul and crawl our way out. That was my one and only encounter with Yorkshire's subterranean world. And it will be my last.

After the mountains the next few miles were sheer self-indulgence along an ancient packhorse trail, one of the green roads that once formed the main links between the dales. Potholes abounded again, some enclosed by walls for safety, others less obvious, lurking open-mouthed in the hummocks. The path skirted the edge of Ling Gill, a two-hundred-foot shadowy cleft in the limestone, before climbing to an old Roman road over Cam Fell. Long views here across Langstrothdale and the graceful twenty-four-arch, 1,328-foot-long span of the Ribblehead viaduct, which has carried one of the most spectacular railroads in the country since 1874. British Rail keeps threatening to close the line and public outcries are led by the ever-vigilent Rambler's Association.

Three pied wagtails stood on a nearby wall apparently awed by the scenery. They ignored me as I began the long descent into Wensleydale, famous for cheese, sheep auctions, and dairymaids. The charms of the last were once so overpowering that monks, who administered vast monastic estates in the Pennines from their dale-end abbeys during the twelfth to sixteenth centuries, were given strict instructions to employ "only old and ill-favored females."

"You'll be lucky to find any dairymaids nowadays," Elizabeth Calvert of Keld told me. "A few of the lads stop on but t'girls generally go away. I've heard tell of a couple of lady shepherds up in the border country, but they're both married."

A few miles farther on a walker sat studying his contoured map—an elaborate colored confection of whorls, scrolls, spurs, swirls, and sudden edges in the high hills, then a sinking of the land back into the plain, giving up its humps and fissures in a slow, grinding leveling. . . .

"Ice did all this," he said. "The last Ice Age, ten thousand years ago, glaciers moved past here scouring out the valleys, rounding the hills, and dumping great piles of debris all over the place." We sat quietly looking at the land. "Can you see it?" he said.

"Yes," I said. "Yes I can see."

We sat together for a long time, looking. I tried to define what it is that draws me so closely to this land. Although this was my first shot at the Pennine Way, I had been a lover of this part of England for far more years than I care to remember. I'm an Englishman. Better still, a Yorkshireman, and this is my stomping ground, first as a scout, then in my brief career as a rural planner, and now as a writer.

I jotted down some notes in my bog-smeared notebook:

The constant presence of water: in sinister dark pools on the high peat, tumbling down gulleys and gylls, leaping off gritty cliffs in veiled sprays, squelching in moist meadows, scurrying in becks down to the slow, sleepy rivers, easing past village churches, under ancient bridges, where bowed fishermen wait for trout, then sweeping out toward the flattening hills and fat fields of York's plain . . .

•

Dales villages and the green rolling hills all around. Seem to have a natural affinity for one another. Places like Burnsall, Buckden, Dent, Kettlewell, Muker, Askrigg, and to the south, Haworth and Heptonstall, seem "reet suited" to their settings. You feel that with the people too. A true Dalesman away from his dale is a sad sight. "Tha' wants for nothin' round these parts," an elderly farmer from Starbotton told me. "Mayn't look s'much to them as can't see but it's only place I'd ivverbe. I 'ave t' go t' Bradford once a month f' t' bankin' and suchlike and I'll tell thee, I'd as soon as lose me big toe in a rabbit trap as stay down yonder a minute more than I 'ave to. I don't feel reet till I'm on't backside of Kilnsey (Crag) and smellint' fells again."

•

The empty moors: unruly land, soggy with acid water, raped of everything but color; the moors that nourished the Brontë sisters, that kindled their love of its secrets and its deep, wild melancholy—that killed Emily, victim to their eternal indifference; places of purple gloom broken by patches of dazzling green and burnished bronze; lands loosed from the silly structures of men.

•

A melding of things: farmers with faces like old walls and hands veined with heather-colored lines; sheepdogs as wise as witches and witches (yes—they're still here) as mystery-filled as ancient caves; bowed churches—some a thousand years old—full of pre-Christian secrets; fragments of lost ley-lines as straight as today's power lines (but once tapping far greater sources of energy?).

From my wallet I pulled out a worn fragment of a poem by a friend who loved this unique part of Yorkshire and who is no longer around. I always carry it with me:

> Listen, and I shall sing a spring song;
> Not in the muted flats of sterile fashion,
> But on the major notes of all
> The old melodies. I move to sing
> And praise the flap of a half-made wing,
> The sky in the stones, and the wobble
> Of calves and foals in an air of full,
> powerful emanations, rising.
> (From "Spring Song" by James Mayer)

Once you spend time in these Yorkshire Dales, you never quite lose them. . . .

Coming down to Hawes through the huddled hamlet of Gayle I met the "old men on the bridge" lined along the parapet, watching the waterfalls of Duerley Beck cascade over a series of stepped ledges. The peaty brown water frothed and foamed and Eddie, the most vocal of the group, explained: "It's bin a bit clashy an' floudby on't tops recent' but river's bin reet daan— just drippin' offt' rocks int' summer—nobbut nearly dried out it was." The Wensleydale dialect is decidedly thick, and it can take time to decipher even simple sentences. I asked if he thought the unsettled weather would improve for the day's big event in Hawes, the Great Annual Sale of Mule gimmer lambs. "Alopod tha'll be alreet lad," Eddie assured me with absolute authority. "It's when that can't see yon moor tha'l have rain—when it's packy an't mist's rollin' abart."

And he was right—the day turned out just fine. As the local saying goes, "T'old men on't bridge know afore thee knows."

The fell side was one enormous parking lot for Land-Rovers and sheep trucks, and the aroma of bacon "butties," hot meat pies, "mushy" peas, and chips fried in beef drippings rolled up the hill and around the beaming Ron Goodwin, a farmer from Staffordshire who had just acquired fifteen "bonnie whites." "You usually get good deals at these big sales—they're auctioning close on thirty-four thousand over these two days and Mules are good breeders—cross between Swaledales and Blue-faced Leicesters. I could have got Black-faced gimmers (females)—they don't show their age so quickly, but they're more expensive."

Farmers and shepherds in flat caps, deerstalker hats, and Wellington rubber boots clustered together around the pens, leaning on carved horn walking sticks and discussing with almost biblical reverence the relative merits of the lambs, most of whom seemed nervous about the whole affair and bleated pathetically. One farmer described a hobolike character on the other side of the pens as "bow-legged wi' brass," and they all nodded, impressed by wealth worn modestly.

Clouds scudded across the Wensleydale fells, and shafts of sun moved over patches of browning bracken, purple heather, brilliant gold gorse, and a palette full of greens in the fields—exactly the same colors worn by the farmers in their tweed and oiled-cotton jackets, olive anoraks, and twill working trousers.

The auction room was crowded and distinctly muttony. The sale had started at 9:30 A.M. prompt, and the auctioneer was now hoarse. His pretty female assistant, who recorded sales in a large brown register, seemed far more interested in the contents of her Cornish pasty lunch than in the subtle nose-scratching, chintickling bidding antics of the various lineages of Crabtrees, Pratts, Masons, Baines, Beresfords and Metcalfes, ranged in tiers on posterior-polished benches.

The sheep were driven in, usually in lots of thirty-five or more, and circled the ring warily until released in a flurry of butting heads and flying tails. It was all very quick and business-like; the auctioneer obviously knew that by evening he'd have to sell over sixteen thousand animals and at 1:30 P.M. the prospect ahead seemed daunting.

I started sketching some of the faces, an encyclopedic array of Dales characters, but was distracted by two girls who sat in equestrian finery on the far side of the room. Hardly more than teenagers, they projected an aura of landed wealth and power and were obviously known to the local farmers, who tipped their hats respectfully. I tried to be surreptitious but one of the girls spotted me, blushed, and turned to speak to a very large, red-haired male companion, equally well groomed and holding a riding crop. He was distinctly unamused. I decided to stick to farmers' faces.

Hawes itself has a hard, gray charm that brightens on market days when the broad main street is lined with stalls selling horn-handled walking sticks, Wensleydale cheeses from the creamery just up the hill, hand-knit sweaters using wool from valley sheep, and a motley assortment of lotions and potions for animal husbandry.

The Crown pub was filled with farmers supping pints of strong Old Peculier ale from Theakston's small brewery down-dale at Masham. I wandered across the road into Kit Calvert's one-room store of second-hand books looking for "the complete Dalesman," as they call him locally. I'd met him here in the past when he entertained customers from his battered armchair, telling tales about the "old life" in the Dale he loved, while puffing on a white clay pipe. All from personal experience he would describe the local hirings of farm laborers at the market outside, the baking aroma of big flat "havercakes" made from oatmeal, the intricately carved "knitting sticks" used by the "terrible knitters" of nearby Dent, the "witchstones" that farmers hung around cows' necks to ward off evil, and the special spades used for cutting peats, a different design for each dale.

He was always reticent about his own achievements, particularly in saving and expanding the production of Wensleydale's famous cheese ("just a bit of cheek and chivvyin' "). But someone obviously noticed, and he went to Buckingham Palace for an MBE (Member of the Order of the British Empire) in 1977, in honor of services to his dale.

"Why me, for th' Lord's sake," he once asked me bashfully as he pulled his battered trilby down over his large ears and lit his pipe again, scattering sparks all over an ancient waistcoat.

But things had changed since my last visit. Kit had died a few months previously and someone else was running the bookstore.

There were other, happier changes in Hawes. "It's that vet chap, James Herriot, with all his books on the Dales," said John Jeffryes at Simonstone Hall hotel. "He's put the whole area on the map." Brian and Cherry Guest at Cockett's Hotel in the town center, and the Jutsums at their newly refurbished Rookhurst Country House, all agree that a new surge of tourism has raised standards. "It's not just a whistle-stop any longer," said Susan Jutsum. "People come to stay now and walk. It's very different from before. Very exciting too. We can serve dishes we'd never dare to ten years ago."

A constant source of curiosity to explorers of these hills are the often bizzare traditions still proudly maintained by towns and villages in and around the Northern Pennines. Appleby in the Vale of Eden hosts a week-long Horse Fair in June, which attracts hundreds of gypsies, complete with Romany caravans and palm readers, and the tiny community of West Witton down Wensleydale dramatizes the *Burning of Bartle* in late August. Allendale Town celebrates New Year with a Norse pagan "fire festival"; serene and secluded Semerwater holds a "blessing of the water" ceremony in August, and at Ripon, a market town on the eastern fringe of the Dales, a centuries-old custom of horn-blowing every night in the main square is still preserved. A similar ritual takes place every evening at the nearby village of Bainbridge.

I hitched a lift to this model twelfth-century village built for foresters around a broad green. Every night at 9:00 P.M. prompt, from September 28 to February's Shrovetide, a villager (invariably a member of the Metcalfe family) has given three long blasts on a horn for the past seven hundred years. Originally it was intended as a guide for travelers in the forest but the forest has long since gone and the tradition is kept alive by ten-year-old Alistair Metcalfe, who dutifully steps out onto the green and blows the three-foot-long South African Cape Buffalo horn "just before I go to bed." His uncle, Jack Metcalfe, who died in 1983 after thirty-six years of horn blowing, was once asked if it was true that a good blast carried over three miles. His reply was typical Yorkshire: "How should I know? I'm at this end."

A few miles farther across more wind-torn wastes, the Pennine Way does its vanishing act again, and then comes Tan Hill Inn, the highest pub in England. Scattered around in the heather were the tops of stone-lined shafts, relics of "brown-coal" mining, which has flourished here since the thirteenth century, when the soft peaty coal was transported by packhorse to the great abbeys down-dale.

A chart inside the cozy pub indicated more than one hundred miles of tunnels on the plateau, and a blazing fire suggested the landlord is never short of supplies. "He can nip out and just pick it up," said the barman, stroking the comb of Eric the cock and the neck of Nasher the dog simultaneously. It's a zany kind of place, ideal for bedraggled hikers looking for light relief. A group in the corner huddled over dominoes, a bearded giant snored on the sofa with a tiny waiflike girlfriend in his arms, and a woman with wild eyes told witching tales to no one in particular by the fire. A well-dressed couple arrived, took one look at the odd mélange, and vanished.

After Tan Hill, I descended through a silver world of moist mists, and in the buzzing silence I sensed the timelessness of these ancient hills—flickers of infinity rarely found in the frantic little worlds far below.

At the reservoir in Baldersdale I celebrated the Pennine Way halfway point with handfuls of ice-cold spring water and then— just as my ankle gave way for the third time that week after another tumble on tussocks—came Hannah.

"Tha's gone and hurt thisself, then?"

A middle-aged woman in a tattered purple pullover and baggy black trousers held up by a loop of string stood with a shovel in a pile of manure. Her cheeks were holly-berry bright, her hair, brilliantly silver, haloed her head.

"Come n' sit thisself down a bit, please" she said, indicating a tiny milking stool in the cow byre. "Just give me a minute.

Bessie's got excited and made messies. I'm a bit particular and I hate walkin' in clarts. If there's one clart about you carry it around all day."

She cleaned up meticulously and let me into her dark farmhouse where she'd lived alone since her mother's death in 1958. The kitchen was crammed with cardboard boxes piled halfway to the ceiling, and it was only later that I found out what they all contained. We huddled around a tiny electric heater and she served me glasses of fresh milk while her Jack Russell terrier, Tim, pranced around trying to get a sip.

She told me about her love for her little valley. "I don't go far but I don't need to. There's nothin' I like better than goin' through that iron gate and down among the trees and the water. That little stream by the first bridge. I go there a lot."

We talked about her five cows. "I can't afford more but I enjoy what I have. They're just like people—some have a calm temperament, others are excitable, and a few can be downright bossy and nasty."

I wondered if she ever got lonely. "Oh never, never. I've so many things I want to do. There's the wallin', slatin', there's weedin', muckin' out. I'm going to make jam. I used to make butter too. I can still hear that sound when it, what we call, 'broke'—a lovely slushin' sound as it got thicker. Oh no, I'll never catch up with myself. Some people free themselves up and they've got lots of time and no idea what to do with it."

She noticed I was still limping. "I'm a great one for walkin' sticks," she said and vanished. Five minutes later she was back with a fresh-cut ash stick. "It's a clumsy brute," she apologized. "I'll just dress it up a bit to neaten it, please." I held it while she stripped the bark from the handle and tip with a pocketknife.

She seemed one of those people gifted with a natural earthy wisdom. "Success seems to me to be much more than just a lot of things lying around—there's as many ways of success as there are people."

Very reluctantly I left Hannah and limped up the long hill from the farm with my new stick. She stood waving all the time. "Come back, please, if it hurts" was the last I heard.

Later that night the barmaid at the Rose and Crown Pub in Mickleton told me I'd just spent the afternoon with Hannah

HANNAH HAUXWELL
on the Pennine Way

Hauxwell, whose happy face has become the stuff of legends following a TV documentary on her life. And the cardboard boxes? "Oh, they're full of letters," she said, "from people all over the world. She's living in a house bursting with love."

Middleton-in-Teesdale, a nineteenth-century lead-mining center, has a demure charm, and I should have remained there safely sketching under the shade trees on the green. Instead I hurried around buying sugary supplies (for instant energy I told myself) and was quickly alongside the cascading river Tees on what I hoped would be one of the big walks of the journey.

The day sparkled and the light seemed to have its source not in the sun but in the valley itself which glowed a fluorescent green below the darker fells. Near High Force, where the narrowed river tumbles dramatically over an outcrop of hard dolerite, there were people peering intently at the ground looking for the last summer showings of rare plants. At Widdybank Fell, a rare band of "sugar" limestone creates special alkaline soil conditions ideal for the elusive spring gentian, the pink bird's-eye primrose, the bog sandwort, the purple mountain pansy, and a host of other species. Botanists flock here, and the construction of the vast Cow Green Reservoir above the Cauldron Snout falls in 1971 brought howls of protest from around the world. The bleak geometry of the dam wall seemed out of place in the wild scenery, and I was glad to be climbing into the hills again.

High Cup comes as a surprise, an abrupt dropping of the land down dolerite cliffs and a graceful easing of Pennine hills into the Vale of Eden, edged on the far horizon by the dramatic fells of the Lake District. This is one of the most impressive vistas along the Pennine Way, and I sat for an hour in a patch of wild thyme, watching the weather. I counted five simultaneous patterns from valley floor mists to thunderstorms in the Scottish border country where lightning played over the hills like snakes with broken spines. I waited in vain for the Helm wind, a unique local phenomenon caused by the abrupt meeting of mountains and plain.

"Waitin' for t' Helm?" A tall, rake-thin figure with a gray beard hanging down his chest appeared suddenly from behind a tumble of boulders near the precipice. His torn coat and trousers were the same muddy brown color as the rocks, and he walked slowly with a limp, supporting himself on a stick as angular as the lightning in the distance.

"T' Helm—it's a wild wind that blows here where t' mountains drop off to t' vale. There's a cloud too—hangs over t' fell for days."

"Oh," was all I managed. I was still wondering where he'd come from.

"Aye well, you won't get none today. It's all wrong for it."

And then he was off, limping around the edge of High Cup like some wild prophet in the wilderness.

Later I made the long descent past Narrowgate Beacon and Peeping Hill down to the pink-stone village of Dufton nestled around a sycamore-shaded green.

"Did you see Moses?" two young hikers asked as I dropped my rucksack by an enormous pink fountain. "He gave us a hell of a scare!"

We asked one of the locals about the odd character in the hills.

"Well we get strange ones now n'then on t'tops. Likely some old shepherd."

The three of us sprawled on the green, rubbing weary feet and waiting for the youth hostel to open. A raven joined us, legs wide apart like a gunslinger and staring with eyes like black holes until we offered it the remains of a beef sandwich. It gave a look of disgust, shook its head violently, and flapped off across the treetops.

"Moses in disguise!" said one of the hikers.

Why the dog bit me I shall never know.

It was a docile-looking creature, hardly more than rabbit-sized—lolling in a muddy hollow by a barn wall (obviously his favorite resting place, a comfortable earthy couch shaped by years of lolling). I smiled and mumbled some gentle endearment as I strolled by, but it just lay there, watching me, indifferent to my greeting. But it was all an act. Suddenly the fickle creature leaped up, gave a sudden sharp snarl, and sank its teeth into my calf. I whirled round, backpack flying off my shoulder, but it was already in retreat, scarpering around the corner of the barn. I

215

gave half-hearted chase but it knew its game well and vanished.

My leg stung so I sat down, opened up the first-aid kit, and quickly poured some purple iodine over the teeth marks. They were not deep (it takes quite a lot to penetrate two layers of thick walking socks) but I've always had a dread of rabies ever since I witnessed the agonies of the traditional injection cure given a friend of mine many years back. He couldn't sit down—or do much of anything else—for almost two months! I poured more iodine on the wound and it ran down into my boots. The dog was nowhere to be seen but somehow I felt it was still watching me. As I hobbled away I turned for a last look, and there it was, brazen as brass, back at its muddy hole, preparing for the next victim.

The next day was anything but balmy. The morning hike back up onto the open moors was in a petulant drizzle, which became a pitchforked rain as I climbed higher. On the summit of Cross Fell, at 2,930 feet, the highest point of the Pennines, the clouds suddenly descended in clammy tentacles, and I was swallowed up in the first snow of the season—a howling white fury. I could see only a few feet ahead. The path became confused with sheep tracks, and my compass failed to reassure me. I felt very lost and cold on this "Fiends Fell," its ancient name until St. Augustine brought his Christian influences here in the sixth century and chased out the bogeys by sticking a cross on the summit. I groped around through remnants of old lead mines. There was supposedly a hiker's hut somewhere for emergencies like this, but I never found it and, looking like a snow monster, I burrowed behind a wall until the storm eased. Much later I sloshed and skidded down the mountainside to the pretty village of Garrigill.

At the George and Dragon a morose group of grouse-shooting "guns" sat around the fire on high-back benches conducting a postmortem on the day's activities.

One stout gentleman in "plus twos" (breeches-like trousers), with a tiny deerstalker hat perched on his head, explained, "I never shoot well when I have to look after others." The group nodded and went on to moan of wet shooting butts, slow beaters ("a bunch of lazy school kids"), wily ground-hugging packs of grouse that were hard to spot, and half-blind pickers-up who collected the "bag." "I know for a fact they missed four of mine," grumbled one elderly participant with a purple face. A game-keeper sitting nearby had heard it all before and winked slyly at the barman.

The "glorious twelfth" of August—start of the grouse-shooting season—is a key date for Pennine landowners who depend on the substantial income from wealthy "guns" (many from the United States, Germany, and Japan) for effective moorland management. Anti-blood-sport groups and Ramblers protest the occasional closure of moors for shooting, but Lord Peel, owner of a 32,000-acre shooting estate around Swaledale, gave me his emphatic rationale: "Shooting is part and parcel of good moor management. The heather habitat is very vulnerable, and its retention falls squarely on the shoulders of the landowners. Overgrazing of sheep and inadequate 'burning' can soon ruin a good moor." I didn't quite understand the logic. Spending small fortunes just to bang away at a few harmless grouse still seems the epitome of idiocy to me. But I suppose it fills the coffers of wealthy landowners.

I stayed that night at the Alston Youth Hostel sharing a room with five other Yorkshire walkers and learned a terrible secret in the morning. I awoke around 6:00 A.M. to find all eyes on me.

"Tha's kipped well then?" asked the biggest walker.

I thanked him and said I'd enjoyed a splendid night's sleep.

"Well—tha's one out'a six then."

Five puffy-eyed heads nodded in unison.

The penny, as they say, had not yet dropped.

"Tha' snores like a bull in heat," said the big one.

I was stunned. Could it be that my wife has never told me the terrible truth or was it just a chance occurrence? I mumbled apologies and decided it might be more considerate to fellow walkers if I slept rough or used farmhouse bed-and-breakfasts for the rest of the journey.

Alston was once known as "the town of widows" after the high proportion of married men killed in the lead mines that litter the fells here. It is also the highest market town in England, set on a ridiculously steep hill—a lumpish huddle of bowed roofs and thick stone walls; a place with a sturdy enduring character.

And Alston has surely needed endurance. A few years back the town's steel plant, the major source of local employment, closed with the loss of hundreds of jobs. But rather than dismay here I sensed some of the same optimism and determination that helped bring new life to the Calder Valley. Small businesses seem to thrive; the Congregational Church is now a craft gallery; there's a narrow-gauge railway (one of several in the Pennines) for tourists along the beautiful South Tyne river to Haltwhistle; Moira McCarty runs a second-hand bookstore with a café where people can drink tea and browse through books by the fire, and Kate Webb produces 180 pounds of cheese a week at her home in The Butts, a tiny square behind main street where local archers once refined their long-bow skills.

"Hold your nose," she warned me as we entered the tiny dairy complete with pasteurizing machine, brine vat, and cheese presses. She produces three distinct types: a pungent and crumbly goat cheese, a Tynedale from Jersey and Ayreshire cow's milk, and a blend "for those a bit nervous of a real goat cheese." Upstairs in the aging room were around sixty cheeses on the shelves (traves), all at various stages in the aging process. "I never keep many more than three months, they go so fast. The problem is the goat's milk—I can't get enough locally. So this winter I'm going to France to find out more about the small co-operatives they have over there with the goat owners. I'm sure I could do the same."

Other residents here take their gardening very seriously, particularly in the fall when most pubs around Alston hold their leek and onion shows. "Blood, beer-barrel dregs—you name it, ivrywoon has their ooon concoction for feedin' the soil," said David Thompson in a singsong Northumberland ("Geordie") accent as he laid his three-foot-long leeks on the judging table at the Miner's Arms show in nearby Nenthead.

Ken Armstrong was bashful about his first prize at the Turk's Head show but was impressed by what one of his competitors had just offered him for half a dozen of his shoots. Jimmy Walker, who came in second, nodded and smiled: "Aye well, its the Swan's Head show next week and my best'll just be ready for then."

The woman serving at the fish-and-chip shop across the road was fed up with it all. "Nothin' but blinkin' leeks and onions for weeks now. Roll on Christmas!"

I had intended to take a ride on the narrow-gauge diesel railway, but the lady in the ticket office whispered: "Someone's gone off with the key," adding mysteriously, "and I know who it is!" So, no train, and instead, a slow walk through flowery pastures, along a section of the Romans' Maiden Way, to the ruins of Thirlwall Castle and the great bastion of Hadrian's Wall.

The Wall takes a while to become impressive. For centuries local builders found a source of cheap cut stone in the abandoned structure, ordered by Hadrian in 120 A.D. to mark the northern limit of the Roman empire. In addition to the wall itself a series of milecastles with gates every Roman mile were constructed along with major forts, a parallel ditch to the north, and the great Vallum ditch to the south. If all this elaboration were not enough, the central section follows the craggy undulations of the Whin Sill, an enormous sheet of dolerite that emerges in a waved line of shattered cliffs—such a natural form of defence that Hadrian's additions seem almost incidental.

The partial reconstructed wall rollercoasts along the sill, offering splendid opportunities for photographers and artists, who (if they sit atop the wall as I did) have problems holding their sketchpads steady in the wind that always seems to blow here.

Another one of those ravens joined me for lunch—large, shaggy, and obviously ravenous. It stood, giving me the most unnerving stare from eyes like black holes until I submitted and shared my cheese and onion sandwich. When finished, it took a lopsided look at my apple, shook its head, and flapped off over the crags.

Turning north from the remnants of Housesteads Fort, I could see little else but angular blocks of Sitka spruce massed along the ridges like legions. I had reached the southern tip of the vast three hundred-square-mile Border Forests. The Forestry Commission has often been lambasted for blanketing popular tourist landscapes with its "pole factories" of spruce and pine plantations and chose these hills and heaths for their remoteness and inaccessibility to car-borne travelers. Walkers however must contend with muddy tracks through dark crypts of conifers, shadowly regimented.

Silence reigns here; sounds sink into thick blankets of pine needles. All that can be heard are the soft sighings of breezes in the highest branches, like ocean lappings on a lonely seashore. Mosses and fungi flourish and the most delicate of mushrooms with stems as thin and straight as horsehair. Warty toadstools ooze a deadly looking black fluid, and puffballs wait to explode under piles of pine cones. In the gloom, nothing moves, and it all smells of a slow rotting death. I was glad to be out on the open moor again.

Down in cozy Bellingham the menu at the Cheviot Kitchen restaurant read like a poacher's priority list—venison, hare, wild duck, grouse, teal, partridge, woodcock, pheasant, and pigeon. I ate every nuance of a very gamey grouse in front of a roaring fire and wandered off over the bridge to enjoy an hour at Jubson's traveling fair, newly arrived in town. But something had gone wrong. Poor Luke Jubson stood by his motionless dodgems gazing at the empty shooting galleries and unclaimed Teddy bear prizes.

"If I could just get the men's wages I'd be satisfied. My father did this most of his life. Started just after the great war when it used to be really good, but this is just plain daft." Luke's displeasure was shared by the three other families who traveled with him around the small villages of "Geordie-land" (Northumberland). They agreed it was the evening dance that had eradicated trade although in their hearts they knew times were changing and little fairs were not so popular nowadays. So I went to the dance and pranced the floor with the village lovelies until my blisters burst for the second time.

At the Upper Redesdale Show the next day in the hamlet of Rochester I peered inside the main exhibits marquee where a dozen granite-faced judges were testing a wonderful array of homemade sausage rolls, scones, rock buns, slabs of treacle toffee, swiss rolls, "edible necklaces," chutneys, and fruit wines.

Up the hill, beyond sheep pens full of Swaledales and Blackfaces "bonnied-up" for competition, the three judges at the sheep dog trial sat huddled in a horsebox lunching on beer and hefty beef sandwiches. Six shepherds stood around, leaning on crooks, waiting their turn in the pasture.

John Dixon, a local farmer, quietly explained the essentials. "The shepherd stands by that post and his dog's got ten minutes to get the three sheep round and do a 'shed'—he gets the sheep facing all one way and sheds the last one before taking them into the pen. Looks easy when it's done well." He stroked the head of his dog Phyl. "There's no dog in the world with a brain like a border collie. She's not too fit though, are you lass? Pregnant again. You've got to look after 'em—a good one can cost you over three hundred pounds nowadays."

We watched a competition shepherd become irritated by the erratic behavior of his dog. Whistles and angry commands of "come-by", "away-here," and "stand there" seemed to make no difference. "Dog's either got a bad 'eye' or he's not just payin' attention," said John. "They're like that at times, showin' off. Now look—he's sniffed at something and he's lost the sheep again. He took his eyes off and lost 'em." The dog failed to complete the course in time and the disconsolate shepherd, reluctant to blame him, complained, "that Blackface had it in for us."

I was curious how conditions were changing for the hill sheep farmer. "Well there's still a lot of shepherds around," John explained, "but they mostly whip about on motorbikes now. Some farmers have a hard time with three hundred acres—that's enough for more than two hundred sheep, but even with subsidies it's tight work. Ideal size is around six hundred or so ewes with ten tups for breeding in autumn—about seven hundred hill acres and some good inbye land near a stream for hay. Cheviot sheep are good but Blackfaces and some of your Swalesdale mixes breed better. A while back we got quite a lot of these rich 'dentist farmers' playing around but most seem to have gone into forestry now. It was a bit more complex than they thought. You've still some 'heafing' going on, especially on the open moors where you've got to teach the flocks their territory. In the past the shepherd used to live up there with 'em and then the farm was always sold with its heafed sheep. Then there's still the dipping and clipping in May although wool's lost a lot of its

221

value now, and the September dipping, which used to be done by salving each sheep by hand with a mix of tar, Brown George (old fat), and buttermilk! Messy business that was!"

The little country show rolled along into the evening with a Punch-and-Judy show for the kids, a fell race, a pet dog competition, and a husband and wife bagpipe-and-drum team ("They couldn't afford the whole band!").

Off in a corner of the field the ancient game of quoits was being played using 5¼-pound cast-iron rings to encircle an iron post (hob) in the ground. The pitch was the traditional eleven yards in length and a skinny teenager, David Milburn, was impressing the old-timers with his skill as a "ringer," and his ability to land the first of his two throws as a "gater," which usually blocked his opponent's quoit. His second throw, hurled in a flat "wibbly-wabbler" fashion, was aimed at knocking his own "gater" into a ringer. He was very modest about all the attention —"Jus' been gettin' th' hang of it this year."

The equally popular sport of Cumberland wrestling was the star attraction at the larger Alwinton Border Shepherd's Show a few days later in the eastern foothills of the Cheviots. And here I made a big mistake.

"We need more in the All-Weights," said the tiny woman keeping the lists of competitors. So I volunteered. It looked simple enough—one arm under and one over your opponent's shoulders, nice tight lock grip across the back, then a bit of skipping and tripping to fell him. Best of three falls wins. Simple.

But no one mentioned I'd be matched against George Harrington, a Cumberland and Westmorland champion.

"It's my first go at this," I said lightheartedly as we walked to the wrestling area, ringed by scores of spectators.

"Makes no difference to me," said George.

And it didn't. I heaved and tugged and tried fancy footwork but I was soon back in the changing tent having been felled twice by this blond giant. "You didn't do so bad out there," he said peeling off his vest and colorful pants.

My shoulders and back ached for a week.

The walk north to Byrness offered more bouts with tussocky moors and segments of dank spruce forest. I saw three roe deer looking as fed up as I felt in the mushy earth but managed a grin at a place with the longest single name on the Pennine Way for nothing more than a modest farm. They call it Blakehopeburn-haugh, a wonderful kit-of-parts word consisting of "Blake"—a familiar place name in Northumberland; "hope"—a sheltered valley; "burn"—the border term for a hill stream; and "haugh"—a Norse term for flat land beside a river. As it was a farm they could have added a "garth" and a "helm"—Norse words for enclosure and cattle shelter.

Byrness came and went in a wink. I decided not to dwell on the fact that the last twenty-nine miles of the walk are said to be the hardest and loneliest of all. I was up over Windy Crag and Ravens Knowe and came to a rather undistinguished gate marking the border with Scotland. A brief moment of complacency, then off again across the grassy remnants at Chew Green of a vast complex of Roman camps, built alongside Dere Street, a major Roman supply road to the border country.

By evening it was obvious I'd never make Kirk Yetholm. My knees had gone to jelly and the sky was darkening rapidly. It was cold too. A mile or so below the trail I could see a barn in the claw of a narrow valley and decided to sleep there.

Part of the roof was missing, but there were bales of straw and hay stacked inside for winter sheep feed. Out of the wind, the place felt cozy, shards of cold moonlight flecked the hills outside and a freckling of stars filled the darkness. I made myself a warm niche, slipped into the sleeping bag, and would have been asleep immediately except for scurryings in the straw. I dislike invisible things that move in blackness. I whipped out the torch but the batteries were dead. Something eased up the groundsheet. I kicked violently and heard a squeal. Then came tiny mews and two fist-sized kittens nuzzled wet nosed, near my neck. I went to sleep, pacified by purrings.

At dawn a milky mist hung over the hills. The sun was no more than a dull ball, ghosting in grayness. Groping through half light I climbed back to the trail, strangely tired. Usually, when I'm in high gear, the landscape seems to do the moving for me; I float along, buoyed by breezes. But on this last morning, my legs seemed lifeless. The carrot at the end of the stick had withered.

For days I'd been promising myself a place for rest and quiet contemplation but the momentum of the walk itself would not let up. Now it had ceased, twelve miles from frothy pints at the Border Hotel. I wandered with all the alacrity of a two-toed sloth, raddled and boned-out, merely wanting to lie down on the damp grasses and sleep.

Then suddenly it all changed. The sun yolked out from behind clouds, the mists slipped off the shoulders of The Cheviot like veils, revealing a soft summit and the long slope down through Hen Hole toward Kirk Yetholm. It was a day brighter than polished silver. I had to contend with a few boggy bits across the aptly named Black Hag, but after Burnhead Farm my springy step returned and I followed a good road for the last couple of miles.

I was joined by Tom Smith, a lean middle-aged man with a quick smile, who told me stories of cattle raids and ferocious border wars between the Scots and English during the fourteenth century and the gypsy "kings" who once ruled this part of Scotland.

Tom lived next door to the pink house in Kirk Yetholm that was the "palace" of Charles-Faa-Blythe, the last king of the gypsies. "They were so powerful round here in the mid-1500s that James V agreed to let them maintain their own laws even though they didn't own any land. They were called muggers on account of they made mugs and pots and baskets and things out of horn. After Charlie died, his daughter Ester became queen in 1861, a real firebrand—she could out-shout anyone. We did a reenactment of her crowning last year at the Yetholm festival. They were quite a few gypsies came for that—it was so good to hear Romany spoken again—I got so much of it when I was a kid."

So, full of tales and glorying in the crisp Scottish air, I came down into the pretty village tucked away in a fold of hills. I was now ready for a little mothering and warm muffins.

The bar in the Border Hotel was crypt quiet. Two old men, both with shocks of white hair, sat on stools sipping whisky and murmuring together in an unintelligible Scottish brogue. They gave me the briefest of glances and the barman looked nervously at my boots, suitably unmuddied for the occasion.

"A celebration pint, please" I said with pride. "I've just walked the Pennine Way."

"Oh aye" was the noncommital reply.

"Took longer than I thought," I said in what I hoped was a modest tone.

The two old men continued their conversation without pause.

"It can," said the barman, and slowly filled the glass.

And that was it.

No flags and no fanfares.

But a pair of weary feet wriggled in anticipation of gentler times ahead.

9. GREECE—KEA
Looking for Zorba

"If a man doesn't break the string, tell me, what flavor is
left in life."
—*Zorba the Greek* by Nikos Kazantzakis

In spite of John Donne's sonorous admonition that "no man is an
island," most of us possess a longing to find our own seclusion
in the perfect secluded place. It's a typical wish-list item, to discover the ultimate unspoiled island, preferably Mediterranean,
ideally Greece.

226

The criteria are straightforward: it must be ignored by jet-setters, hidden from tourists, ethnically authentic, gastronomically pure, with friendly locals, beautiful scenery, and perfect weather. Most of all it must stimulate that essential spirit of Zorba—an anarchistic "only-one-life" perspective, exemplified by an enthusiasm for ouzo, a lust for lamb in all its forms, and an intense sense of harmony between land, ocean, and the individual spirit.

Well—I found my perfect Greek island entirely by chance. I'd planned an exploration of Skiros, Sifnos, and Folegandros, all of which I'd been assured possessed the epitome of the Zorba mood. But something somebody said on the flight to Athens, a whispered aside from a man who obviously knew his islands, sent me off in an entirely different direction. To the island of Kea.

So here's my perfect island in a series of vignettes, glimpses of a small world that is sure enough of its own heritage and integrity to remain just the way it is for a long time to come.

I could have traveled from Athens airport to the ferry departure point at Lavrion by taxi but chose the local bus instead. I hoped for hoary locals, chickens, piglets on old twine, outbursts of ethnic folksongs—all the hullabaloo of foreign bus journeys that travelers love to relate to envious friends at home. In actuality the bus from Athens turned out to be an ultramod affair with tinted windows, red velveteen seats, and a bevy of well-dressed citizens carrying shopping bags from up-market Athenian stores. No folk songs with this lot.

But things improved as we left the interminable concrete boulevards of the capital and moved beyond the suburbs into the olive groves and village-sprinkled hills. The city shoppers disappeared, to be replaced by groups of black-shrouded widows hidden in shawls, sun-bronzed farmers with fat drooping mustaches, and a huddle of aromatic fishermen carrying yellow nets and food baskets brimming with fat loaves and bottles of wine. The driver had ceased his horn blowing and cursing at the antics of city motorists and settled snugly into his niche, surrounded by all the comforts of home—little colored lamps, two plastic Madonnas and five saint cards, family photos, a row of international flags above dusty postcards of European capital cities, a neat compartment for tissues and cigarettes, two sets of amber worry beads (*komboloi*), a Playboy rabbit sticker, and a rhinestone-studded holder for his can of soda.

Out of the city he was now king of the road, pausing in one village to negotiate some shady deal with one of the locals (lots of winks, nods, and handshakes), graciously helping old ladies on and off the bus, joking with the conductor (who held his book of multicolored bus tickets like the Gutenberg Bible), pausing again for a tiny cup of pungent Greek coffee delivered through the side window of his cab by an admiring taverna owner.

Every once in a while he'd reach into his tissue box and pull out a fresh white flower, smell it, suck one of the petals, and replace it carefully next to the worry beads. In between there were waves to people we passed, murmurs of admiration at the spritely young girls in the villages, and effusive greetings to friends lounging in the endless outdoor tavernas along our route.

A bus driver's lot is indeed a happy one on the byways of Greece.

Lavrion seemed to be nothing but tavernas, lining the shady squares and boulevards of this otherwise undistinguished port town. How the Greeks love their leisure—sipping the days away around rickety sidewalk tables laden with milky glasses of ouzo, cups of thick Greek coffee and frappé (iced coffee), cold glasses of Amstel beer, and the inevitable retsina wine.

Beyond the town I could see olive groves on the dry hillsides, hazy and shimmering in the midday heat. Some of the groves had existed for centuries, filled with wonderfully grotesque trees whose trunks have exploded into separate serpentine forms, twisted and writhing beneath elephant-hide bark. They seemed tangibly alive like the contortions of an emerging Rodin creation, eternally in agony beneath delicate filigrees of silver-green leaves.

Eventually the ferryboat to Kea arrived. The *Ioulis Keas II* was a substantial two-deck affair, which until 1977 had been the famous "Ferry across the Mersey" in Liverpool, England. Gerry and his mop-top Pacemakers had sung her praises (she was then known as the *Royal Daffodil*), and now, here she was, making her two trips a day to this lovely six-by-twelve-mile island, an hour and a half from Lavrion. There were only a dozen or so passengers and a couple of cars. She looked very empty.

"Weekends you'll see a difference," one of the passengers told me. "A lot of Greeks in Athens have relatives over there. It gets pretty frantic Friday nights."

The cooling *meltemi* summer wind from the north was blowing ("the Aegean air conditioner"), and we eased out into the evening light, rounding the barren bleached hills of Makronisos island, heading fifteen miles due east for the port of Korissia.

One of the crewmen decided to practice his English on me. "I like Kea very much. Not many people there—maybe fifteen hundred now. But it has much history—they have digged—dug —up a town near Korissia more than four thousand years old. Also on the back of the island, on the east side, there is—are— remains of a famous Greek city. They call it Karthaea. It is hard to get there if you don't have a boat. You can still see pieces of three temples. This was a very important island—once many famous writers and strong runners came from here."

I had bought a small guidebook on Kea in Lavrion, and my informant was indeed correct. The island had been a flourishing cultural nexus of the western Aegean around 500 B.C. And in spite of long periods of subsequent occupation by the Romans, the Byzantines, the Venetians, the Turks, and more recently the Italians and Germans, the island seems to have survived as a hotbed of nationalistic pride. Even as recently as the 1940s, it boasted a population of over 40,000, supported by a rich agricultural base on terraced hillsides and its role as a wood and coal refueling center for trading steamers from the north.

"There she is," my crewman-companion pointed through the silvery evening haze at the island's mountainous profile. It looked larger than I'd expected. As we came closer I could see the lines of ancient farming terraces supported by enormous boulder and fieldstone walls. Scores of tiny white farm-chapels dotted the slopes. The main town, Ioulis, was set well back from the coast on a steep hillside, in traditional Cycladean fashion. Sections of huge stone walls surrounded the 1100 B.C. "Kastro" castle and remains of a thirteenth-century Venetian fortress—an ideal defensive position against the once interminable pirate attacks.

On a hillside near Ioulis is one of Kea's principal archaeological attractions, a twenty-foot-long lion carved from a solid slab of island sandstone in the sixth century B.C. I was too far away to see it.

"Never mind," said my companion. "It's not very good carving."

Korissia hid her charms until the very last moment, as the ferry eased into the sheltered harbor. Then she appeared as if by magic, a tight, white huddle of houses, shops, tavernas, and *kafeneion*, lit by little lamps, alive with bouzouki music, fishermen mending nets, chickens and pigeons pecking among the quayside stones, and people walking together in the traditional evening stroll, the *volta*. A perfect picture of Greek island life.

I had planned to stay at one of the two modest hotels here but instead was lured away by villagers to inspect rooms in private homes overlooking the harbor. Literally within minutes I was sitting on my own broad balcony, a glass of ouzo in my hand, my bags strewn across a pleasant apartment with kitchen and bathroom; the aroma of roast lamb wafted up from the two quayside restaurants. I had finally arrived and was already infatuated with the place.

The following morning I found an embryonic Zorba on the quay at Korissia. His name was Dimitrios, and he traveled with his friend Leos in a tiny ramshackle fishing boat around the Aegean. (Their craft was hardly visible among the dozen or so fancy yachts tied to the quay.) They were both in their twenties and went wherever the mood—and the fishing—took them. If the people of a particular island were friendly and bought their fish, they would stay awhile, docked each day at the quay, fishing every night from dusk till dawn.

I sat with them as Leos untangled the mile of hooked *paragadi* lines they used and chopped inky squid for bait. Dimitrios labored intently under the hot morning sun, filleting four mid-size skates, which, along with a few kilos of mullet, were his total catch after ten hours at sea. He was disappointed.

"They won't buy my fish. The taverna owners here do not like skate."

These mini manta rays must be the most difficult of creatures to clean, with their leathery hide, enormous bones, and their vicious clawlike hooks embedded in the flesh.

"So why clean them?"

"We eat them ourselves!" said Dimitrios, and for the first time he smiled and his eyes flashed with life. "It doesn't really matter. If we sell our fish then we usually eat at the tavernas, if we don't sell, we eat our own fish. What's the difference?"

He took a long drink of retsina and handed me the bottle. I passed it immediately to Leos, having failed miserably to acquire a palate for pine resin–enhanced wine. Natural Greek wines are light and enjoyable—why eradicate their flavor in this way?

Both young men spoke some English, and I wondered why they'd chosen this life. Was it just a little flurry of freedom before settling down?

"No, no," Dimitrios laughed. "We live this way all the time. We like it. We fish in the summer then in the winter we go home to Crete. We have a friend with a little house there. There is no winter in Crete."

"What about the future?"

"Who knows? We have many good friends"—raised eyebrows and wide smiles—"and the people—especially the people of Kea—are good to us. We like this life. Every day we have fresh fish, fresh bread, fresh figs, olives, cherries—we dance if there is dancing, Leos is a good singer, I play bouzouki, we meet new people all the time. Our life is good—very good! We have everything we need—no problems!"

A grin covered all his face and he handed me a pink fish steak. "Here—tell Siphos at the taverna to cook this for you!"

Later on I took the bus up the long winding road to Ioulis. Sitting with my sketchpad above the little tight-knit town I felt how simple is pure contentment: a bag of dark cherries, a handful of pungent kalamata olives, a few slices of garlicky salami, a still-warm loaf from the bakery, and the sound of the wind in the almond trees. Far below the ocean flashed like scattered diamonds; cows and goats munched slow paths along the ancient terraced hills; a farmer scythed the last of the early summer hay in long slow strokes, and the old broken windmills on the ridge watched over it all as they have done for two thousand years.

It was far too tempting: I could rent a little hillside cottage here for next to nothing, plant a garden, have my own goats, my own vine arbor, sketch, paint, and write to my heart's content— maybe become part of the life of this small place and maybe produce something true and good out of the whole experience.

I always seem to have been driven by one desire: to see and touch as much as possible of the earth before leaving this one life. "All that can be enjoyed must be enjoyed here. A mind must decide to conquer its weaknesses and meanness, its laziness and vain hopes, and cling with all its power to every second which flits away forever. In eternity no other chance will be given to us." The spirit of Zorba speaks again.

Then there are the moments that come so unexpectedly it's, only later you wonder at their intensity.

I was walking—more like climbing—up through the winding stepped streets of Ioulis. There was no breeze; the meltemi wind is a fickle friend, strong and steady some days, cooling the body and mind, and utterly absent on other days. Today it had got sidetracked somewhere on the Russian steppes and the poor little town baked on its amphitheatrical hillside in 100-degree sledgehammer heat. I should have stayed down in Korissia, safe in the shade of the harbor tavernas enjoying the tasty mezes (snacks), and crisp-broiled fish, but instead I decided to go sketching in this beehive town of Cycladean architectural complexity.

I was most happily lost as usual in its labyrinths, passing the old mustached men in the vine-trellised tavernas playing tavli (backgammon), smelling the hot fresh bread from the bakeries, watching the old women knitting in open doorways or huddled in gossipy groups, keeping a perpetual eye on village antics and mores.

Suddenly I spotted an old woman trying to negotiate a set of dangerous steps down the side of a steep fieldstone wall leading from her garden patch. She was dressed in ritual black with black shawl and black stockings and carried a bunch of fresh-cut daisies.

With only one hand free she looked in danger of falling. I scampered up a dozen more whitewashed steps and helped her down. Her face had all the dourness of the island's mythical widow-witches, deeply furrowed with lines and creases, scorched into hide-leather texture by decades under the Aegean sun. But as she reached the bottom step, she turned and smiled such a brilliant smile that the wrinkles seemed to vanish, the stony eyes sparkled, and her head turned coquettishly like a young girl's.

Neither of us seemed to know what to do next. She clung to my hand and just kept on smiling. I mumbled a badly pronounced greeting of *"Kalimera"* (good morning), which came out sounding more like "calamari," which in turn made her giggle. Then the little moment came; she looked down at her bunch of white-petalled daisies, carefully selected the biggest one with a bright golden center, broke off a portion of the stem and, standing on her toes, pushed the flower into the hair behind my ear. She gave my hand one more squeeze and vanished down the steps, into the shadows.

I left the daisy where she'd put it for the rest of the day. The villagers doubtless thought the sun had addled my brain, but wherever I went I was greeted by smiles and nods, and that was just fine.

I thought I'd seen just about every kind of moon there is to see: blue ones, big cheesy harvest moons, scimitar-bladed crescents, haloed, halved, eclipsed . . . but this one was something unique. Over dry hills and dark brittle cliffs rose a balloon of pure pink edging slowly up into a violet-black sky and casting a pink shimmer across the still waters of the bay. The tiny night-fishing boats were edged in pink. The olive trees were shrouded in a pink fuzz. The breeze had died; there was no movement anywhere— just that big balloon moving slowly upward. . . .

"Asti nichita ina mahiki" (this night is magic), said Sophocles. He was usually a man of far too many words who considered himself something of a philosopher-poet but spent most of his days grilling fish over brushwood chips for his always-hungry

Ioulis
Kea Greece

admirers at the taverna. He was enormously proud of Kea's history as a cultural nexus of the Cyclades during Greece's Golden Age—birthplace of Simonides (556–468 B.C.), the lyric poet who wrote elegant epitaphs for the Greek warriors who fell at Marathon; home of the poet and playright Bacchylides, the physician Evasistratos (founder of the science of physiology), the sophist, Prodikos, and the wandering philosopher, Ariston, who considered Kea to be second only to Athens in the sophistication of its ancient culture.

"*Asti nichita ina mahiki,*" said Sophocles again. The smoke from the fire swirled around his long curly strands of hair and goaty beard. He had the face of a young child in spite of all the hair; his eyes gleamed in the flames. This was a night for poetry, and he knew it.

The islanders seem uncertain about Vourkari. Not long ago this was your traditional picturesque Cycladean fishing village, a mile or so around the bay from Korissia, with a population of fifty and maybe a dozen or so small boats. Across from the village are the excavated remains of Ayia Irini, portions of which date back to 4300 B.C. In the last year or two Vourkari has become something of a hit with the sloop-set, and the boat bums who arrive daily in their gleaming fiberglass and chrome yachts to party the night away in the quayside tavernas and the two nearby (dare I write it) discos. While the revelers seem to have little impact on the rest of the island, Vourkari is a warning that Kea's idyllic isolation may not endure forever.

One incident here was reassuring though, suggesting that the traditional courtesy and kindness of the Keans still flourish intact. An Australian sailor, who had regaled fellow yachtsmen with tales of his nautical prowess around the world for most of the evening, stayed on at the taverna after his company had left, enjoying a series of strong nightcaps. He eventually paid his bill and wobbled over to his boat to sleep. When he began climbing the steep gangplank, his sense of balance left him and he looked ready to fall between the boat and the dock. Before I could even rise from my seat, the taverna owner and his three strapping sons scampered across the quay and caught the inebriated Aussie in midfall—a fall that almost certainly would have been fatal.

Gradually they eased him over the rail into the boat whereupon he collapsed in a heap on the deck and promptly sank into sleep. The owner hesitated, wondering if he should put the poor man to bed but decided that may be a little too much intrusion on his privacy and returned to the taverna to the rousing applause of the customers. The sailor never knew how close he'd come to a watery end.

It was not my idea of the perfect ride but I had little choice during the 2:00 to 5:00 P.M. siesta when the island switches off every day. For over an hour I'd been walking a shadeless road from Korissia in the direction of Panayia Kastriani monastery, stuck way on a rocky promontory up at the northeastern tip of Kea. Three cars had passed, all full. My water had run out and I was peering into a roadside shrine, wondering if the bottle of wine and ouzo inside could be used by strangers in an emergency. These shrines are all over the island, placed as tributes to the saints for fortuitous events. You often see them on dangerous bends in the mountains in recognition of someone's miraculous recovery from a death-defying accident. They are often constructed like minibasilicas, two or three feet high, complete with towers and domes, and containing icons, photographs, votive offerings, oil lamps, and bottles of alcohol.

I had almost decided that the saints would applaud my initiative when along came this battered truck carrying a huge black bull, bowlegged by its own enormity. Surprisingly the truck stopped and two equally enormous bull-necked men gestured that I could join the animal in the back if I wished. My "beggars can't be choosers" attitude prevailed, and I spent a most uncomfortable twenty minutes dodging the lashing tail and restless hooves of the bull as we passed the lovely Otzias beach (flashes of nude bathing here) and climbed higher and higher into the brittle, tawny hills.

Eventually we reached a small whitewashed farm overlooking the western beaches and bays. The two large men, obviously brothers, invited me to join them under the vine arbor. We sat on benches in the shade with our backs against the rough fieldstone walls of the house. Inside the rooms were small and bare with stone floors; a woman was moving around in the shadows; enormous sunflowers waved outside the rear windows. A cock crowed and a donkey replied and they began an extended dialog of brayings and doodledoos. The brothers laughed.

"That is the new donkey. The best on the island!" He told me he'd paid over 70,000 drachmas for the animal, more than $500. "A car is very expensive. The government double the price with taxes. This donkey—it will go anywhere. Very strong!"

The woman emerged with a bottle and glasses on a tray. Her wrinkled face was shrouded in a black shawl. The elder of the two brothers, Yiorgio, poured the ouzo, and we added our own water, watching the liquid turn milky. "*Yaisou!* To your health!"

I felt utterly at home. Below the farm, terraces descended to a dry valley filled with pink-flowered koumara bushes. They say witches used to eat the leaves of this bush before casting spells. Halfway down were twenty or so blue-wooded beehives (Kea is famous for its thyme honey). The terraces were still golden with barley stubble; the crop had just been cut and lay in high piles on the circular threshing terrace near the house. Cicadas buzz-sawed in the fig trees; dozens of baby green figs peeped from under the big leaves. Grapes dangling from vines above our heads looked almost ready to eat.

Yiorgio stretched out his arms expansively. "We have every-thing—yes? We have the figs, grapes in September, maybe we make *tsipuro* (a fiery liquor derived from grape pips and skins), we have the olives in October, we hunt for rabbits and partridge, we have hay for the cows, we have goats, we grow tomatoes and cucumbers, my cousin has a fishing boat so we have fish all the time—and my mother makes the best bread on Kea!" He pointed with pride to the huge domed oven streaked with wood smoke at the side of the house.

A bright lizard flashed across the courtyard and vanished behind a line of flowery plants set in colorful ten-liter olive oil cans. Over the terraces a hawk hung in the sky, floating on the spirals, slowly circling, waiting to drop like a stone on some un-suspecting creature far below in the valley. "*Yaisou!*" said Yiorgio again. We all smiled together, and kept on smiling.

Much, much later I arrived at the Panayia Kastriani monastery perched on the top of towering cliffs overlooking a violet-blue ocean. Pappa Leftares, the Orthodox priest who oversees the little citadel, was away, but I was treated royally by a matronly caretaker and six children. The moment I arrived they rushed me off to see the cell-like rooms with tiny balconies overlooking the sea (the monks are gone and visitors can stay here for a few dollars a night). The ornate domed chapel in the center of the compound was being restored, but in spite of all the internal scaffolding the icons and frescoes sparkled in a soft white light.

One of the children who spoke a little English told me the tale of the monastery: "There were some shepherds on this hill, a long, long time ago, and they saw a glow in the earth and were very frightened and ran to bring all the people of the island. And when they all came they walked into the glow and found the beautiful icon of the Madonna so they built a church."

I marveled at the faith of the islanders to construct this ornate complex in such a remote place but—there again—Kea has hundreds of tiny white chapels built from fieldstone on the isolated terraces. And even today, in an increasingly secular world, each chapel is whitewashed every year, the icons and altars are cleaned and candles lit every week, sometimes every day. Faith is a tangible reality here; the old ways still have meaning.

When I eventually returned to Korissia that evening I saw the village priest walking toward the quay in his long black robes and inverted stovepipe hat. He was a small stocky man with a huge grizzly beard, his long brown hair was tied in a knot at the back of his head below his hat. I wished him "Kali spera" (good evening) and he paused, looked very intently into my face, and smiled. In fumbling Greek I tried to explain that I had just visited the monastery, and in the middle of my garbled monologue he stepped up to me (his head only reached my shoulders) and gave me a truly rib-cracking bear hug. Then he shook my hand, smiled the brightest smile, and continued on toward the quay.

There were moments when all the little magics of this place coalesced...I lay in the warm ocean at midnight, just floating there, with the water tickling my toes and the night breeze sending briny ripples across my stomach. The smell of wild sage and thyme wafted down from the hills around the bay. I could hear

239

the chatter of the boat riggings from the harbor dock and the endlessly plaintive bouzouki songs; I could smell the lamb roasts and grilling souvlakia from the quayside tavernas; I could hear Savros bawling out the orders in his sandpaper voice to a never-ending array of family members sweating over hot stoves. . . .

I just floated, utterly weightless, with all these sounds and smells mingling together, and the moment seemed to go on and on . . .

Many lazy days later, just before dawn, I reluctantly left tiny Kea. The ferry eased out of the harbor and into the Aegean. Korissia quickly disappeared behind its sheltering bluff, and as we gathered speed the sun slowly rose from the ocean in a violet-pink haze. I saw the terraced hills of the island for a final time, layer on blue layer, before they slowly disappeared into the early morning mists.

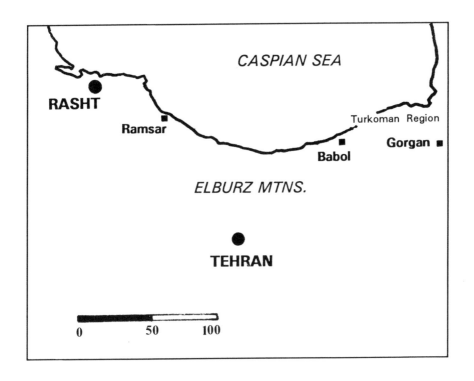

10. IRAN

Boar-ing Days by the Caspian Sea

Don't ask how I got there.

It's a long story and I'm in Tehran only sort of semilegally. The problem in post-Shah Iran is that almost everything is illegal or dangerous or "not advisable" for western "Satanists."

Fortunately, in another lifetime there, I had developed many strong friendships during my two-year stint as an urban master planner working under the hovering eye of the Shah and the Shah's wife, the Empress Farah (once a trainee architect), on the future plan for Tehran's growth. Having a king and queen as overseers led to many strange occurrences, and I can't resist relating one of them before the tale of this particular adventure begins.

241

It was sometime back in 1968 and we were all in the Shah's palace, the Saltan Atabad, high in the foothills of the Elburz Mountains that tower over the city. We had been summoned to present our projection for population growth in the city over the following thirty years or so. The figures were alarming. Even assuming a scenario of moderate growth, we had concluded that by the end of the century, the capital would find itself home to over sixteen million Iranians, up from a mere two and a half million at that time.

The Shah stared at us incredulously. (The Empress smiled benevolently as she always seemed to do.)

"And this is the basis upon which you would design your plan for the city?"

Our team leader coughed. "These are the projections, Your Majesty, following a very careful analysis of population characteristics, longevity factors, migration trends, birth rate statistics, and..."

The Shah raised his hand and our leader stopped abruptly in midflow.

"I will issue an edict."

A sudden flurry of activity. Ministers shuffled papers, assistants opened large red books, two finely dressed gentlemen, who appeared to be acting as scribes, stood formally by their high desks, with pens poised over single sheets of gold-edged paper.

The Shah looked around to ensure that all was ready and slowly made his pronouncement as the scribes scribbled.

"This is my edict. By the year 1995 the population of the city of Tehran shall be no more than five and one half million. We shall create other alternative growth centers in other of our major cities, and the plans for the future of the capital shall be prepared based upon this edict."

Utter silence.

The ministers bowed their heads, and then bowed lower in acknowledgment of the edict. The scribes underlined the statement. We could hear pens scratching on fine parchment.

"I will expect to see the first submission of your draft plans in one month," said the Shah and then waved his left hand as a

242

sign that the meeting was over. The Empress continued to smile benevolently.

So the audience was at an end. And that's how decisions were made in Iran in the era of the Shah's "White Revolution."

We looked at our team leader, an Iranian architect with many years of hardball planning negotiation experience in the United States. His head was bowed as low as those of the ministers. The Shah rose; we rose and were led off by uniformed protocol pilots back into the richly decorated antechamber where we could do little except stare at one another in utter disbelief—and dismay.

But those days were long gone. Many of my friends in Tehran were gone too, some to safer havens in the United States and Europe, others caught up in the tangled terror of the Khomeini purges and never heard of again.

"Why on earth have you come back?" I had found one of my old colleagues, a brilliant architect, and now a lowly official in some sub-subdepartment in a bureau of a division of a ministry that had nothing at all to do with city planning.

"I wanted to see what has happened since the revolution."

"You're mad." He looked at me, worried and thoughtful. "You shouldn't stay in Tehran."

"I don't want to."

"Good—I think it's best for you to leave as quickly as possible."

"That's fine. I want to go north again. To the Caspian Sea."

"Why?"

"I spent a lot of time there once with some people on the marshes west of Rasht. I'd like to go back."

"The passes are still blocked. Spring is late. You won't be able to get over the Elburz Mountains."

I hadn't expected this. Usually by May the passes are clear.

"Okay. I'll go east on the Mashad road and cut across near Shahrud. The mountains are lower there."

"You'll be in Turkoman country—almost in the U.S.S.R.!"

"Great. I've always wanted to see the Turkomans."

My friend was not impressed by my casual itinerary.

"Well—at least you'll be able to buy some hats," he said,

referring to the exotic Persian lamb headgear of the Turkoman tribesmen.

"Fine. I'll buy some hats—I'm getting two adventures for the price of one."

"Depends on the price you're willing to pay."

He always did have a kind of gloomy Iranian humor, that friend of mine. But he was also dependable.

Somehow he arranged for me to borrow a well-worn Peugeot, and I was ready to set off a couple of days later. I'd seen little of my old haunts in Tehran; my friend had made me a welcome guest in his house on condition I stayed indoors. Irritating but sensible I suppose. I had no wish to see the inside of one of Khomeini's houses of horror.

The little bit I'd managed to see of Tehran was depressing. The fancy boutiques and European fashion stores that once lined select parts of the broad avenues had virtually disappeared. Some of the hotels were still open but rather down-at-the-heel, their swimming pools closed and their bars, once packed with Western oilmen and get-rich-quick entrepreneurs, were seedy laughterless places now, serving mainly doogh (a sort of fizzy sour milk) instead of their once notorious cocktails.

The killer taxis were still around though, clapped-out Mercedeses and Iran's own Peykan, using the 1960s British Hillman design, careering wildly along the graffiti-lined boulevards (anti-American slogans were still a popular form of street art) with their drivers surrounded by dangling worry beads, family photos, gaudy-colored postcards of Islamic religious leaders, and plastic dolls dangling on beaded threads.

Scattered along the dusty, dreary sidewalks were the old peddlers' carts crammed with ballpoint pens, razor blades, matches, batteries, cheap lighters and cheaper sunglasses, flaky wafer-biscuits, watch straps, and cigarettes sold individually. But gone were all the statues and framed portraits of the Shah's father, Reza Shah, and the Shah himself. The Ayatollah was everywhere, his stern gaze watching over every house and every shop, ensuring obedience to all the strict Islamic codes of behavior. No more primped Tehrani females from the affluent mountain suburbs of Shemeran displaying their newfound wealth in the latest Milan and Paris fashions. Chadors were obligatory now, those black head-to-toe shrouds that the Shah had tried so hard to discourage. Women had been slammed back into Islamic modesty to become shadowy and submissive looking once again.

Ah—but at least one delight remained. Iran's wonderful national dish, the chelo kebab, still provided daily sustenance in the form of barbecued strips of lamb served with broiled tomatoes, segments of raw onion, dishes of pungent torshi pickle, and those succulent mounds of the best rice in the world, mixed into a rich risotto with melted butter and raw egg yolks and sumak spice. One could still live well on such a feast in spite of all the changes.

Once on the road, I felt better.

Tehran dribbled out across the desert in a chaotic plethora of unpaved highways and half-finished buildings (so much for our grand master plan). Vistas of mountains and sandy plains opened up as I banged through the potholes, heading east toward Mashad, an ancient city filled with religious fanatics and a place I hoped to avoid.

After a hundred or so miles, any pretence at paved road ended, and I was back on the once-familiar sand tracks, leaving dust clouds in my wake as I bounced along under a hot afternoon sun.

Over the desert hung a peculiar light, a steely sheen that crisped the contours and made flocks of wandering goats seem stereoscopic against the gold-beige wilderness. The old Peugeot bumped and rattled under a flaying sun. A distant shepherd, leaning on his staff, seemed to be dancing to a slow steady rhythm in the heat shimmers; inverted cones of spiraling sand, a string of dust devils, joined in the gyrations. One of them left the formation and headed straight for me with malicious intent. I'd had experience with these devils on other journeys and slowed down to a crawl as it swirled across the quivering plain. It didn't make much difference. The creature had aimed itself well and hit the car with the force of a demolition derby pileup, knocking it briefly onto two wheels and smothering us in a sandy maelstrom, before scampering off again to do battle with a line of low dunes on my right.

Feathery plumes of gold-edged clouds floated above the desert. It was so empty: A few bleached bones at the side of the track; two scrawny camels blown up to Spielbergian monsters by the gyrations of the air; mirages of great lakes spread everywhere across the flats; a single hawk, or an eagle, riding the thermals in sweeping Art Nouveau curves.

As the heat intensified the desert seemed to lose whatever minimal color it had retained in the morning, as if the sun had sucked at the last of its life and pounded it on an anvil into a flat, ringing nothingness edged by malevolent black-boned ridges of brittle rocks.

There was little traffic, but the huge Mack trucks that once thundered by the hundred across these empty wastes had left their souvenirs in the form of endless corrugations in the roadbed. Now, as desert travelers often relate with complacency, driving corrugated roads is merely a matter of pacing, finding the right speed so that you ride them as if in a hovercraft, rather than hitting each one like a dinghy in hard surf. And in theory, they're correct. Given a straight sand road, the corrugations usually form an even wave pattern. But unfortunately, with typical Iranian illogic, the road twisted like an inebriated boa constricter across the level empty land. There was no apparent reason for its ridiculous alignment, but it meant that the corrugations constantly changed wavelengths as the trucks had slowed and then accelerated after each of the inane curves. No sooner had I achieved a nice steady rhythm, usually around forty mph, then there'd be a bend and then another bend, and the flow was lost in a welter of ruts and rocks.

After three hours of this nonsense I felt like a burst bag of Kitty Litter, and what made it worse were the knocking sounds, metal on metal, coming from the front of the car. Crankshaft, burst gasket, cracked cylinder? I'm not much of an auto mechanic, and my mind boggled with the possibilities. After another one hundred miles of tortuous track my patience was shot and my cursing had increased to blood-vessel-bursting intensity. I had to get whatever it was fixed!

I was nervous. My direct contact with Iranians had been very limited on this trip. I wanted to be as anonymous and inconspicuous as possible. But there was no choice now.

After another twenty miles a gas station appeared, a typical desert setup with a single hand pump and the owner's house, a mud brick affair with four beehive-domed rooms facing onto a muddy courtyard. And that was all. Beyond the house was desert and more desert and hazy outlines of distant mountains.

I wasn't sure what to expect and certainly not the welcome I received. The owner greeted me like a long-lost cousin, leading me to his house for tea (chaii) and serving slabs of elongated pizza-shaped bread (nan-e-barbari) baked by his wife in a domed oven. She sat, wrapped in a chador, on the doorstep of one of the rooms, carefully sorting rice for the evening meal on a blue cotton cloth. Each grain was examined thoroughly. Broken grains and other extraneous bits of straw and dirt were pushed off to the side. The pile of acceptable rice grew very slowly. Five children, lined up by height, stood watching.

The owner inspected the car carefully and returned to the house to explain that one of my shock absorbers was damaged and needed immediate attention.

"Do you have any shocks here?" I asked in stumbling half-forgotten Farsi.

He laughed and repeated the question to his wife who began giggling behind her chador, along with her children.

"No—no shocks. We have nothing!"

Wonderful. Stuck in the middle of nowhere again.

The owner, whose name was Hassan, then began a long explanation that I found hard to follow but which seemed to indicate that he had a friend who was expected that evening who could fix everything so don't worry, have some more chaii and stay for dinner.

So that's what I did. The friend didn't arrive until dusk, by which time Hassan had set me up in my own room in his house (three of his children were quietly instructed to remove their bedrolls into their parent's room) with a freshly beaten carpet on the mud floor and some pillows for lounging on. The friend didn't have any new shocks either but possessed the Iranian skill for improvisation. Somehow with a lot of hammering and cutting up of strips of old rubber tire and more hammering he managed to salvage what was left of my own shock and make it workable again. By the time he left it was dark and dinner was cooking.

247

"You will stay with us tonight," Hassan insisted. "We are pleased to have you in our home and to share our food."

And what food! The most exquisite needle-grained rice served with golden fragments of *tahdeeg* (the crisped rice from the bottom of the cauldron), a slow-cooked *khoresht* (stew) whose basic ingredient was a whole goat's head (no, I didn't eat the eyeballs) and tiny kufteh kebabs of lamb mixed with spices and broiled over a charcoal stove. *"Kheili khub!"* I said to Hassan's wife when we had demolished the meal. "Very, very good."

Later on Hassan brought a plate of sweet honey cookies smothered in yogurt *mast,* which we ate slowly, sitting by the courtyard and looking across the desert. The moon was out, full and silver, and stars filled the sky. The children had gone to bed. A warm breeze blew in from the west... I suddenly missed my wife very much. This was the Iran we had known and loved together so long ago, and in spite of everything that had changed in that country I was happy to be back. Only one wish. I wished Anne could have been there with me.

After a breakfast at dawn of fresh-baked flat bread, honey, and mast, I thanked my hosts profusely with presents from my bag (I often wonder what Hassan does with my red Moroccan leather spectacle case. He didn't own any spectacles, he just loved its rich color), and set off again for Gorgan and the land of the Turkoman.

More ruts, more skidding around sharp bends, a muddy stretch where a downpour of night rain in the mountains had made surging rivers out of a string of dry streambeds—but no more knocks. The improvised shock absorber repair worked fine. I passed ghostly ruins of two caravansarys, ancient resting places for camel trains on the great trading routes between Afghanistan and Turkey.

Eventually I arrived in Gorgan, a rambling town on the edge of a vast green plain. Unlike the mud-walled enclosures of most desert villages, the buildings here were mainly two-storied constructions with large balconies. Heavy roofs, covered with pantiles, gave protection to the balconies and often to a large part of the street below. This was particularly noticeable in the bazaar, a long rambling lacework of tiny streets where one could gaze comfortably at the small shops and remain perfectly dry even in the worst rainstorm. Actually, it was in the bazaar that I saw my first Turkoman.

He was bargaining for a bundle of coarse rope. He had high Mongolian cheekbones and almond eyes, a browny yellow complexion and a magnificent curved beard, which started abruptly below his bottom lip and swung in a scimitarlike arch to a pointed tip.

But it was his hat that caught my attention. Like a huge black upturned Persian rice pan, it immediately conjured up pictures of cossack horsemen, dancers, balalaikas and cries of *"Ra!"*

I tried to engage him in conversation, "conversation" being a polite way of explaining my hand-waving antics combined with a very limited vocabulary. In desperation, I pointed to his hat. *"Kojast?"* (where?) I asked. He smiled, lifted it from his head, and put it into my hands. Made from closely coiled Persian lambs' wool, it was a beautiful thing to look at and to hold. I put it on—much to the amusement of the rapidly increasing group of spectators. I should have known better. It was impossible to give it back. He insisted, almost in a menacing manner, that I keep it (an Iranian custom, actually more of a social obligation, when any possession is admired by a stranger). I shall never forget the proud way he smiled, bowed, and left me rather embarrassed, holding his prize possession. A Turkoman without his hat. Impossible!

On the following day, the weather changed. The clammy mist disappeared, revealing soft tree-covered hills. Below the town, a great green plain stretched northward toward the border. A fresh, clean breeze blew in from the Caspian Sea.

I had made many inquiries about the Turkoman people and had been advised to travel first to Pahlavidej, fifty miles into the plain, where a market was held in the town every Thursday. Unfortunately it was Sunday. Nevertheless I was determined to buy some more of those hats and a few of the locally produced shawls made from crude cotton and printed in brilliant oranges and greens.

The road to Pahlavidej from Gorgan was a rough dirt track, posing no problems in a dry summer but not quite so straightforward during a wet spring. After the third river crossing, when at one stage the water reached halfway up the doors, I began to wonder whether I should ever reach the town.

On either side, wheat fields stretched as far as the eye could see. There was no one about. No sign of movement anywhere except for a gentle almost hypnotic waving of the young wheat. Gorgan had long since faded into the heat haze. It was not without some anxiety that I lurched across the next flooded stretch, the car bravely pulling itself through the mud on three of its six cylinders.

A crazy little humpbacked bridge formed the entrance to Pahlavidej. The town consists simply of two wide streets crossing at right angles at the central maidan. The buildings were mainly two-storied brick and wooden structures. At first sight a dusty, uninspiring place.

Then I began to sense its character. I felt as though I'd passed into another country, seemingly oblivious of the rest of the world. The women walked freely in the streets wearing brightly colored dresses and shawls. Their Mongolian heads were adorned with the most elaborate earrings and necklaces. Almost all the men had beards, some carefully groomed to a fine point, others dangling in great matted masses onto their chests. Some even had long Mandarin-type mustaches that hung limply from the outer edges of their upper lips. And every man had a hat, huge inverted pyramid hats; high narrow ones; short, stocky ones, and flat, wide ones, but all, nevertheless, true Turkoman hats.

I was regarded initially with what appeared to be amused contempt, at least until I made it known that I'd like to purchase a few hats. Suddenly, everyone became very friendly, and I was led off by a small boy into the narrow streets behind the maidan.

I bought six. They were so beautiful and so cheap (about $4.00 each), made by a little wizened black-cloaked man who looked more like some mysterious magician than a hatmaker. His eyes were narrow slits, and a continual smile flickered over his lips and his face. His wife was wrinkled, plump, and equally cheerful in appearance. She wore what appeared to be at least four brightly colored dresses, surmounted by a huge bright red cotton shawl. Her smile was as infectious as the old man's.

The bargaining completed, I was literally forced to sit down cross-legged on the crudely made Turkoman rugs and join them in their meal of local goat's milk, cheeses, yogurt, eggs mixed with rice, and flat chapati-like bread. Glass upon glass of hot tea was pressed into my hands. I felt like royalty.

After lunch, the old man led me proudly round "his" part of the town, pointing out the magnificent Turkoman stallions, famous throughout the world as racing horses. In Pahlavidej, they form the only satisfactory means of personal transport and are also used extensively as plough horses in the wheat and cotton fields. He told me, through one of his English-speaking sons, of his younger days when the whole of Turkomania was part of Iran. He had led a nomadic life rearing horses and sheep. He used one beautiful phrase: "My life was like the air."

Now, he said, since the division of the Turkoman area, most of the tribesmen on the Iranian side had settled down in permanent villages scattered throughout the plain—Gomishan, Crupan, Fenderisk, and many others. Their nomadic yurt tents were now used to protect the harvested wheat from storms. Cooperatives were being established. Many of the young men were moving to the cities along the Caspian coastline and to Tehran. He was watching a way of life disappear. And he was sad.

I left Pahlavidej in the evening. The sun was a great red ball slowly dissolving into the wheat fields. I passed a few Turkoman riders sitting proudly on their young stallions and saw women gathering water from a well, their red-and-gold shawls softly gleaming in the dusk light. I waved at some of the children as they gazed at the car. When they grow up, will they be riding the same stallions and wearing the same hats and looking every evening across those vast green-and-gold plains?

Like the old man, I too was a little sad, and also curious about the future of this isolated corner of Iran, recently involved in border disputes with the USSR. "My life was like the air," he had told me. But now there were new storms brewing in the north. . . .

I headed west, along the coast of the Caspian Sea toward Rasht. The Elburz Mountains rose to snowy fourteen-thousand-foot peaks. Their southern slopes facing out over Tehran and the great Salt Desert, Desht-e Kavir, were dry and cracked, but on this side they received abundant rain and were covered in dense subtropical jungle.

I finally found my village again, at the marshy edges of the Caspian, beyond Rasht. The headman M'mad recognized me in spite of a new beard, expanded midriffs, and all the signs of an overindulgent Western life.

Nothing much had changed. Their homes were still simple affairs of wood plank walls and reed-thatch roofs, and I went fishing again in the early mornings in a wooden canoe, catching catfish with an ease that almost made me feel guilty. They just seemed to lie there in the shallows waiting for me to toss in the bait, almost as if they wanted to be caught. Oh, and did we eat! Fat catfish steaks sprinkled with ground sumak, cauldrons of lobster-red crayfish, cracked open and dipped in melted butter, fresh salty slabs of goat cheese, thick dollops of mast and honey on hot flat bread and—God how I'd missed it—pungent, gray caviar (the villagers made their own caviar illegally, from sturgeon caught a few miles away in the Caspian Sea shallows). We spread it thickly on small rice flour pancakes cooked by the women on a griddle over a log fire.

And then someone suggested a boar hunt.

Well, I'm not much of a huntsman type, but the idea of photographing wild boar out in the marshes was too tempting a prospect to reject.

"Fine," I said, having no idea what I'd let myself in for.

"Good," he said. "We leave after breakfast tomorrow."

It was a warm clear morning, hardly a cloud anywhere. We left the village in three *quayk* canoes. The first carried four beaters, young men who had volunteered to arc through the northern edge of the outer marsh and drive the boar toward us in a shallow lagoon. They knew the place well. It was a favorite village hunting locale, the scene of regular forays for meat. The other two boats carried five older men, experienced hunters, and me. Their guns seemed old and rusty, but they'd obviously performed well on previous trips if their tales were anything to go by.

We paddled slowly through fields of water hyacinth, waves lapping placidly under a rapidly warming sun. Unfortunately the mosquitoes were up as early as we were, waiting for us in biting clouds as we entered the lagoon. They were impervious to repellent and seemed much more attracted to my fleshy torso than the lean, muscular bodies of my companions. I lit a cigar. That didn't seem to make much difference so I lit a second. Then everyone in the boat wanted one and in the other boat too. Pretty soon we were all paddling across the lagoon under a cloud of Jamaican cigar smoke, and the mosquitoes went off in search of other less aggressive antagonists.

We beached the boats on the far side of the lagoon at the edge of a forest of reeds, well over head height. M'mad imperiously handed out rubber boots and gloves to ward off the razor-edged reeds, and then issued instructions. The hunters were to move north toward the beaters; I was to remain near the boat in a narrow stretch of lagoon to photograph any boar that made it through the gauntlet.

The voices of the hunters faded away into the reeds. Soon I had the place to myself. There was no breeze. The sky was cloudless and the sun oppressively hot. And it was so quiet. I have rarely known such a stillness. The only sound was my heartbeat and the murmur of blood in my ears, rather like the kiss of a soft shower at dusk. There were no mosquitoes either. I felt an enormous surge of peace.

I seemed to be there for hours. Occasionally, far, far away I'd hear the noise of the beaters, and then nothing more for long periods.

Sometime around midday my troupe of frustrated hunters returned for lunch, complaining about the lack of boar.

And it was then I noticed the leeches.

In spite of my thigh-high rubber boots those cunning little black threads had switchbacked through every available gap in my loose clothes. I could see them in the green water, like discolored spermatazoa, but I missed them on the lily leaves and the overhanging fronds of marsh palm. The hunters' legs were dripping in them. I thought I was safe until I pulled off my boots during lunch and found a dozen or so happily sucking away on my shins. They'd somehow slipped over the tops and down through two pairs of socks to find flesh.

The local custom is to leave them alone until their sticky

MY CASPIAN BOAR
— Iran

bloated bodies, ballooned to full finger-sized capacity, sealed up the wound and dropped off involuntarily. But some customs are hard to honor. I couldn't bear to see them slowly increasing in girth with my blood. So I tried the other remedy of burning their tails with a lit cigar until they wriggled and fell. The only problem then was that in their haste to evacuate, they forgot to coagulate their incisions and I was left with oozing wounds. Khusrow, M'mad's son, shook his head at my stupidity, scooped up a palm full of soft marsh mud, and placed little piles of the stuff on each sucker hole.

"Five minutes, then wash," he said.

He was right. In five minutes I washed off the mud to find the holes sealed and only a few purple bruises left as souvenirs.

After lunch I was alone again.

The beaters had moved to another section of marsh further to the west and I had been placed in a shallow pool about fifty yards wide, away from the main lagoon and surrounded by reeds.

"If we miss," M'mad had told me, "boar come this way. Be careful. Very mad sometime."

He had presented me, proudly, with a double-barrel shotgun of indeterminate age and held together with twine.

"If he comes at you—shoot!"

Shoot! I hadn't come to shoot. I'd come to take world-class photographs. I accepted the gun rather disdainfully.

It seemed as if our hunt would be a flop. But it was pleasant in my pond anyway scribbling notes to myself and thinking how little had changed in this remote part of a restless nation.

The beaters seemed to be getting closer. Maybe they were packing up, and we'd be home for more caviar and catfish steaks sooner than I thought.

But there was another noise too. Someone was running through the reeds. I tried to peer in but they were too dense. Then I saw the tops of the reeds shaking a few yards beyond the edge of the pool. Maybe it wasn't one of the hunters.

It wasn't.

It was a boar. I could hear grunting—a very irritated type of grunting. And then it came. The biggest piglike creature I'd ever seen, but much more muscular and alert than any farmhouse porker. Its tusks projected a good four inches out of its mouth and hairs bristled along its thick neck and back. I stood very still and quiet and focused my camera. The boar, way out at the far side of the pool, paused and seemed disoriented. I extended my zoom as far as it would go. What a ferocious thing! I could see its eyes clearly. Angry, cruel eyes. One hell of a fine photograph!

And then I dropped my lens cap.

I don't know how it happened, and it didn't make much noise. Just a little splash in the water. But it was enough. The boar turned. I must have moved. He saw me and gave a furious grunt. Oh God! He was coming at me.

I'd heard all the tales of these creatures. They can do terrible damage to a body when angered, particularly in the area of the crotch, which seems to be inconveniently placed at their jaw height.

He was coming fast. I could hear the hunters too, splashing back in the reeds and shouting. The boar was mad and scared. I dropped the camera and tore the gun off my shoulder. The sights seemed all buckled. I didn't know how to use one of these damned things, and the boar kept coming, roaring across the shallow pool, white spittle blowing out the side of its mouth. I pulled one of the two triggers. Wham! An explosion of water erupted way off to the boar's left side. The noise was deafening and the jolt almost knocked me backward into the water. And still it was coming, faster now...

One last chance. I lined up the battered sights on its forehead. Wham! This time the recoil sent me sprawling into the pool. My ears were ringing with the sound of the blast. I'd had it. I should never have come on this dumb hunt. All I wanted were a few photographs. I closed my eyes...

But nothing happened. I'd expected to feel...God knows what I'd expected to feel, but it wasn't going to be pleasant.

But nothing happened.

I opened my eyes and the pool was empty. The reeds were shaking again all across the far side. Lots of shouts. I stood up very shakily. My legs were wobbling, like wonky pistons. My camera lay in the water. The gun was still smoking in my hand.

M'mad was the first to break through the reeds.

He stopped, but he wasn't looking at me. The others burst through and he pointed. They cheered and leaped around in the water. Then M'mad called to me: "Davi, Davi. You got him! You got him!"

He pointed again to a spot in the pool about ten yards from where I was standing. "You got him!"

Something very black was floating just below the surface. Something with bristly hair.

"You—big shot," Khusrow called out.

They approached cautiously. A wounded boar is notoriously dangerous. One of them jabbed the animal with the barrel of his gun, and rolled it over on its back, its legs sticking in the air. It was definitely dead.

"Two shot—dead!" M'mad said.

Blood was slowly returning to my head. I felt dizzy.

"One shot," I said. "The first one missed by a mile."

"One shot! Ah—you big, big hunter." M'mad slapped my shoulder hard and I almost fell back into the water again. The others were admiring the wound on the side of the boar's head. He looked harmless now—and smaller. Even the tusks in his open jaws seemed harmless. I felt sorry for him. He was just a rather large pig. I didn't feel like celebrating at all.

But they obviously did. Three of them were still shouting and dragging the boar by its legs out of the pool and back to the lagoon. The meat would last them for a week or more.

M'mad and Khusrow insisted on lifting me onto their shoulders but hadn't allowed for a combination of my weight and my waterlogged thigh boots with the result that we all came crashing down into the pool, laughing and spitting water like a bunch of drunks on a Friday night blowout. Then M'mad stood up looking very serious and pulled out his belt knife and said, "Wait." He marched across to the poor dead boar and then marched back again. "The tail. Is yours now."

It was a rather pathetic little thing, about six inches long with a brush of brittle hairs at the end. I felt a bit silly accepting it but he looked so formal about the whole affair that I smiled, said thank-you, and vowed to dispose of it later.

It's still around the house somewhere in a box of travel trinkets. Not much of a souvenir really, but I never seem to get around to throwing it out.

AUTHOR'S NOTE

I have not been able to return to Iran since the terrible earthquake of June 1990. Rasht was one of the hardest hit cities and my friends' village also suffered severe damage. I have written to them but—not surprisingly—have received no replies to date. I send them all my sympathy—and my love. Along with a promise to go back again as soon as I can.

11. TRAVELS IN INDIA

The Travails of a TET

I'm usually a mellow fellow, a tolerant world traveler, familiar with all the wackiness of errant schedules and the permanent out-to-lunchness of petty officials. But in the heat and hectic pace of India, agitation and aggravation sometimes smothered my benevolent nature, and I occasionally became your typical Western TET—Totally Exasperated Traveler. And what was even worse— I discovered fragments of a true colonial Englishman lurking in my subliminal regions and didn't like him at all. . . .

Hot! It's unbelievably hot in Allahabad, as only India can be, leaving you drenched, drained, and wandering in a druglike trance between infrequent patches of shade. I was so glad to be leaving. Just a couple of things to do—make an important phone call to the United States and catch the 7:30 P.M. train to Delhi. I had two hours, more than two hours. Plenty of time. No need to rush in this interminable heat.

The manager of Allahabad's best hotel was a skinny little weasly faced man with a penchant for pomposity that exceeded the absurd. He was obviously fully aware of the power of his position and loved every disdainful moment of his dealings with guests. A true Indian Basil Fawlty in miniature.

"I'd like to call New York, please," I said with a bright smile.

"Ah." (His eyes closed to slits and his thin lips curled under a full black mustache into a sneer.) "To America?"

"Yes—New York, U.S.A."

"Ah." His sneer became a wide smirk and he seemed to be preparing himself for a most enjoyable interlude.

Now this was a hotel recommended in all the reliable guidebooks and it didn't seem a lot to ask.

"I can wait," I said pleasantly. "I have plenty of time."

He smiled patronizingly. "Is not possible . . . sir."

"What's the problem?" I asked gently, entering his snare.

"The problem, sir, is Calcutta."

"Calcutta?"

"We must go through Calcutta, sir, and they will not take our calls."

"Well—shall we just give it a try and see what happens?"

His sigh and uplifted eyes were truly Shakespearian in gesture.

"Sir, Calcutta does not answer us. Calcutta is so very badly lazy. Much, much time."

"I'm quite happy to wait in the dining room until you get through."

"Is not possible, sir. Please go to Central Telephone and Telegraph. Very quick there."

"But listen . . ."

"Sir, I must attend now to other businesses, please."

He swept into his tiny cubicle of an office, delighted with his performance. Another anticolonialist victory.

The taxi driver outside the hotel had apparently never heard of Central Telephone and Telegraph. The doorman instructed the driver, who stared blankly until the correct dialect was discovered for the conversation. Then he nodded, opened the door for me, and roared off (literally), using his one working gear.

We drove for mile after mile with the taxi engine squealing in protest. My driver pointed out the key city sights with incomprehensible exuberance. My impatience increased. Time was getting short.

Finally, after stopping three times to ask directions, we pulled into the forecourt of a large, distinctly unimposing concrete building at the far side of a stagnant and stinking drainage channel. On the roof was an appropriate array of telegraphic equipment, which gave me confidence that our mission might be accomplished. However, we had problems from the start. The large gates were closed and there was no sentry in the box at the left side. On the opposite side a watchman lay asleep on a low trestle bed. My driver called out to attract his attention, but he was dead to the world.

Five long minutes later a man dressed in military guard's uniform sauntered down the steps and into the sentry box. He paused, ignored our presence, and then returned to the building. My driver, whose power of patience seemed endless, just waited. Another five minutes later the man returned to the box, shuffled some papers on his desk, finally opened the gate for the taxi driver to walk through, and closed it abruptly in my face.

My driver explained our need at great length. The guard seemed disinterested but eventually picked up a phone to call someone. Having received no reply, he strolled nonchalantly back into the building. Ten minutes later he reappeared, sauntering down the steps, and said it might be possible to place a call, although they were very short of staff. He asked me, through the driver, the location of the call. I offered to write down the number, but he said that was not necessary, he just needed the country and city. I told him, he nodded and disappeared again up the steps of the building. Eight minutes later he reappeared with a little torn piece of paper and asked the driver to tell me to write down the telephone number.

"How long do you think this will take?" I asked the driver.

He asked the guard. The guard had no idea and said he would find out. Before we could stop him he vanished into the building again. Four more minutes passed. He returned slowly.

"Is not possible to call quickly. Calcutta is always difficult."

I asked if I could accompany him inside.

"That is not possible."

"So you mean I have to wait outside here until you get New York and then you come all the way back to fetch me? That could take a lot of time. It will be very expensive for me."

The complexity of this logic eluded him.

"Okay. Please tell me how long they think the call will take to place." I tried hard to hide my impatience but didn't succeed. The guard noticed my rising belligerence, turned, marched back to his box, and slammed the door shut behind him.

The taxi driver turned and shrugged his shoulders.

"It is better I think we go to the other office."

"There are two telephone offices!?"

"Yes."

"What's the difference?"

The driver smiled and shrugged his shoulders again. Time was definitely running out.

"Okay. Let's go. Fast. I've got to make that call."

We clambered back into the taxi, a faithful reproduction of a 1950s British Morris Oxford, made in India and renamed "The Ambassador." He switched on the ignition. The engine gave two ghastly howls and died. Silence. Utter silence. He tried again. Nothing.

"This is ridiculous," I groaned.

The driver turned and predictably shrugged his shoulders.

We sat for what seemed forever. Then he opened his door and walked toward the guard to ask for assistance. The guard was deaf as a slab of granite. As far as he was concerned we had never existed.

The driver returned, opened the door, sat down, and started thinking again.

"I'll push," I said.

He turned, smiled, and nodded.

So I got out of the car, pushed it across the bridge, over the stinking moat, and into the street. Some passersby stood watching, amused by this rather overweight foreigner struggling with a bulbous, dilapidated taxi. Finally two men on a moped stopped and came to help push-start the car.

We all had the impression the taxi driver was not familiar with this method of starting a car (or the car had no workable clutch as he seemed to drive in one gear all the time). After thirty yards of sweaty pushing, he still hadn't let in the clutch. We stopped and the moped driver explained what he should do. On the fourth go the car burst into something approaching life, with two cylinders banging and clanking.

It was now 6:30, an hour before my train was to leave.

"We have no time," I said. "Forget the telephone. We must pick up my bags from the local station—then drive to the main station for my train."

Again the driver looked perplexed. Fortunately the moped driver was able to clarify my instructions.

We set off, the car lurching and jerking like some kind of apopletic bull, down the dark streets.

Ten minutes later he was well and truly lost. I felt he'd taken a wrong turn way back, but as I'd only been in the town for one day I wasn't at all sure of my way around.

The driver stopped to ask directions to the station (in his own town!). We set off, only to become completely lost again, in a narrow alley blocked at the far end by half a dozen white cows, wallowing in pools of muddy rainwater.

More enquiries, too exasperating to recount.

In another ten minutes we finally found the station, and I hurried off to collect my bags from the left luggage office.

The clerk was a delightfully impish elderly man with a betel-stained toothy smile and eyes sparkling behind the thickest spectacle lenses I'd ever seen.

"There's no key, sir. So sorry."

"You have lost it?" I asked.

"It has been taken," he said firmly.

"Do you have another?"

"Oh no, I do not, sir," said the clerk, smiling. "But the stationmaster does."

"Can we get it?"

"I cannot leave the office here."

"Can we telephone him?"

"His telephone is not working." He was still smiling brightly.

"Can I go and fetch him? I'm in a great hurry. I need my bags."

"He may not be where he normally is, sir," he said.

"Well, can I try?"

"By all means, sir, by all means."

"Where should he be?"

He drew me a little map of the station on the back of an old luggage chit, and I went to find the stationmaster. He was not where the clerk thought he would be, but I eventually located him sitting with a group of turbaned porters in a room behind a room, behind another room, drinking tea.

I explained the urgency of my predicament.

"This will be settled," he said smilingly, "in a moment." He continued to sip his tea, finished a tale he was telling his friends, lifted his very substantial bulk off the tiny wicker chair, and accompanied me back to the left luggage office.

When we arrived, he placed his hat officiously on his broad head and adopted a mantle of absolute authority.

"Where is your chit?" he asked.

I explained that I had already given it to his assistant, who was grinning and bowing and apologizing, all at the same time, for any inconvenience caused to the stationmaster.

"Give him his chit," the stationmaster said, ignoring all the obsequiousness.

The old man handed it to me like a wafer at holy communion.

"You must sign," said the stationmaster.

"It says here I should sign only after recipt of the luggage," I said.

The stationmaster's authority was obviously not to be questioned.

"You must sign now."

I signed.

"And here." He handed me the clerk's copy of my chit.

I signed.

"And here." He flung open an enormous ledger and pointed to where my name was entered in meticulous script.

I signed.

The stationmaster handed the ledger to his assistant imperiously and swept out of the left luggage office without another word.

I looked at my watch. I'd never make the train.

"Look, I'm running very late. Can I please have my bags—now!"

I must have panicked the poor man. He moved too quickly and fell against a shoulder-high pile of ancient left luggage ledgers near the door to the baggage room. In a wonderful explosion of dusty and crumbling paper, they collapsed in total disarray, blocking the door.

"I'll help you move them. Let's hurry!" I said and looked for a way to reach his side of the counter.

"Please, sir." He struggled to reach his full height. "Please, sir, no, I will call my assistant to move them."

"Look, I can help you. I don't have time."

"Sir, I do not lift ledger books." His manner suddenly became just as imperious as the stationmaster's. To him my suggestion was outrageous, an affront to the meticulous system of behavior and protocol in India.

"Where is your assistant, then?"

"I will send for him, sir," he told me. A young boy was passing with a tray of tiny tea cups. He ordered the boy to leave the tea on the counter and go to find his assistant.

His dignity and authority restored, he turned smilingly to me and offered me a cup of tea. I declined. My patience was gone. I stood staring at the fallen ledgers, sweating and fuming. Within a couple of minutes his assistant arrived, and he began to sort out the ledgers in date-order.

"Please," I almost shouted, "just move them and let me have my bags!"

My imperiousness appeared to work. They pushed the ledgers aside, opened the door, and dragged out my bags. I was amazed to find them intact. But there was yet one more hurdle.

"Where is your chit, sir?" asked the old clerk.

"I already gave it to the stationmaster."

The poor clerk must have lost it in all the confusion.

I could see he was going to hold on to my bags. My tolerance was used up. I broke all the taboos, lifted the counter flap, pushed between the two men, picked up my bags before he could say a word, and stormed out of the office to my taxi.

Fortunately, the next bit went smoothly. The driver actually remembered the way to the main railroad station. I was so amazed I tipped him far too much and left him smiling benignly like a minor Hindu deity.

At last—the sound of trains, blowing steam, and people (lots of people!). Stepping over, between, and around the (now familiar) array of sprawling sari and dhoti-covered bodies in the main concourse of the railway station, I scampered to the ticket counter at the far end of the "safe drinking water" stand.

"First class to Delhi, please. The train leaves very soon, I think."

The clerk was another elderly man, slightly deaf and obviously unimpressed by my disheveled, sweaty appearance.

"It is too late."

"No, I don't think so. I've got twenty minutes."

"You wish reservation?"

"I'd like a sleeping berth, yes."

"In which case you need a reservation."

"Fine. May I have a reservation, please."

He pointed to what looked like a minor mob scene across the concourse.

"Go there, please."

"But your sign says 'First Class Tickets.' "

"That is a different matter. You go over there, please."

More running of gauntlets between bodies, snagging people, clothes, and infants with my ridiculously overstuffed bags. The crowd is pure chaos. There are five windows but only one is open. Everyone is shouting, cursing, hacking, spitting.

The clerk is oblivious of it all. I catch occasional glimpses of him smiling and chatting to his colleagues and then turning back to snarl at his customers. He writes very slowly in a huge ledger. It's twenty degrees hotter over here, and I'm beginning to hallucinate about quiet hotels, soft easy chairs, air-conditioning, and ultra-dry martinis.

Five minutes of sardine-can serendipity. Then suddenly I'm

at the grille. Only the clerk is gone. I can hear him laughing somewhere behind the rickety tables piled high with browned ledgers. As soon as he returns the smile vanishes and a mask of utter disdain slides over his face like a gray film.

"Please, I don't have much time. Can I have a first class birth reservation for Delhi?"

"It is too late."

"I can just make it, I think."

The clerk sneers.

"Where are your forms?"

"What forms?"

"Your reservation forms."

"Look, can't I just buy a ticket? Forget the berth."

"All first class is for berths."

Stalemate. The big clock over the platform entrance ticks on, aloof as Victoria herself.

"Okay. What do I need?"

"You need reservation forms."

"Where do I get them?" (I already know the answer.)

"At the last window" (another sneer). "Sir."

Stumbling over more bodies. More waiting. Finally I am handed a long sheet of stained paper with enough questions to justify a mortgage.

I shall obviously miss the train, but I'm in too deep now to think about anything else.

Back in line again, my form completed. I'm allowed to go to the front of the queue and face the same sneering clerk.

"All berths are booked . . . sir."

I'm about to have a fit. I'll never get out of this place. Then the clerk peers more closely at my form.

"You are British and you live in America?"

"Yes."

"You are a tourist?"

"Yes—why? Do I need more papers?" (My turn to sneer now.)

"Oh no, no, sir. Not at all. But you should have informed me."

"Why?"

"There are special seats for tourists."

268

"You mean you're not fully booked?"

"Oh no, sir. You can have a berth. No problem at all."

"Wonderful!"

"Yes. The office next to your previous place will be dealing with this, sir."

"You mean—I go somewhere else!"

"Yes, sir. Of course. You are special category."

"You can't give me a ticket?"

"No, sir."

We stare at each other. I'm close to bursting point.

A man in a large red turban steps up.

"You will be requiring of a porter, sir?"

"What? No! Wait. Yes. Okay. Let's go! I've got five minutes!"

The sprawling bodies moved for him (they never did for me).

Another queue. Another clerk. More disdainful looks. Obviously "special category traveler" doesn't impress him, he sees them all the time. But I do finally get my ticket.

"You must be hurrying, sir," the porter says.

"Where do we go now?"

"Please to follow me. Your name will be on the list."

Scampering onto the platform. A huge steam-spewing behemoth faces me. Train lovers would melt at the sight. I'm far too tired even to look at it. We run together down the length of the train. The carriages are bulging with bodies. Second class looks like a turbulent Hieronymus Bosch fantasy. The porter pauses by long lists of printed names (nonalphabetical).

"Please to tell me your berth number, sir."

"I've only just bought a ticket. My name won't be on any list." I was fed up with the whole ridiculous process.

"You do not have the reservation?" the porter asked with a worried frown.

"I don't know what I've got!"

The porter looked utterly confused. Now I know I'm in trouble.

"Can you ask somebody?" I know it's a dumb idea. The platform is one mass of jostling humans, not a uniformed official in sight. "Look," I said, mustering all my remaining sanity, "is this a first class carriage?"

"Yes, sir."

"Well leave the bags here. I'll work it out."

He was obviously glad to be let off the hook and almost forgot to take his rupees before disappearing into the crowd.

Somehow—I actually don't know how—I found myself being led to a seat in a six-berth carriage by a very plump and smiling guard, obviously used to the ineptitudes of foreign travelers.

I sank into my seat and closed my eyes.

"You have your bedding chit, sir?" Another official!

"My what?"

"Your bedding chit, sir. For your sheet and pillow."

"You mean that's not included?"

"Oh no, sir. That is extra, you see. You must have a chit."

"Forget it. I'll manage without bedding."

"It gets very cold in this train, sir."

I gave him ten rupees and asked him to do what he could to obtain bedding. The other five passengers were staring at me as if I were some kind of extraterrestrial being. I closed my eyes.

The train gave a great scream, whistles were blowing, doors slamming. Two hefty jerks, and it began to ease out of the station. I opened my eyes again. It was 7:30 precisely. I'd made it!

One of the passengers leaned over. "Ah, sir. You are from?"

"U.S.A. I'm from America."

"Ah." Five faces nodded expectantly.

"This is the Delhi train, right?"

"Delhi, sir?"

"Delhi, right?"

Much murmuring among the five faces. Oh, no! Don't say I've got the wrong train. That would be the absolute last straw.

"I was told this was the Delhi express."

Grins, laughter, and snorts. They all started talking at once.

"Well, yes, sir, that is the name, but I don't think it is what you would call a true express, sir. Oh, no, not at all, sir."

"Oh, no, by no means. Very slow train, sir."

"You should have got the 10:30 P.M. Much better, sir."

"Oh dear, dear sir, you have a long journey. Very difficult."

Who cares? The train's moving. It's going in the right direction. What's a few extra hours? All I want is sleep anyway. I close my eyes again. My bedding man shakes my shoulder roughly. Another guard is standing beside him along with a large Indian businessman, looking very worried.

"This is not your seat, sir. It belongs to this man."

"Well, this is the one I was given." I felt utterly drained.

"The other guard should not have done this, sir."

"Well, where is mine then?"

"I don't know, sir. We have no record of your name."

"Look, I've spent far too long waiting in lines for my ticket to be told you've got no record of my name."

And then someone else started talking—a very angry, officious Britisher, pouring out pompous phrases about the chaos of Indian rail travel, the terrible condition of the stations, the abysmal attitude of the clerks, and the appalling ethics of guards who accept tips for obtaining bedding and don't produce any—all topped off with a lot of froth about the climate, the food, the incompetence of petty officials...a real colonial tirade. A bit overblown, I thought, but certainly hitting all the bases—and eloquently. Surprise! Surprise! It was me doing the talking! A full, fulminating, postcolonial persona had suddenly emerged from my deep subconscious. I stopped him in full flow, wrapped him up, and popped him back. I didn't like him at all. I was very embarrassed.

But it must have worked. I was left with my berth. The businessman shook my hand, and told me that other accommodation would be found for him. I began to apologize but he would have none of it. The porter appeared with my bedding. Someone helped me pull down the bed. The second guard returned to ask if I would like a cup of tea, which I gracefully declined. The five men in the carriage were very quiet, staring with some trepidation at this split-personality character in their midst. I smiled as charmingly as I could, bid them good-night, and slept the sleep of the gods through the long rocking night.

Delhi was a long way away but "Sufficient unto the day are the trials thereof." In India it's a good phrase to keep repeating to yourself, over and over and over again.

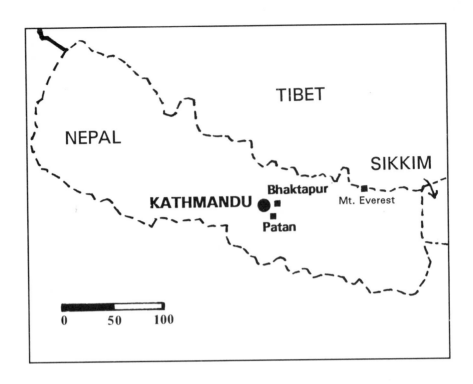

TIBET

NEPAL

SIKKIM

Bhaktapur

KATHMANDU ●■   Mt. Everest

■

Patan

0   50   100

12. NEPAL—
KATHMANDU
An Unfinished Experience

I had to come to hike in the high Himalayas. Another dream of youth. Every serious traveler has to journey to Nepal, at least once. True, there are other intriguing Himalayan destinations—Ladakh, Pakistan's Hunza, Bhutan, Sikkim—but Nepal and its mystical top-o'-the-world capital, Kathmandu, always seem to have a special place in the hearts of world travelers.

I decided to fly from New Delhi. I could have roughed it with all the other backpacking trekkies and taken the notorious fifty-five-hour bus ride from New Delhi to Kathmandu but, as I was planning to return later by bus back to India, it seemed a waste of time (admittedly a rather contrived rationalization). And anyway I'd waited long enough to get there—twenty-one years, maybe more—so I felt I owed myself a celebratory form of arrival, a sort of fanfare flight for fantasies realized.

Prior to the flight I'd planned to stay overnight in New Delhi, but I'd forgotten the travails of travel in India. There was some kind of film festival going on in the city, and I couldn't find a room anywhere. Even the $3.00 a night variety were crammed with Indian movie maniacs. So I thought, "When in Delhi..." and went to see a movie instead. An Indian movie.

The film was an enlightening experience. After two hours it showed no sign of ending. We'd gone through the full repertoire of the producer's art—five murders, gory mayhem, fallings in love, fallings out of love, family retribution, a stickup, a punch-up, three songs (they came out of nowhere for no apparent reason; the action just stopped, the fat lady sang, the action started up again), jealous wives, jealous husbands, faithful lovers, unfaithful lovers, a car chase, a car crash, a suicide, an odd little Arabian Nights dream-fantasy, two sex scenes (very delicately handled—the softest of soft porn), a comic character who kept falling down and pretending he was a dog, three gaudy sunsets, a fabulous banquet—in fact, a bit of everything for everybody, and still the damned thing kept going! The audience didn't seem to mind at all. They laughed, applauded, wept, went out for sticky snacks, came back...

I'd had it and left.

I should have remembered a joke told me by an Indian businessman on a train between Varanasi and Jodhpur. (This came well after the traditional greeting: "Hello and how are you today and would you be so kind of telling me the country of which you are from and of which good name you are having and your special qualifications as a professional person and I hope you are well, thankyouverymuch.")

"At a conference for press," he began, "a pressman asked from a film producer, 'Can you be telling the story of your latest film?' Producer looks very surprised. 'What are you meaning by "story"? Having you ever seen me make a film with any story? I have a special formula—a recipe for the success of my films.'

" 'And what is your recipe?' said the pressman.

" 'It is very simple,' says the producer. 'One hundred grams of love affairs, two hundred grams of weeping and screaming, three hundred grams of violence, and four hundred grams of sex. I mix together well and my film is complete.' "

They make hundreds of these "recipe" films every year in India. Same characters, same basic variants of plot, running the same gamut of emotional highlights—and the same audiences. "Just keep 'em coming" seems to be the motto (usually at an average rate of eight hundred films a year).

The flight was on time and uneventful. A very odd circumstance in India. It was clouds, clouds, and more clouds—impressive formations, beautiful—but only clouds nonetheless. I'd hoped to see a bit of India from the air. This might be my only chance. But all I got was clouds.

An hour or so later something appeared on the horizon that looked like clouds but was too hard-edged. The color was the same, but the shadows were complex and striated.

Mountains! Glorious panoplies of snow-capped peaks towering above the clouds. The Himalayas. A vast white wall broken into sky-scratching diamond peaks, stretching across my window and all the way as far as I could see across the window on the other side of the aisle. Magnificent! Real lump-in-the-throat stuff.

At last—I was coming in to Nepal, until a few decades ago one of the remotest kingdoms on earth, closed to outsiders. And now, since the hap-hippie days of the sixties, a definite must-see for all true adventurers.

The energy of the place slams like a shock wave. I had no idea what to expect. Everyone I'd talked to who'd been to Kathmandu went sort of sloppy-eyed when asked to describe the place, rhapsodizing about its "special magic," its justified reputation as "hippie heaven," the way the city "just sort of hooks you." They almost always ended sounding like born-again religious converts with phrases like "You'll understand when you get there." But they were right. Kathmandu is so overwhelming, so packed with images, that succinct summaries seem almost impossible—certainly inadequate. Like them, I'm tempted to say "You'll understand when you get there," but I suppose the role I've given myself requires a little more than that. Carefully measured prose wouldn't do it though—at least not my prose—so all I've got left are my tape-recorded notes . . . shards of googly-eyed wonderments:

A green valley couched in hills and behind those hills, that line of bride-white peaks in the bluest of blue skies, not a cloud anywhere; tight-packed villages among the high terraces, perched like rock piles on the ridges . . . then sinking into the city, filigreed with spires and the tiered roofs of temples . . . you can feel it closing in . . . streets wriggling and narrowing the deeper you go, bound by houses and lopsided stores of raw sun-baked bricks . . . getting tighter now, old men sucking hookah pipes in shadowy doorways, women in black skirts with red-embroidered edgings, a child's eyes, full of wonder, watching me from behind the ornately carved latticework of a wooden window screen; thick wooden doors into the houses, scratched and worn, with locks the size of jewelry boxes . . . smells of hot oil and baking *pauroti* bread . . . sudden pyramids of bright color—a spice seller on a corner, half hidden by his minimountains of turmeric, cardamom, cumin, and coriander . . . a swath of formal tree-shaded spaces as we pass the palace of Nepal's King Birendra Bir Bikram Shah Dev (the young Harvard-educated incarnation of Hindu Lord Vishnu) and past the fancy hotels and restaurants of Durbar Magh.

Then back into a medieval tangle of alleys, muddy, unpaved . . . temples everywhere—cramped candled caves splashed with blood-red paint, shadowy gods inside, all glinting fangs and wheelspoke arms . . . noise—so much noise—crowds pressing against the cab as we drive deeper, past the flute sellers and the tanka shops and wood-carvers' workshops and trinket carts sparkling with polished Gurkha knives, bracelets, heavy Newar jewelry . . . rickshaw cycles, winging like angry wasps through the throng . . . howled greetings from the peddlers—"*Namaste!*" ("I salute the God within you," "Namaste—to you too.") The gods are everywhere, holding up cornices, carved on the ends of protruding beams, peering from gaudy posters in store windows—scowling, smiling, fighting, snarling, or caught in the middle of erotic acrobatics . . . holy lingham shrines in

275

dark courtyards, lit by smoky strands of light and wrapped in blood-red cotton sheets...more peddlers selling the skulls of long-dead monks decorated in silver, brass prayer wheels crammed with written prayers that you spin like a child's toy and "make-merit" (*tamboon*) with Buddha all day long...fruit stalls piled high with apples, pomegranates, green oranges, grapes...a street of side-by-side dentists' parlors overlooked by Vaisha Dev, the god of toothache, his shrine a mass of hammered nails (each nail a plea for pain relief)...bookshops galore—vast repositories of guidebooks and used books from the backpacks of trekkies and the social hubs of world-wanderer gossip...yak-wool jackets, very de rigueur with the "only-got-three-days" trippies...past the Rum Doodle restaurant (ah—Rum Doodle, the world's highest fictitious mountain, ten thousand feet higher than Everest and subject of a wonderful travel book!)...

We're really stuck in the crowd now, hardly moving; I can read the notes and flyers pinned to every available post and door: "See the live sacrifices of animals for Kali—every Tuesday"; "ENLIGHTENMENT NOW! Retreats in Buddhism, Massage, and Meditation. One day to three weeks..."; "BUFFALO STEVE AND TERRY—I'm at the White Lotus Guesthouse. Leave note where I can find you guys for a few beers"; "WE NEED URGENTLY—unwanted trekking equipment for staff to make follow-up visits to children living in remote areas of Nepal."

We pass old hippies in dingy cafés sipping fruit-filled lassi and mugwort tea, playing with graying strands of matted hair, coddling their neuroses...a hundred brightly painted mandalas on laurel bark paper fluttering like summer butterflies...we're really approaching something special, you can sense it, everything's getting frantic—jugglers and boys banging on little *tabla* drums, saffron-cloaked monks with dye-daubed faces, ancient Hindu wanderers in dhotis carrying only wooden poles and mud-stained cotton bags, the spacy faces of old-young hash-heads...all crammed in this alley of Hobbit houses piled high on one another, leaning and cracked, beehived with tiny rooms, ladder staircases, encrusted with carved-wood images of tiny gods and peacocks and Byzantine tracery... surely it can't get any more claustrophobic than this—a sweaty tangle of bodies, trishaws, street markets, hooting cabs, howling peddlers, and grimacing gods... this is too much... I'm suffocating...

Then, like a torrent tumbling off a precipice, we're all suddenly spewed out into the living heart of this crazy place, a great sprawl of spaces and shrines and palaces and monasteries and pagoda-roofed temples, soaring into the sunlight with bells and gongs and cymbals and all the wonderful clamorous cacophony of Kathmandu's throbbing center—the great Durbar Square itself—ending place of pilgrimages, center of enlightenment; the most wondersome place in the world!

It's a dream. I've never seen anything like it. I leave my cab and wander across the stone-paved plazas like a gawking child, openmouthed and oggle-eyed. Everywhere are the encrustations of excess—expressions of the tangled complexity of Nepal's Buddhist-Hindu heritage—great sculptured orgasms of carved stone and wood and gold-spired stupas and chedis and arched doorways buckling with the weight of swirling decorations—and everything splattered with red *sindur* (red dye mixed with mustard oil) or betel nut juice stains and the piled detritus of rice offerings and ashy incense sticks and melted candles, all in a soaring forest of tiered buildings, swooped by flights of white doves, sparkling against a high blue sky.

It's too much. You need days to begin to understand all the riches and symbols and intracacies of this place where everything has a meaning, a significance (no empty Rococo decoration-for-decoration's sake here). The images just keep piling up like the carved layers of the shrines. I caught a glimpse of the tiny living goddess—the Kumari—peeping out of the ornate wooden windows of her chamber in the Kumari Bahal. Selected as a child, she is considered to be the incarnation of the virgin goddess, Kanya Kumari (just one of the sixty-three various names given to Shiva's shakti, Parvati), and maintains her status until her first period, at which time she becomes mortal and is replaced by another god-child whose horoscope aligns with that

THE DURBAR SQUARE
— Patan. Nepal

of the king. Official forays from her palace are limited to religious festivals when she travels in an elaborate chariot and is carried everywhere to prevent her feet from touching the ground.

White, red, and gold temples are everywhere—the soaring extravaganzas of the Taleju, the Degu Taleju, the octagonal Krishna Mandir (the ferocious black figure of Kal Bhairav, holding a skull as an offering bowl, lurks here behind a huge lattice screen), Narayan, Shiva-Parvati, Jagannath. And beyond, in all the teeming alleys leading to Durbar, are hundreds more temples and shrines.

In the misty distance, on a hill at the edge of the city, I can just make out the great white stupa of Swayambhunath, topped by a golden spire and the all-seeing eyes of Buddha. Here, among the incense and gongs and bells and spinning prayer wheels and bowls of burning oil and pushy peddlers, scores of monkeys frolic while Tibetan Buddhists transact precise rituals on this sacred site, more than 2,500 years old.

And there's more. Kathmandu has two sister cities close by —Patan and Bhaktapur—each with its own mysteries and medieval charm and its own equivalent of Durbar Square.

Wisdom, knowledge, enlightenment—all hang like thick incense in Durbar Square. It's a spiritual nexus attracting crowds of fluttery devotees, swarming like moths around the stupas and temples lit by a million flickering oil lamps. Some are harmless, gentle people, moist-eyed and moist-minded, floating somewhere slightly above the dusty plazas and murmuring to one another in free-flowing, stream-of-consciousness, ganja-laced sentences—always half finished, left dangling in the air like wisps of hashish smoke.

And then come the instant Buddhists and Krishna-cultists prattling on endlessly in caterpillar watta-batta-mutta sentences about the incarnations of Vishnu and the eight-fold path and the colors of Hindu deities with a facile familiarity that seems to have come from intensive spring break crash courses in "got-it" enlightenment at some hip ashram, paid for by poor unenlightened Mum and Dad back in old Satanland. Their transformations are often short-lived and when the rigors of meditation and abstinence begin to pall, they return home, leaving little and taking little of value back to the old familiarity of their own cultures.

280

A few remain though—die-hard stalwarts, long-term converts, moving in slow gurulike movements, eyes fixed on some
infinite place, immersed in their Karmic devotions. These are the
ones you remember most, wisping like wraiths through the great
square, past the remnants of the old psychedelic "pie shops" and
hash-houses with their age-stained posters of The Doors and the
Jefferson Airplane, past the cracked honeycomb windows of the
Hobbit houses and the ragged alleys and the lopsided guest-
houses and the gaudy signs for Star beer and "genuine Buff-
burgers." They move tirelessly, endlessly, floating through the
Jackson Pollock canvas of Kathmandu, part of the splash, daub,
and trickle of the place.

I was hungry for something sweet.
    Alas—the famous cakes and cookies of Kathmandu no
longer contain the mind-expanding ingredients of the seventies
when weary trekkers and wannabe gurus would fill the pie-
shops along "Pig Alley"—gorging on ganja-laced confections
and rejoicing in the liberated attitudes of the Nepalese. Today's
ingredients are a little more on the conservative side, but KC's
restaurant, up in the northern part of the city, still attracts some
of the old loyalists and has kept its appeal with the mystic in-
crowd.
    "She's going to do it. She's going to do it." A young girl who
said she was from Manchester, England ("But that was ages
ago—I mean absolutely ages."), bounced excitedly on her seat
next to an older woman, also from England, who had spent the
last half hour or so firing barbed darts of philosophical epigrams
at her companions. She seemed very aloof. Her wiry hair was
drawn tightly back over her scalp into a bun, her face had a
gaunt profile, and her eyes seemed a long way away, somewhere
in a cold dark place. I've seen that look before in the faces of
long-time world travelers. But there was something not quite
convincing here—she was like a queen under seige, peering
down imperiously from high battlements atop loosely mortared
walls. There's undoubtedly safety—even occasional serenity in
such heights—but unresolved fears can eventually eat like acid
through the cracks and bring the whole elaborate fortification
crumbling down. And that's what I sensed: someone feigning

enlightenment in that arrogant way peculiar to Western truth seekers, and yet still fragile, vulnerable, incomplete.

The tiny room of cake eaters became very quiet. The woman closed her eyes and performed a little ritual of breathing exercises. No one spoke. She took one last long breath and began to recite a kind of blank verse in a slow raspy voice (in transcribing from the tape I've tried to give it the poetic form I think she intended):

"We are
but shards of a great whole
bits of eternity, spewed out briefly
to traipse, and wobble, and bungle and bravado our way
(in a state of induced forgetfulness called consciousness)
through the ritual three score and ten
(and hopefully less),
trying to know the already known
to fight the unfightable,
play games with our devils,
fool with our so-called minds,
praying for personal peace,
sighing for spiritual bliss in the crypts of crises,
appealing for perfection
and hopelessly longing to love ourselves and others—
unquestioningly, unconfused, complete and eternal—
so that we may return to the whirling wheel—
the endless in and out—and lose our "me's"
in the great whole again.

So why?
Why all the ballyhoo and bullshit
and the braggadocio and the bombast
when we already know—down deep in our deepest—
that there's no "me" in me—that all is dross—
mere bagatelles—that help to pass the days
until there are no more days left
and we return from where we came
having relearned (and maybe not—for what it matters)

some of what we knew we knew.
So why?!"

Her eyes were still closed and she sat very still as the murmurs of her admirers filled the room. Heavy stuff. Wagnerian gloom and doom. Outside in the muddy street there it was all laughter and noise and sunshine. I left the rest of my cake and rejoined the hullabaloo.

Surely it needn't be that ponderous or pointless. I know that Buddhism has its downside, "All life is suffering," etc. etc., but up here in Nepal, with the sparkling white peaks soaring above the temples and the crowded streets and the emerald green rice paddies and the tight little mud-walled villages perched on terraced hillsides, surely here there's also rejoicing and joy in the fun of life itself.

I decided I had to dream up a response to her rather woeful litany. So I sat on the steps of a temple and scribbled away merrily to a spritely tune that ran through my head:

Life's just a vacation—
see it that way—
a gay celebration
everything's okay
and there's no need to pray
for wealth, and forgiveness
and bliss and delay in divine retribution
for life—
is a time to play
making love in the hay
gazing up at the day
letting come what come may
(and never saying nay)
but rather
hey hey—
and "Hey Hey!"
And when its all over
(there'll be nothing to pay)
you'll merely return, just the same way,

to where you once loved
and lay
in a peace, in a place, far far away
(and right now, today)
And maybe—who knows—
you'll come back here someday. Hurray!
So—don't you delay
Just say . . . (and repeat the whole thing all over again!)

Well, it's hardly grand philosophy but it seemed to fit the mood of that moment. At least the gloom was gone, and I was free to explore the city again with a bunch of newfound friends.

One was a young man, a Buddhist scholar, who had lived in Kathmandu for a number of years working with the rural blind out in the Himalayan valleys, far beyond the city. His task was not an easy one. Buddhism teaches that bodily afflictions and other ailments are divine retribution for past karmas, punishment for acts in previous lifetimes, and the idea of trying to overcome such afflictions is considered by many believers to be ill-advised. But, with great charm and tact, my friend has persevered and changes were coming slowly to the villages. The blind were being encouraged to assert their independence, become full participatory members of the community, operate small farms and businesses.

It was slow, slogging work but in Nepal nothing changes quickly in spite of the thousands of dedicated field-workers sponsored by well-meaning organizations from the West. And they were all here—agricultural specialists encouraging tree planting on the rapidly eroding slopes of the foothills; health workers; engineers; financial whiz kids trying to untangle the complexities of Nepal's subsistence economy; missionary teachers; medical technicians; dam builders; Peace Corps volunteers. It seems at times that there are as many foreign volunteers and specialists as tourists. There's something about this little nation that warms the hearts of wealthy philanthropists. The people, the scenery, the still-dominant royal family, the endurance of its varied cultures, locked in time, away in the remote valleys, reachable only by long weary treks on difficult mountain paths. A wonderful place!

Back in the boardrooms of Europe or America, Nepal seems manageable—a compact kingdom hardly larger than New England. Send some cash, a few enthusiastic specialists backed by a bevy of volunteers, and the job will be done in no time. Great public relations, a satisfying tax write-off, and a chance to spend some time in one of the world's most beautiful remote hideaways.

Only it doesn't always work out quite so easily. Nepal is Nepal and Nepalese ways of life are not as malleable as the "let's-make-some-changes" guys would like to think. And there's another problem. Nepal is very seductive. Centuries of slow, isolated cultural development have produced a beguiling mélange of architectural form, spiritual intensity, and societal richness, unique in the world. Just as I was, outsiders are often overwhelmed by the power of the place; half-baked schemes for "modernization" and social enlightenment suddenly seem inappropriate—even threatening—in a place offering itself as a touchstone to these more eternal values and truths, which Western nations have often forgotten in their wild pursuit of wealth and material abundance. The teachers are often the taught here. It comes with the territory.

My friends entertained me royally, and I remember one afternoon in particular that three of us sat drinking *chhang* (homebrewed millet beer) served from a communal bowl in the shady garden of a restaurant famous for its Tibetan wontons or *momo*s. We had gorged our way into a pleasantly loopy state. Over the garden wall I could hear the spinning of prayer wheels in a temple courtyard. A flight of white pigeons curled over our heads. The ceaseless prattle of the city seemed a long way away.

"I'd like you to meet an artist," the girl said, filling my glass with chhang for the umpteenth time.

"Lovely," I said. I had no special plans. Kathmandu does that to you. Time becomes seductively elastic and nothing seems particularly urgent in this lovely rice-paddied valley under the mountains.

Eventually we finished the bowl, and she led the way past the temple and into a monastery at the end of a muddy track. We were greeted by monks in orange robes and led to a small cell at the rear of the compound. And there he was, a tiny elfin creature sitting on a stool in a bare room furnished only with a bed and an old wood chest. A single bulb hung down on a frayed wire from the ceiling.

He turned and smiled, and the room seemed immediately brighter. It was a smile I shall always remember. His whole face shone, his eyes sparkled and seemed translucent; I felt as if I'd been immersed in silky warm water. We were all smiling. I looked at my friends and their faces shone. The whole room was one big grin.

The girl introduced him to me, but I've long forgotten his name. It doesn't matter anyway. I was mesmerized by him. His aura was almost tangible, evoking stillness and joy and something much deeper.

"He's from the Dolpo," she said.

Now, like many of the ancient Himalayan kingdoms that once existed all along the Himalayan range, Dolpo is still a remote and unexplored region, three hundred miles to the west of Kathmandu.

"How did he get here?"

"He walked."

Of course. Even Nepal's single major road, the "Rajpath" to India, one of the most tortuous mountain roads in the world (and one I was to experience first-hand later), was only completed in 1959. The rest of the country is still virtually roadless, bound together only by a spiderweb network of narrow paths.

"That must have taken a while."

"Three weeks."

"Alone?"

"Oh no," she laughed. "He is a very famous artist in the Dolpo. Two hundred of his followers came with him."

"Why did he come?"

"He was invited to paint a series of tankas for the temple here."

Now tankas (or thangkas) are one of the major art forms of Nepal's strange blending of Buddhist and Hindu faiths. They are a written record usually composed in circular mandala form, depicting the lives, deeds, and incarnations of the various deities and the supreme power of Brahman, the metaphysical absolute,

286

the beginning and the end. They are works of the most exquisite detail painted with tiny brushes and using natural dyes made from cinnabar, lapis lazuli flower petals, and gold dust. While the broad themes are constant, artists are given unlimited freedom to interpret all the various facets of Buddhism's four truths —pain, suffering, desire, and nirvana—and all the entangled attributes and activities of the deities—erotic, comic, cruel, demonic, loving, and lethargic (the gods are often appealingly human in their foibles).

The result is a staggeringly rich panoply of teeming images, pulsing with life—an artwork of great beauty and subtlety but also an important visual aid to meditation and religious insight.

The smiling artist said something in a soft singsong voice.

"He's asking if you'd like to see one of his tankas."

"Yes, I would, very much."

The elfin nodded, opened up the wooden chest in the corner of his cell, and carefully lifted out a rectangle of stretched canvas, about four feet high and three feet wide.

Slowly, almost shyly, he turned the canvas toward us.

It exploded with color—bright emerald green mountains, golden-edged clouds, pink and sapphire-blue lotus blossoms, curling traceries of leaves, haloed gods, some black and fierce, some with elephant's faces, others with huge mouths and horns and a welter of gracefully waving arms, some almost transparent with long-fingered upraised palms and gentle almond-shaped eyes, and all clad in meticulously detailed robes. There were scores of separate images, each one tingling with symbolic gestures that I couldn't begin to comprehend. And yet the painting possessed a swirling unity of composition so that each detail could be enjoyed separately and yet still form an integral part of the whole. Far more structured than the rambling fantasies of Hieronymus Bosch, but just as filled with life and movement— and humanity. These were gods, but gods reflecting all the kaleidoscopic miasma of human experience and knowledge.

My friends had seen tankas before, hundreds of them (you can buy ones of questionable quality throughout Kathmandu), but even they were silenced by the power and vitality of this little artist's work.

"How long . . . ?" I began.

287

The girl asked how long the tanka had taken to paint.

"He says about three months—three months of twelve-hour days."

"And he's painting more?

"Six. He's been asked to do six."

"And then?"

"He'll go back to Dolpo."

"Walking?"

"Walking."

"Three hundred miles."

"Right. Three hundred miles."

"And when he gets back?"

"He'll paint more tankas. This is his whole life."

We thanked the artist. His smile felt to be warming my shoulders as we left the cell.

Outside it was dusk and the Himalayan ridges were flushed in a peach glow. Prayer wheels were still turning in the temple courtyard, spun by worshippers as they walked clockwise, round and round the white stupa, topped by the eyes of Buddha. Endless circling. The great mandala of creation, slowly turning, through all the centuries, ever changing, always the same. A universal centering here, in this little isolated mountain kingdom.

I wondered about the wheel spinners. Most were dressed in layers of old, poor clothes. Maybe they were peasants from the lonely valleys making merit by their long pilgrimages, living hard lives in a harsh climate, snatching subsistence crops from tiny patches of cleared earth in a land of broken rocks, ice, and burning summers. Surely it couldn't be hard for them to recognize the *dukkha* of Buddha—the teaching that all so-called reality is empty and full of the "suffering of desire." But had they found *sunyata* by being awakened (*buddha* is the Sanskrit word for *awakened*) to the freedom that exists beyond hopes and fears and desires? Their faces were shadowy in the half light. It was hard to detect emotion in them—any emotion. Maybe that's what enlightenment looks like. A blank indifference to reality. Merely a part of the cycle, moving slowly around the stupa, turning the wheels. . . .

* * *

Time to head for the hills.

I'd spent a day with a group of weary but starry-eyed trekkers who had just returned from a three-week hike to the base of Everest, way to the northeast of the city.

First came the warnings of littered trails, unreliable and greedy Sherpa guides, altitude sickness, the overabundance of other trekkers, expensive supplies, wild dogs, smoke- and animal-filled mud-walled houses, and, of course, diarrhea (the notorious "Kathmandu crud"!).

Then they told me the things I wanted to hear—of crisp nights spent in sleeping bags under the stars; meals of *tsampa* (ground roasted barley mixed with chilies) and dhal bhat, and mellow intoxication from home-produced brews of chhang and *rakshi* (rice liquor); the endurance of their barefoot porters carrying loads in bamboo baskets (*dokos*) hung on straps from their foreheads; tattered lines of prayer flags and *mani* walls—piles of stones carved with the Buddhist inscription "Om Mani Padme Hom" ("Hail to the Jewel in the Lotus"); stumpy stupa shrines topped by Buddha eyes; the incredible wild beauty of valleys, glaciers, ice fields, and glimpses of Himalayan peaks across meadows brimming with alpine flowers; flocks of snow pigeons, pheasants, choughs, eagles; strange dhami shamans (spirit mediums and medicine men), and the one feature that set them all nodding and smiling—tremendous pride in their individual feats of endurance.

I left them, elated by the prospect of days among the mountains. The sun was shining. The high white peaks behind the city beckoned. All the arrangements had been made...

And then cancelled.

This was one dream that didn't materialize at all. I was hit by a full barrage of bad luck—an ankle twisted badly in one of Kathmandu's muddy potholes on a night when all the lights went out, a roaring pneumonic cold, and another Costa Rica–type attack of dysentery, which left me flat on my back for days, weak as a baby.

I was unable to muster much of the Buddhist capacity for acceptance of fate. This wasn't predestiny. This was just bloody unfair! To come all this way to fulfill a boyhood promise, and then to be stuck in a cold hotel room, hearing all the trekker talk outside in the street and the thump of boots and the final fare-well of a friend.

"Tough luck, Dave. There's always next time, mate. Those hill's ain't going nowhere!"

Right.

And apparently, neither was I.

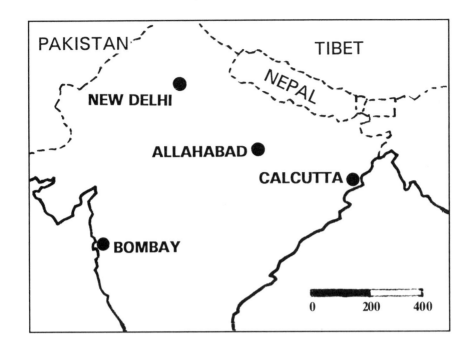

13. INDIA—THE KUMBH MELA
Swamis, Sadhus, and Instant Salvation

The ultimate cleansing of body and spirit! At Allahabad in north central India one splash, paddle, and body-wash in the fast-flowing Ganges—the holy mother of rivers—at the right moment of the right day "reaps the benefit of bathing on ten million solar eclipse days." It's an offer any self-respecting Hindu cannot possibly refuse. A whole lifetime of sin, debauch, and spiritual uncenteredness, washed away in a few wet moments. A new beginning, a promise of eternal bliss, salvation, Nirvana!

"You should see the Kumbh Mela at Allahabad," I'd been advised by a friend in Kathmandu. "It's an incredible festival of cleansing. Fifteen million people—all coming to the Ganges once

291

every twelve years. Incredible. You might just make it. It's worth a try!"

At first glance Allahabad is not a particularly prepossessing city. (Second glances don't help much either.) Nonetheless this dusty, hot place is a renowned center of learning, an intellectual nexus, for students from all over India. But much more important, it is the meeting place of the three most sacred rivers, the Ganges, the Yamuna, and the "invisible river," Saraswati.

"From time immemorial," reads the local brochure, "Prayag (Allahabad) has been regarded by pious Hindus as the most sacred place in the country and as the God Brahma performed many yajnos or sacrifices here, it is called Tirthraj or the holiest of the holy places." (Usually I don't enjoy the language of guidebooks, but this one has such a pleasant, almost Victorian English flow to it.)

"King Harsha Vardhana, the beloved emperor of India, used to hold at Prayag, where the fair water of the Ganges plays with the blue waves of the Yamuna, a quinquennial fair, at which rich and poor, saint and sinner from every part of India gathered. These gatherings had great advantages. People from different provinces met together, exchanged their thoughts, and profited by discourses with learned men from places other than their own. Those who came from backward districts were imbued with advanced thoughts and ideas and returned home with changed minds. Sadhus and saints solved the queries of many an inquirer. Trade flourished and wealth circulated." (This is always an important criterion of Indian festivals.)

The brochure continues in its delightful prose: "The Mela or fair is a very old Indian institution. A number of pilgrims, not to be reckoned in thousands of lakhs [Note: The Indian system of counting is a rather confusing conglomeration of hazars (thousands), lakhs (one hundred thousand), and crores (ten million).] assemble here to bathe at the confluence where a temporary township springs on the riverbed. Some of the pilgrims live there in temporary huts in order to obtain religious merit by taking a plunge in the river every day during the whole month and they are known as Kaplabasi."

Apparently there's some uncertainty about the origins of this amazing gathering of up to fifteen million devotees from all over India, but the Chinese traveler-historian Hinen Tsang described his experiences here in 644 A.D.:

> The pilgrims were people from all ranks of life, from the Emperor Harsha Vardhana with his ministers and tributary chieftains, down to the beggar in rags. Also among the participants were the heads of various religious sects as well as philosophers, scholars, ascetics, and spiritual aspirants from all walks of life. The emperor performed all the rites with great eclat and ceremoniously distributed the wealth of his treasury to people of all denominations... The people responded enthusiastically for they were given a three-fold opportunity of improved personal wealth, winning fresh inspiration through consorting with the sadhus, and redemptive bathing in the sacred rivers.

And all this for a river—the great river Ganges—symbol of all rivers and all water in India. Legend has it that by bathing or drinking the sacred Ganga water, one attains salvation. The water itself is said, even by scientists, to contain mystical properties. A quote from *The Times of India:*

> The Ganga water, even when it is polluted, becomes pure again after traversing a distance of 8 km. It is considered that the mixing of various herbs in the water is why it has such qualities. The Goddess Ganga expressed the fear that the people of the earth would pollute its waters but Bhagirath promised that coming generations would cleanse it again. This task has now been commenced by the Government of India...

From the distance it looks like a vast military encampment: Thousands of square white tents with four-sided pyramidal roofs lined up in endless rows fill the dusty flats around the Triveni Sangam, the confluence of the three rivers (you can actually see only two but in India nothing is what it seems and everyone insists that it is the third, invisible river of Saraswati that endows this place with unique significance).

It's very hot. A white dust hangs in a cloud over the site, giving a haloed, mystic feeling. I've been walking for almost an hour now from the cordoned-off entrance to the Sangam. Actu-

293

ally, walking is not quite the word, more like half-carried, half-trampled by a thick mélange of humanity filling the hundred-foot-wide "corridors" between the tents and the fenced encampments of the sadhus, the gurus, the sanyasins, and the swamis. Each encampment has its own ceremonial entrance made up of rickety scaffoldings and tied bamboo poles topped with painted symbols, logos, and depictions of Hindu deities. A vast supermarket of salvation specialists. Hundreds of them from all over India, each surrounded by his own faithful disciples and followers. The women in their bright saris feverishly cook and clean outside the square tents, while the men, bearded, ascetic, and clad in dhotis or dark robes, gather in hunched groups around their chosen wise man to listen and debate and nod and sleep and listen again.

And the crowd churns on. Once in it's almost impossible to break free without the risk of being squashed to a sweaty pulp by a million shoeless and sandaled feet. I'm not even sure where we're going but I'm part of the flow, and there's nothing I can do to stop it.

"Are you understanding the significance, sir, of this event, sir?"

A young man in long white robes links his arm in mine and smiles brightly into my dust-smeared face.

I don't really feel like talking (I'm far too busy trying not to trip on the pebbly track), and I mumble something about having read an article in *The Times of India.*

The youth smiles sympathetically.

"Ah the *Times,* sir. That is a good paper. But I think it is possible that you don't understand everything, sir. It is a very long history."

"Yes," I mumble again. "Yes, I suppose it is." Everything in India has a long history.

"The spiritual tradition, sir, of *tirthayatra,* the bathing at sacred river crossings, can be traced back to the Vedic period of our history, sir, about 1500 B.C. There are quite a few important bathing places, sir, but here—the Triveni Sangam—is the most important. And the Kembh Mela is the most famous holy festival—and this one"—he pauses for drama—"this one, today, is the most important for one hundred forty-four years due to the astral signs, sir, which are the same as when Jayanta dropped the liquid of the Amrit Kumbh, sir, on this very place."

He looked closely to see what impact this startling information had made on me. His eyes gleamed; he was obviously very excited and I felt it only fair to let him continue.

"The Amrit Kumbh. I haven't heard of that."

A great grin cleaved his hairless jaw. "Ah, sir. That is why everyone is here, sir. All these people. They say fifteen million. Maybe many more. How can one know, sir?"

That was one of the reasons I'd come. It was a substantial detour from my route to Rajasthan and the remote western regions of India. But I wanted to see what it was like to be among such an incomprehensibly large crowd of believers, all converging for the simple act of bathing in the Ganges. I wanted to feel the force, the power of such numbers. So many people all sharing the same purpose, all here at substantial cost and inconvenience and discomfort, all of one mind and spiritual intent—surely something miraculous would happen with all this centered energy. A river might stop flowing, apparitions might appear, the skies might turn black, and a god might descend. . . .

My informant smiled again. "I am your friend, sir. I do not want money, sir. Just to be your friend."

I'd met many of these so-called "friends" throughout India but this one seemed to be less grabby than most. He hadn't even asked the ritual string of questions yet—country of origin, qualifications, profession, salary, wife, children, address—"in case I should ever be fortunate enough to visit your country"—and the old clincher, "I collect foreign coins, sir; if you happen to have any . . ."

"Sir, are you hearing me, sir?" My friend looked hurt. He had been talking.

"I'm sorry I missed that . . ."

"Yes, sir, it is very difficult. Too many people. Too much commotion, I think. But nevertheless I was saying to you about the Kumbh, sir. The Kumbh means a jar, sir, a thing for holding liquids. And according to my religion, sir, there was a time, many many many long times ago, when our gods were all very tired and weak and the great Brahma told them to make a special 'liquid of life' to help them become strong again, but they used the bad spirits to help them and the bad spirits wanted to keep the liquid in the Amrit Kumbh—in the special jar, sir."

I nodded, trying to focus on his words, still nervous about being pulped on the rough track.

"But then, sir, then Jayanta, a young god, sir, flew toward heaven with the jar and was chased by all the bad spirits, and as he flew he split drops of the special liquid at four places on earth —in India, sir. Now at each one of these places, in turn, they hold a festival of life, sir, every three years, a different place every three years, and on the twelfth year they come here, sir, for the purna, the most important kumbh and, as I have told you, this one now, today, is the very special one because of the astrological signs, sir."

"That's quite a story."

"Yes, sir. It is a very famous story. All Indian people know about this. It is good for you to know this too, I think."

"Yes, it is. Thank you."

"You want to meet sadhu?"

"A wise man?"

"Yes. Very famous sadhu, sir. You can see his sign."

He pointed to one of a line of camp entrances, this one was painted a garish red, topped with a triangular pediment on which was painted numerous ferocious Hindu gods.

"Come, sir, we go and see sadhu."

Somehow he tugged me sideways out of the churning crowd and through the entrance. It felt wonderful just to pause on soft sandy ground and not have to move.

"Wait here, sir. I will find out where the sadhu is, sir."

A few yards away the crowd serpentined on, sheened in dust haze, down the long slope to the Ganges herself, gleaming soft silver in the sun. There were police everywhere and other more military types bristling with guns and grenades. Apparently previous melas here have produced outbursts of "cultural divisiveness" (a *Times* euphemism for outright revolution) in which scores lost their lives. Also fires, drownings (the Ganges is not always a tolerant mother), and anarchistic outbursts from students of the Allahabad universities. It was obvious in the amazing organization of this tent city of millions and the stern-faced wariness of the guards that the government was determined to make this particular one a model mela.

I could see the black superstructures of the pontoon bridges across the river, smothered in pilgrims. The smoke from thousands of cooking fires rose to mingle with the dust haze. I could smell the hot oil in which the chapatis and papadums and samosas and a dozen other varieties of deep-fried delights were being prepared and sold.

Near the entrance to the sadhu's compound, an old man in a large pink turban used a tamed canary to pick fortune cards at random from a line of little boxes set in the ground. A group of spectators stood solemnly and silently as he read the fortune text to a client, another equally old man who fingered a string of black beads and tugged nervously at his long gray beard. He didn't seem at all happy with the reading. The fortune-teller took his coins, shrugged, and gestured to the canary, which had nimbly hopped back into its cage and closed its own cage door. The crowd snickered, pleased it wasn't their fortune that had just been read. The old man painfully pulled himself to his feet, grumbled at the reader, and was swallowed up in the slithering crowd.

"He is over here, sir."

My friend had returned, bright-eyed and smiling again. We walked between the rows of tents toward the center of the compound where a large green canvas awning stretched over a low painted platform.

It was cool and dark under the awning. A score of men sat in a circle around a central dias. They all had long beards and were dressed in layers of crumpled cotton robes, black and gray. They shuffled around a bit to make room for us. I felt self-conscious in my jeans and checked shirt and pushed the bulging camera bag behind me. Cameras seemed out of place here, like laughter at a funeral. And it felt funereal. Everyone looked very glum except for the sadhu himself, a tiny, virtually naked man with spindly ribs and arms seemingly devoid of muscles. His matted black hair tumbled in sticky tresses over his shoulders. Offerings of rice and fruit and books and brass vases and painted pendants lay all around his feet, but he seemed oblivious of everything and everyone. His eyes were closed. His face was turned upward, his mouth curved in a half smile, and his hands rested limply in his lap.

It was very quiet.

"They say he has not spoken for six hours," my friend whispered.

"And they've been sitting here all this time?" There was something almost sculptural in this hunched bunch of devotees.

"I think so."

So we sat. And sat. And sat some more. My legs had gone numb but no one moved, so I tried not to fidget.

"What do you think they're waiting for?" I finally asked my friend.

"Something," he whispered mysteriously. Then he giggled softly. "Anything."

More sitting. Now my arms were numb too. I was hungry and hot and thirsty. And bored.

"I think I'm ready," I whispered. I'd never make a guru lover. A bit of meditation once in a while is all right, but I suffer from an overactive brain and an underdeveloped sense of patience.

"Yes. We'll try another one." Even my friend seemed perplexed by all the silence.

"They usually talk more," he explained as we rejoined the throng. "He was one of the silent ones."

As the heat and dust rose together and the crowds grew thicker, silence became hard to find. This was a strange affair—part carnival, part religious revival, part showcase for the nation's cream-of-the-crop gurus. A high-hype commercialized religious romp—or something else?

My Kathmandu friend had lent me one of his religious books, a delightful nineteenth-century account of an English Victorian woman's wanderings with a swami in the Himalayan foothills. I sat with my new friend in the shade of an empty canvas tent as the crowds milled by and read a few fragments of Sister Nivedita's (her Indian name, given her by the swami) truth-seeking experiences:

298

So beautiful have been the days of this year. I have seen a love that would be one with the humblest and most igno-rant, seeing the world for a moment through his eyes. I have laughed at the colossal caprice of genius; I have warmed myself by heroic fires and have been present at the awaken-ing of a holy child . . . my companions and I played with God and knew it . . . the scales fell from our eyes and we saw that all indeed are one and we are condemned no more. We wor-ship neither pain nor pleasure. We seek through either to come to that which transcends them both . . . only in India is the religious life perfectly conscious and fully developed.

I looked up. Among the crowds were the occasional Western faces, the faces of seekers, coming to the mela to find answers to all the mysteries, coming to find comfort, coming to "play with God," coming to experience the "perfectly conscious religious life."

Singing, chanting, dancing and discordant sitar sounds ex-ploded from a score of pavilions. Babies rolled in the sand while sari-clad mothers washed and polished huge copper rice caul-drons at the water taps; ancient hermitlike men displayed them-selves in the most contorted positions in little tents with hand-painted signs nailed to bamboo posts: "Guru Ashanti has sat in this same position without moving for eight years." "Ras-tan Jastafari eats only wild seeds and drinks one glass of goat's milk every 8 days to the honor of Shiva." A fairground of fakirs! There were men with necklaces of cobras and pythons; a troupe of dancing monkeys playing brass cymbals; more fortune-tellers with their little trained birds; peanut vendors; samosa stands, reeking of boiling oil; groups of gurus huddled together deep in gossip ("So what's new in the enlightenment business, Sam?" "How's your new ashram going, Jack?" "Harry, can I borrow your cave up on Annapurna for a couple of years?")

There were special compounds for Tamils, for Tibetan refu-gees, for Nepalese pilgrims from the high Dolpo region of the Himalayas, for ascetic members of the Jain religion, and a hundred other far more obscure sects.

* * *

A GATHERING
OF GURUS
— Kumbh Mela
India

Sometime in the middle of the afternoon a scuffle occurred near the river. A bronzed Swedish cameraman had just had his expensive video camera smashed into bits of twisted metal and broken computer chips by a crowd of irate Bengali tribesmen. Generally everyone seemed to tolerate cameras and tape recorders but this unfortunate individual had broken some taboo of propriety and now stood towering head and shoulders above his antagonists, gazing at his ruined machine in disbelief. The police arrived, then the army, and together they formed a flying wedge to rescue him, while the shouting, cursing, and spitting roared all around them.

"You have to be very careful," my friend whispered. "You never know what can happen here."

A few minutes later there was another commotion on the far bank. Thousands of dhoti-clad bathers were running around, shouting and pointing at the fast-flowing river. Loudspeakers were urging calm and I could see another phalanx of police and soldiers scurrying down the dusty slope to the water where they stood helplessly gazing at the water. Stories spread like a brushfire through the tent city. Someone had been lost in the river. An old woman, a young child, a famous sadhu—someone—had stepped beyond the cordoned-off section of shallow water into the main flow of the current, eddied with whorls and churning froth. He, or she, had been caught in the undertow and had vanished. People strained to spot the body. But mother Ganges swirled on, India's eternal stream of life and death, filled with the ashes of cremated bodies, bestowing fertility on the flat lands, rampaging over them in furious floods, swirling and whirling its way from the glaciers of the high Himalayas to the silty estuaries of the Indian Ocean. Omnipresent, indifferent, endless.

My friend had to leave (suitably rewarded with rupees and two rain-stained copies of *Newsweek* "to improve my English"). I sat on a bluff overlooking the merger of the two rivers. The sun sank, an enormous orange globe squashing into the horizon, purpling the dust haze, gilding the bodies of the bathers.

The moon rose, big, fat, and silver in a Maxfield Parrish evening sky. There were thousands of people by the river now. The bathing increased but everything seemed to be in slow motion. I watched one old man, almost naked, progress through the careful rituals of washing. He was hardly visible through the throng and yet he acted as if he were the only person there by the river, unaware of everything but the slow steady rhythms of his cleansing. After washing every part of his body he began to clean his small brass pitcher, slowly rubbing it with sand, polishing the battered metal with a flattened twig, buffing its rough surface with a wet cloth, until it gleamed in the moonlight. Then he disappeared and other bodies took his place by the river.

I sensed timelessness and began to feel the power of this strange gathering. Each person performed the rituals in his or her own way and yet from a distance there seemed to be a mystical unity among all of them, all these souls as one soul, cleansing, reviving, touching eternity in the flow of the wide black river, linking with the infinity, becoming part of the whole of which we are all a part.

I made my way slowly to the river and knelt down. For a moment there was no me left in me. The river, the people, the movements, the night breeze, the moon, life, death, all became as one continuum. A smooth, seamless totality. An experience beyond experience. A knowingness beyond knowledge.

I washed my face and arms and let the water fall back to the flowing river where it was carried away into the night.

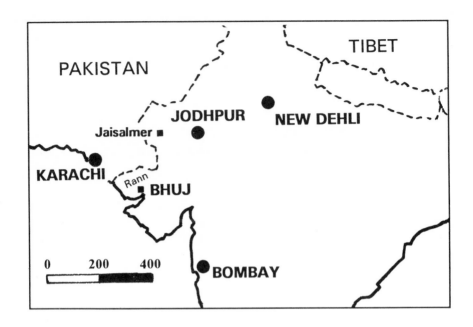

14. INDIA—THE RANN OF KUTCH

A Long Journey into Nowhereness

Close your eyes and imagine the utter emptiness. A white nothingness—a brilliant, frost-colored land—flat as an iced lake,
burning the eyes with its whiteness. Not a bump, not a shrub,
not a bird, not a breeze. Nothing but white in every direction,
horizon after horizon, on and on for over two hundred miles east
to west, and almost one hundred miles north to south.

This is the Rann of Kutch (or Kachchh), the largest area of
nothingness on the planet; uninhabited, the ultimate physical
barrier, separating India from Pakistan along its far western
border. Only camels can cross these wastes, and at terrible cost.
During the monsoon seasons it's a shallow salt marsh, carrying
the seasonal rivers of Rajasthan slowly out to the Arabian Sea,

304

just south of the great Indus delta of Pakistan. Then for months it's a treacherous quagmire of molasses mud under a brittle salt skin. Periods of safe crossing are minimal. Occasional piles of bleached bones attest to the terrors of this place. Tales of survivors, reluctantly told, are unrelieved litanies of human (and animal) distress. There is life out here—herds of wild asses the size of large dogs and vast flocks of flamingoes encamped in mud-nest "cities"—but very hard to find.

"It is a strange place." An old man in one of the baked-mud villages on the southern edge of the Rann had finally agreed to talk about the place through a local interpreter.

"I crossed the Rann many times when I was a young man. Now the only people you will find on it are people carrying drugs or guns. The army tries to stop this trade"—he flung out his small, cracked hands—"but what can they do? The Rann is so vast, the army cannot always use their trucks or their jeeps. They get stuck in the mud, even in the dry season. You can never trust the Rann. Every year it is different. It is very hard to know which way is safe for a crossing. One year"—he paused and studied the endless horizon—"many years ago, I lost my brother and eight camels. He was not so experienced as I was and we had a disagreement. I told him we had to go the long way because the monsoon had been late and the mud was not dry. But he was in a hurry. His family was very poor..." The old man smiled sadly, "We are all poor but he wanted to buy land and build his own house ... he was in a hurry."

He paused again and we all sat staring at the shimmering whiteness. Even the sky was white in the incredible heat. "He was a good man. I was his older brother. He should have listened to what I told him." Another long pause.

"What happened?" A stupid question. I knew the answer.

The old man shaded his eyes. "He has his eldest son with him, twelve years old. A fine boy..."

There was a wedding in the village. We could hear the music over the mud-walled compound. Later there would be a procession and a feast of goat, spiced rice, and sweet sticky cakes.

"He went a different way?"

The old man looked even older. His face was full of long gashed shadows.

305

"You must go to the wedding," he said. "They will be proud if you go. Not many people like you come to this place."

"I've been already. But I think it made people a bit uncomfortable. I seemed to attract more attention than the bride and groom. One man looked quite offended, a man in a bright blue suit."

He laughed. "Ah! Yes. I forgot he was coming. He is with the government—very important. He likes to take charge of things . . . just like my brother."

"So what happened to your brother?"

The old man shrugged. "He took the wrong path. We found two of his camels on our way back. They were almost dead but we brought them back home to our village."

The music of the wedding faded. It was hard to find shade from the sun. I looked across the Rann again. Almost one hundred miles to the other side, with no oasis, no water, no shade, just this endless salt-whiteness.

"He could have reached the other side. Maybe he decided to stay for a while?"

"His family is here. His wife and his children."

"Maybe the army arrested him?"

"No, this was nine years ago. The army was not here so much at that time."

"So you think he died."

The old man drew a slow circle with his finger in the sandy dust.

"He became a 'white,' like so many others."

"A 'white'?"

"We call that name for men who do not return from the Rann. Part of their spirit remains in the Rann. There are many, many of them. Who can tell. Maybe hundreds of men. Hundreds of whites."

"Back home we call them ghosts—the spirits of the dead still trapped on earth."

"Yes I know about your ghosts. Here it is a different thing. We are not afraid of the whites. When we cross the Rann we remember them. They protect us. Sometimes they guide us."

"But you never see them?"

The old man smiled and spoke quietly. "As I told you, the

Rann is a very strange place and you can see many strange things . . . it is difficult to explain. The Rann is not like other things on earth—not even like other deserts. It has its own nature and if you listen and look and think clearly, you will be safe . . ."

"Your brother didn't listen?"

"He was a good man but much younger than I. And he had many worries. His mind was full of many things. He could not hear clearly."

"Do you think about him a lot?"

"He was my only brother. We had five sisters. But he was my only brother."

"So, in a way, he's still here."

"Of course. He is a white. He will always be here."

My long (very long) journey to the Rann began on the Nepalese-Indian border, in the gritty, noisy little town of Birganj. Sixteen hours of bone-crushing bus travel had brought me south from Kathmandu, over the passes and down through the gorges, and deposited me at this nonentity of a place. We were late arriving, not a particularly surprising occurrence in a land where precise bus schedules bear little relevance to reality.

"Sir, please be on time, sir." I had been instructed in Kathmandu. "At six-oh-three A.M., sir, the bus will leave the square, and you must present your ticket ten minutes before departure, sir, otherwise there may be many difficulties."

I had left my warm bed near Durbar Square, one of the most overwhelming urban spaces in the world, and arrived in another chilly fogbound square to find no sign of the bus at its alloted space. It was very dark and wet, and repeated inquiries always brought the same inevitable smile and shrug—the Nepalese equivalent of our "no-problem" response. But for the initiative of one small boy who told me the departure point had been moved to the other side of the square (I couldn't even see the other side in the cloying gloom), I would have missed the bus and been obliged to start the whole rigmarole of ticket buying all over again.

The ride began with the barefoot bus driver praying to the various Hindu deities that decorated his tiny cab, and then rapidly deteriorated into a series of Looney Tunes crises, each more potentially disastrous than the previous one. The cyclist we ran into, a pothole we hit the size of a mine shaft, and the fruit seller's cart we spilled to avoid a cow, were mere warm-ups to the chicken runs against mammoth Mack trucks, the race against a still-sliding landslide, the near spill into a sixty-foot gorge when a section of roadbed gave way, and the ultimate fury of our driver, who leaped out of his cab to confront another driver traveling at sloth pace up a steep ravine (only he forgot to set the handbrake first!).

All I wanted when we finally arrived in Birganj was a simple bed and sleep. A simple bed came easily enough (a square of plywood and a sheet in a freezing cold $3.00-a-night hostel), but sleep was hard to come by in a room also occupied by an enormous Australian earth gypsy whose snoring seemed to shake plaster off the walls and made the windows rattle. Haggard and dizzy with fatigue in the early dawn, I tried to sort out my papers for the border crossing while he insisted on telling me hard-luck tales of his injuries, illnesses, and illicit dealings, all the way from Darwin ("best place in the land of Aus, mate") to Dar es Salaam. His pessimism and chronic dislike of almost everyone he'd met and everything that had happened to him made me wonder why he bothered traveling at all. His ultimate tirade was directed at "that bunch of bastard wogs" in Bombay who had managed to relieve him of all his worldly possessions except his sleeping bag and had even run off with his money belt crammed with dollars from some emerald-smuggling escapade in Malaysia. The air was purple with his profanities, and I was tired of him.

"Isn't there one single place you've enjoyed?"

His mood changed. The swearing and cursing subsided, and this hairy giant of a man became almost teary-eyed as he told me about Bhuj, the idyllic Gujarat coast ("Not a bloody soul for miles. The best beaches in India, mate. No one ever goes there.") and the mysteries of the Rann of Kutch.

So, thank you whatever your name is; I forgive you your snoring and your jaundiced outlook on life and your self-pitying tirades, and will remain ever grateful for your introduction to this truly fascinating corner of India.

Now the only thing I had to do was get there.

Traveling by bus is the only real way to experience India. You just lean back (actually leaning is a rather difficult thing for the average-sized Westerner because of the cramped space between the seats), stop trying to drive the bus in your mind (you couldn't anyway—it takes total Indian logic and faith to negotiate even the quieter country roads littered with tractors, cattle, bicyclists, lines of basket-carrying pedestrians, and wild dogs. And as for the towns—forget it!), and let the whirligig of impressions roll by. Here's a transcript of one of my tapes, a bit garbled, but I think it captures the flavor of bus travel in India well enough:

> ...a truck on its side in a hole in the road, didn't he see it, did it just open up? We're slowing down to get through all the spectators; kids are selling us Cadbury's chocolate bars, newspaper cones full of peanuts for three cents... here's a woman with enough branches and lumps of wood bundled on her head to break the proverbial camel's back... a guru-seeking English couple behind me speak in pungent epigrams, out-Zening each other (one-up-Zenship?)... a cartoon sign indicates that spitting is prohibited on the bus so everyone's hacking and spitting... enormous dew-covered spiders' webs in the bushes by the roadside... behind another bloody white cow again in the middle of a twelve-foot-wide road and all the driver's honking doesn't make any difference at all... now he's put the tape back on, the same one of Indian music we've had for hours and hours over the same cracked speaker. It seems to keep changing speed—or is that the way it's meant to sound?... ah, stopping again. The beer isn't bad. But I can't take any more dhal bhat and curried eggs. A glass of mango lassi—beautiful. This is nice and crunchy—what is it? I said what-is-it? Little birds. Sparrows. Oh boy... off again now past a street market under umbrellas—six men in a line operating sewing machines; open-air dentistry—that's novel; a barber

plucking out nose hairs one at a time; bright-painted pedal-cabs all over the place; piles of beautifully ornate saris on a table; a herd of goats gone crazy; the smell of little bits of dough deep-frying in an old oil drum over a pile of red hot charcoal . . . cabs like tiny temple shrines dripping with ornaments . . . elaborate washing rituals at roadside taps—such a concern with cleanliness, especially the feet . . . towering posters for Indian films (you can spot each of the ritualized characters a mile away: the black-faced villain with scimitar mustache; the lovelorn hero; the shy, modest heroine; the plump, plotting matron; and the comic—there's always a comic) . . . piles of lemons and limes for sale on the steps of a very old and very lopsided temple . . . a riverbank smothered in drying laundry . . . drying chilies on rooftops, brilliant reds . . . odd little dog kennel–sized stores selling pens, cigarettes, matches, combs, perched on platforms supported on four wobbly wooden legs (temporary businesses, no property taxes?) . . . signs everywhere for Campa Cola, Thumbs Up Cola, Frenzi ice cream . . . latticed beds by the roadside for sleepy store owners . . . so many, many people. You never seem to get away from crowds . . . we're playing chicken again with a truck, the road's only wide enough for one of us, he's coming straight for us—jeez—c'mon pull over—wow! How the hell did we miss him? . . . the bus driver's mate leaning out and shouting at the truck driver, banging instructions in code on the side of the bus (one for watch out; two for *watch out!*, three for what?). Too late, we've hit it (only we never hit anything, or at least nothing that we notice. It's like magic. A constant barrage of inevitable accidents that never happen).

Out in the country again, very flat, rice paddies I think; a few mud houses with round cow dung patties drying on the walls . . . men performing their most intimate toilets out in the open fields, trousers down a short way, chatting to one another . . . a teacher sitting cross-legged on a stool outside a mud-walled school lecturing to a class of thirty, forty children . . . a swarm of preschoolers, gleefully naked, frolicking in a green pool . . . the body of a very old man dressed in rags and clutching a long pole at the roadside. (Is he dead? We miss him by inches and he just lies there.) A sense of all these scenes repeated endlessly across all of India, beneath a patina of colonial organizational officialdom that has long since clogged up and atrophied—and yet— still a vitality here, a frazzling pace of life, colors, laughter, variety; an acceptance of the unchanging nature of things; a calm in the midst of unending chaos...I'm worn out just watching it all—it's like a TV docudrama. How would I feel if I were actually out there, in it, trying to do something, to accomplish something...?

Gandhi marveled at all this energy. What was it he said? Something like "We must be Indians first and Indians last." Well it looks like he got his wish. India flows on and on, as Indian as it's always been and possibly always will be, at least in these vast hot heartlands. And another telling quote, this time from Rudyard Kipling: "And the epitaph dear: A fool lies here who tried to hustle the East."

It was rather sneaky of me. But I couldn't resist it. The zap-Zen-ing of the English couple I'd heard in the seats behind me had merely been a preparatory duel, a prologue to the real battle. I could sense the tension. So could the Indian passengers, although they couldn't understand a word of their brittle exchanges. I was tempted to turn around and study them but that would have to wait. The contest was about to begin—a mutual masterpiece of bickering between two lovers who may have known and loved each other a little too long:

SHE: I told you I don't have them.
HE: Yes, you do.
SHE: I *never* had them.
HE: I brought them for you. You asked me.
SHE: I've never seen them.
HE: They were on the pile.
SHE: Did you move them?
HE: No. Did you?
SHE: How could I if I never knew they were there?

311

(Long pause and sounds of searching through backpacks. Then a sort of embarrassed silence.)

SHE: I've found them.
HE: I told you they were there.
SHE: I must have forgotten.
HE: I wish you'd listen to what I say.
SHE: Why? Are you always right?
HE: More often than you think.
SHE: Why are you being nasty?
HE: I'm not being nasty. I'm being honest.
SHE: You're getting angry now.
HE: I'm definitely not getting angry.
SHE: Why are you so angry all the time?
HE: It's things like this that make me angry.
SHE: You must have a very deep anger inside.
HE: I do not.
SHE: Why are you so defensive?
HE: You make me defensive, saying I'm always angry. You always assume I'm wrong.
SHE: I don't always assume you're wrong.
HE: It's a pattern. You always do it.
SHE: What a horrible person you make me out to be.
HE: You're not horrible. You just act unpleasantly at times. Like I'm being dishonest. It hurts.
SHE: Well you're not always honest.
HE: Neither are you.
SHE: And you've often hurt me.
HE: You often hurt yourself.
SHE: No, I don't.
HE: You do. I did nothing to hurt you intentionally.
SHE: Well—you did anyway.
HE: I'm sorry. But sometimes that's your problem, not mine.
SHE: Oh—very clever.
HE: It's not clever at all. It's the truth.
SHE: I must be a terrible person.
HE: No you're not. You just keep dumping on me, and I'm getting tired of it.
SHE: I don't mean to dump on you.

HE: So why do it?
SHE: I don't know.
HE: Do we have a problem? Something we should talk about?
SHE: I don't know.
HE: Do you still love me?
SHE: Yes. Do you still love me?

The rest of the conversation was lost to the din of the traffic. We were passing through another village and chaos reigned as usual. They seemed to reach an amicable hiatus though. When I finally turned around they were both asleep, her head on his shoulder. (It's amazing how little non-incidents like this helped pass the time.)

Bus travel seems endless. People get on, people get off, but the journey goes on forever. The only thing that changed were the occupants of the seat beside me. So far I'd had three Indian companions, each of whom had slept through all the noise, heat, and confusion. I envied them their tranquility.

Then came a spritely young woman, a nurse from Eire, with a wonderful singsong way of talking. All her sentences ended in an upswing of Irish brogue. In spite of five months of backpacking around India from ashram to ashram, she still retained that bright-eyed enthusiasm of the novice traveler. Nothing seemed to phase her. She was totally in love with her life on the road— not a bit of the tired TET anywhere. I envied her too and was sorry to see her leave.

And then Dick Davies arrived, a young Welshman with a prematurely old face, deeply lined and flecked with dark scars. He wore an old suede hat, Australian style with one brim turned up, baggy green corduroys, and a torn leather jacket so stained with grease, food, blood, and mud that it was difficult to tell its original color.

At first I thought that he too would sleep out the journey like my three Indian companions, but our conversation became animated when we compared notes on Kathmandu and the Himalayas.

"I'm a real white-water nut," he told me with a grin that made his old face suddenly look very young. "Himalayas, Central America, New Zealand, Africa, you name it. I've been kayaking there."

He was a true world wanderer, who had spent most of the last decade of his life seeking out white-water wonderlands all around the globe. I felt envious once again.

"I've never done any white-water stuff," I said. "Somehow I don't think I'd enjoy it that much."

He laughed. "It doesn't make that much difference what you do really. Like anything good in life, you end up pretty much in the same place."

"And you get there by kayaking."

"Yeah. Listen, I'm not one of the religious types. Y'know. You've met them. Nepal, Ladakh, the south. They're all over India. They're all looking for something that makes everything make sense."

"Centering?"

"Centering? Okay—that's your word. Call it anything you want. It's all the same. You know what it is when you get there."

"And kayaking. That's what you do."

"Yeah. But it could be something else—anything."

The driver had finally turned off the tape. It was really hot now in spite of the breeze through the open windows of the bus. Everyone seemed to be asleep.

"What's it like? Kayaking."

Dick smiled and sighed. "It's a bit of everything. It's good some days, lousy other times. Like life. You take a knock and you get up and you go again. Each time, it's better. You learn to trust. You learn to trust yourself, and you learn to trust the water. You never fight her, try to beat her. She'll always win. You've got to read her right—understand her."

"And how do you do that?"

"Hard work, boyo! You walk each set of the rapids first."

"Walk?"

"On the edge, on the boulders. Try to see the next one and the one after that. Try to see it all, find out where the rocks are, how wide the chutes, where the keeper waves are—they can be rough—they go backwards—they'll spin you like a top—like a bloody blender. If there's rocks underneath, you can bust your legs—chop, chop, chop—smash 'em to pieces. It's those that don't do their homework that never get back to brag about it."

"But what's it really like? When you're actually in there heading for the rapids?"

"Lousy. Like you're going to piss your pants—or worse."

"Every time?"

"Almost. Sometimes it happens too fast and you don't have time to think what you're thinking. You trust your memory— and your instincts. You've never got time to make second decisions. If it's a string of rapids—those are the best—and you come out wrong from the first one, well, you've just got to improvise. That's when you need your instincts. All the stuff you've ever learned. One paddle wrong and the bloody thing can be upside down in a twinkling and then you've got problems. A whirlie'll get you sure as mustard if you're not ready for it. You get in a hole, under a rock and you're there forever!"

"Is this what you tell people?"

"Hell—that's just the start!" He paused and lit a bidi cigarette. "You've got no idea. You've always got to be ready—for anything. Stopper rocks—they flip you, and they're hard to miss if you don't get enough of a warning. Then there's haystacks, souses, satins, eddies, fillies, and spinners. If you hit them wrong they'll send you twisting all over the shop, right into an eye or something."

"What's an eye?"

"You'll only get to look into a good one once. When you're being sucked in, round and round, like on the inside of an ice cream cone. And there's the eye—the black eye—right at the bottom. If you get that close its bye-bye bay, bye-bye."

"You do this kind of kayaking often?"

"Often as I can."

I knew I was going to ask him. And I did. "Why this? Why not something a bit safer?"

"Hell, if I knew the answer to that one . . ."

"You get a high or something? Adrenaline?"

"Yeah, yeah. You get high. Later. But when you're in it—I don't know—it's hard to say what it is. But it gets into you. Even if you don't do it for weeks—months. There was a year once I never went near white water. My legs were shot. One broken in two places, the other mangled up below the knee. But I knew I'd be back. Once you've done it for a while, and once you get the hang of it..."

He paused and sucked on his bidi.

"You're alive. I'm not kidding. You're so alive you could bust a nut. I don't get that feeling from anything else. Not even in bed...y'know. Doesn't matter who I'm with. I never get it like I get it on a ride—when you're heading for that edge, right after the riffs, and—even if you've done your homework—you still don't know, there's no way you can tell—what the hell's gonna happen next, except that you're going down, you're going over the drop, down the chute, and you're not going to finish until you're finished—or until she's finished with you."

"Why she? Why not it?"

"Oh, it's a bloody 'it' sometimes. Most times it's an it. You curse the bastard. But like I said...she gets you, she gets into you, and you can't stop going back. And when the ride's over. When you get to the back end and she's calmed out and you're floating around feeling great and dead cocky.... Well—you know, she just feels like a woman...."

"Like she knows what you've done."

"Yeah. Yeah that's something like it. Like she knows what you've done. Like you're okay. You got through again..."

"And that you'll be back."

"Oh yeah. Hell—yeah. She knows you'll be back. Just like a woman knows..."

We both sat quietly for a while. Something he'd said brought back a memory.

"Y'know, I almost drowned when I was a kid," I said. "Near a waterfall. I fell under and couldn't get back up. I'm sure that stupid experience put me off the idea of messing around on white water."

"Oh yeah. Well—that can do it."

"You never got close to drowning?"

He nodded but didn't seem to want to talk about it. The smoke from his cigarette curled around his hat.

"One time I think I did drown." He spoke slowly.

"Meaning?"

"Well, I don't know really. Something strange. Still don't know what happened...."

316

I knew he wanted to tell me so I just waited. He lit another cigarette.

"Ah—it was a long time back. When I first got started. I'd only been doing it a few weeks. And I was lousy. I mean lousy. I couldn't get the hang of it. I wanted to, but I couldn't. It wouldn't come right. Anyway, this one day I was up in Scotland by myself, the Cairngorms, trying to get it right, and everything's going okay until, hell—I was under the boat and then out of it and I couldn't touch the bottom and I didn't know where the hell I was. And jeez, was it cold! Real brass monkey stuff and churning away like mad. Currents all over the place, and I was flippin' over like a hooked fish. I'd sucked in a lot of water, I couldn't find the surface. It was black as pitch. I'd got no air left. I knew I was drowning. And all these weird things were happening. You get flashbacks like they tell you—I was crying because I'd broken my mother's best plate. Then I was on a soccer pitch with the mates. All kinds of stuff. Coming home down the lane from church past the pub and hearing them all singing . . . and then it all sort of went quiet and it wasn't like I was in water or anything . . . it was just okay and there didn't seem to be much to worry about anymore. . . ."

His cigarette trembled in his fingers. The afternoon sun flickered through a filigree of tree along the roadside.

"And then. Well everything got weird. I wasn't in the water. I was on the bank, sitting on some sand, and the boat was right by me and it looked fine and I felt fine . . . I wasn't even coughing or anything."

He shook his head and grinned.

"Hell—I dunno what happened. Still don't. I thought I'd drowned, lost it. Into the great yonder and all that. Weird. I don't know how the hell I got to be sitting like a Sunday afternoon fisherman on a riverbank with the boat and everything—all together in one piece."

My spine was tingling. That was my story. The accident that had happened but never happened in Iran, twenty years ago. One of the strange events that changed my life and my way of looking at life.

We sat quietly for a long time listening to the hiccupy rhythm of the bus engine.

"So that didn't put you off going back in?"

"No—I've been kayaking ever since. I learned fast after that. Seemed to come naturally."

"And you don't get scared about drowning?"

"No. I've never thought about it since that first time. I've been banged about a bit y'know. But that's all part of the game. But no. No, I don't think about drowning."

"She must have liked you a lot."

He laughed. "Yeah. Yeah she must. She still does!"

For the next few days there were more buses, and then there were the trains—eternally slow, lumbering steam-powered relics howling their way across the empty desert (maybe the driver just gets lonely and turns the horn on for company) with dining cars whose only offering seemed to be rice and lentils (more dhal bhat) and bottles of warm fizzy Limca and Campa Cola. They said I could order meals, which would be picked up somewhere further down the line, but for some reason, the system never worked for me.

The days were oven hot and the fans rarely worked. If you opened the windows the sand and dust poured in; if you left them closed it just sort of filtered in and took a little longer to cover you and everything else in the compartment in layers of fine grit.

Relief came in the form of frequent—very frequent—pauses at little desert stations where you could buy eggshell-sized clay cups of milky tea for a couple of cents and then smash the cups against the wheels of the train (the cups were never reused by the vendor and were made of the ideal biodegradable material— a perfect "dust-to-dust" recycling).

I tried to read an English-language newspaper left behind by a previous occupant who insisted on giving me the ritual Indian interrogation and then spent an hour describing the horrors of government red tape when he attempted to establish a cement factory in the desert. The newspaper wasn't much better—endless exposés of political corruption "in the highest of echelons"; terrible statistics of female infanticide and fetacide due to the disproportionate emphasis on male offspring in India ("It is reliably estimated that more than half the girl-children conceived in

318

India are killed at or before birth...") and shrieking half-page ads: "TOUGH MEN have real feelings. For feeling sensation she'd love to experience, it's CHAMP ribbed condoms!" Even one promoting vegetarianism, that began: "The stomach of a human being is a graveyard of animals..."

The nights were worse. Wrapped in two blankets over a double layer of clothes, I sat freezing and sleepless, trying to read in the one light of the compartment that flickered on and off with the bouncing of the train. I mentioned the light to one of the guards, hoping he'd try a replacement bulb. He smiled instead and pointed to a sign you see often on trains: PLEASE RECORD COMPLAINTS, IF ANY, WITH GUARD OR ASSISTANT STATIONMASTER. THEY HAVE COMPLAINT BOOK.

"Do you have a complaint book?" I asked.

He shrugged and smiled again. Of course not. What a dumb question.

I finally arrived in a golden city.

Jaisalmer, in the far western reaches of India and only a couple of days' camel ride from the Pakistan border, is a golden stone mirage. Spread across a rocky hill and bound by battlements and unbroken walls more than one hundred feet high in places, the city resembles an Indian version of France's Carcassonne.

Driving by car for hours overland from Jodhpur, across three hundred miles of scorching desert, I had become accustomed to the barren monotony of burnt plain. The Indian landscape is always writ large. Scenery changes slowly here, and time flows seamlessly. There are few surprises. It's not boring though— more a pleasant kind of mind-numbing neutrality in which the brain switches off and you're left with a floating sensation, similar in some ways to deep meditation.

So, for a long time, there was nothing. And then suddenly —something. A vague blur on the horizon that slowly took on form and substance. It could be a dust cloud, or an isolated butte not quite worn down to the interminable sandy plain. But the shadings were too evenly spaced. Those were walls and towers, I could see. It was a castle, a fortress, a Tolkienesque fantasy.

The road was heading straight for it. A few low houses appeared off to my left, poor mud-walled places with conical roofs and dusty compounds bound by fences of cactus and piled sagebrush. I passed a line of figures carrying huge bundles of twigs on their heads like enormous, comic hats. Some goats; some children playing in the yellow dust; women in bright red saris and ornately embroidered waistcoats; the rasp of sun-shriveled stalks and brittle grass.

Now the golden blur on the horizon had taken on a finer form. It was a city, it was Jaisalmer—ancient enclave of the Rawals of Western Rajasthan—alone in this vast wilderness; a golden fantasy, and one of India's most unusual and unspoiled, hidden places.

Even close up it maintained an illusion of fantasy. The evening sun was turning the miles of perfectly masoned walls into a soft pink confection. I stopped the car by the side of the road. What history behind those walls—what records of Rajasthan's past glories, etched into the fabric of its palaces, temples, and merchants' mansions. . . .

Rajasthan has always been a "place-apart" in Indian history, particularly in these arid western deserts. Evidence of civilizations here have been traced back to 2500 B.C., but recorded history really began with the tribal "republics" and warrior clans of the sixth century A.D., led by the fierce Rajputs. They were constantly at war with one another, although the still-existent "ballad-histories" of later centuries suggest highly structured and chivalrous battles, until the protracted and fierce campaigns against the occupation of India by the Turks from Turkistan during the twelfth to sixteenth centuries.

Constant duplicity, double-dealing, and complex family infighting finally led to the erosion of Rajput morale and power. The tribal states became mere protectorates and later allies with the British, who began their conquest of India in the mid-eighteenth century. British "residents" were appointed "to ensure the welfare of the Rajput princes and the tranquility of their country." In turn the Rajputs returned the favor by loyally supporting the British during the great national rebellion of 1857 and later during the First World War. But British power waned, and by the time of Independence in 1947, the Rajasthan royal families agreed to relinguish much of their independent power in exchange for generous pensions and privileges. Even today, after Indira Gandhi's abolition of those perks in 1970, the population of Rajasthan still holds the descendants of the "ancient Rajputs" in high esteem.

A man on a bicycle interrupted my musings. He was neatly dressed in a tweed jacket, with baggy slacks folded around his ankles and held by metal bicycle clips. His black hair was crisply combed forward over a bald patch and he carried a small canvas briefcase. He explained that he was a representative of one of India's largest tire companies and was in the city "to make businesses." I'd only got in a couple of nods and a friendly hello when he began this remarkable monologue:

"I am wondering if I might be assistance to you . . . for India, d'you see? Of course you are British I am thinking by the little flag on your bag, and you are our ex-rulers . . . I'm not going to talk about that . . . that is just a joke between the friends of our two countries . . . these are all things of the past. Those who are understanding of India are very much with us and those who cannot are very much gone. Irrelevant. So we don't have to look back, d'you see?

"I see it as my duty to look after you. We are all in this world—one world for all, everyone, of course. I find, moving around all the places, that my country is still far, far behind. So far. They talk very much loudmouth things—they say they are doing a lot of things for the downtrodden and all. But it is not so—not so at all. Things are not changing at all . . . all poppycock, as I think you are saying.

"If you have money in my country you will get what you want, and if you don't have, you will not get anything. VIPs all over. Too much. Always secret, isn't it, under the counter d'you see?

"I am pleased to offer my services. Really—I wanted. If I can do it I am pleased. You are not asking me money. You are not asking of anything at all. I have plenty of time, and I think you are looking something. God takes me here. God takes you here, d'you see? And it is nice to know that I have a friend in England who I can call when I come to your airport.

JAISALMER
India

"Please do not belittle me by thanking me. If this were my city you would be welcome to my small residence—in my small way I would offer you Indian hospitality, but I am snookered by being in this city, which is not mine. But we have planted seeds for the future, d'you see? And now please tell me—how it is that I can help you?"

I hadn't said one word throughout this masterly, all-encompassing preamble. It was far too eloquent a speech to be interrupted. And I really didn't need any help, but it seemed a shame not to think of something after such an introduction.

"Well—I was wondering where I should stay."

"Ah, yes. Always a problem in my country, isn't it? Where to stay is one of the most difficult things. It is so easy to make a mistake, and then you pay for it, by jove. Very difficult it can be."

"I presume there are hotels here."

"Oh yes, by golly. Many places but not places for you, if you don't mind, d'you see? Only three places I think—no, I am mistaken. Four places. First there is the palace up there, on the hill by the gates. Actually it was really a caravansary—for the camel trains, d'you see? But some people call it a palace. Then there is another palace behind the city, d'you see? Very nice. Then a new hotel, just finishing I think, up by the temples. And then there is the Circuit House—and Tourist Bungalows in India—very good places and very cheap for traveling persons. But it is difficult there because it is being filled by Indian people. I am staying there. Very cheap price—30 rupees ($3.00) with a very nice dinner—thali—you know thali—plenty of rice and dhal and curry vegetables and chapatis. Eat as much as you like. But I think there will be no room. If you wish I will be asking for you."

"No, no. Don't worry. I'll go and look at the palaces."

"Yes. I think is a good idea. Very nice places. Not too expensive. Very clean. Let me show you how to go there."

And so, he did. I followed my businessman friend, pedaling away happily on his gearless bike, and was introduced to the luxuries of the city hotels. Finally I selected a large and inexpensive room in the pleasantly seedy eighteenth-century Jowahar Niwas Palace on the edge of town. Some of the fine trimmings were still in place, but I had a feeling that the great days of the

Maharaos had long since passed, and that their descendents had to be content now with meager pittances from passing travelers.

But the fortress city was everything it appeared to be from a distance, a magical golden stone masterpiece of walls-within-walls palaces; dark and complex little Jain temples filled with white statues of *tirthankaras* (saints), all with jeweled third eyes in the center of their foreheads (a sign read: "USE OF EGG, MEET AND VINES PROHIBITED HEAR"); narrow, winding alleys ending in impregnable battlements and sentinel towers; a richly decorated temple to the Goddess Bhavani where the fierce Bhatti Rajput warriors, "the wolves of the wastes," once worshiped before embarking on their innumerable battles with desert tribes—and all climaxing in the main square by the Jawahar Mahal, the Jeweled Palace, where the regal Rawals gave blessings to their armies and entertained the populace with spectacular extravaganzas after each successful expedition.

Of course, not all battles were successful. The ancient oracle's prediction that Jaisalmer would be sacked "two and one-half times" proved to be true, and traveling historian-bards (*charans*) still sing of the great seven-year seige of 1295 A.D. in the reign of Allud-din Khiljii. Recognizing imminent defeat, the Bhattis slaughtered their own women and children, smoked their ritual pipes of opium, and stormed out of the great Elephant Gate to be massacred, in the thousands, in an infamous *johar* by the invading armies. A similar johar was repeated a few decades later, followed in the sixteenth century by a "half-johar" when a "friendly" leader of a desert tribe managed a sneaky attack as far as the palace gates. The Rawal of Jaisalmer killed off most of his own royal family to prevent their capture before the invaders were finally beaten off and he was left heirless in his broken citadel.

Below the broody walls of the fort, built of huge blocks of unmortared golden sandstone, is the Manik Chowk, the hectic marketplace of the city, teeming with peddlers, fruit sellers, goatherds with their flocks, camel drovers (*raiskas*) offering expeditions way out into the Thar Desert to the great silky Dunes of Samm or, in late August, a long journey to the Ramderra Fair to see the famous "tera-tali" acrobats and the "horse-worshipers" at the Ramdevra shrine. I had hoped to arrange a journey to the great Tilwara Cattle Fair way out near the Pakistan border at Barmer, but that is in January and I was too late.

The streets nearby are lined with exquisite eighteenth-century *havelis* or merchants' houses, all honey colored and dripping with ornately carved stone façades, the work of Jaisalmer's *silavats*. A few are now museums or showrooms for the city's richly embroidered brocades and silks and carved marble statutory. Their cool interior courtyards are as richly decorated as the façades, soaring slabs of sandstone chiseled to lacelike tracery by the skilled silavats.

"Pleased to come in, sir." A small, age-bent gentleman in long flowing robes caught me trying to photograph the courtyard of his haveli. "This is my private house, sir, so very neat and clean as you can see. You, I can perceive, have been made wary of the havelis by all those cheap salesmen people. It is understandable, but you are welcome here to photograph my own house."

He was charming, leading me through all his finely painted rooms full of late Victorian furniture and bric-a-brac and lit by dusty chandeliers—a combination of a Vincent Price film set, Dickensian town house, and antique-lover's paradise.

And then he pounced. In a small room on the upper level of the house overlooking the courtyard, he switched on the flickering lights and announced. "And this, sir, is my little shop. All things very good and very cheap. Not like other places . . ."

I should have known better. Everyone seems to be a merchant in India!

Later that evening I rested on the rocky hill of Barra Bagh, watching the setting sun bathe the walled city in a brilliant gold wash. Here among the templelike *chhatris* and tombs lie the cremated remains of all the famous Rawals of Jaisalmer. Flute players and tabla drummers strolled among the ancient stones; a herd of black goats wandered home between the smaller shrines at the base of the rock, leaving pink-gold streamers of dust behind, haloing the young goatherd boys.

* * *

Everything was fine during the night in my palace-hotel. Except for one thing. The dogs. Those damned, mangy, sly-eyed ribby wretches, slinking in the shadows of every Indian street. During the day they're tolerable, usually dozing in the heat, making no more noise than the occasional snarl at unguarded ankles. But at night they become interminable, maddening surges of canine cacophony from dusk to dawn, piercing the thick sleepy silences with the sear of wasp stings.

One begins: a sudden rumbling bass rising rapidly to a quavering high C (or, in India, never quite hitting the note, like one of those unnerving quarter tones), which is then picked up by another one, determined to outdo the instigator, followed by another and yet another, until the whole world becomes a resounding disharmonic orchestration of yowls, yelps, growls, grunts, and howls rising to a climactic fever pitch and ending as abruptly as it began—in a short, spongy silence.

You lie still, trying not to make the slightest sound that might set off the whole maniacal chain reaction again. But it starts anyway. Maybe a minute or two of glorious respite, and then again and again, like the jarring surges of pain from an abscessed tooth. Except you can always pull a tooth or douse it with a few glasses of the hard stuff. But these damned dogs go on forever, every night, in every community, all across the vast subcontinent of India.

On my third day in Jaisalmer there was a sandstorm. A real roustabout out of the desert; screaming winds and the air so full of sand that the city vanished completely into the maelstrom. I decided to stay in my room and listen to the local radio station.

It was all music. Indian music. And I just couldn't get the hang of it. I listened to the squeaks and grinding noises, the staccato improvisations on the sitar, and all the banging and hissing of drums and cymbals but, no matter how hard I tried, I heard only noise. And not a very pleasant noise at that. It was only when I read a mellifluous critic in an English-language newspaper I'd found in the lobby describing a recent concert in Bombay that I began to understand a little of the subtleties and complexities of this ancient art form:

Viplau Bhattacharya, a budding Saptak pupil, played a composition in Raga Durga, on sared which was followed by a scintillating tabla solo by Siddhartha Seth. Peshkar, kaydas, tukdas and chakradars were vigorously rendered in Benares style. Then Pt. Jasraj took the stage with his retinue of disciples. With a deep bass voice he chose to delve into the depths of Kharj octave with astonishing ease. The nishad of ati kharj was clearly audible. A lapi, ornamented by murki and meend, was steadily done in a rising movement and the primary goal of the octave shadja was impressively attained along with vertical swava patterns much to the amusement of one and all. Layakari and tans effected through gamak were clean and forceful: some storzando tans had the effect of a raging storm. Dhanesh Bhavsar provided melodic accompaniment on an out-of-tune harmonium... [poor Mr. Bhavsar]

The New York Times couldn't have said it better! However the *Times* editorial staff may have had problems with some of the unusual advertisements on the facing page:

Educated young handsome Vaishnar-Baniya boy of 30 having Bank assignment invites correspondence from parents of graduate, smart, fairly religious Vaishnar-Baniya girl with horoscope.

Horoscopes invited from parents of cultivated good-looking girls for chartered accountants.

Wanted: Beautiful girl 18–24 years. No dowry. Caste no bar.

Wanted: Alliance for Captain Merchant Navy. Foreign company, own flat, young, Goan Catholic marriage annulled, issueless, invites Goan graduates below 31, no dowry.

Those having no issue please contact for sex and vitality World Famous
Dr. SUBHASH SIGH
Thousands, Disappointed, Issueless persons have not been

blessed with issues or only daughters for lack of vitality and skin diseases and male and female disorders, cured on the basis of 110 years of vast experience and special services.

Ah—but what services? I should have called the World Famous Doctor for more details.

I love Indian newspapers! A nation bares its soul. Behind the seemingly simple pastoral rhythms of predominantly rural life lie centuries of traditions and faith-bound mores—layer upon layer upon layer, heaped high as a hindu shrine, as complex and convoluted as temple carvings. It sometimes makes our freewheeling rainbow-hued dabblings in societal plurocracy seem like baby doodlings in loose sand: uncentered, unattached, meaningless.

But then, occasionally, you get a paragraph of real *National Enquirer* stuff like this glimpse into the antics of a high government official:

CABINET MINISTER OR MAFIA KING?

Did Dr. P. Patil, the Minister for Irrigation, brandish his revolver before Chief Minister S. Patil-Nilangekar? And did he, while in office lead a similarly vicious criminal assault on a manager of a district cooperative bank? When asked if he would seek legal action against the rumor-mongers the Minister said: "I don't have time for such funny things. I have a lot of social work to attend to."

And finally, this delightful tale:

SNAKE MAN COMETH

Professor T. Velayudham, a resident of Calicut, Kerala, began his ten day sojourn with poisonous snakes on Friday in his specially constructed glass chamber in the Sabha sports grounds. He was to keep company with over 80 poisonous snakes gathered from all over the country. Some members of the audience however complained that Professor Velayudham was not staying in the chamber, as has been advertised. He only goes inside the chamber, they said, when the crowd is sufficiently large enough. Poor show, Professor!

On a long bus journey south from Jaisalmer to Bhuj, across miles of deserty wastes, I did some homework about the Rann of Kutch. The owner of the hotel had very generously lent me a few books on Gujarat, and I scribbled away, delighted by one descriptive passage from a booklet by a Lt. Burns in 1828:

> ... Rann comes from the Sanskrit word "ririna" meaning "a waste"... a space without a counterpart on the globe, devoid of all vegetation and habitation... its surface shines with a deadly whiteness; the air, dim and quivering, mocks all distance by an almost ceaseless mirage. No sign of life breaks the weary loneliness. Stones and bones of dead animals mark infrequent tracks... passage at all times is dangerous, travelers being lost even in the dry season. Because of the heat and blinding salt layers, passage is made at night, guided by the stars from dawn to dusk...

Just my kind of place for a dry-season ramble!

Gujarat has also been a "land apart" on the Indian subcontinent. Ruled for centuries by powerful and fierce Maharaos, the "Kutchis" have long had an outward-looking attitude to the world. Their fame as seafarers, merchants, traders, and even pirates has made them a major presence in East Africa, Arabia, and the Persian Gulf. Recent development here by the Indian government of the new port of Kandla is beginning to increase Gujarat's links with the rest of the country, but the Kutchis still value their own history, traditions, and independence.

The ruined castles of feudal chieftains, set high on the crags of Gujarat's Black Hills, are still revered places. So too are the remote shrines of local saints, whose pious meditations and fierce penances (*tapsia*) were said to give them power over gods and the local warrior-kings.

You can see that power here in the bleakness and broken ridges of the hills. Fragments of ancient fiefdoms still dot the sun-bleached desert and, as Bhuj suddenly appears—a gray, solemn bastion of towers and high stone defence walls—I wondered how much had really changed in this remote region since the wild rampages of a ferocious duo known as Mod and Manai in the ninth century A.D., and the cruel vengeances of the warrior Ful in the next century.

Tales of cunning, intrigue, murder and massacre are the very stuff of Gujarat legend. Our contemporary scandals and conspiracies of financial finaglings and political philanderings seem like schoolboy pranks when set beside the tangled complexity of regal power plays in and around Bhuj.

Take one of Ful's little escapades. When he was a child, his grandfather, the powerful king Dharan Vaghela, decided to slaughter most of his power-hungry relatives. Ful only escaped the massacre when his maidservant dressed her own son in the royal infant's robes and sacrificed his life to save the baby prince.

Revenge later became Ful's main aim in life, and when he reached fighting age he challenged Dharan Vaghela to combat and neatly lopped off his head in the first blow. That may have been enough for most warriors, but Ful's vengeance was not satiated. He had the skin stripped off the corpse, flayed, stretched across an enormous chair, and then invited one of Dharan's pregnant daughters, an aunt, to join him for supper. When she realized she'd been tricked into sitting on the skin of her murdered father, she committed suicide. Her unborn infant was cut living from her body and became known as Ghao, "he that born of the wound." And not surprisingly, the vendetta continued into the next generation and the next.

The "memorized history" of Gujarat is full of such legends, piled up like rock strata, hard and thick. "Ages shall wear away," the Kutchi bards sing, "but our stories shall remain."

And what wonderful stories: a princess turning herself into a mosquito to drive a king mad; the tumbling of mighty fortresses by magic catapults; the mysterious "cursed city" of Padhargadh whose ruins can still be seen today; the brilliant Troylike invasion of the poor city of Guntri by soldiers hidden in hay carts. All great stuff!

What surprised me was that in all the tumult and vengeance wreaking and city annihilation of Gujarat history, Bhuj still stands intact, surrounded by its high walls and impregnable gates. Until only a few decades ago, the city's ruler, Maharao Khengarji III, had the keys to the five gates of Bhuj delivered to him personally every night, and every morning he would have them returned to the guards so that the citizens could conduct business beyond the walls, and the long lines of bullock carts and camels camped outside could enter with their produce from the desert villages.

Known as the "Jaisalmer of Gujarat," Bhuj is a medieval maze of tight, winding streets, flurried marketplaces, ancient palaces (now museums), and Hindu temples decorated with gaily painted gods, abandoning themselves to the joys and terrors of all their incarnations. Someone described it as "stepping into a Salman Rushdie world of mystery and intrigue." I didn't sense much of the intrigue except in the intense secretiveness of the Gujarat shopkeepers and merchants, whose agile abilities with the abacus and whispery deal making confirmed their reputation as India's most skillful traders.

But mystery—definitely. Everyone seemed to have a mission. There were few beggars or loiterers. You sense constant purposeful movement here with little time to notice foreign travelers. People were friendly, but in a kind of indifferent way. It was as though this remote city, rarely visited by outsiders, responded to a higher agenda of purpose, reflecting centuries of accumulated tradition and independence from the rest of the country.

For once, I enjoyed the anonymity. I felt like a floating camera lens, recording scenes, capturing the flavor of the place, but almost invisible. No lines of chattering children followed me around; no hands grasped at my elbows demanding handouts; no merchants leaped from their tiny trinket, tailoring, and "traditional art" shops to snare me inside.

The Indian government has one of the largest military bases in the country just outside the city, purportedly to keep a wary eye on the Pakistanis and their always imminent invasion across the Rann of Kutch. But somehow you wonder if they're also watching the mysterious Bhujis and Kutchis too. . . .

"Ah yes, Bhuj is rather different from other Indian cities." I'd been lucky enough to meet one of the descendents of the royal family here who lived in a few simply furnished rooms with an English country house feel to them, deep in the recesses of the Rao Pragmaljis palace. He was a tall, thin-featured man, who spoke with quiet English public school eloquence: "We have always possessed a certain reticence about our role in the Indian nation as a whole. Gujarat for centuries has been an outward-looking region—we were seafarers and world traders while the rest of the country was a conglomeration of introverted, subsistence agricultural states. Gujurati merchants and entrepreneurs are all over the world, little colonies everywhere—India is just one of our many homelands, so to speak. Our outlook is somewhat broader."

We were walking in stocking feet along the dusty passages and halls of the "new palace," built early this century in mock-Gothic, town-hall–style. The palace had obviously been unused for years. Pigeon droppings encrusted the ornate tilework and carved stone traceries. The main audience room, rich in baroque trimmings, possessed a cobwebby melancholy. An ornate (but very mildewed) throne stood on a raised platform at the far end. Stuffed tiger and antelope heads on the walls dribbled sawdust from cracks in their hides as we shuffled across the dusty floors. It was very quiet. The sounds of an always hectic city were shut out by windows crusted with grime.

My royal companion was obviously a well-traveled and well-read individual, and somehow our conversation had switched to a comparison of Western and Eastern attitudes toward life (as it so often does in India).

"Western man is a crisis-torn, self-divided, cosmic misfit. Excuse my saying so, and a terrible generalization I admit, but I have found it to be often true. Western man tends to be bound up, imprisoned, by his materialism and the limits of his conscious mind. Unless one has the urge and the means to find out what is beyond mind—the conditioned brain, so to speak—to discover what is beyond the experience and the act of experiencing; beyond the act of observation and the observer; the thought and the thinker; what is beyond space and time, in fact—what is beyond all these symbols. Unless one has an innate passion to find out, to discover for oneself, one will never be equipped to live in a full way—a full life."

He paused to point out a collection of music boxes and

clockwork toys cocooned in dusty spider webs and scattered randomly over an enormous Rococo table, a gift from the French royal family prior to the revolution that rocked Europe.

"You see, you must have understood this from all your travels in Nepal and India. Meditation, detachment, and self-control are the steps by which human beings remake themselves closer to their origin. Unless outside the mind and in touch with the timelessness of being—what is man? What is the point?"

We were now at the top of the palace tower (after climbing a hundred or more steps whitened by decades of droppings). Bhuj lay below us, a tight winding warren of streets and alleys bound by those gray walls. One of the main gates ended by a broad man-made lake in which the towers and turrets were reflected. The water was gold in the late afternoon sun. Women were pounding clothes on the stones at its edge. There were tree-lined walks and little temples and oxcarts and bell-ringing pedicabs. And beyond stretched the bare land, rising to the fort-encrusted ridges of the Black Hills, and then fading into the silver haze, out across the edges of the great Rann.

"But I'm not a pessimist. Honestly, I don't think I am." The prince (in name only) added, "The world is becoming a small, better place, I think. I believe we are on the threshold of a new time when man—particularly Western man—will come face to face with the boundless energy in himself. We are all moving toward the inward and the beyond. At least"—he smiled and shrugged his shoulders—"that is what I would like to hope."

We stood quietly watching the timeless scenes in this strange little city on the edge of the world's greatest nowhere-ness.

"Now, come on. Let me show you the real palace. Come and see how the Raos once lived when all this was ours."

The contrast with the dusty hollowness of the new palace was immediate. We walked past the "Ladies' Palace" with its finely carved wooden-lattice windows ("so the ladies could see everything but not be seen") and stepped through thick studded doors into an Aladdin's cave of regal splendors. Enormous silver-encrusted thrones; ornately carved carriages for state occasions; doors of the most intricate inlaid teak and ivory designs; displays of jeweled swords and fans; more hunting trophies and lions' heads from the Gir Forest. We ended up in a magic place, the Pleasure Hall, deep inside the palace where fountains once played and a miniature moat of cool water ran around a central dias covered in gold-and-silver-threaded cushions. Here the Maharao would recline, reflected in mirrors all around the walls. "There was so much fun," the prince told me, "singing, throwing water, games—and other things—all in lots of candlelight reflecting off these gold decorations. Can you imagine how it was?"

I could indeed. What a life these Maharaos must have lived in this Pleasure Hall, conveniently close to the Ladies' Palace, enjoying all the perks of seemingly boundless power, plotting new glorious battles, parading around in those elephant-drawn carriages. I wondered if the titular prince was perhaps a little envious. But he was far too self-controlled to let on.

And I had other things to think about anyway. I wanted to get to Rann.

On the way back to the hotel, a little event occurred that made Bhuj a warmer place for me, a touch more accessible than I'd first thought.

I was passing a baker's shop. The smell of hot flat bread was enticing, and I paused to buy a small chapatilike round, toasty hot and bubble crusted. And then I noticed a street vendor nearby cooking up all kinds of vegetarian delights in black iron cauldrons over charcoal fires—kormas, palaks, bhaturas, and masalas, brimming with chunks of eggplant, peas, lentils, and beans. For a few pennies I bought a large spoonful of eggplant curry and asked him to place it carefully on one half of my chapati. I folded the other half over, pinched the edges and made a sort of Indian version of an Italian calzone. It was delicious! All those rich spices locked inside a patty of hot bread.

The baker was watching me and smiled as I filled my mouth with my improvised snack. Then I had an idea. Why couldn't the baker make some more of these by layering the thin raw dough with any kind of curried filling and then baking them for the normal ten minutes or so in his oven.

He seemed a friendly type so I stepped back into his store and explained my idea. At first, and quite understandably, he seemed reluctant. I mean after all, who the hell was this crack-pot foreigner to suggest changes to his centuries-old, father-to-son-to-son traditions? But when I explained that I'd buy half a dozen of these custom-designed calzones for double the selling price, he laughed and agreed to perform the experiment.

The street vendor joined in the fun, suggesting the various fillings, and we watched as the baker pushed the little dough creations deep into his oven. Ten minutes later they were done —and they were magnificent! The flavors of the bread and the curry melded together in a hot, fist-sized snack. No mess, no fuss. A perfect Indian fast-food concept.

I shared my six "Bhujizones" with the curry vendor, a nearby tailor, two wide-eyed children, and a man on a mule who had stopped to enjoy the fun. I only got to sample one of them. The others were gobbled up in a few minutes. Then the tailor ordered two more; another man in long brown robes, who seemed very self-important, ordered three; more kids clustered around, and pretty soon the baker had a street-blocking audi-ence as he stoked the fires and set about baking fresh batches. Everyone was laughing and chewing and ordering more. Sud-denly the city seemed like a fun place to be.

Later on in the evening I passed again and the baker was still churning out his new creations. I waved and he came run-ning over carrying two of them wrapped in little squares of newsprint. He gabbled something very fast (complimentary I think), shook my hand vigorously, and vanished again to tend his baking Bhujizones. I have often wondered since if, together, we'd added another variant to India's wonderful street-food of-ferings.

The following day brought another unexpected series of inci-dents.

"Please, sir, do not forget, if you wish to visit the Rann, you will be required to carry a permit," the hotel manager advised me.

Getting a permit. Okay—no problem. I was more familiar with Indian behavior now and forsaw no difficulties. . . .

"It is best, sir, if you will get to the office early," he advised. It was not even two o'clock in the afternoon. Plenty of time.

But I should have known better.

The process required visits to three separate government offices; endless filling out of forms (and filling them out twice due to a clerk's inability to spell my name correctly); langorous pauses for betel nut chewing and tea; returning to previous offices to "clarify" form entries; minute inspection of every detail of my passport (including the binding!); an impressive display of seal-making using a stick of red wax and a candle (only to have the seal snapped into half a dozen pieces a few minutes later by the next official on my list—in the next room); constant confusion over the forms themselves, which were all in English, only hardly anyone spoke English; meticulous compiling of papers (at one point I carried fourteen different sheets of paper from one department to another held together by sewing pins); a warning from the next to the last official that if the forms were not all completed by closing time at 6:00 P.M. I would have to start the whole process over again the following morning; and finally, at five minutes to six, waiting for the last signature from a man who looked very imperious and sat on a tall chair raised on a carpet-covered dias and seemed to be far more interested in the condition of his fingernails than in my pile of wilting, ink-stained forms.

But I was proud. Throughout the whole four-hour ordeal I had never once raised my voice or played the arrogant colonial (whom I'd discovered deep in my psyche while traveling in India). I smiled. They smiled. They shared tea with me. They offered me betel "pan" and I accepted (it took hours to get all the little pieces of nuts and spices and whatever else goes into its elaborate preparation out of my teeth). I offered them bidi cigarettes, which they accepted (but on one occasion politely mentioned they would have preferred Marlboros). And then— clutching my precious papers like winning lottery tickets—I returned to the hotel for a traditional vegetarian *thali* dinner (usually the only food available in Bhuj hotels).

Tomorrow I'll finally be off to the Rann, I told myself. I celebrated by ordering a second enormous metal tray of thali and was just finishing off my rice, dhal, vegetables, and paratha when someone started beating on my door with the urgency of a fireman in the midst of a blazing inferno.

337

"Police. Open."

Now what? I opened the door.

Two neatly dressed policemen stepped promptly into my room with the worried manager trailing behind, shrugging hopelessly.

"Passport."

Keep calm, I told myself, don't blow a fuse. Be like you were earlier on at the government offices.

So I was.

I answered all their questions, let one of them search my luggage, smiled as they meticulously inspected all my permits, and smiled again as they saluted smartly and left. The manager was very apologetic.

"They very nervous, sir, of people going to Rann. Much trouble with drugs and weapons."

He couldn't seem to stop shrugging his shoulders.

"That's okay. I'm just a tourist."

"Yes—I am knowing that, sir. But they..." His twitching shrugs completed the sentence.

"Honestly. It's okay. And thank you for looking after me."

He left, bowing and shrugging simultaneously.

Five minutes later, another knock on the door. This was becoming an Inspector Clouseau nightmare. I opened it. And behold—another enormous tray of thali with two bottles of Thums Up Cola.

"Complimentary manager," the young boy said.

What a nice way to end the day. Three dinners!

This had been a long journey, one of the longest of my world-wanderings. All the way from Kathmandu to the far western limit of India to the vast nothingness of the Rann of Kutch.

And was it worth it?

Definitely.

The drive north from Bhuj began as sensations of diminishing stimuli, leaving the city and then the Black Hills behind, easing further and further out into a flattening desert plain. I paused in one of the few villages on the edge of the Rann and was entertained by the headman while his wives and daughters paraded past me in brightly embroidered jackets decorated with hundreds of tiny mirrors. I watched them sewing and sifting rice in the shade of their mud huts and among the circular granaries topped with conical roofs of reed thatch. Out under the thornbushes beyond the village, herds of white cud-chewing cattle sat in statuesque groups, guarded by naked, gold-skinned boys.

Nearby were two camels commencing the rituals of courtship. At first it seemed gentle enough—a bit of nudging and polite nipping of flanks—but then the screaming and spitting began. Either the female was in desperate heat or she was merely trying to discourage the gallant male who was now attempting to mount her. The more he tried to climb on her back, the more she spat and screeched. The boys lay on their stomachs, laughing. Finally the male forced his seemingly reluctant mate to the ground where she quieted down and just sat on her haunches with a kind of "Well—c'mon then, get on with it" look. But the poor male was obviously past his prime and for all his mounting and bellowing, just couldn't seem to make it. So they ended up together, side by side, eyes closed, like a couple of old pensioners ruminating about prior conquests in the virile days of youth.

Further on, way out across the salty flats, a herd of over three hundred camels were being led by a group of raiskas to a market near the coast. Raiskas have a notorious reputation as fly-by-night seducers of village women as well as their more traditional roles as balladeer-historians, news carriers, and nomadic traders. I wondered what the decibel reading would be for a herd this size enmeshed in mating rituals.

Later on, at another village close to the edge of the Rann where this story began, I joined in a wedding until I felt that my presence was taking the limelight away from a visiting dignitary. He was being lauded to the skies by a "walking historian" (a *charan* or *bhaat*) whose job it was to act as the official greeter and sing long—very long—ballads in praise of the achievements and successes of each important visitor to this desolate region. A role similar to that of a wandering bard in medieval England.

The elders of the village sat around the dignitary, nodding agreement, as the historian sang his homage-filled rhymes. I always love to watch these old men of rural India. They seem to live such gentle, quiet lives, respected by their families, cared for

339

by their children, sleeping the hot days away in the shade of their homes, or huddled in whispery bunches, seemingly involved in the slow resolution of weighty matters.

I sat a distance from the wedding party so as not to interrupt their celebrations and chatted with a young man who had just returned from Bombay to his village to attend the festivities. We sipped tiny glasses of "dust" tea made from finely ground tea leaves mixed with cardamom, sugar, and milk. Very sweet but refreshing, particularly on hot days like this. He seemed a little bored by the endless (and to him) sycophantic, antics of the singing historian.

He spoke an English I could understand so I asked him about the daily routine of the old men of the village.

"Oh this is very much our tradition, this taking care of our grandfathers and great-grandfathers. A young man of the family will always be looking after him. The old man knows how things should be, and he sees that everything in his house and in his farm is in good order. When he is at home—the women have cleaned up and all those things—and he sits down. People come to call on him and take advice. If there is any calling to be done then he goes out and calls on them. Ladies of the houses, they are doing household work, grinding millet and corn, giving children their bath, making the bread, and seeing for all things for a rainy day. They clean up. If there are any rats here then they will see that a cat is there who finalizes everything. Then, if it is very hot, the old man may sleep—whenever the body requires it—and before sunset he eats his food and usually goes to sleep after sunset because there is no electricity here, you see. . . ."

I asked about the younger men too.

"Oh, a young man is very strong. He will go to the fields every day. He will take the animals out for grazing—or he may not. He may have a little porridge in the day to keep his reserves, then he will pay social calls, and the rest of the time they are sitting, discussing, talking. It is not a very hard life. But when it is time for cultivation, then you will find everyone out in the fields. Then it is very hard. But it does not last for long."

In an adjoining courtyard I could see four men in the shade of a line of round-walled granaries, furiously weaving blankets, which were stretched out on wooden trestles and using bright red, purple, and yellow threads of wool. They had obviously not been invited to the wedding and seem to be ignored by everyone.

"Oh, they are not of this village. They walk around, all over, and make blankets when they are asked."

"They seem to be working very hard."

"Well, yes. They work whatever time they wish but they must complete each blanket in three days or they will starve. God will not give them food. But the talent is there, isn't it, and as long as the talent is there, they do not have to bother about anything. No red flags of communism here y'see!" He laughed at his own wit. "And that is why we in India are safe from all that because it is embedded into us that we are satisfied with what God has given us. The cycle of karma plays a very important role in our day-to-day life and we say, if I don't have it, it is because God did not will it. I must do something good in this life for my rewards in the next one, d'y'see."

The singing historian was coming to the end of his ballad. His voice rose, the nodding of the old men increased, and the dignitary sat very straight and stern as the last refrains rang out. My companion translated (with a sly grin):

"And you have been just, with authority, with kindness and with love for our village. Here you sit in these four walls and we feel proud when we see you here, a descendent of the old house of our rulers that began here in the year 1212 A.D., in this place. But do not forget your duty. You are a political power and you are also a social power of great importance and we are all standing here and respecting you and remembering all the great deeds of your revered family."

The nodding reached a crescendo; the dignitary nodded gravely too, waved his hand limply at the wedding party, indicating that the celebration could now continue, with his blessing.

I wandered on around the village of tight-packed mud houses surrounded by high mud walls, trailed by a snake of children who giggled as I walked and then scampered and ran when I turned to talk to them.

A group of old men, in huge grubby turbans, sheltered in the shade of a goat-nibbled tree, the only tree I'd seen for miles, drinking something black in finger-long glasses. My English-speaking companion was still with me.

"That tea looks odd," I said.

He laughed, "It's not tea. It's a kind of opium. Only the old men drink it. It strengthens the weaknesses of the body."

"Really?"

His city cynicism flashed again. "Well—that's what they say. I think it just makes them sleepy."

The men invited us to join them in the shade of the tree. One of them pulled a heavy mortar of black rock from under his gray robes and placed a thimble-sized piece of something that looked like broken obsidian in the bowl.

"That's opium?" It wasn't at all like the little greasy balls I was to see later among the hill tribes in Thailand's Golden Triangle.

"Yes. Watch him now."

The old man, whose sulphur-colored turban seemed to be unraveling as he moved, pounded the hard black substance with a brass pestle into a fine powder. Then he added water, mixed it thoroughly, and strained it through a piece of white cloth into a clay bowl, which he offered to me.

"I'm not sure I really want any," I whispered to my companion.

"Oh, that's not a problem. Just pretend to drink," he whispered back. So I accepted the bowl, lifted it to my lips but kept them closed. I handed the bowl back. The men nodded, smiled, and extended cupped hands toward the man with the unraveling turban. He proceeded to pour a little of the muddy fluid into each set of hands. There was a murmur of ritual acknowledgments before they leaned forward and drank with eager sucking noises and licked the gravelly remains from their fingers.

"Now they all go asleep," said my urbane companion.

And that's just what they did.

A little later I met the old man whose brother had been lost in the Rann many years ago. After his sad tale of the terrors of the place and the spirits of "the whites" that haunted its barren wastes, I was anxious to drive on deeper into the blazing nothingness, past the sun-cracked skins of stone mountains, peeled off like onion layers. I wanted to see the herds of wild asses said to roam the eastern portion, the Little Rann, and the vast gatherings of flamingoes living and laying their eggs in "cities" of conical mud nests way out in the whiteness. So I drove on, leaving the village far behind.

Now there was not a tree or a shrub or even a single blade of grass anywhere. Nothing but an endless eye-searing blankness in every direction. The track was a vague incision in the salt, but beyond that was what I'd come all this way to see—nothing at all. Twenty thousand square miles of perfect flatness. No clouds, no movement, no life. Nothing.

It was like vanishing into some vast realm beyond the mind, way beyond thoughts, beyond feelings and sensations and all the convoluted tangles of consciousness. Even beyond awareness itself. A space so colorless, so silent, and so infinite that it seemed to be its own universe. And I just simply vanished into it. . . .

The sun was so hot in the dry air that I almost felt cold. I noticed this odd sensation at one point, about twenty-five miles into the whiteness, when I got out of the car and walked out across the cracked surface of the salt. After a couple of hundred yards or so the heat shimmers were so violent that I could no longer see the vehicle. I couldn't even see my own footprints due to the hardness of the salt and the intense shine radiating from it. Then I noticed the shivering, similar to the sensation of a burning fever when the hotter your body becomes the colder you feel. It may also have been a flicker or two of fear. I realized that I had done something rather stupid. Two hundred yards away from my landmark was the same as a hundred miles. I didn't know where the hell I was. I was lost!

I remembered tales of arctic explorers caught in sudden blizzards and dying in frozen confusion a few blinding yards from their tents. A few yards in a blizzard is infinity. This was infinity.

In retrospect the whole incident seems ridiculous, but at the time I sensed panic and the horrible reality that if I didn't retrace my steps within the next half hour or so I'd become a raving sun-sacrificed lunatic lost in this utter nothingness. Given shade I could have waited for the sun to drop and the shimmers to dwindle. But shade was as impossible as alchemist's gold here. There was no shade for two hundred miles.

And then, as suddenly as they had come, the shivers ceased and I felt an unearthly calm. I was neither hot nor cold now. The purity of the silence rang like a Buddhist bell, clear and endless. Here I was in the loneliest, emptiest place on earth, smiling inwardly and outwardly, utterly at peace, as if in some sensationless limbo state between life and death.

I burst out laughing at the zaniness of the whole predicament and my feet, without any prompting and guidance from the conscious part of me, walked me surely and certainly right back through the shimmers and the vast white silence to the car.

The Rann is still with me now. In times of silence I return to its silence; in a strange way I find it comforting and reassuring. We should all carry a Rann somewhere in our minds. A place of refuge and utter peace. A place of the mind but far beyond the mind.

I never did see the asses or the flamingoes or anything else out there. If I'd taken a camel rather than a car I could have continued further and deeper but, as it was, I was hampered by thick mud below the salty crust about thirty miles in. The monsoon had been late that year and the Rann had not yet been thoroughly baked by the sun to make it safe for my way of traveling. But that was fine. I'd found what I'd come looking for.

Absolute nothingness.

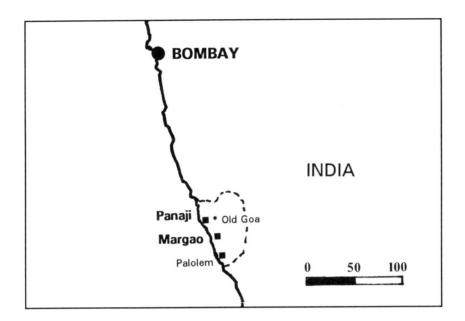

BOMBAY

INDIA

Panaji ■ • Old Goa
Margao ■
Palolem

0   50   100

15. INDIA— GETTING TO GOA

From Dreams, Into Dreams

What an enticing prospect.

A little piece of Portugal plopped down on the Indian sub-continent. Stucco and red pantile-roofed houses. White manue-line churches tingling with Baroque extravaganzas; shaded and shutter-windowed manor houses hidden in palm plantations; a redolent compost of cultures mellowed like fine-crusted port to offer outsiders the life and fire of India tamed by the grace and gentility of old Catholic Europe.

And beaches.

Ah, the beaches. The best in India (with the exception of a few in the southern state of Kerala); most of them undeveloped, golden white strands edged by dunes, tickled by sloppy surf,

345

where you can lie, naked as a babe if you wish, sipping aromatic cashew or coconut *feni* liqueur, wasting the days and nights away and waiting for the great Christmas psychedelic *pujas* of would-be hippies, wanna-be rock stars, world-wanderers by the buffalo cartload, and long-limbed nymphettes with blue eyes and golden hair—a world reunion of wackiness, once a year, every year. Guaranteed to tantalize the gypsy in your soul and galvanize the guru-gush that flows here like spiritual syrup, sweet and cloying but somehow liberating, invigorating. All a part of the life force in Goa for those who have settled in this ideal penny paradise; a wild, mind-stretching bacchanal for those who must soon trade their sandals for Florsheims, pop the bedroll back in the closet, slip off the bandana, and reenter the grist and grind of workaday worlds back home.

Goa has always been a goal. Way back in the scintillating sixties I worked for a while as an urban master planner in Tehran (long before the vengeful era of the Ayatollahs). The window of my office overlooked a small square or maidan in the heart of the city, a hundred yards or so down the road from the American embassy. And as I grappled at my desk with the challenges of the capital city's future growth, the eradication of its slums, the routes of metro systems and freeways, and the implementation of all of the Shah's grand schemes for the education and titillation of his "adoring subjects" (a phrase often used in the local Farsi newspapers), I would look down enviously at the travelers sprawled with their backpacks and tattered maps beneath the shade trees in the square. They were there every day, a different bunch, but strangely the same—Americans, Canadians, Europeans, Australians, all in the ritual garb of dusty jeans, discolored T-shirts, sweat-stained bandanas, torn boots, all coffee-bean brown from weeks of world-wandering, all making the great sixties "grand tour" from their homelands, through the wilds of Turkey, across Iran and Afghanistan, into the mythical nirvanas of Nepal, Kashmir, Kerala—and Goa.

Often I'd take my lunch down to the square and talk with these starry-eyed earth gypsies. A few were rapidly deteriorating into rambling dope-heads; others were young men, hair ponytailed by elastic bands, with weary boned-out faces, and young

346

women, leached of sensuality, sharp-edged and stern like gangly governesses, guarding their shrunken souls with Fort Knox imperiosity. But most were still road-fresh, bursting with the energy of exploration, kicking out the edges of their experience, in love with all the boundless possibilities of life and their own lives in particular. They spoke of the high Himalayas with the same reverence that a monk might use to address the sacraments. Truth would be found in those rarified regions, they believed; great wisdoms and insights awaited their arrival; they would discover a higher existence in these netherworlds far from the hedonistic bondage of our get-and-grab society. To them Kathmandu would be a lofty paradise, a place of visions in a land of simple centeredness. Sure, they demurred, drugs may form a part of their rituals of passage, but only as a means of release, you understand, not escape.

And then they'd talk about Goa. An idyllic corner of India where you could rent an old Portuguese beachside villa for pennies a day, feast on a pick-it-yourself vegetation diet with occasional banquets of lobsters and tiger prawns scooped up in bucketfuls from the warm surf—a place to sprawl in the sun, singing freedom songs, listening to long-haired gurus and dreaming dreams of perfect peace in the world.

I would return tingling with possibilities to my cramped office. Much as I loved my work and believed in its ultimate value, the frustrated wanderer inside kept up the old melody—there's more, there's more, there's so much more to see, there's so much more to be!

I knew that one day I'd be in Goa. It was just a matter of time really. . . .

Twenty-one years. It took twenty-one years and as I look at these words on the page I feel that familiar flicker of fear—time wasted, time passing, mortality, the terrible inevitabilities of life. But at least I had arrived. Not for the Christmas orgy though. In my years of travel I had developed an aversion to crowds—even crowds of flower-power people trying to resurrect the "good vibes" of the youthful sixties and seventies. I had become a seeker of quiet places—the hidden corners, the backroads, the nooks and crannies of the earth. Even in unspoiled Goa I intended to avoid the northern beaches—the hippie enclaves of Anjuna, Baga, and Calangute. I'd heard through the world-wanderers' grapevine of far more tranquil places to the south of the capital, Panaji, and the Mandovi River. "Go beyond Margao," I'd been advised. "Almost to the southern edge of Goa. Go to Palolem, my friend."

But first, I had to get out of Bombay. I'd only intended to stay in the city a day or two making travel plans. But Bombay is not an easy place to leave. A casual conversation on a bus traveling south from the state of Gujarat had led to meetings with prominent members of the Jain sect (a religion appealing particularly to the more affluent and literate members of Indian society). Next thing I knew I was a houseguest in some elaborate mansion on Bombay's "gold coast," dining on fine vegetarian fare and spending time with one of the sect's ascetic gurus.

"This man was a very famous businessman, owner of many hotels," my host explained. "But he was also a great thinker, much respected by his peers, and he decided to take *mukti*, to become a sadhu. He sold all his possessions—his houses, his hotels, all his lands, he made his wife and his children comfortable, and then he said good-bye and set out to walk across India dressed only in a dhoti and eating only a little rice every day. He was not a young man at all, he was over sixty when he did this, and he could not—he is not permitted—to travel any other way but on foot, sleeping on the ground or at the temples as he walked. And now he is with us for a while at my temple—yes, I and my family built this special temple for the Jains of northern Bombay—and we are very happy indeed to have him here. You will meet him. You will like him."

And I did like him. He was rather similar to Gandhi in appearance; small, thin, spectacled, and with a smile that was not so much enlightened as entertaining. His eyes sparkled. We had a wide-ranging discussion, touching on everything from Jane Fonda and the international implications of the McDonald's empire to the problems of Sri Lanka and the nutritive properties of Indian rice.

Then he began, at first a little formally, to explain the tenents of "Arhat Darshana" (Jainism) in a lilting speech full of Indian-English phraseology: "You see it is very natural for the intelligentsia to strive to free themselves in all ways possible from the pains of major diseases of the soul in the form of births, senility, and death existing in the putrid body-cell, which is full of impurities, and it becomes inevitable to have various thoughts and musings in this behalf."

He paused and smiled that enticing smile. He seemed to be amused by everything around him—himself and me and particularly a group of nearby worshipers who hung onto his every word. He leaned over and whispered, "I don't think they understand my English very well but they listen to everything so— what can one do? I am hoping you understand what it is that I am saying to you."

I nodded. "Two days ago," I said, "I'd never even heard of Jainism, and I appreciate your taking time to help me understand."

He giggled, then he reached over and touched my shoulder. "My friend. I am now a sadhu; I own nothing, I owe no obligations, I have only time. Nothing else is of any importance."

He sipped some water from a paper cup. My host, who sat cross-legged next to me, whispered, "He is not well. We are bringing in a doctor this afternoon. He has just returned from a walk of over one thousand kilometers. We are worried about his health."

I looked at my host's face. He was also an important Bombay businessman and years of worries and deal-making and financial tanglings hung heavy around his eyes and over his furrowed forehead. The guru, on the other hand, seemed so full of life and energy he almost floated on his raised wooden platform. It was questionable who needed the doctor most.

"And so," the guru began again, "we Indians are a peculiar people you know. Especially on account of our powerful culture and instinct of self-confidence, there has always been considerable reflection, cogitation, and imitation in the field of philosophy. This I think you must agree on?"

I nodded again. It was the Indian capacity for rapacious thought and vibrant spiritual values in the midst of seeming societal chaos that attracted many of the Western world-wanderers here in the first place.

"Consequently, you see, the quest for Muktivada—you

might call this liberationalism—has become the staple hymn of our country, and that is why only knowledge, which is liberation, reverberates and resounds. And Arhat Darshana—Jainism —came about to make the path of liberation smooth, unobstructed, and easily available. The reason for this is that in no other religion, as in Jainism, is found so exquisite an arrangement and composition of means and materials, so rationalistically and methodically devised for the realization of the path of salvation. You understand?"

An eloquent preamble I thought and nodded. But what of the essence?

He looked at me and smiled. "You have a phrase in your country—not a popular phrase with us Jains of course," he giggled, "but your politicians say it—was it Mr. Reagan, no I think it was your Mr. Mondale—'Where's the beef?' "

We both laughed. This was no cave-dwelling hermit. Only two years ago this man had been your typical high-flying, newspaper-reading, three-piece-suit Indian entrepreneur.

"Well—you see—in the doctrine of the Jain philosophy we believe that the ultimate principle is always logic and there can be no principle devoid of logic, you understand. We call this *Syadvada*—the means by which one acquires the full and complete knowledge of any state of things from all different and diverse points of view.

"Syadvada is known as the 'compromising system of philosophy'—the great theory of relativity by Dr. Einstein is in many parts only a mere shadow the doctrine of syadvada. In this philosophy there is not even an iota of space for imaginary conceptions or superstitions. Many wonderful discoveries of science—so-called 'new' discoveries—are to be found long before in Jain doctrines. We are rationalistic philosphers you understand? Theories of sound waves; the interpenetration of matter; the instinct and feelings of vegetable life; theories of atoms and molecules—all these and many more detailed 'scientific' descriptions you can find in the most ancient—and I mean truly ancient—Jain readings."

The sadhu sipped again from his glass. My host nudged me.
"Ask him about Atma," he said.
"What's that?"

"The soul. It is the foundation of Jainism."

So I asked the sadhu to explain Atma and he smiled that smile again.

"Long or short?"

"Long or short what?"

"If you can spare me two days I will prove to you without any doubt whatsoever the existence of the soul. Otherwise . . ."

"Let's try the short version."

"Yes. Very wise. Life is also short."

However his explanation was not so short or so 'scientific' as I had hoped. I became rather lost in his complex philosophical knots.

". . . and so you must conclude," he said finally, "that the soul in all living things is like the soul in us. There is absolutely no difference between the soul of an ant and the soul of an elephant and your very own atma or soul. Contraction and expansion are the characteristic attributes of every living being, and due to the bondage of karmas, a soul finds itself born again and again in any one of millions of forms of existence."

My host had previously explained the great length to which Jains will go to avoid disturbing the soul of any other living creature, even to the point of placing gauze masks over their mouths to prevent the accidental intake of flies.

The sadhu continued: "As fire in firewood and ghee in milk are not perceptible to us although inherently latent in them, the soul is also not perceptible though it exists in your body. And when the soul comes to know its true nature, it evinces inclination to practice Dharma—it breaks the bondage of the cycle of life and death, the karma—and becomes free. That immortal soul becomes the enjoyer of permanent, continuous, uninterrupted, and infinite happiness in the region of final absolution, which we call the state of mukti."

I've always had a problem with the concept of perfect bliss —harps, haloed angels sitting on clouds, thinking nothing but blissful thoughts in the perfect and heavenly Hollywood filmset. I've tended to assume that happiness exists as a relative state, as an antidote to unhappiness: The peace after the pain; the reward after the effort; the kiss after the crisis. But maybe that short-changes life. Maybe "the pursuit of happiness" is really not the point at all—it's the attainment of happiness, untrammeled happiness, here and now, that is our birthright.

The man sitting in front of me had cleared away all the irrelevancies of his life—even his wife and family—to take mukti. My host had told me he himself would never have the courage to go so far. "I'm what we call a Shravaka Dharma—a religious layman. And even that is very difficult, like trying to be a good Christian. Enjoying worldly things, but in moderation. That is why sadhus like our sadhu are so very important. They remind us of what is possible in this life. He is a tangible example. His way is very hard—he cannot use fire to warm himself; he cannot eat any living thing including vegetables; he lives in absolute celibacy—even if he touches the garment of a female he must undergo painful expiation, Prayashchitta—he can only wear unsewn pieces of cloth; he cannot use any form of transport, or any umbrella or shoes; if he wants to remove bodily hair he must pull each hair out by himself, he can only eat once a day and cannot even enjoy a glass of water after sunset. . . ."

The sadhu was smiling again. "I think I have spoken too long. You must be tired."

I was. But he looked even more spritely than when we arrived. "You possibly understand far more than you think you do. It is always hard to see things from a new direction. As I told you, in Jainism we believe in Syadvada—the need to understand and tolerate many different ways of seeing things. I think you have a story about two blind men trying to define an elephant from a few little bits and pieces. Each conceives something entirely different from the other and yet, to a limited extent, each is perfectly correct. Given the appropriate additional information they would arrive at the same conclusion. We believe that to comprehend the real nature of anything one must pay due regard to all points of view and recognize that we may all be correct. So many philosophies—and religions—emphasize only one way of seeing and reject all other interpretations. We believe in complete tolerance—the unity of larger truth—an all-encompassing truth in which everyone, everything, is a part. The greatness of the state of Siddha—true universal brotherhood through tolerance—or, if you wish, love!"

* * *

Bombay certainly requires tolerance. In spite of its Anglo-European façade of monolithic Victorian buildings, graceful parks with round-the-clock cricket matches, double-decker buses, fancy high-rise apartment towers, elegant world-class hotels, and remarkably clean beaches along the ocean waterfront—in spite of all the trappings of a vibrant cosmopolitan city—there lurks eternal India herself. Beggars, countless thousands—maybe millions—of them in their sackcloth and tin-walled shanty towns behind the broad boulevards; the night streets littered with sleeping bodies; the endless offerings of "friendship" from drug pushers and sidewalk hustlers; the chaotic prattle and screech of traffic mixed with bullock carts and cows and mangy dogs and rivers of jostling bodies; the gross extravagances of the wealthy meeting head to head (but never perceiving) the utter degradation and squalor of the lower castes and the untouchables and the burnt-out dope-heads heaped like corpses under the Gateway of India (an enormous basalt arch across from the Taj Hotel), commemorating the 1911 visit of George V, during India's heyday as Britain's "jewel in the crown."

But it's time to go to Goa! Peace and palms in a true penny paradise. And a boat to take me there, a big one with three decks. I chose the middle level—second class—and arrived early enough to stake a claim to a section of wooden bench in readiness for the night. Talk about time warp. I could have been back in the sixties. Even out of season, the deck soon became a playground for a full range of hoary world-wanderers; dewey-eyed students fresh out of first-year college; a video team from Japan who insisted on interviewing everyone even though no one could understand their questions; two elderly ladies in horsy tweeds and brogues, fully equipped with umbrellas, binoculars, and a small library of guidebooks neatly packed in a pigskin case, and the inevitable group of sullen Germans, bronze-bodied and bored.

Green canvas sheets, salt-stained and torn, were stretched over the deck to give some relief from the afternoon sun. The water moved as slow as syrup, slammed into submission by the heat. Lukewarm soft drinks were offered at outrageous prices; the smell of curried cooking and little acrid bidis—the universal

353

Indian cigarette—wafted up from the lower deck where I could see brown bodies crammed together like Coke bottles in a bottling plant.

On our deck everyone seemed rather subdued at first in the flesh-melting heat. But then the whistles and bells and hoots began and, with an alacrity remarkable in India, we were off, wallowing out into the Arabian Sea. Everyone suddenly started talking excitedly like children on a day outing from school; fishy breezes blew in and sweat dried; someone started up with a guitar, and illicit aromas floated around under the canvas awnings. All we needed was a chorus of "Kumbaya" or "This Land" and we'd be back in the heydays of Seeger and Baez and Dylan and Beatlemania and Kerouac and flowers in our hair and love in the air and hardly a care—anywhere.

At dawn, Panaji is pure Graham Greene. Sprawled lazily along the banks of the Mandovi River, the capital of Goa presents a shadowy, moss-flecked façade to the newcomer. Parts of a collapsed bridge across the river peep out of the slow rosy-red waters; a ferry now provides access to the other side, the only way north to the twenty-mile-long stretches of old hippie beaches. But behind the sultry river frontage, Panaji possesses colonial charm. Small parks and squares with parasol shade under banyan trees and palms; swathes of jacarandas, flowering bahuinia, and gulmohars (with fire-bright red blossoms) softening the sharp edges of the newer construction. And in the center, the oh-so-Portuguese triple white towers of Our Lady of Immaculate Conception rise up over the city, atop an elaborate staircase of carved white stone. Behind the church is the old town of clustered yellow and ochre stucco houses with white trim, verandahs, and red pantile roofs. Narrow cobbled alleys wind up around a steep hill; flights of worn steps lead higher to once-elaborate mansions, now a little unkempt, but still utterly Portuguese in flavor.

During the Portuguese occupation, which endured for over 450 years following the arrival of the conquistadores under Afonso de Alburquerque in 1510, this little fiefdom of Goa (a mere thirty by fifty miles in size) was known proudly as "Goa Dourada"—Golden Goa. Cut off from the rest of India by the tangled mass of the Sahyadri mountain ranges in the east, Goa has always been a "place-apart," a green, forested "pearl of the Orient," said to have been created by the Sea God when Parasurama—an incarnation of the Hindu's Lord Vishuu—shot his golden arrow into the Arabian Sea to determine the site of the perfect place for penance. Traces have been found of neolithic occupation as far back as 2000 B.C., and for over 1600 years, from 300 B.C., to 1200 A.D., tiny Goa was ruled by Hindu kings and their vassals. Later known as the "Paradise of India," the state flourished as a prosperous mercantile trading center, the "Emporium of the West Coast," famous throughout the world for its Chinese silks and porcelain, Persian pearls, Indian spices, cotton, and indigo.

With the arrival of St. Francis Xavier in 1542, a relatively compassionate melding of Hindu and Christian cultures occurred, manifested in magnificent Catholic churches and palaces and unique Hindu temples that somehow managed to combine both architectural influences in a vibrant mélange of Baroque, classic-revival and Indian styles, complete with octagonal campaniles. True, there were anticolonialist tensions and Inquisition-style Portuguese purges against the Hindus, but Goa seemed to avoid many of the worst atrocities of European occupation in other parts of the Orient, and even after Goa's hasty bloodless "liberation" by India in 1961, the proud populace insisted on maintaining its unique cultural identity.

"We are Goans first, then Hindu or Christian—or maybe a bit of both." I was lucky. On my first afternoon I'd found a guide with his own car and a very benevolent attitude about daily rates. Angelo Fernandes was pure Goan—blithe-spirited, open-faced, and devoted to his little Rhode Island–sized country of a million or so inhabitants.

"So—where do we go?" He seemed as ready for adventure as I was.

"Well—I don't particularly want to visit the hippie beaches up north, and I'm not really interested in the resorts. I want to see Goa as it was before the sixties—the real Goa. Maybe the south?"

"But nobody goes there."

"Good. Then that's where we're going."

And so we did. But not without a token visit to the strange colonial remnant of Old Goa, a few miles east of Panaji. I'd heard about this place from one of my many fleeting companions on the Bombay ferry.

"Weird place, man. I mean—really spacy. All these old palaces and cathedrals—they had about six hundred churches there once—can you believe that—six hundred! All left to rot. Just like someone came in and said, forget it, man, and they left it, sort of half-ass finished and spooky. You gotta go there. India's a weird place, but this place is really something, man."

Actually it was a little too familiar. The spookiness may have existed when Old Goa, Velha Goa, "The Rome of the Orient," was abandoned as the capital in 1843 in favor of Panaji. At that time, the place was rife with disease and plagues and people refused to trade there. As the vines and weeds and moss took over the stern classical-style edifices the city must have had a decadent ghostly charm. "Those who have seen the glories of Old Goa have seen Lisbon," goes the old saying, but I found it hard to see the correlation in today's few scattered, primped-up remnants of convents and churches set in dull engineer-inspired gardens. Even the great Basilica of Bom Jesus, where devotees used to congregate once a year on feast day, to kiss the toe of St. Francis Xavier's "miraculously incorruptible remains" (a custom now discontinued following the removal of the toe—actually it was bitten off—by a fanatical female worshiper a few years back) had little of the grace and delicacy of Goa's other Portuguese churches. Possessing the bulk and bombasity of a fortress, external ecclesiastical accoutrements seem to have been added as an afterthought. Only the wild Baroque exuberance of the sixty-foot-high carved altarpiece and the shimmering cherub-graced silver casket of St. Francis gave it authenticity as a serious house of worship.

But the little church at Sancoale, a few miles to the south, is the epitome of Goan grace and architectural sensitivity. Angelo had been saving it as a surprise, and as we wound along the road beside the River Zuari, here she was—a tiny white confection, set by a small bay against a hill of eucalyptus and palms. Frangipani and flowering bougainvillea provided flecks of color, which made the delicately pinacled exterior appear even whiter, and lacy, with filigrees of decoration around its modest pediment. A perfect miniature creation, in perfect scale and harmony with its setting. No wonder people fall in love with little Goa.

Time to eat.

It was a modest beachside place, nothing fancy and not far from the Charles Correa's Cubist Cidade-de-Goa resort, one of a handful of such enclaves on Goa's still undeveloped eighty-mile coastline.

We were the only customers and sat at a window table overlooking the ocean. I'd eaten nothing of any interest since my farewell bacchanal at Bombay's Taj hotel luncheon buffet (one of India's most extravagant culinary displays) and expected the worst in this empty restaurant.

My fears were utterly unfounded.

Two little palate-cleansing bowls of a spicy seafood broth known as *tomyupkung* and a plate of steamed mussels in a garlic, cumin, and wine sauce appeared within minutes of our arrival, along with two loaves of crusty Portuguese bread, hot and smelling of San Francisco sourdough. We obviously didn't eat fast enough. Another appetizer followed in a couple of minutes —this time delicate slices of home-smoked mackerel wrapped in little pouches of palm leaves. Then, with hardly a pause, came slivers of perfectly cooked suckling pig, crisp-skinned and juicy.

Even Angelo seemed surprised by the speed of delivery. We considered asking them to slow things down a little, but whoever was creating these magnificent degustation dishes back in the kitchen was well and truly on a roll. We decided to let him be and just enjoy his handiwork.

The chef was tireless. Tiny crisp-crusted vegetable samosas redolent with familiar Indian spices were followed by slices of *apa de camarao,* a sort of pie with a golden rice crust over a succulent mix of whole prawns cooked in coconut milk. Then a slight pause before the main dish, Pomfret Recheiado, a whole fish filled with a rich pungent stuffing of sour red masala and grilled until the skin crackled like cornflakes when you cut it.

This was too much. But whoever it was working back there hadn't finished with us. Small bowls of vegetable vindaloo were accompanied by tiny crushed rice and lentil pancakes and, before we could raise our hands in defeat, out came a masala of miniature pink crabs in a sauce brimming with coriander, flecks of chili peppers, cumin, and garam masala. All this washed down with *capitos* of heavy Goan red wine, a little like young port but far more pungent. Angelo staggered to the kitchen and returned a few minutes later.

"Oh—she is so beautiful!"

"Who?"

"The cook—it's a girl who is cooking all these things. She is . . ." he sought the most complimentary adjectives but failed. "You must see her. I will ask."

He vanished into the kitchen again and seemed to be gone a long time.

And then she emerged.

She couldn't have been much more than a teenager. A dark-eyed, golden-skinned Goan madonna, blushing a little, and carrying a round dish of something resembling crème caramel. Angelo was grinning like a gibbon.

"You know what this is?"

"No, but it looks good."

"This is bebinca. She can make bebinca! This takes hours of work. It's eggs, coconut milk, sugar . . . what else?"

The girl whispered something in a voice that sounded like a spring breeze.

"I don't know how to say in English. Special spices—a special mix. Every cook makes a different mix. This is a very traditional Goan dish—but very, very difficult to make."

He looked at his new love with adoring eyes.

"Isn't she . . . ?"

The girl blushed even more, placed the dish on the table, and scampered back to the kitchen.

And that was the last we saw of her. The bebinca was superb—light as a cloud, a melt-in-the-mouth creation that left the palate sweetened and refreshed. But Angelo's only thought was for the girl, and he set off for the kitchen again.

This time he was unlucky.

A large man with a thick black mustache, large by Goan standards at least, stood by the door. Angelo made some complimentary remarks about the food, the man nodded but seemed aloof and wary. My friend returned with the bill. It was for a ridiculously small amount, hardly more than you'd pay at a roadside hamburger joint back home. He looked utterly forlorn and defeated. Love has teeth behind a pair of pretty lips, and he'd been bitten. His plate of bebinca sat untouched; his romantic urges had been crushed. The man was obviously guarding the door. Protocols had been infringed, and it was clear there'd be no more dallying with the pretty cook today.

"You can always come back," I said.

Angelo seemed not to hear me and we drove away in silence.

It's the green you notice at first, particularly the bright sparkling green of the rice paddies between the palms and eucalyptus, and the lacquered leaves of the cashew trees and the frilly fronds of bamboo. Everywhere you look is green, receding into turquoise as the land rises to the jungled hills along Goa's eastern border. And peeping coyly through the plantations are the shuttered windows of the old Portuguese farms, mansions, and occasional stately palacios, mostly single-storied and set in gardens of flowering bushes. Many have central courtyards, usually with a small fountain where the sound of playing water combined with deep shade offers respite from the summer sun.

Village market stalls brimmed with fresh fruit—coconuts, bananas (from clusters of thumb-sized beauties to the famous foot-long giants from Moira), jackfruit, papaya, pineapples, chickoo, custard apples, and mangoes. And every community, no matter how small, had its own feni distillery producing the araklike liquor that is the lifeblood of Goa. Coconut feni tends to be the most popular—too popular, according to the government, which has seen the export crop of coconuts dwindle to a trickle as farmers leach the sap from fronds where green coconuts should have been maturing in great bunches.

I preferred the cashew feni, which uses the cashew "apple," normally discarded or used for pig food after the removal of the nut. A widespread cottage industry now exists where locals ferment the crushed apples in battered copper vats, usually in a barn or the back room of a taverna, and distill the heated mash through a crude system of coiled pipes into earthenware jars.

The first run is a relatively mild concoction known as *urrack*, which sells for pennies a glass just about everywhere. But connoisseurs await the second distillation, when urrack is mixed with more fermented juice and run through the pipes again to produce the far more potent feni, which is then aged (a couple of weeks is usually considered more than adequate) in four-gallon earthenware jars known as *causos*.

Feni and fry-heat sun don't mix. A few samples in a village near Margao left me an unusually passive passenger for most of the afternoon.

My awakening came rather abruptly. Our windows were down to catch the cooling breezes as Angelo drove through the narrow streets of a nondescript village north of Chaudi. Suddenly the windshield was awash in colored water—bright splashes of blue and red as little bags burst on the glass. Then they were coming through the side windows. A red one burst on Angelo's forehead and he looked as though he'd been shot at point-blank range. I opened my mouth to laugh and received a blue one in midchest, which exploded with a pop, spraying my clothes, my notebooks, the inside of the windshield. More followed. We were awash in blue and red.

"The windows! Up!" gurgled Angelo, spitting out the sweet dye.

Too late. More bags whizzed in before we could raise our defences.

I was fully awake now. "What the hell . . ."

"Holi! Holi!"

"What?"

"It's Holi—it's the Shigmo Festival. I forget. They said it had been banned this year."

We had reached the edge of the village. Our attackers were way back down the road, roaring with laughter, waving masks and colorful cloaks and beating drums. Angelo couldn't decide whether to be angry or join in the fun. Then he giggled.

"You! You're all blue."

"And you, my friend, are very red—and blue."

"I should have remembered." He was still giggling.

"What's it all about?"

"It's spring. February is the beginning of spring. People

360

sprinkle each other with packets of colored powder—they're supposed to be flower colors. Spring flowers. Sometimes they mix the powder with water. It's okay. It washes away."

I looked in the mirror. My beard, nose, and cheeks were bright blue, not to mention most of my clothes.

Angelo's giggles had got the better of him. He was becoming quite hysterical looking at me.

"You are a crazy man!"

I looked down. In my lap lay a little bag of blue dye, unexploded.

"Angelo. Look at yourself in the mirror."

He turned the mirror. I couldn't resist.

Thwack! I burst the bag on top of his wind-blown hair, and the blue water exploded down his neck, round his eyes, and ran in rivulets down the red dye already coating his face. Now he was purple!

"Two crazy men now."

We were like kids. He dipped his hands in his streaming face and flicked the spray at my beard. I retaliated. It became a water battle. The inside of the car was dripping with the stuff. We couldn't stop laughing.

"Happy spring," he bellowed, spraying me again.

"Happy spring to you too!"

Goa and the Goans take themselves quite seriously in spite of their penchant for enjoying life and smiling all the time. They consider their little country, relatively affluent in Indian terms, to be distinct from, and superior to, most of Asia and the Orient. You can see it in the popular roadside sign:

MORE WORK, MORE FOOD, MORE ELECTRICITY.
LET'S MAKE GOA A LAND OF PLENTY.

Even the man selling gaudy postcards on the beach by the classy Oberoi resort at Bogmalo seemed far too well dressed and disinterested for the job. As soon as the tourists left, he leaped on his bicycle, combed his black hair, and departed with a professional expression on his face as if he were off to something far more worthy of his time and intellect.

361

An elderly gentleman in charge of a food concession at Miramar (wonderful Indo-Chinese-Thai concoctions at these places) left the cooking to his young assistant and joined me at my table to discuss the revival of *Life* magazine and the intricacy of British politics.

Goa is a little weary of its image as a cheap haven for freaks and potheads. Beach signs issue strict warnings:

DON'T DABBLE IN DRUGS
IT IS A SOCIAL EVIL AND CRIME
PUNISHABLE WITH 10–30 YEARS IN PRISON
BEWARE OF THE MENACE!

And they remain proud to the point of paranoia about their own language, Konkani. Whatever you do, you don't call it a dialect. They see it as a distinct and separate language, well over a thousand years old, and once subject to ferocious persecution by their Portuguese overlords.

"It is a perfect language for poetry," I was informed by a man who ran a newsstand in Margao. "We have many literary prizes for Konkani and many fine writers like Bakibab Borkav, R. V. Pandit, Nagesh Karmali—and of course, Manohar Sardesai. But it is a struggle. The Indian government does not encourage its use, so," he laughed, "we use it even more."

He showed me a piece of yellowed paper with finely inscribed print in Konkani. He translated:

Into the realm unknown to man
Into the heart unfound on earth
Into the eternity unread in life

"I keep this," he said, and patted the pocket next to his heart.

While officially Goa is now a part of India, the Goans insist on maintaining their rich cultural identity. Angelo had been correct. There had been efforts made to suppress the celebrations of Holi—"In some places there were some problems last year with protestors and riots, so the government said it must be banned. But Goans don't like to be told what to do. We are free people—and it must stay that way!" Angelo insisted.

Up north, at Ajuna and even Mandrem and Arambol beaches, you'll still find the remnants of the flower-power days —defiant freaks, mellowed monks, overlanders, gypsies, poets, guitar pickers, seers, searchers, artists, punks, all dancing, philosophizing, hash-happy under the light of the great silver Goan moon. Maybe one day I'll go and play hippie-for-a-day or a week or join in the riotous pujas or dance naked with the wild ones. But not this time. I wanted seamless days for a while; no distractions, no diversions. Just me and the sea and the frangipani and a glass of feni and maybe some prawns and fresh fruit picked from wild trees by the beach. . . .

At Palolem, way to the south near the border with the state of Karnataka, I found my paradise, a true "pocket of singular languor": This was the Goa I had come looking for. The Goa before the world-wanderers and truth seekers arrived. An arc of sparkling sand on a bay no more than a mile wide, bound on the northern edge by a jungle-covered headland that kept the water calm. A village of simple palm-frond-and-bamboo homes, similar to those in Samoa, set under the palm trees; a few fishing boats carved from tree trunks; surf nets drying on the white sand; a tiny taverna with its own feni shed, a plain room where I could stay for a dollar a day if and when I wished; a young girl who cooked the best banana pancakes I have ever tasted and made fresh curry sauce every day, carefully mixing it from hand-pounded spices she kept in little cotton bags.

Angelo had to return to Panaji. He told me I'd have no problem getting back up north when I was ready. In a way I was sorry to see him go. In another way I was delighted to be here alone, not a part of anything and yet feeling to be a part of everything.

Maybe I'll write a bit. Maybe take some photographs or sketch. Maybe read a little about Syadvada (the sadhu in Bombay had given me one of his own books on Jainism).

Or maybe not . . .

The days would define their own rhythms—new thoughts, coming and going as they may. Life doesn't offer too many opportunities like this, even for a travel fanatic like me. Time seemed unimportant. Plans would be remade. Later.

PEACE AT PALOLEM
GOA

I remembered the little Konkani saying shown to me by the newsstand man in Margao:

> Into the realm unknown to man
> Into the heart unfound on earth
> Into the eternity unread in life

16. THAILAND'S GOLDEN TRIANGLE

Vagabonding Among the Hill Tribes

It's just like moon walking. The last few miles on this almost-invisible jungle path have been relatively free of obstacles and we bounce along on cushiony ground. There was a bad patch an hour or so ago—nothing but creepers, vines, roots, rocks, and nasty little hollows that you couldn't see until it was too late. San, my guide, has stumbled a couple of times but keeps on smiling (he never stops smiling); my tumbles are rather more regular and my smile is buckled. I have no idea where we are, but the mossy smoothness of the path has mellowed me into "mai pen rai" ("it doesn't really matter"), a typical state of mind in Thailand.

In the dense, dark underbrush of the teak forest, there are

clicks and cracks and crackles, but we don't see anything. I've been bitten all over, but I never see the biters. It's an odd feeling, to be so intensely part of something and yet to feel aloof, as if I were floating a few feet above my battered body, bemused by the whole effort.

"Soon be coming," says San. (He's said that for the last two hours.) But maybe this time he's right. The jungle seems to be thinning out, and I can see flickers of hills ahead with tiny fields scattered over them.

If someone had told me a couple of weeks ago that I'd be hiking through the notorious "Golden Triangle" of northern Thailand, smack bang in the middle of the world's most lucrative opium-growing region, I'd have laughed and continued to enjoy the pampering pleasures of Bangkok. But now here I am, within spitting distance of Burma and Laos and the famed Mekong River, doubtless trespassing in some drug warlord's territory, and being strangely unperturbed by my arrogance. San has warned me about Khun Sa and his army of five thousand ferocious "opium soldiers," telling me a few unpleasant tales of their penchant for bamboo torture and the casual dismemberment of intruders. " 'S'okay now. Wrong time for poppies. No problem."

In contrast to the bright, rich patina of twentieth-century Bangkok and the more affluent southern region of Thailand, the wild hill country of the north hides hundreds, some say thousands, of tiny primitive villages inhabited by tribal migrants from Burma and China who have been easing southward into this wild territory for centuries. The broken, virtually impassable terrain of deep valleys and jungle-clad mountains has allowed the seven basic tribal groupings to retain most of their ancient cultural trails.

It's an anthropological paradise up here, and courageous observers often venture into this wilderness to study the contrasting mores of the primitive peoples. They compare the desire for "mutual spiritual harmony" of the Karen with the egocentric "me-oriented culture" of the Lisu and the "decorum-at-all-costs" attitudes of the Yao. They are boggled by the contrasts of tribal dress: the dour blacks of the Lahu contrasted with the colorful extravaganzas of the Akha and embroidered richness of Meo costumes. They are intrigued by the wide variety of sexual customs, even among different tribal groups living close together in the same valley. The Karen, for example, believe that one of few appropriate times for courtship is at funerals, whereas the Yao and Meo encourage relatively "free love." The Lawa have very strict taboos against licentious activities and, after marriage, Akha couples often have to limit their lovemaking activities to a tiny isolated hut raised high on stilts so as not to offend their house spirits or one of the ten thousand "codes of conduct" that govern every aspect of their lives!

Those who take the time and trouble to explore the hill country gain fascinating insights into the way our ancestors must have lived thousands of years ago. And while Thailand's popular present-day King Rama IX provides modern-day citizens with a treasured link to the country's rich heritage, the hill tribes are an elusive reminder of far more ancient cultures and origins. In these hills you walk hand-in-hand with prehistory.

The twelve-hour overnight public bus ride north from Bangkok to the hill country was a marvel of modern comfort (they take bus journeys very seriously here). The modest ten-dollar fare included a supper packed in a ribbon-wrapped box, constant refills of Coke with Thai "scotch," a video TV screen visible from our reclining seats, a stop at 3:00 A.M. for a second supper (five courses) in a huge roadside restaurant, and personal pampering all the way by three beautiful stewardesses.

We arrived in the northern city of Chiang Mai, Thailand's second largest city. It was cooler here with a pleasant breeze tumbling down from the hazy hills. I wanted to be off immediately but was told my guide had been delayed. So I agreed to make the ritual round of the city's famous craft workshops, visiting silversmiths, umbrella makers, silk weavers and teak carvers. I found myself impressed by the skill and patience of the artisans (but annoyed by the "tourist trap" tone of the tour).

Soon Chiang Mai was far behind. I sat happily with San in the front seat of a four-wheel-drive Jeep as we headed for the hills, across the flat paddies where peasants winnowed rice in huge straw baskets, past mud holes occupied by wallowing water buffalos, pausing to buy fresh lychees from a roadside stall, watching villagers fish with a hammock-net (and avoid the local alligator!). We switched to a boat for a journey north up the Mekong River (memories of Vietnam), warily taking photographs of tribal people on the Laos side. Our boat carried the likeness of Che Guevara on its prow, which seemed most appropriate in the circumstances.

Finally we were on our own to find the hill tribes—just the two of us, slogging up steep mountain tracks, going deeper and deeper into the dense jungle, hacking at bushes, skirting fallen trees, crossing turbulent streams, cooking bits of dried chicken and rice on a battered butane stove in the evenings, and sleeping on lightweight plastic sheets spread out on piled leaves.

San always seemed to know where we were going even though he claimed our route as a "first" for him. On the third day we were hardened hikers but we realized we had better watch out for ourselves in the heart of this mysterious Golden Triangle.

We scrabbled over the next ridge, down into a more open valley where trees had been cleared and small fields were planted with corn and beans. A few men in black trousers and waistcoats sat around in groups watching the women hoe and weed the rows. Higher up a village of large thatch-and-bamboo huts perched on stilts a few feet above the steeply sloping hillside. The place seemed poor and bedraggled. Smoke wafted through the thatch roofs, big pigs waddled around or lay like fat black cushions in dust holes under the houses, children in black pants and skirts watched us curiously. At first no one seemed particularly interested in our sudden arrival, but gradually the children began to cluster and a large stern-faced woman with short-cropped hair approached us, talking staccato fashion in the local dialect. San listened intently.

"She asks to know if we've come to buy."

"Buy what?"

"Opium."

We both laughed, shook our heads, and San explained politely that we were hiking the hills and taking photographs. Her face became even more stern; she stood straight and pointed to her head (she was obviously used to giving orders).

"I think she wants you to take photo of her."

So I did. It was not one of my classics though; the subject stood as if defiantly waiting for a final firing squad volley and seemed definitely displeased with us.

Then, wobbling down the hill, came an elderly man in black, carrying an old contraption of bamboo pipes bound together with twine. The stern woman shouted something at him, and he began to play an eerie melody of half tones and quavering minors while a dozen kids danced around him in the dust.

"He plays the 'Kaen' for our welcome. They do not understand who we are but they play this for visitors from other villages," San explained.

I was starving and hoping for an offer of food. But then San suddenly went very still again. He watched the woman talking to two men a few yards away. Something was not right. People were moving in from the fields below and climbing up toward the village.

"David, I think we should go now," he said quietly. "Smile and hold your hands together and do wai."

I felt ridiculous but trusted San's instinct. We walked slowly backward up the hill doing our bobbing wais. The man with the bamboo instrument played louder and louder—it didn't seem like a welcome at all now, more like a wailing siren echoing in the hills.

"David" said San, "when we get past this house we must run to the trees. Please do this."

As soon as we were out of sight we ceased all the wai-ing and scampered into the jungle. It was suddenly cool again as we crashed through the brush following a pig path. We were both panting, and I could hear that strange wailing way back in the village. I knew we had made the right decision but didn't understand San's reasons. A long time later, after we had run ourselves to a standstill, he explained between great gulps of air:

"It is my mistake. I missed the sign. They were waiting for someone special. I think they think we are spies—from the government—maybe it was the cameras. And that man was not playing hello on his kaen, he was warning the village about us. . . ."

We panted in unison.

"It's a good thing we left, San."

"It is a very good thing. Yes," agreed San.

A day or so later, what could have been a disastrous expedition turned into a delightful interlude with the Meo tribe. Many long jungle miles away from our dangerous encounters we began to enjoy a more mellowed experience. Hardly had we entered their village than we were made guests of honor at the headman's house and for a few days were allowed to watch and talk with anyone we pleased about anything that came to mind.

I was amazed by the cleanliness here. In the middle of the jungle, in thatch houses shared with dogs and chickens (and other less domesticated creatures who kept popping in unexpectedly), the women were always washing their hair and sweeping it up into tight topknots, preening their faces, polishing their ornate silver jewelry, hanging out their beautiful hand-embroidered skirts to dry after strenuous washing on rounded rocks, cooking in cast-iron cauldrons on fires at the center of their earth floor inside their homes, and then washing the pots on the steps outside.

No one seemed to have heard of chimneys so the smoke just hung around the house, giving flavor to chunks of meat, corn, and chilies suspended above the fire, and blackening everything else inside. Each surface had a sooty patina but that only seemed to make the urge for cleanliness even stronger.

The headman's home was the worst of all. His status had enabled him to build some of his walls out of cement block carried by hand for miles from the nearest jeep track. It looked relatively impressive but the concrete only kept more of the smoke trapped inside, with the result that San and I spent most of the time in other split-bamboo-walled houses where there was a chance of breathing more freely.

Here we heard tales of the mysterious Phi Thang Luang, "people spirts of the yellow leaves," who were thought to be mythical beings haunting the deepest parts of the jungle, until their recent discovery by a jungle expedition. We were also told of the tremendous efforts by King Bhumiphol Adulyadej (Rama

IX) and his government to replace opium growing with more useful (but often less lucrative) crops.

One old man with no teeth and crazed smile explained how intricate the January opium harvest used to be. "You must cut each poppy pod correctly—just the right depth—then let the gum drain slowly overnight and then come and scrape the gum with a special knife the next day..." He paused and chortled. "Can you guess how many pods we used to cut? It was very hard work. Corn is much easier!"

Having extolled the virtues of corn at length he lay down on a blanket in a corner of his house and began the slow elaborate process of opium smoking. He placed each round pellet of dark oily substance on a long stick and heated it until it bubbled, then inhaled the smoke through a long bamboo pipe, all the time prodding and pushing it with his thin stick.

His wife seemed unconcerned. "It is a Meo tradition for men. We chew betel instead," she laughed, exposing the brown-stained mouth and teeth, and then added quietly "...and we do all the work too!" (Emerging liberation tendencies among the Meo?) But then she rose to move a smoking kerosene lamp closer to her prostrate husband as he struggled to light his fifth pellet....

In many of the houses we saw special "spirit shelves" (*dhat-jee-var-neng*) on which sacred objects—bones, horns, dried animal intestines—were placed for animistic worship of the sky, the wind, the forest, and family ancestors. The husband and the eldest son would usually pause in silence at their own shelves before sitting on the earth floor for their evening meal of rice with vegetables laced with ground coriander, chili peppers, and maybe a little chicken or smoked pork (not particularly gourmet fare, but for two jungle bums like San and me, a feast indeed).

Life was simple here, the people open and friendly, and the mood decidedly mellow. There were about twenty rattan-and-thatch houses in the village, sprawled loosely over a hillside deeply etched by water channels (a remnant of the last monsoon season). The headman's house sat at the top of the rise against a backdrop of dense jungle, which rose layer on layer, like green flames, behind the stockade where he kept his prize pig. The

A
MOUNTAIN
VILLAGE
— Thailand

other houses were large structures, each at least thirty feet square, with wide roof overhangs on two sides. Someone was always dozing in their shade. The pace of life in the village (particularly for the men) was pleasantly slow.

Long before the sun rose, a pink light filtered through the high wall of trees surrounding the village clearing. Cocks crowed like alarm clocks in jarring disharmony, and you could hear the always-ravenous pigs shuffling around the house, which smelled of charred meat (at least it kept the flies and mosquitoes away).

The headman, who told us he was forty-two but looked double that age, lay sleeping on his split-bamboo bed, raised a foot or so off the ground on little bamboo legs. His wife, Nao, rose to wrap her long black hair into the traditional beehive-shaped topknot and adjusted her rich hand-embroidered skirt, while her two tiny daughters scampered off in their sarongs to bring water from the well in long bamboo tubes. On hot days, Nao would wear her red-and-black turban but, as we were on the edge of the monsoons, the weather felt a little cooler.

San and I watched with half-open eyes as she tied around her forehead a scarf embellished with strange embroidered symbols. She saw us smiling and explained: "This is my magic for hunting. We are short of meat so I'm going hunting with two other women if the signs are good."

Nao went outside to grind rice between two enormous stone wheels for breakfast cakes, which she later served with sweet tea in cups made from round bamboo segments. We sat with the family on the earth outside the house enjoying the early sun. The headman joined us, and during the meal, he leaned forward to rub the scarf around Nao's head. She smiled again: "He has seen the signs and it is good to hunt." (I had watched earlier as he stood by the spirit shelf gently touching the horn and each of the old bones. Apparently he had decided that the signs favored the hunt.)

Observed by a bunch of curious piglets, three young boys practiced target shooting with crude crossbows. One had been selected to accompany the women in their hunt and strutted like a peacock in front of his peers. He wore his newly washed black waistcoat and knee-length baggy trousers proudly like a knight's armor. The other boys watched enviously as he left. (San and I had been told firmly that guests did not join the hunt but would be expected to enjoy the results.)

Most of the women and a few of the men left early to work in the tiny rice and tobacco fields below the village, scattered alongside the stream that bubbled down the hillside in miniature cascades. One small bunch of elderly women sat outside a lop-sided house at the edge of the jungle. I had noticed them there for a couple of days, sitting silently and looking very dejected. The old women looked up, one pointed inside, and we stepped through the open door. The air was almost unbreathable—thick fumes combined with black smoke and an odor of something sickly sweet, presumably opium.

An elderly man lay naked on his bamboo sleeping platform breathing heavily. His eyes were closed and his skin yellow. Sitting cross-legged at his head and wrapped in a richly decorated red shawl was the village shaman—an even older man with enormous hands and two deep scars across his left cheek. The earth around his feet was covered in offerings brought by the villagers: tea, smoked meats, two silver neck rings, a large pumpkin, and piles of sweet potatoes. He was fast asleep.

We talked quietly with the group outside. They told us the shaman had been asleep for almost three days and that when he woke, his "patient" would be cured. There was total trust in their eyes; faith was tangible and I felt ashamed at my Western scepticism. San smiled and nodded with them. "I have seen it happen. These people know many things the big city doctors have never been taught. Belief is very powerful medicine in the hills."

By late afternoon the weary hunters returned carrying two scrawny wild chickens, a number of enormous gourds and taro roots, and a sad little collection of dead frogs, which are enjoyed as delicacies by the Meo tribe.

Within an hour or two the rather modest foraging trove was transformed into a wonderful feast serving four families. Somehow over twenty of us ate long and well and lay on the warm earth watching the sun sink behind the hills, turning them scarlet, and listening to the birds singing. Someone played a kaen and two young girls danced a sensual "corn dance" by the grinding stones, their bent-back fingers fluttering like butterflies and their eyes filled with smiles beneath silver headdresses. They danced so lightly they seemed to float over the dusty earth. The villagers, who had seen the dances so many times before, sat as mesmerized as San and I. The women even stopped their ceaseless embroidering and the old men grinned like young boys. It's a scene you carry with you forever.

But eventually after a series of these long slow days we had to leave. The old men of the village forecast rains—the beginning of the monsoons—and we still had a lot of jungle walking to do. Somehow though, the trek seemed much easier now. The blisters had burst and healed, the bites had stopped irritating, and my mind was full of bright images of life in these wild hills.

We made one more impromptu pause in an Akha village where everyone turned out in magnificent headdresses to worship their "great all-power God"—Apoe Miyeh. The feast afterward included such jungle delicacies as wild boar, porcupine, roasted cicadas (locustlike insects), and (oh dear!) local tribal dog, which is considered a key ritual ingredient.

A few days later we were back in Chiang Mai among the noisy scooter-taxis (known locally as *tuk-tuks*) and street salesmen and all the tiresome trappings of modern Thailand. It doesn't take much—even now—to make me think of my days in these mountains where life-ways have changed little in thousands of years.

And who knows, maybe I'll go back one day.

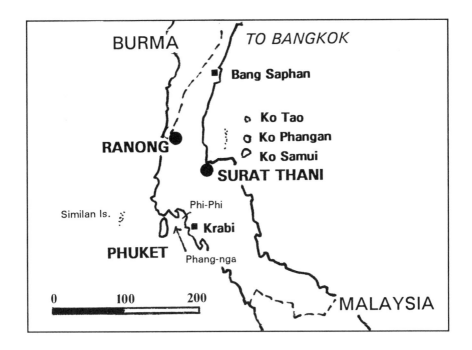

17. SOUTHERN THAILAND

Sea Drifting and Other Serendipities

"You want to drive to the south!?"

"Why not? It's only six hundred miles or so," I said.

My host in Bangkok was an ex-Peace Corps worker, familiar with the zany antics of newcomers to Thailand and usually a man of placid nature.

"That road is crazy. Honestly. It's a 'chicken-run' all the way. Those trucks don't brake for anything. You're just asking for trouble. Why not forget it this time? If you fly down you'll be there in a couple of hours."

"Yes, I know that. But I'd like to see what's in between."

"You've never even driven in Bangkok! You'll be lucky to find your way out. . . . You don't understand what it's like . . ."

"Listen," I said, "why don't I give it a shot, and if I find it's not what I want, I'll come back. And then I'll fly."

He paused and played a final card. "It's my Jeep you're driving, you know."

Dirty move.

"Ah, yes." He'd got me. "You're right. It's not fair on you. I'm being selfish. I just thought with you being away on vacation . . . the Jeep'd just be sitting there . . ." Silence. We'd reached the crux. He sighed one very exasperated sigh.

"How long will you be gone?"

"Couple of weeks. Tops. I'll be back before you are."

More silence. A fan whirred. I needed all the air I could get. Bangkok melted in that overwhelming wet heat, and I was desperate to get back on the road.

"You're crazy. You know that."

"Yes, I know."

He smiled a wry smile and kicked the keys across the low bamboo table with his bare foot.

"Two weeks?"

"Yes, two weeks. And I'll have dinner waiting for you here when you get back."

"Lobsters?"

"Lobsters, chateaubriand, caviar. The lot!"

He laughed. "You're crazy. And please, David. Remember I said that."

Of course he was right. It was a crazy idea. Even getting out of Bangkok was a nightmare. I left early in the morning before the rush-hour chaos of clogged streets, gridlocked intersections, useless traffic signs, one-way systems that became Escher labyrinths, sending you every which way only to bring you back where you started. And leaving early didn't seem to make much difference. I became disoriented, then lost. My glossy map seemed to bear little relationship to a street system that would test the patience of a Tokyo taxi driver.

But hours later, using the smoggy sun as my only orientation, I was out. Windows wide open, fresh breezes blowing in off the rice paddies, clusters of villagers in coolie hats tending the bright green shoots in a shimmering heat.

I paused for a Coke at a roadside stand. Bottles are a valued commodity in Thailand so the young girl poured the soda into a plastic bag, threw in a couple of pieces of ice, added a straw, and bound the top tightly with an elastic band. What a novel form of conservation!

Only it didn't work. I took a couple of sips, placed the bag on the passenger seat and rejoined the busy throng of traffic on the narrow main highway to the south. Next time I looked the bag had fallen on its side and the soda was gushing out from around the straw all over the brushed velour fabric.

I wondered what the poor Jeep would look like when it finally arrived back in Bangkok. If it ever did.

It's hard to resist the little roadside stands. A lopsided table piled high with just-picked pineapples: you stop; a lady in a wide-brimmed palm-frond hat tells you to make your selection; you hesitate, so she carefully picks one for you, slices off the skin to reveal the golden flesh, dripping with juice, and whops it all into bite-sized pieces, deposited neatly in another plastic bag. Five cents please. You give her double the amount. And why not? It's a beautiful bright morning, and the day is all yours to do with what you will.

More snack stands, each cook specializes in his, and her, own delicacy: tiny chunks of barbecued chicken dipped in crushed peanuts, sesame oil, and chili paste sauce and served on a banana leaf; boiled chunks of soft-textured snake meat in a soy, ginger, and coriander sauce; rubbery strips of squid pounded flat as pancakes, brushed with a chili and fish-sauce marinade, and roasted over hot coals; slivers of crisp-skinny wild duck with melt-in-the-mouth flesh; a couple of crabs, scooped from a roadside marsh, baked in salt, and cracked open to release their aromatic delights. A bonanza of totally new taste experiences for this footloose gourmand!

The first hundred miles were the worst, jousting with convoys of trucks hauling pineapples and sugar cane (and invariably topped with piles of baskets and huddles of placidly smiling Thai fieldworkers). Disabled scooter-vans and battered cars became a familiar sight. One young man flagged me down and asked for a lift to the next village to fix a flat. His English was remarkably

381

good, and he sat happily next to me, oblivious of the Coke-soaked seat, nursing his torn tire and telling me tales of South Thailand. He seemed to have a particular grudge against his Burmese neighbors who share occupancy of the long narrow finger of land linking southern Thailand with the Malaysian peninsula.

"You wanna hear joke?" he asked.

"Sure," I said. I hadn't heard—or at least I hadn't understood—many Thai jokes.

He pointed to the ranges of wild mountains on our right, across the verdant rice paddies.

"That Burma there."

I looked at my map. He was right. The border was somewhere in that jungly wilderness, a mere ten miles away.

"In Second World War, forty years ago, okay, much fighting. Japanese. Burmese, Thai," he pounded his fists together. "Okay? So, plane carry many soldiers from many different countries. And when plane up to the air, pilot says in announcement, 'Attention please. Now we have overload. Should be three of you soldiers jump out of the plane. Okay?' And all soldiers—many, many soldiers—keep quiet. Nobody wants to suicide. Right? So then American soldier—very brave—the first one, he says, 'Okay, I go first.' Before jumping off plane, he shout—very strong shout—'Long live President of America'—and then he falling down out of plane. Okay?

"Second one—soldier from England—before jumping he shout, 'Long live for King of England'—and then he jumping.

"The third one, Thai soldier, like to do like that but thinks it crazy, so, he shout, 'Long live King of Thailand' and kick Burma soldier out."

His laughter carried us all the way to the next roadside village and a tire-repair shack.

"Okay. I thanking you. Don't forget joke—he kick Burma soldier out! Good joke eh?"

By late afternoon I had the road to myself. Strange cone-shaped pillars of eroded limestone, hundreds of feet tall, rose from endless rice paddies. I was entering karst country, the eroded stumps of a once-vast limestone plateau formed under ancient oceans and then lifted high by restless tectonic plate movements. Everywhere I looked I could see tiny villages—clusters of mahogany-plank and bamboo-walled houses raised on stilts and topped with palm fronds, gathered around the soaring profiles of layer-roofed temples adorned with patterns of gold, green, and ochre tiles.

Vignettes of delight were all around: Two young children riding the back of a lumbering buffalo home to their village, haloed in a golden evening sun; a line of straw-hatted paddy farmers moving slowly in silhouette across the muddy rice fields; a young girl in a bright red sarong leading a procession of waddling ducks on a raised path between the paddies; the ubiquitous spirit houses—tiny dollhouse-size temples raised on posts and littered with candles, flowers, and daily offerings of fruit and rice—outside many homes and roadside stores; the delicate spires reaching skyward from stumpy domed chedis.

The images never cease: Five children whispering to one another as they lift four-cornered fishing nets suspended on a bamboo frame from the shallow waters of a roadside stream; the placid, otherworldly smile of a golden Buddha sitting cross-legged on a raised plinth in a village temple; a young mother lying by the side of a rough-carved, hollowed-trunk fishing boat watching her two naked children frolic and splash in the slow-moving evening ripples of the ocean across a palm-fringed bay.

I was saturated in images. Time to rest for the night. Bangkok was well and truly banished from my senses now. The spirit of the road had returned. The days were mine again and two weeks was a wonderfully long period to be free and frisky, to go anywhere I felt like going, soaking in all the serendipities of Thailand.

It couldn't have been better. A beachside bungalow in the small village of Bang Saphan for the price of a hamburger dinner back home. The Gulf of Thailand stretched out beyond my front door, purple and gold in the lingering sunset.

The sand was evening-pink, and palms rattled their welcome in a warm breeze. A long cool shower, a change of clothes for a stroll in the dusk along the beach to a small bamboo and thatch snack-shack for a dinner of squid soup, tiger prawns baked in a clay-pot casserole, and a plate of fresh-cut pineapple, banana, and papaya. I returned to my little house, read for an hour or two until the moon shone, big and silver, through my window. A perfect night for a swim. So off I went, blissfully naked, splashing through the soft water and then floating, happy as a sea otter, lying on my back, looking at the stars. . . .

Morning was just as good. The dawn came in right through the window. I could hear the sloppy surf and smell breakfast cooking down by the beach. None of your cornflakes and waffles here. Instead, a typical Thai spread of rice porridge flecked with chilis, onions, and shrimp; a plate of crisp wok-tossed vegetables in fish sauce with fried rice, and more fresh fruit.

Dull thuds kept coming from a plantation of coconut palms near the beach. I could see a bunch of men standing around the base of trees holding long lines of rope that disappeared into the treetops and shouting instructions into the high palm fronds. Coconuts fell, hitting the shadowy ground, and the men moved slowly, kicking them into piles.

I was curious to see how the coconut pickers worked, fifty feet up in the swaying tops. How did they get there? How long did they stay up?

One of the men shouted a warning. I jumped sideways and a coconut missed me by inches. Lots of Thai giggles. I could have been maimed! Surely the picker had seen me coming. I looked up and a pair of anthracite eyes stared back. A pair of eyes set in a furry face with a big nose. A monkey! And apparently a very belligerent monkey getting ready to aim the next coconut right at me . . .

So that's how they do it down here. A labor force of trained monkeys with the men just standing around bawling out instructions. I moved back out of firing range and watched. The monkeys were tireless, leaping from one bunch of coconuts to the next, moving each nut from side to side to test its readiness to fall, spinning the looser ones with one hand until the stalk snapped and the fruit came tumbling to the ground. They'd cover the whole treetop in a matter of minutes and then scamper down the vertical trunk, listen to more shouted orders, and vanish up another tree to repeat the whole performance.

Between the falling coconuts and the shouts I managed to

piece together bits of information from the men about their monkeys. These were very valuable creatures, worth hundreds of dollars each. Even a young graduate of the three-month-long coconut-picking course could be worth as much as twenty thousand baht (eight hundred dollars), and its untrained offspring around four hundred dollars. Work in the trees usually begins when they're around two years old and lasts for up to seven years, at an expected rate of at least five hundred coconuts per day, seven hundred for the real stars of this unusual labor force.

Someone neatly sliced the top off a newly dehusked nut with one blow of a panga knife and offered it to me. The sweet water inside was cool and delicious. I smashed the shell on a rock and used a finger to scoop out the soft gelatinous flesh (the best part of the coconut) that covers the harder meat.

I couldn't leave this little village. It had everything the perfect hideaway should have—simple beach bungalows, excellent fresh fish and fruit, a cluster of bamboo shacks for the fishermen further up the beach, maybe a trip out into the bay with one of the fishermen later on . . .

Eventually—much later than I'd planned—I was on the road again. The vegetation was more lush now. Jungles surrounded the bases of the high karst towers and rubber plantations took the place of rice paddies, each tree trunk neatly scarred with cuts that allowed the white latex sap to drain into coconut shell cups.

Doormat-like rectangles of coagulated latex were drying by the thousands along the roadside. The deep, almost black, shade of the plantations offered delicious relief from the pounding sun.

Another form of relief came quite unexpectedly in the form of a roadside ashram—a place of Buddhist meditation and worship—set in thick jungle and open to anyone. The architecture was unusually zany for Thailand. None of the traditional curved roofs decorated in golden tiles here, rather a Corbusian fantasy of concrete temples and dormitories, one of which was fashioned after an ocean liner and surrounded by a turtle-filled moat. Most peculiar, and with an even more peculiar mélange of orange-robed Thai monks mingling with a truly international representation of bearded world wanderers, sparkle-eyed freshmen from

European and American colleges, and "just-for-the-day" tourists armed with cameras and tape recorders.

"We're on a meditation course," a young California student explained quietly while his companions sat staring blankly around a picnic table. "Ten days of silence and meditation."

"I'm sorry. Should I be asking you questions?"

"Oh, no, that's fine. We start after lunch."

He seemed to be taking the course very seriously. His scalp was shaved and his forehead was marked with ochre dye.

"Can anyone participate?"

"Well—yes, I suppose so. We made arrangements, though, months ago to come here." He looked disparagingly at some of the other visitors, wandering around the neatly kept grounds.

"When you come here you're expected to participate in the schedule. Fasting, meditation—no talking. It's not a summer camp y'know."

I nodded. The sorting had begun in his mind. Serious seekers from the merely curious; the pecking order of spiritual purification. I sensed an unpleasant conflict of Western competitiveness with traditional Buddhist tolerance.

"Have you seen Emmanuel Sherman's paintings in the temple?" he asked.

"No. I've just arrived. Who is he?"

"He isn't anymore. He was a recluse. He lived for years in a cave on Ko Phangan Island in the Gulf of Thailand. Then he came here and did all these paintings. They're pretty famous."

"What happened to him?"

"He got malaria. Wouldn't take any medication. Went back to Phangan and died there."

The paintings were certainly powerful, executed in sweeping Japanese-style brush stroke monochromes, vibrant with themes of Western decadence and the "eight-fold path to freedom" and accompanied by Sherman's Zenlike verses:

> Oh boundless joy!
> To find at last
> There is no happiness in this world.

In the still mind
One can listen to the grass
Growing

My single hand claps the sound of thunder
My hand-sound echoes universally

My mind responds only to silence
It is loud beyond all description
How sublime!

The silence of the forest behind the temple encouraged introspection. I walked on winding paths, past tiny huts raised on stilts. ("They're for the monks and long-term residents," I'd been told by the Californian. He seemed envious. "We get the dormitory.") Butterflies bounced on the warm, wet air. Foot-high statues of Buddha and fragments of carved bas-reliefs marked the path to another open-walled temple set in a clearing. Blackboards and piles of notebooks suggested this was some kind of classroom for initiates.

It was all so quiet. Vines and creepers hung in lazy loops from the trees. I could see a young girl in a white robe sitting among a swirl of banyan tree roots. She was quite a distance away, but I could sense her total stillness. Just watching her made me feel enormously peaceful.

I was glad I'd come.

The next phase of my journey is hard to describe. I still dream about Phang-nga Bay, and it's difficult to separate the reality from the dreamscape.

I'd reached the town of Krabi on the west coast of the southern peninsula, overlooking the Andaman Sea. The town itself offered little inducement for dallying, but the nearby beach of Noppharat Thara is one of those earthly paradises that encourages you to make a serious reappraisal of worldly ambitions and wonder—quite honestly—why you would ever wish to go anywhere else. And this is only one of a string of deserted strands all along the indented coastline, some with talcum powder–soft sands, others littered with millions of multicolored seashells, and one in particular, Susarn Hoi, aptly named "cemetery of shells." Not much sand here. Instead the sea bed itself has risen up to display vast rock platforms consisting entirely of petrified shells more than thirty million years old. Strange place.

Only forty or so miles to the west, beyond the hazy profile of Yao Yai Island, lay Phuket Island, one of Thailand's most over-crowded bits of recreational real estate, packed with package-tour tourists. But here, on the eastern side of the bay, there's no one—no distractions, no girlie bars, nothing but these beautiful beaches, the occasional junk sailing by from Penang or Singa-pore, a few fishermen, and dozens of scattered offshore islets, jungle-shrouded and mysterious.

Oh—and the Phi Phi Islands.

In recent years this fantasy-shaped archipelago, full of soar-ing limestone cliffs, crystal-clear coral reefs, and turquoise bays edged with silver sand has become a little too "discovered" for travelers seeking solitude. But in spite of a couple of small re-sorts and a few beachfront restaurants, those willing to rough it can take off over the jungled hills with a sleeping mat and a few basics and soon discover their private corners of paradise.

I was taken by a local Phi Phi fisherman toward the southern tip of this arc of islands. His pitch had been simple: "You like bird ness soup?"

"Not particularly."

"You want see caves where ma' get ness?"

"Not really."

"Good. We go."

So we went.

It was hot on the main island and a breezy five-mile boat ride in a "longtail" didn't sound like such a bad idea. I'm a push-over for pitchmen anyway.

And what a strange world we entered.

Incised near the base of towering limestone karsts were dark caves, full of eerie shadows and dripping with enormous tiered stalactites. Our voices echoed in their murky interiors. As my eyes became accustomed to the dank gloom I saw a spidery web of bamboo pillars and catwalks, lashed together with rope and vines, rising from the floor of the cave and disappearing high into the darkness.

"For ness," the fisherman explained in his singsong English. "Ma' climb for ness. Ve' high."

"They climb these things?" I gasped. They didn't look strong enough to support a monkey—even a parrot.

"Li' bird. Swiss. Have ness."

"Swiss?"

He grinned, revealing a toothless mouth. He was having problems with the word and tried again.

"Swisses? Lil' birds." He flapped his arms like wings.

"Oh—swifts!"

"Ya, ya—swiss. Ve' li'."

"Very little. Yes, swifts are very little. And this is where they build their nests?"

"Ya, ya. Ma', climb."

I must have looked a bit sceptical. Next thing I knew the fisherman leaped onto one of the vertical bamboo scaffolds and began climbing—almost dancing—upward, pulling himself up by the dangling vines, his toes outstretched like fingers. The bamboo poles creaked and swayed. I expected the whole gossamer construction to fall apart and placed myself to catch my falling guide.

In seconds he was up more than fifty feet, on the edge of the deep shadows. He pointed into the far recesses of the cave. The scaffolding seemed to be everywhere. "Ve' far. Two kilomet."

"Okay. I believe you."

"Ma', climb." His voice sounded miles away.

"Yes, I understand. Come on down now."

He was looking around. "All go. No swiss."

Then he spotted an object on the side of the high cave wall. He reached out, touched the mossy rock, and something white floated down to the floor. I picked it up. It was a bit like sponge tissue—webbed strands of soft fiber.

He was down again. I hadn't even heard him coming.

"Ness," he said.

It was a tiny fragment of a swift's nest, left behind by one of the pickers. Apparently the birds build them out of strands of saliva, which later coalesce into tangled rubbery strips, rather like transparent vermicelli.

"Ve' goo." He grinned and rubbed his skinny belly, then flexed a sinewy bicep. "Mak' stron'."

I tore off a tiny piece and tasted it. Nothing. A texture like sponge with no discernable flavor whatsoever. It reminded me of the soup fiasco in Hong Kong when, unwittingly, I'd eaten a bowl of the most innocuous broth laced with gelatinous strips and been charged an outrageous amount for the honor of ingesting the finest shark's fin soup on the island. Birds' nests obviously fell into the same category. A dish for the purist, offering promises of virility, energy, longevity, and all those other virtues so anxiously sought by Oriental epicures.

It seemed like an awful lot of trouble and danger to go to for something so—well—bland.

The fisherman was now firing an imaginary machine gun at me and laughing. "If you ta', me go..." (more machine gun sounds). "Bi' dollas. Man', man', dollas. Much money."

Apparently these nesting caves are very valuable and jealously guarded.

The fisherman stopped firing. "Is alri'—no more swiss."

The cave had been abandoned by the birds. These were old bamboo scaffolds and presumably even more dangerous than they looked. The fisherman was even crazier than I'd thought. One or two rotten bamboo poles or some broken vine knots and the whole fragile construction could have collapsed. But he didn't appear to mind. He was firing his machine gun at invisible birds' nest looters again.

A few days later I was sixty or so miles to the north of the Phi Phi Islands, drifting in my own longtail through the dreamscape of Phang-nga Bay. The limestone karst pillars that had followed me most of the way south from Bangkok congregated here in the hundreds, rising like an abandoned city of eroded skyscrapers out of shallow waters. The largest were over a thousand feet high; great gray monoliths, sheer-sided and topped by scrubby jungle and vines, showing yellowed scars where slices of eroded limestone had fallen off recently and tumbled into the coral beds at their bases. They receded into the heavy haze of the bay like solitary hooded monks on some strange and lonely pilgrimage.

Well away from the tourist boats, I drifted for hours among these eerie formations peering down into a translucent ocean, watching parrot fish flash their gaudy colors. Some of the pillars enclosed tiny coves etched with arcs of white sand. No one lived here. They beckoned. "Stay awhile," they whispered. "Why not?" I wondered. "Why not?"

Toward evening I paused at the only village out in the bay, an odd clustering of wooden houses on stilts occupied by a group of devout Muslim fishermen set against the rocky islet of Ko Pannyi. A blue minaret rose up above lopsided bamboo cat-walks. A muzzein chanted the call to evening prayer, and the sounds echoed off the rock pillars, now turning scarlet in the sunset.

I drifted on, at one point right through a towering karst pillar, where the sea had opened up a tunnel dripping with stalac-tites. As I emerged from the other side the bay was bathed in gold-and-purple light. And the whispering was there again: "Stay. Stay." Plans, schedules, timetables, itineraries, all seemed so utterly pointless. Southern Thailand had so much more to show me, so many little "lost worlds"—clusters of islands out in the Andaman Sea, other hidden islands I'd heard about on the world-wanderer's grapevine in the Gulf of Thailand. . . .

The decision made itself and who was I to argue? I'd planned to return early to Bangkok and surprise my host, but that would have to wait. I had to find these places. The islands beckoned, and I had no choice but to respond—happily.

I feel motionless but by the size of our frothing wake we seem to be traveling pretty fast through this heat-hazy limbo. Land is far behind. The pounding discos and gorgeous-girlie bars of Thailand's Phuket Island are way to our east, long gone in the early-morning mists. In spite of impressive world-class resorts and superb beaches, Phuket depresses me. Thousands of European, Australian, and American bronze-skinned Buds and Chucks flying high on cheap beer, grass, and exotic female companions. The food's good—some of the best seafood in the world—but the fun and the pace palls fast and you soon begin to wish for

PHANG-NGA BAY
—Southern Thailand.

silent white coves and the shimmering eternity of an empty blue ocean.

It's 9:00 A.M. but the sun is already hot. Boat breezes create an illusion of coolness, but that won't stop your skin blistering like a paratha if you don't smother yourself in high-spf lotion. The ocean is alive. Tiny flurries of fish, bright as hummingbirds, leap together in rainbowing sprays. The captain looks out for sailfish, the prize of deep-sea fishermen who work the waters in the cooler November-to-March season.

I don't feel like fishing. I really don't feel like doing much of anything except sitting in the shade of the cabin and watching our knife blade prow slice through turquoise waters.

For an hour or two that's all there is to see. It's fifty miles from Phuket to the first of my island discoveries, the Similans. There are nine of them and only two have any kind of native population.

"Very quiet," my captain assured me before we left Phuket. "You like to snorkel or scuba?" I admitted I'd never tried either seriously. He gave one of those endearing Thai grins. "Best in world. Better than Barrier Reef. Australians told me. Better than Maldives, better than Hawaii. You try." I promised I'd try.

Way out on the starboard side, something was moving across the hazy horizon. "Chao Lae, 'Sea Gypsies,' " the captain told me. "Not friendly. Only like the sea."

Little seems to be known, or at least understood, about Thailand's elusive colonies of Sea Gypsies. One of those ponderous surveys conducted by some obscure division of the United Nations recently concluded that they were "unsuitable for conventional social integration and assimilation." (I had this picture of tropical-suited census-takers and bespectacled sociologists being chased out of Sea Gypsy territory by harpoon-waving natives unpersuaded by the benefits of "assimilation.")

There were two longboats, maybe three, low in the water like alligators. Each had four fishermen, silhouetted against the silver sea. They showed no interest in us.

"Some come from Burma and China. Some have very black skin and fuzzy hair, like Andaman Island peoples." The captain grinned again and wagged his head. "A bit slow. Not educated. Don't even know where Bangkok is!" I on the other hand knew all too well where Bangkok was, having spent a week in that city's interminable heat and traffic before driving south to Phuket. I envied the Sea Gypsies' ignorance.

Soon they were gone, vanished into the haze. We nibbled on cold cooked shrimp the size of baby lobsters and slices of fresh mango. The captain offered me a mug of "Genuine Thai Scotch Whiskey" (which tastes exactly the same as "Genuine Thai French Brandy" and "Genuine Thai Jamaican Rum"), but sun and alcohol don't mix for me. I borrowed his panga, sliced the top off a big green coconut, and drank the sweet colorless milk.

This is exactly what I'd been waiting for—days of happy hedonism among the outer islands of Thailand, eating when hungry, snoozing when the sun scorched my eyes, being part of this empty ocean for as long as I chose.

"Similans coming." I woke and peered over the rough wood sides of the boat, scoured by rope burns. He was right. Way in the distance, tiny blips of land floated like mirages.

"We do snorkel off Ko Payang. Good place."

This was to be my first real snorkeling experience, and I was as excited as a young child, peering into the clear ocean as we approached the shore. I could see the coral reefs below us rearing like prehistoric forests; patches of white-blue sand lay between them, silhouetting hundreds of fish of all shapes, sizes, and colors.

Khun (the captain and I were now on first-name terms) gave me a cursory explanation of snorkeling techniques, which to him were as obvious as breathing. But it was the breathing bit I couldn't quite master. I didn't trust that tube as my only air supply and wasn't used to having my nose trapped uselessly inside a glass fishbowl. I jumped (actually Khun pushed me) into the warm ocean. Looking back I blush at my flailing antics as I choked on the sudden rush of water. I even forgot how to swim properly while struggling to breathe. I pulled off the mask and sucked in great gulps of fresh air. Khun was in hysterics.

"Put on, put on. Try again. No problem."

Slowly—far too slowly—I became accustomed to this strange suffocating device. I learned to clamp my lips tightly around the rubber mouthpiece and breathe evenly and regularly. My nose gradually accepted its redundancy and I began my first exploration of the undersea world of the Similans.

Below was a universe of infinite color and form, lit by dappled sunlight. The higher reefs were flat and gray, topped with hundreds of sea anemones; lower down the shelf corals glowed deep orange and purple. Great filigrees of sea fans waved slowly in the half light. Butterfly and damsel fish floated by nibbling at the coral, ignoring me completely. I swam further and further from the boat. I was in my own world now, weightless, full of wonder at the wealth of things to see. Ahead loomed an enormous vertical reef topped with delicate tubastrea. The colors changed dramatically as the reef descended into the gloom — brilliant golds and greens became blood-red crimsons and bronzes. I wanted to dive deeper, scuba-style, but one more choking session with the snorkel tube convinced me to remain close to the surface.

I felt something brush against my legs and turned quickly. Two parrot fish, decorated with brilliant patches of scarlet, emerald blue, and white, retreated a little and then sort of hung there, as intrigued by me as I was with them. Slowly I extended a hand and very gently let it rise to touch the underbelly of the smaller one. It didn't move; in fact it seemed to rest peacefully, with a vague smile on its face, cupped in my palm. The larger one drifted closer, its dorsal fin hardly moving. I could see every detail of its dark eyes and fluttering gills. Then ever so gently it drifted up to my mask and planted a big soft-lip kiss on the glass. I just lay there boggle-eyed, meeting its gaze until I was attacked by the giggles and had to surface, laughing like a jackass. Kissed by a fish! What a novel experience in the middle of this bright blue nowhere!

Far in the distance I could see Khun fishing over the side of his boat with a homemade bamboo rod. Behind him rose the surf-rounded rocks of Ko Payang, edging a beach of brilliant white sand. The vegetation was low and thick, shaped by the sea winds until it looked almost like land. Behind, dense vine-laced jungle rose to a thick green canopy. The island was only a mile or so across at its widest point; most of the others were smaller, strung out in a line of receding blues north to Ko Similan.

I returned to my hidden world, hoping to see one of Thailand's famous (but harmless) coral sharks. Instead I was the only spectator at an impromptu ballet by a shoal of tiny fish, thousands of them, performing precision-formation rolls and tumbles, turning silver, then gold, then shadowy green in quick succession. Even the larger fish paused to watch this little afternoon delight in a flickering amphitheater of meticulously carved coral.

I don't know how long I was down there. Time was irrelevant. I forgot my own body completely and became a part of this magic water world. A spectator turned passive participant—an honorary member of a secret society engaged in ageless rituals. . . .

Much later, when I swam back to the boat, Khun proudly displayed our dinner-to-be in the form of six filleted fish lying on the warm wood deck. We ran the boat up onto the sand in a hidden cove surrounded by more rounded rocks. I chopped pineapples, bananas, and mangoes while my friend prepared a simple fire of driftwood and cooked the fillets in an ancient cast-iron pan he'd carried in his boat for twenty years. He sprinkled them with spices from an old rusty Balkan Sobranie tobacco tin. When I asked about the contents he became aloof and mysterious. In a country where food is an important art form, Thais protect their private recipes jealously and Khun had no intention of giving away his family secrets. Suffice it to say, whatever he added to the fish gave them a piquancy and zest unmastered by any of those gourmet restaurants in Bangkok. We ate without talking for almost an hour as the sun sank slowly behind the rocks. Our grins were conversation enough.

A few days later I traveled north from Phuket to Ranong. This important fishing port and growing commercial center sits on the east bank of the Pakchan estuary overlooking the hazy hills of Burma. I'd hoped to make a brief foray into that still-mysterious country, but recent internal problems and student uprisings had (once again) resulted in tight closure of all borders. Even the local fishermen, who rarely concerned themselves with territorial infringements, were taking particular care not to trespass across the invisible centerline of the estuary.

I wandered down to the harbor to sketch the frantic activity at the fish auctions and managed to find a small boat to take me to one more group of Thailand's magic hidden islands—Ko Surin.

We left very early the following morning, edging nervously down the Thai side of the estuary, well away from the Burmese gunboats, past Ko Chang and Ko Phayam, and finally out into the blue ocean again.

Just like the Similan journey, I felt I had the world to myself along with occasional flurries of flying fish. After an hour or so we made a brief stop at the tiny island of Ko Gum Yai and swam in one of the most perfect little bays I'd ever seen. A few hardy adventurers were camping on nearby Ko Gum Noiey—otherwise it was just us and the parrots and the monkeys. All was idyllic, at least for a while, until I noticed the old captain casting uneasy glances at a handful of high clouds way off over the Burmese outer islands. But surely we were still in the dry season. So why was I worried?

An hour later my apprehension was transformed into full-blown fear. Our tiny puffball clouds had turned into ogreous hammerheads, the afternoon sky had become deep dusk, and a furious hot wind rolled the waves like battering rams into the side of our tiny wooden boat. Everything movable was tied down or thrown below into the galley. Then, without even a sprinkly introduction, the rains came, and came and came. Blinding curtains of the stuff, even battering the sea into submission with their sodden pounding. The galley was rapidly filling with water—the boat seemed to have leaks everywhere. The pump wasn't working so we baled by hand, using two battered buckets (even at the height of the storm the captain managed one of those hapless Thai grin-and-shrug combinations). Keeping dry was useless; keeping a hold on anything firm was essential. What a ridiculous place to disappear, I thought, on my way to an island no one knew anything about and maybe didn't care anyway.

Eons later the storm drifted eastward, leaving us floundering in swells and steaming under a hot evening sun, too exhausted to even consider clearing up the mess below in the galley. . . .

Fortunately Ko Surin was beautiful, more lush and laden with flowers and fruits than the Similans. And the diving! This time I tried a little scuba and vanished into an undersea world even more dramatic than Ko Payang, with more fish, reef caves, and those famous coral sharks whose sleek, sinister presence I never quite trusted. A few fellow divers joined us. They had traveled on an organized tour from Phuket with mountains of diving gear. Two Australians (Australians seem to get everywhere), who had enjoyed a couple of years of Asiatic wanderings, took me night-diving off Ko Sindara. Armed with powerful torches we frolicked among the reef caves like water babies, amazed by the dazzling colors of the corals. Some reefs resembled Bangkok traffic jams—countless thousands of fish hovering, scurrying, swooping in shoals or lurking in shadowy anemone-encrusted passages. It was almost an anticlimax to crawl back to our sleeping bags under the stars. In dreams of vivid color I returned to those reefs again and again, floating endlessly with the fish through coral canyons and fantasy cities far more dramatic than anything created in science fiction.

A week later I was scampering over the soft white sands of Ko Samui and playing tourist again. A few years back, the island, fifty miles north of Surat Thani on the east coast of Southern Thailand, was an undiscovered, palm-growing paradise. But word travels fast among the travel fraternity, and soon tiny banana frond A-frames were being built (in a day or two) by starry-eyed dropouts seeking another Goa for their endless revelries. And for a while it truly was. Money was virtually unknown on the island; the locals were friendly, sharing people; coconuts (the best in Thailand), fruit, free-range marijuana, psychedelic mushrooms, and fish were available in endless supply. What more could a true earth gypsy ever want? But gradually—maybe inevitably—the developers arrived with their upscale A-frame colonies, followed by trendy beach bungalows offering nightly beach parties, and finally the five-star resorts with every imaginable comfort at amazingly reasonable rates (relative to Western standards at least).

I'd been advised to avoid Samui's notorious psilocybin mushrooms. They were officially illegal anyway, following the deaths of a couple of overindulgent tourists. The tales of their demise varied. Some said they were convinced they could fly and had leaped off a high cliff on Samui's eastern coast; others claimed they'd tried to play Neptune among the coral reefs and never returned. Whatever. Sadly they had died, and it was all blamed on the island's hallucinogenic mushrooms, so the police decided it was time for a crackdown.

"Try some omelet."

I'd met a bunch of free-wheeling Italian travelers. Now Italians seem to have a knack for finding places that everyone else seems to miss—hidden beaches, unmapped mountain paths, an old woman in a palm-frond shack who cooked the most exquisite Thai curries brimming with prawns and lobsters, the quietest out-of-the-way places to camp. Wherever I go I look out for Italians—kindred spirits in my nooks-and-crannies ramblings.

"Is very good omelet. Have a piece."

I should have known something was not quite right. There was too much giggling.

"Not bad," I said. And it wasn't. A rich creamy texture, laced with black flecks of what I thought to be truffles.

"Oh yes. Truffles. Just like truffles," they all assured me.

I ate a few more slices. We were all sharing our dishes, Chinese style; it seemed the sociable thing to do. Everything tasted so good: rice noodles laced with coriander and small pieces of Thailand's fiery orange chili, *prik kee nu luang;* a whole rainbow fish cooked with basil, cardamom, and garlic and liberally sprinkled with *nam pla,* a variant of the ever-present fish sauce; finely chopped vegetables with lemongrass in coconut milk; little bowls of *tom yaam gung,* a spicy shrimp and lemon soup; fat juicy chunks of *gy pat by gaprow,* chicken roasted with mint, cloves, and coriander, and plate after plate of tiny sweet banana fritters known as *gluay twat.* A wonderful spread, served by two beautiful Thai girls in a lopsided beachfront house of palm and bamboo, miles from anywhere.

We all ate slowly. There was no rush.

The only problem was my chair. I kept looking down to see if the legs were straight. I felt I was slipping sideways. Maybe it was the heat. Or those fiery little chilies—they can make your head spin.

And then I was sitting on the sand, quite a distance away from the table. I had no idea how I got there. I had no recollection of leaving the feast. But it felt okay. The sand was warm, enticingly warm. Sensual. My legs moved backward and forward, digging deep into its softness. So soft. Like duck down. And I was bouncing up and down—ever so slowly—like a baby on a puffy cloud. I could hear soft laughter behind me. Or was it a waterfall? Or a breeze in the palms? No matter. It was a lovely gentle sound, trickling over my head like warm water, tickling my ears.

Someone put a glass of coconut milk in my hand. There was a face—one of the Thai girls. Peach-colored with tiny pearl eyes and a coy smile. Her small oval mouth was moving slowly; I couldn't take my eyes off her teeth. Such neat, white, tiny teeth; like a miniature keyboard. I could reach out and play them and make wonderful music. But my hand didn't seem to want to move. I watched my fingers ease through the pink-gold sand like wriggling worms. . . .

The sky was a blue I'd never seen before—a brilliant silky turquoise with a texture of soft tofu. It looked—well—it looked, edible! As if I could reach out and cut pieces from between the cotton-candy clouds. And the clouds were different too—moving backward, then forward—gracefully, as in a slow minuet, leaving little images behind like lace petticoats.

Thoughts tumbled. Cascades of twirling perceptions, each one a different color and shape. Wouldn't it be fun, I thought, to slice through them and look at their cross section—all those colors and forms, all intertwined, all changing.

And then I was in the water. Again, no recollection of moving. I remember thinking how nice it would be to float in the sea. It undulated like a big rubber waterbed. Inviting. Promising. Tiny silver and gold fish moved between my toes. I heard a voice saying "f-i-s-h" very slowly. Sort of a surfy sound. "Fishhhh." Then a breath. Then "fishhhhh," again. It was my voice. I could feel the vibrations in my throat. Fishhhhh. A beautiful sound. The most beautiful sound in all the world.

I was on all fours now. Some kind of creature. A large lizard? Playing in the shallows, seeing finger-long fish dart in shoals, scores of them turning as one, one mind controlling them all. My hands became flippers. A seal now? As each flipper entered the water the shoals would move away in sinewy curves and then curl back to look more closely, then curl away again as I moved forward, my body swaying from side to side. I could feel the sun's heat on my back, like massaging fingers, moving up my spine and outward across my waist and shoulders and tickling the underside of my chest.

Round pink boulders at the water's edge became enormous scoops of ice cream, piled on top of one another. A huge sundae. Particles of quartz sparkled like sprinkled sugar. I splashed water on the rocks and they darkened to a deep red. Raspberry syrup! How lovely.

Then my giggling began. Just ripples at first; it all felt so soft—pillowy—to this sea-frolicking lizard (or seal) or whatever I was supposed to be, faced by all this ice cream. Except that I was changing now, rising up out of the water. I felt as light as a breeze. Lifting. As I moved my head, I seemed to lift even higher leaving my lizard body behind. Floating. Really floating. I was looking down at my ice-cream rocks and the water and the beach from up high. And I felt no weight. Nothing at all. I stretched out my arms, tilted to one side, and floated sideways. I lifted my neck and looked at the sky and moved upward, toward the blue tofu. I looked down and my body slid down through the warm air like a seagull riding the thermals. I was utterly free. I have never known such sensations except in dreams. I could feel the giggling rising from my stomach, up through my lungs and throat, and right out the top of my head—waterfalls of laughter, bringing more laughter, like a child, lost in the moment, in the fun of floating and laughing and soaring and diving...and the earth had never looked more beautiful....

Much, much later I landed gently and found myself sitting on the sand again. The sky was a more normal blue now and the pink rocks were—pink rocks. Pretty things, but rocks nevertheless. Certainly not ice cream sprinkled with sugar and laced with raspberry syrup. Silly idea.

My companions were all around, sprawled on the beach, asleep. One of the Italians rolled over, opened an eye, and smiled.

"Good omelet, I think."

The omelet. Of course. Those truffle-like flecks had been

Samui psilocybin mushrooms! Sometimes I worry about me. But that floating bit really had been very, very pleasant. . . .

Ko Samui began to get to me. Too many people. Time to look for quieter islands again.

Eighteen miles or so off to the west I explored one of the world's most beautiful archipelagos, Ang Thong. Here in the clearest of turquoise-blue waters sit forty jungle-shrouded islets, each with its own secret beaches of white coral sand. Towering pinnacles of eroded limestone rise hundreds of feet, fantasylike, from dense tangles of trees, vines, ferns, and creepers. Recent designation as Thailand's second Marine National Park ensures preservation of Ang Thong's pristine delights and the safety of the nation's favorite fish, the *pla tu,* or short-bodied mackerel, which spawn here in countless billions in March. The head-quarters island of On Koh Wua Ta Lap (Sleeping Cow Island) has a few bungalows for rent and abundant fresh water, but all the others are virtually untouched. Most visitors come here from Ko Samui to snorkel and fish among the blue lagoons. A handful of hardy ones visit Moe Koh (Mother Island), to swim from the tiny beach surrounded by spiked cliffs and scale the tallest one to catch a glimpse of Talay Noi, an emerald green salt water lake trapped among soaring karst pinnacles. From here the whole interlocking beauty of the archipelago stretches for miles into the brilliant silver haze.

I've left my favorite place until last. When the overabundant distractions and delights of Ko Samui began to pall I hopped a ferry to the less-developed island of Ko Phangan for a couple of days' quietude in a palm-frond bungalow on a little cove, taking occasional walks on jungle paths to the hidden waterfalls of Thaan-sadet and Pang.

Finally I decided to go completely native. A small fishing boat chugged me even further north to the ultimate escapist islet of Ko Tao. Here I discarded all trappings of our so-called civilized ways and gave myself up to the sun, the ocean, the warm breezes, and the company of a handful of travelers who seemed to have discovered the ultimate in peace and simplicity, living lives as gentle as gossamer. There were few luxuries and organ-

403

ized distractions here. Most tourists would never enjoy the "nothingnesses" to be found here. All you really have is you, your own experiences and your own perceptions.

And that was just fine with me.

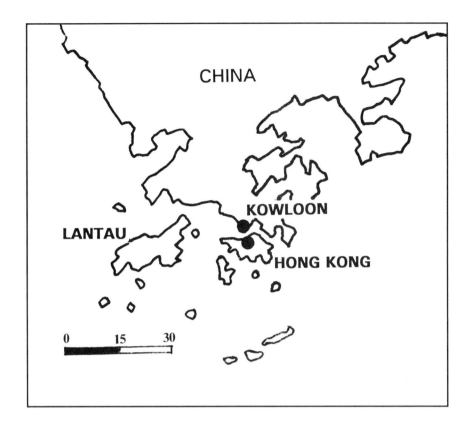

18. HONG KONG
Way out among the Islands

Somewhere deep in dreams comes the echo of bells and the rumble of gongs—long booms followed by the chitter of cymbals and then silence; I wake up suddenly; I can see branches swaying outside my window. I'm lying on a wooden board covered by straw matting and my back aches. It's very dark and hot, mosquitoes are doing kamikaze imitations and I can't remember where I am.

Slowly the real world returns. Right—I'm a guest at the Buddhist monastary of Po Lin (Precious Lotus) on Lantau Island, way out in the bay west of Hong Kong, and it's 4:00 A.M., time for the first service of the day.

I light my candle in the cell-like room, dress quickly, and

creep downstairs to the courtyard. The air is cool. A breeze rolls down from the dark hills, rattling leaves and bringing scents of early morning. The richly painted walls of the main temple, brilliant crimsons and golds, are illuminated by strings of tiny lights. Inside I can see the serene profile of a twenty-five-foot-high Buddha flickering in the glow of tiny candles, and down the ornate stairway I peer directly into a smaller temple lit by more candles. Fifteen black-robed monks chant in a low, slow monotone, like an endless mantra that seems to ease its way across the cobbled courtyard, over the pagodas on the high terraces above the temple compound, up the empty hills, and out into the starry blackness.

Hong Kong seems a galaxy away. Yet, a mere twenty sea gull–skimming miles to the east was one of the earth's most frenetic cities, the money machine of Southeast Asia, the "get-ahead-or-you're-dead, eat-'em-up-and-spit'em-out" nexus of our little blue planet. If I'd looked I would have seen the glow over the black hills, but I preferred to be just where I was, and so I didn't look.

I had left that frantic whirligig behind three days ago, bidding farewell to its million scurrying residents, its twenty thousand exotic restaurants, its neon strips, endless open-air street markets and food stalls, and its huddled sampans, jammed shantytown fashion in the typhoon basins. I'd jumped aboard a ferryboat and waved good-bye to the organ-pipe jumble of chrome and glass towers and moved out into the mists of the bay, heading for a few days of walking on Lantau.

This sparsely populated place is the largest of all the 235 outlying islands (even larger than Hong Kong island itself) but more than half of its 155 square miles has been designated as protected areas, many with lovely secluded beaches, and all linked by sinewy networks of footpaths.

First stop was tiny Peng Chau Island. Here the air was cool, and I began strolling the narrow, winding alleys that smelled of brine and noodles and drying fishnets.

"Hey, mister, you wan' sampan?"

My ramblings were cut short.

"Sampan here now. You take."

I had ordered a boat for the crossing to Lantau so—farewell Peng Chau. An old Chinese gentleman, very wrinkled and bent, scampered up to me, grabbed my knapsack and scampered back to the pier.

"Sampan go. Quick, quick."

He pushed me off the dock into a tiny wooden contraption bobbing around like a cracked eggshell and into the arms of an Oriental beauty wearing a broad rattan hat tied under her chin with a purple scarf. She smiled and lowered her eyes in that demure way Oriental women have of sending your heart pounding. Then she sat gracefully, adjusted her hat, snapped the engine into life with a quick tug on an old rope, and we were off, roaring across the choppy narrows. The engine sounded like a swarm of very angry killer bees.

I gazed across an ocean dotted with small wooded islands as far as the eye could see. Directly ahead were the high hills of Lantau, burly green peaks rising layer on layer—a real walker's island; touches of Scottish highlands tinged with Irish emerald green, floating in a Mediterranean-blue ocean.

I had decided to begin my hike from the northeast coast at the Trappist Haven monastery, and within minutes of leaving Peng Chau my charming captain bounced us up on the shore below the church, perched on a bluff. I clambered out unsteadily. She handed me my gear, smiled that smile again, and vanished in a swirl of spray.

For a few moments I was alone; big blue butterflies arabesqued for me in the early-morning air. Then a small truck appeared, banging and clattering down a steep track, driven by Buddha himself. He emerged in rather grubby white robes and stood, plump and beaming at me with a face I had seen a hundred times before in pictures and statues, a face of utter contentment and knowingness. But, like the girl in the boat, he had business to do and started unloading milk churns from the back of the truck. I remembered that the Trappist monks rear dairy cows here and are the main suppliers of Hong Kong's top hotels. I also remembered that Trappists don't talk. So, after he offered me a seat by sign language, we rode in silence up the ridiculously steep hill to the monastery where he vanished (after one last all-enveloping grin) into a cow barn.

407

There was no one around so I strolled over a foot bridge across a deep ravine and into the simple church. A list of resident monks was posted near the door with only twelve names on it. From an adjoining list of eight daily services, starting with Vigils at 3:15 A.M. and ending with Compline at 8:00 P.M., it appeared they must be very busy people.

The views back over the bay and the islands were breathtaking but unfortunately I had little breath to give as I made the long climb up from the monastery, through shoulder-high elephant grass, to the first line of green ridges. The morning seemed to be taking pernicious delight in getting hotter by the second. A yellow snake sinewed into the bushes leaving its ominous imprint on the dust. A single sea gull hovered above me, dropped a little souvenir (it missed), and soared off in the spirals, pretending to be an eagle.

At the top of the fourth ridge the whole of Silvermine Bay (Mui Wo) opened up with its arc of white sand and wooden sampans bobbing near the shore. Kids frolicked in the shallows, and I had such a strong urge to join them that the two-mile descent seemed to go very quickly, at least, until the last section, when I got lost in a mini-jungle of thornbushes all wrapped in sticky spiders' webs with dozens of black spiders the size of campaign medals.

I finally emerged from the sweaty tangle, flung boots and pack on the sand, strode straight into the surf, and promptly disappeared. (The disappearing bit was unintentional—I had walked off the end of a hidden rock ledge.)

The serious leg of my hike began on the hills behind the bay. Local folklore claims that the same Chinese clan (once notorious pirates) has occupied a strange walled village on the north coast of the island for over a thousand years. That seemed a good enough reason for visiting the place.

Finding the correct route from Silvermine Bay was not easy. I made at least four separate starts on different paths before an old man on a mule put me right and I began the long climb up the valley past huddled villages of stones and timber houses. Gradually the country became wilder. Soon there were no houses or people; a cool wind blew down the hills, which now resembled the moors of Yorkshire in their bleakness.

After six long miles I crossed the high watershed and I was looking forward to a spell of easier downhill walking. I paused for water in a hamlet of poor stone houses and could see the trail wriggling hundreds of feet down the slopes to the ocean far beyond. And there in the far distance was the village—a sinister black-walled fortress with massive towers at each corner. A young man sauntered up, dragging a pink piglet on a string, and I pointed out where I was going. He scowled and shook his head.

"No good. Is trouble there. No good to go." I showed him the route on my map. The path was clearly marked. "No. No way to go. No road. People very sick there. You go back now."

Then something very odd happened. The sky ahead suddenly began to darken rapidly and long gray tentacles of cloud trailed across an oily black ocean. I could see sheets of rain obliterating the outer islands, moving toward the cliffs of Lantau and the strange walled village far below us.

"You go back. Now."

I don't usually put much faith in omens and suchlike but somehow I knew that the young man was right, so I thanked him and set off fast on the long trail back down to Silvermine Bay.

As I half ran I could sense the huge clouds crowding behind me, rumbling over the ridges, growing larger and darker. I turned and the hills were already gone in mists. I knew the rain was really coming, pushing the winds over the low grasses, bending the scrub bushes. I tried to run faster but my legs felt like cement blocks. The gale was shrieking now, tearing at my clothes; the first fat drops were here, hitting the trail like quail eggs. And then it was on me, sudden cold dousings of water falling in solid shafts, pounding my head, and making the trail into an instant streambed—pure and wonderful chaos; the land and the elements rolling together in a primeval tag match with me as solo spectator, right in the middle of it all. . . .

I continued running downhill and arrived at a lonely house with stone walls, a tin roof, and a big blue door, which was half open. An old man was peering out, watching the downpour. He saw me, laughed, and beckoned me inside (an unexpected gesture—islanders seem to relish their own privacy). I almost tumbled down the two steps into a tiny dark room filled with pretty little girls who scampered around pushing bundles into corners and piling up cushions on the wooden floor. When all the scurrying ceased, the girls became very shy and an old woman, who sat almost invisible in the far corner of the room, sent them off to make tea in the rear of the house.

I could see a raised platform bed shrouded by a mosquito net and partially hidden by a bamboo screen. The main room was simply furnished with a chest of drawers, a statue of Buddha in a small house-shrine lit by tiny candles, two bamboo chairs, and a chipped wooden table by the door. Light came from a hurricane lamp, which sent flickering shadows across the unpainted walls.

I was served a small bowl of perfumed tea, followed by a much larger bowl of thick noodles in broth with chunks of bok choy cabbage and two sweet buns. The six little girls all sat in a circle on the floor. When I smiled, they giggled; when I ate their lips moved with mine. No one spoke.

Much later, when the storm had passed, I got up to leave. I looked in my backpack for gifts but all I could find was a small flashlight and a box of TicTacs, which they accepted with embarrassment, then grace. The old man came with me to the door and when I turned back to wave, all the girls waved back and giggled in unison. Their lovely smiles kept me company all the way down the long (and now very muddy) path to Silvermine Bay and the comforts of a beachfront hotel room.

Next day, everything was bright and blue again and I discovered one of the most unusual villages I have ever seen on my travels.

I took a local bus along the coast road, past lovely Cheung Sha sands, over the pass by Kwun Yam Shan Mountain, and down to a bay of ancient salt pans in a bowl of green hills. Tai O village is a jumble of tiny fishing shacks perched on stilts alongside a narrow inlet that neatly divides the community in half. Linking both sides is a tiny rope-drawn sampan, which always seems full of locals, wobbling around in upright positions, as the odd little craft is hauled across.

The day I arrived all the fishing boats were decked out in

brilliant-colored banners and streamers in preparation for the great Tin Hau festival in May that celebrates the favors bestowed on the fishermen by the goddess of the sea. "Dragon boats," long thin racing craft ornately carved and powered by eight oarsmen, skimmed up and down the inlet to the beat of drums and gongs. The ferry made hasty crossings between the impromptu races, but then got tangled up with the prow of a large fishing boat that was making a clumsy docking with a large catch of flapping fish.

And fish is really what this zany little place is all about. Scattered everywhere around the hundreds of lopsided shacks are ornate little temples, door shrines, and painted posters pleading to the gods for bountiful harvests of fish, shrimp, abalone, squid, and even shark, whose dried fins and tails sell for enormous sums in tiny stores along the winding bazaar. I watched one bargaining session in progress with a group of casually dressed merchants sitting in wicker chairs around a dozen shark appendages. The price was already at $3,000 (U.S.) and climbing! Some fish here are so valued for medicinal purposes that a single average-size specimen can sell for over $800 (U.S.).

The whole village was redolent with drying shrimp (Tai O is famous for the quality of its shrimp paste), conch, tuna, and dozens of other denizens of the deep hanging like stalactites from store awnings. Combine this with the sight of thin golden sheets of drying tofu, drying seaweed strips, mounds of silvered whitebait, and enticing aromas from seafood restaurants offering just about every imaginable kind of shellfish and huge sea bass you pick yourself from crowded window tanks—and Tai O is one of those special places that lingers in the mind and on the palate for years.

But Buddha must have known of my need for sensory and gustatory relief. By evening I found myself on a wheezy old bus being carried up impossible grades high into the hills again to spend some time at the Po Lin Monastery. I had seen signs boasting of the construction here of "the tallest outdoor bronze Buddha statue in the world," but in spite of an impressive ceremonial staircase and massive marble plinth on a hilltop by the monastery, there was little evidence of activity. (Funds had apparently run out.)

THE PO LIN MONASTERY
— Lantau Island

As soon as I entered the imposing stone gates, I found a tranquil haven of peace where I remained for what seemed like a modest eternity, among the temples, statues, and shrines. I intended to climb Fung Wong Shan Mountain with the monks to watch the sunrise; I planned to have long and convoluted philosophical discussions with the two bearded travelers who had drifted in, but somehow the tranquility of the place seemed to remove all desire for diversion.

Well—until the following day at least when I met a lanky man with a vast frazzle of sun-bleached hair—while piling my plate with all kinds of unusual vegetarian delights in the communal dining room. He had come unexpectedly to this quiet place a few days previously and had decided to stay awhile.

"I don't know what it was. Just a feeling that I was in the right place—like somewhere I'd been coming to for a hell of a long time."

Mike was not one of your religious dabblers—collectors of spiritual shards of knowledge, scrapbooking through the options of Zen, Buddhism, Hinduism, and a dozen or so other more esoteric "isms." I met them all the time on my travels and was often charmed at first by their newfound enthusiasms, their guru-gushings and patinas of centered calmness. Then I'd discover after long conversations that they were invariably as confused and anxious to nail down their spirits as most of us are, to define the edges of experience too precisely, to snigger at the unenlightened with the selfish smugness of eager disciples willing away their souls to the newest—or nearest—guru.

Mike was forty-three. A tall, tough Aussie adventurer, sinewed with life-on-the-road experiences, etched with a thousand traveler's travails and brimming with tales that made my toes curl with envy.

And Mike had the spirit of a child.

Behind the hooded eyelids and bushy beard and leathery face was a baby sparkle, a hardly repressed joy in everything and everybody around him.

Our night-long dialogue in the tiny bedroom cell we shared (the monks believe in spatial economy even though we were the only overnighters at the temple) was as exciting as any in my journeys and adventures. We talked like kids—ideas rushing out of wild minds; new concepts whirling around us like confetti; truths tumbling over more truths in great piles of half-digested wisdoms. . . .

Looking back I see he helped me realize there are special moments when you acknowledge one of the givens of real travel —a desire to leave worldly distractions and allow the child inside to emerge again, open-eyed, open-mouthed, goo-gooing at the mysteries and magic of places unknown. A sudden shining of utter innocence; a rebirthing in the midst of strangeness; a rediscovery of recesses in the brain untouched, unexplored. The salve of spiritual serendipity.

The brain is so full of fun and wonder. Back in the "swinging sixties," rare (and invariably double-edged) dabblings with hallucinogens such as LSD, and other "consciousness-expanders" left me in awe of the mind's amazing resources. We all possess an Aladdin's cave of terrors and truths, memories and repositories of knowledge we never, never even suspected we possessed. Whole filing cabinets of the stuff, libraries; a Pandora's box of power and perception that most of us leave well enough alone.

Blasting through the barrage of "no entry" mind signs, you enter realms of untold riches, touching the infinities of the human spirit, discovering the links that tie us all together like tiny molecules in some enormous entity too vast to comprehend and yet—there! A dim recollection of prebirth embryo states? A reaching back to the knowingness of the newborn babe (Wordsworth's "streams of immortality"?). A desire to build again a new, surer foundation, to bring back the deepest perceptions to the blinkered grind of daily life?

But after all the excitement of such explorations, then come the dangers—the tolls of trespass. The fear of too much truth, too much new "reality," junking the petty patterns of half-lived lives. The alarming consequences of totally changed perceptions. A wish for safe pragmatism versus the bright lights of new being. The fear of losing what you have known and trusted for so long; the fear of never ever finding your way back to the comfortable confines of consistency and discipline and order and the "measured tread" of your previous life. The fear of a whole

new spectrum of options, choices, and possibilities—of unleash-
ing too much of the child again to romp and play and build anew
with new blocks of knowingness. Ah—there's the rub! What if it
was all wrong: what if the accumulated guilts, sorrows, pains
and pangs, beliefs and faiths of the years have only been bar-
riers—even comforting prisons—against the vast possibilities of
humanity and the harmonies of a far larger whole?

Would you want to dabble further? Would you wish to continue the journey or rest in a safe haven? Would you prefer not
to know at all? I'm still trying to answer such questions.

Mike left the cell early in the morning, when it was still dark, to
climb nearby Fung Wong Shan Mountain and watch the sunrise.
I'd planned to go with him but sleep finally came after hours of
conversation and he must have decided to let me rest.

Later I waited for his return, but he stayed up on the mountain or maybe moved deeper into Lantau. I was disappointed.
There was much more I wanted to talk about, to learn from this
particular traveler. But travelers tend to keep traveling on, allow-
ing things to happen as if ordained by a higher power. And that
was fine. I was happy for him and his freedom. I was happy for
the life-child inside him, the child he'd shown me; I was delighted by the child he'd rereleased in me.

I listened to the tape of one of our disjointed, rambling conversations and realized what a strange literary man I'd met, too.
He had a great admiration for William Blake and quoted him
extensively:

In your bosom you bear your heaven and earth and all you
behold; though it appears without, it is within . . . spirit
is in its nature holy because it is life, bliss, energy,
the desire to be of the creative principle.

He blamed so much of today's worldly problems—particularly in the West—on "the wrenching apart of the eternal mind
—a shrinking of humanity from the boundless being of
imagination into a mortal worm of sixty winters and seventy
inches long" (Blake again).

Mike seemed to regard his fellow Aussies as "spiritual savages" (then a little T. S. Eliot) "distracted from distraction by distraction." He added his own: "sham lives disguised by wealth and fashion." And Yeats: "Men are born to die with their great thirst unslaked."

"We're now far too scientifically 'clever' to be able to survive without wisdom," he'd said sometime in the early hours and then paraphrased Salvador Dali: " 'in a world dominated by "techne" we need the forces of psyche to restore the balance,' " and dropped in a fragment of Louis Sullivan: " 'the world is filled with knowledge; it is almost empty of understanding.' "

I found some of his conclusions depressingly negative. While it's easy to be critically glib at some of the more garish outrages of man, particularly Western man, I can't resist a bubbly optimism. I told him of a recent visit to Disney World's Epcot Center where, in spite of all the hype and rosy-colored collages of our collective future, I came away feeling, Hey! maybe we've all got a chance after all. . . .

Mike was cautionary: "Look—the greatest gift you can give the world is your own growth into consciousness.

"But that doesn't have to be at the exclusion of all the potentials we're creating. It took evolution a billion years to change things that we can change in one generation now—or less. Hopefully for the better."

He quoted someone else, I've forgotten who: "The worthiest of men retire from the world to an inner world."

"That's fine," I said, "but remember this bit of something I read last week: 'The key has always been/in your hand,/to open the door,/that you've been raging round the world/always looking for.' You don't have to stay 'raging round.' The world needs you, everyone, to bring back a deeper—a wiser—context for all the possibilities." Then I got in one of my favorite Henry Ford quotes: " 'Each man must live up to his potential for each man has God inside him.' "

"Okay," he said. "Here's another bit of Yeats for you: 'Sometimes I hate reasonable people; the activity of their brains sucks all the blood out of their hearts.' "

"But this *is* heart stuff. I'm not intellectualizing. I really believe that we're on the verge of making the world an amazing place to live in. You've got to be careful about getting stuck too

417

far 'within,' y'know; that thing that Graham Greene said about 'the universal desire to see a little bit further before the surrender to old age and the blank certitude of death.' Fear of the finite can make hermits—or hedonists—of us all!"

"No one expects any more than that we be discreet in our abominations."

"Who said that?"

"God knows." He looked at my serious face and laughed, "I'm joking, y'know. What you're trying to say is, keep a balance; do something with what you bring back. Right?"

"Right."

"Yeah. I suppose that makes sense."

"You really think so?"

"Surely. It's just that there's so much—inside."

"That's great. But it doesn't have to stop you operating—outside."

"Well, let's take you," he said. "You're wandering the world, free as a fly—what do you bring back?"

"Well, I write and illustrate books on my travels. I try to share something of what I've seen and learned—and felt. And, whenever I can, I give Anne help in her work in the field of international blindness. I was an urban planner for god knows how long and . . ."

"Well, okay, yes, all that's great but don't forget your Yeats," he said, still smiling. " 'The best lack all conviction while the worst are full of passionate intensity.' "

"Here's a bit of your Yeats back at you. Surely the balance is the individual who explores both dimensions—inside and out—'a person in whom the center has held.' "

He was honest. "I'm still looking for the center. I'm still on the inside."

So I was honest. "I am too—I often feel like a small boy playing on the edge of an ocean of truth'—that's Peter Matthiessen, by the way. But I can't put everything on hold until I find it."

"Show me a satisfied man, and I'll show you a failure."

"Yes, but what about a happy man?"

"Happy?"

"Yes, happy. You remember happy?"

He roared with laughter like a child. "You mean happy like in dumb blissfulness?"

"In a way—assuming that most of us are all pretty dumb in the great scheme of things. And bliss is a pretty nice thing to have while we keep bumbling along."

"Who said that?" he asked.

"I did."

"I may quote you on that."

"No more damned quotes. . . ."

But he was off again: "Ah, would that we might drift forever into the dreams we dreamed tonight. . . ."

(And so on . . .)

I'm not really sure how many days I spent at the monastery, watching the monks, in their gentle rituals, joining with them for their vegetarian meals, and listening to the temple bullfrogs, chortling and burping in the evening like little mud-happy Buddhas. But even now, deep in dreams, come sounds of cymbals and chanting and the long echoing booms of the gongs. . . .

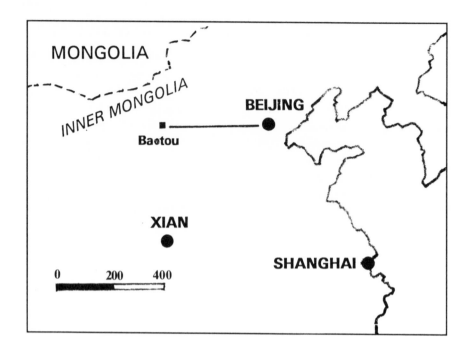

19. CHINA—THE CHINA FLYER

To the Back of Beyond by Train

Absolute chaos!

You wonder if the riders on the seventeen-hour overnight *China Flyer* special from Beijing to Baotou are embarking on some month-long migration to the back of beyond where starvation is rampant and drought assured. For over an hour now the hundreds of passengers crammed on benches and occupying most of the floor and the waiting hall of Beijing's central station (just down the hill from the Forbidden City) have been checking, packing, and repacking their bags and boxes of food, their bottles of beer and flagons of rice liquor *maotai* ("liquid razor blades" is a popular simile). As soon as they discover a tad more space in their bulging sacks they're off to the stores again to buy more

420

dim sum, paste-filled buns, pink cakes with jade green icing, candy bars in fluorescent wrappers, jars of fruits and pickles.

The four of us watch bemusedly, me, Ed Duffy from Los Angeles (a self-made Chinese trader), and our two Chinese guides who are accompanying us to explore the more remote parts of Inner Mongolia.

Duffy is dumbfounded. But there again he's always got that dumbfounded look even after ten years in the import-export business, as if the ways of China are totally beyond his comprehension but worthy of diversionary amusement nonetheless. Our guides, Yves and Barney (their Chinese names are unpronounceable), possess permanently out-to-lunch smiles. I asked Yves if he had bought food and he replies slowly and complacently: "I haave nooooles." (I later discover the man is a noodle freak. He eats nothing but noodles. If there are no noodles around, he'd rather starve.) Barney, on the other hand, never seems to eat at all and just sips tea out of his own personal glass jar in a kind of nipple-sucking stupor.

Then an odd thing happens. It appears to me that, since this is my first time on a Chinese train, the other passengers obviously know far more than I do about the necessities of travel. So my amusement turns to concern and I join the throng, standing up at the stalls, cramming the little bags of food into my pockets, even buying a liter bottle of maotai (twenty-five cents!) in case the night ride is cold. Duffy still looks dumbfounded; Barney and Yves smile at me vacantly. But I feel more secure now. I'm ready for the journey too.

Beijing begins to pall after four days. I feel guilty even thinking this; it had been a childhood dream to visit this mystery-shrouded city, and I never found out why the actuality didn't quite live up to the fantasy. Maybe it was the sprawling vastness of the place. Maybe I'd been spoiled by hustle-bustle Shanghai with its crowded vitality and Chicago-style grittiness.

My journey actually began boisterously in Shanghai, a vibrant port city, as I dodged constant armadas of bicyclists and frolicked through two days of dining at noodle shops and *dai pai dong* (stalls selling delicious stuffed dumplings for five cents a plateful), watching street barbers and elderly residents of the old

421

walled city basking in bamboo armchairs and kids practicing calligraphy on little sidewalk desks, amazed by the frantic antics of live turtles, crabs, eels, mantis shrimp and water snakes in the outdoor fish markets, peering into mysteriously dark herbalists' stores where mixes of stags' antlers, caterpillars, dried frog, lizard tails, and ginseng were mortared-and-pestled into powdered "Herculean potency" remedies for "listlessness, debilitation of the lower limbs, and concerns of the sexual impotency."

Beijing in comparison seemed a little too inscrutable. Unlike Shanghai it didn't really feel a walking kind of place, except in the magnificent Forbidden City itself, which tells you so much about the old China—Rococo riches amid abject peasant poverty; celestially inspired harmony and order in an apparently ungovernable nation of vast deserts, impassable mountain ranges, and far too many people on far too little usable land.

The city was a totalitarian dream of grand monumentality with hidden human undertones. Broad boulevards, enormous ceremonial squares, and shady parks fringed by ancient temples contrast with the intensely intimate *hutungs* (alleys) where families live in almost identical three-room houses set in high-walled courtyards. Here the constant sounds and aromas of cooking (how the Chinese love their food!) and the liquid trills of caged canaries conjured feelings of domestic underpinnings and stability in this imperious capital city. I wandered, unchecked, among the gamblers, the old herbal stores, the endless ranks of parked bicycles, and found the human side much more enjoyable than the great boulevards and vistas of palaces and temples. After four days I was happy to leave and curious about the upcoming seventeen-hour train ride.

The great gates to the station platform are pulled back and chaos reigns again as we are rushed by the crowd, trying to locate our soft-sleeper compartment. After much deliberation about the relative merits of the three classes of rail travel—hard seat, hard-sleeper, and soft-sleeper—we had erred on the side of luxury and purchased the appropriate array of tickets at three different windows.

Then we almost lost them. We forgot you have to make a laborious journey back to the station to reconfirm your tickets even though we had only acquired them two days previously. Poor Yves offered to make the trek; it took him five and a half hours.

A stern-faced female guard in a loose-fitting green uniform (everyone in China seems to wear oversized clothes) led us to our tiny comparment and announced: "This is where you will stay. Please do not move from here."

To emphasize the point she closed the door firmly behind her. It was stiflingly hot. Duffy tugged open a reluctant window. Immediately the door opened again and our guard strode between scattered bags and suitcases and pulled it shut.

"Window not open till we leave station," she said loudly.

Duffy looked even more dumbfounded. Our two guides just sat nursing their smiles. I was the troublemaker. "We need one open window or door. Preferably both," I said.

The woman spoke slow English but understood everything. She garotted me with a glance. But she left the door open.

A minute later two of the prettiest girls I had seen in Beijing knocked gently on the door and offered us a three-foot-high Thermos flask decorated with pink painted primroses. Barney and Yves smiled; the girls placed it in the center of a small window table along with a jar of fresh daisies.

Barney immediately became animated in a kind of blank-eyed way. It was like watching a robot at work. From his bag he pulled out an empty jelly jar with a screw lid. From the top pocket of his shirt he withdrew a plastic bag of something very illicit looking. (Marijuana in China?) But it turned out to be a far more precious leaf. The aroma of black China tea with jasmine and ginger overtones filled the compartment. From another pocket he drew a spoon and carefully measured the tea into the jelly jar. Then he moved to the Thermos flask, opened up a small tap near its base, and out poured the hot water. When the jar was three-quarters full he turned off the water, sealed the jar, turned it twice to mix the tea, and set it beside him on the seat to infuse. He must have been the happiest man on the train.

Yves, who had been watching the whole process impatiently then turned to his bag, pulled out a porcelain bowl and a plastic container bulging with what looked like huge white worms. (Duffy was doing his dumbfounded bit again.) He scooped a

handful of the worms into the bowl, opened a little brown enve-
lope he carried in a separate bag, poured a little white powder on
the worms, and then held the lot under the Thermos tap. A pair
of chopsticks appeared from nowhere; he stirred the mixture
twice, sniffed it, and began putting the worms into his mouth
with the chopsticks in a grotesquely hedonistic manner.

"Noodles?" I asked.

"Nooooles," mumbled Yves. "I laav nooooooles."

Duffy and I decided to start on the maotai. It was going to
be a long journey.

At 3:32 P.M. precisely the train pulled out of Beijing. Steam billowed by the window. Women, selling more of those spongy
buns and lunch packs of cold rice and sliced pork in plastic
boxes, made a last desperate pitch before being rounded up and
removed by the guards. We flung open our windows and the
cool air rushed in along with the steam. Almost immediately a
waiter was at our door to discuss dinner. I say "discuss" because
this was no mere "first sitting" or "second sitting" query; he invited our full participation in deciding the precise contents of our
evening meal, including the nuances of the sauces to be served
with the chicken and the pork entrées, the size and range of side
dishes, the required liberality of seasonings, the type of tea, and
(at Yves's insistence), the thickness and consistency of the noodles. By the time he left we were all salivating with expectation.
All except dumbfounded Duffy, who decided it was time to liven
up the party with more maotai and ribald tales of his ten years as
a China trader.

The train got off to a rip-roaring start, rocking through the
suburbs of Beijing (endless brick kilns and half-built gray brick
houses with gray pantile roofs, set in identical walled courtyards). Then we raced on into green rice paddy plains, wispy
trackside poplar trees flishing by (that's the sound they made,
flish, flish . . .), miles of paddies, like green quilts edged by a
blue border of hazy hills; people in the fields—hundreds of
them—bent double in strange lampshade hats, wading through
the mud, tending each bean shoot like a vine. Every inch of land
was used. Yves watched intently.

"My father did," he said.

"Your father was a paddy man?" I asked.

"Bad back. Finished now. Collects eggs."

I can imagine. Hours every day, bent like that.

Barney slurped his tea from the jelly jar, with closed eyes. Then the pace slowed. For no reason apparent to us, the train suddenly slackened its furious pace and for the next two hours we began a stop-start sequence that left us all sweating and swearing at the ineptitude of the Chinese railroad authorities.

A girl came to refill our Thermos from an enormous tin kettle shrouded in a pea-green cozy. We were all so annoyed by the slow pace that we didn't even smile at her. Barney had seen it all before. He opened one eye: "We arrive on time. Every time. No problem."

He closed his eye and went back to sleep.

There's a commotion. People are hurrying up and down the corridor. A whistle blows. The train speeds up. Ahead I can see a range of mountains rearing like a black tidal wave out of the plain.

"The wall," mumbles Duffy. "It's the wall."

And it was the wall. The Great Wall of China. All ten and one-half seconds of it as we peered through the steam at the ancient sinuous monument snaking up and down a series of rocky hills. Then it was gone.

"That was a bit quick," I grumbled, hoping I'd managed at least one blurry photograph.

"You'll learn." Duffy smiled complacently. "Only slows down when it gets boring. Goes like the clappers when there's something worth seeing."

Dinner was a feast and, for ninty-five cents a head, one of the best bargains in the world. After an enormous porcelain bowl of aromatic broth flecked with tree ears, the dishes just kept coming: chicken with celery and black mushrooms; tiny pungent shrimp with mustard greens, large medieval-banquet-size slabs of broiled lamb, yellow and green beans in soy sauce, wonderful fried potatoes glazed with a sugar-candy coating, stewed duck with bok choy, glazed pork casserole with white slivers of melon. Admittedly the flavors lacked the spicy richness of U.S. cosmopolitan restaurants, but there was an honest earthiness to the gravylike sauces. After five stop-go drowsy hours on the train, eating came as a joyous diversion. Fellow passengers grinned at our enthusiastic devouring of platter after platter. They passed us bits of their own special foods: little bottled sauces brought lovingly from home, pungent pickles, a lemony spice that gave the rice piquancy, a soy-and-sesame-oil concoction with the sear of Szechuan pepper, thick squashy dumplings with delicious pork and black bean centers.... We responded with cigarettes, ballpoint pens, maotai, and a slab of Hershey's chocolate, which was passed from hand to hand like the finest Russian caviar.

Evening shimmers of sunset across endless miles of rice paddies. Figures silhouetted purple against translucent patches of light. A filigree of poplars through the warm air. In the soft-seat compartment the telling of long tales, high-pitched laughter from a crowd of white-shirted Chinese businessmen, slow careful card dealing, smoky shadows next to a flooded bathroom, women in blue uniforms sweeping, always sweeping, and bringing more hot water for the giant Thermos flask.

I sneak down the train to the hard-seat carriage, avoiding the female guards, who love to pounce on wanderers with official glee. The noise increases in the hard-sleeper section (more offers of maotai, cigarettes, and dumplings steaming in hot water) and reaches true cacophony in the hard-seat. Smoke, the smell of cooking food, singing, shouting, spitting of melon seeds, belching, and smiles. Miles of smiles. Bright teethy (and toothless) grins and deep guffaws as I burn the inside of my mouth with a modest-looking dim sum laced with liquid fire. For a few moments I feel aloof from it all, but very soon I become part of the throng: a man shows me his winning hand of cards hidden behind his yellow nicotine-stained fingers; dice players seem hypnotized by the constant click of their grubby cubes; another pulls back a bright red shawl from a baby and shows me the most placid of cherubic faces, plump and pink cheeked; someone gives me half an orange neatly trimmed, each segment open like a flower; an ancient man with thin wisps of gray beard flings back the top of a straw basket to reveal four snow-white ducks,

426

trussed and teary eyed (he smacks his lips and sniffs deeply as if he can already taste them!).

Duffy had described the hard-seat area as halfway between a cattle truck and a college bean feast. John Belushi would have loved it. One cry of "Food-fight!" and the place would have blown wide open. Another sticky bun appears in my palm. I'm beginning to love it all. . . .

A hand on my shoulder. Not a friendly hand. Two female Schwarzeneggers block the aisle and stare at me with outraged grimaces. No "be-friendly-to-foreigners" attitude here. They make it very clear I'm in alien territory. One has her notebook out. I'm going to get ticketed for trespassing? The larger one of the two points back the way I came. Everyone in the carriage is laughing. I start laughing too. Glasses of maotai are raised in salute. I lift my sticky bun in farewell and obediently follow the guards back to the quiet cocoon of my soft-sleeper. They berate Yves and Barney, who look very serious and guilty, like naughty schoolkids. I can see my guides are losing face rapidly. I turn on all the charm I can muster, hold the hands of the two guards, look downcast, and bow a little and mumble inanities softly. That seems to calm them. I look for some token of my atonement, and all I can find are two ballpoints stamped with a U.S. gas company logo. I mumble some more inanities, give them the pens, and they seem confused about what to do next. A final half-hearted reprimand. I smile a last apology. They both smile back and close the door firmly behind them. Duffy opens one eye and laughs. "You got further than most." Barney and Yves ask me not to do it again and resume their tea-sipping stupor.

The last gashes of sunset now. We pass small dusty villages of tightly packed houses, each with a little red sign above the door. "That one says 'Have a happy marriage,' " Yves tells me. "That one 'We love our new son.' " Two cyclists pedaling home pass an old man leading two oxen with enormous horns. Tiny tractors like overgrown lawn mowers return from the long lines of paddies, leaving trails of scarlet dust. A huge moon rises over low purple hills. . . .

Sleep comes easily on our hammocky beds. Through the night I half remember stops and starts and occasional clusters of dusty people waiting under dim streetlights near lonely platforms. Beyond are more long plains bathed in moonlight.

Six A.M. and the loudspeakers begin. Marshal music followed by interminable announcements in Chinese over crackling loudspeakers. Maotai hangover time. Bathrooms (a euphemism for one john and one hand basin) have long waiting lines. Everyone's bleary-eyed and silent. We decide to have an early breakfast and then wonder why: It's only rice gruel in a chickeny stock with flecks of green, and sticky dough buns. Yves slurps away at his noodles. Barney sips tea. Duffy is still sleeping.

Outside, total transformation. No more rice paddies and villages and lines of poplars now. We are deep into desert. Vast vistas of a gravelly wilderness edged by golden dunes and hints of blue mountain ranges. Occasional glimpses of sheep and goats on barren hillsides cut by deep gullies. After the chaos and congestion of the city and the verdant intensity of the plains, this land feels emptier than anything I have ever seen before. An enormous sandy sun shines across all this nothingness—fringes of the great Mongolian grasslands.

Duffy wakes up, takes one look outside, grunts a long, "Oh gawd no," and covers his head with a gray-green Chinese railways regulation government blanket.

A young man steps in our door. "Please, I am student in Shanghai and would much like to practice my..." The green-uniform guards pounce like panthers, and that's the last I see of him.

An older man passes. We had spoken in slow English the previous evening. He is a teacher in Beijing and is coming home to Baotou for a few days' vacation with his family. He pauses at the door. "I wish I could invite you to the house of my father, but there is not time to get permission."

"You need permission?" I asked incredulously.

"Oh yes, of course. And usually they say no. Especially away from the city..."

"What happens if I just turn up?"

He looked startled. "Oh no! There are too many people who watch...they tell...very difficult..."

We both smile sadly and shake hands.

428

Another station stop. Barney and Yves have been waiting for it. "Come, come," they insist, so we tumble out onto the chilly platform and rush to a tiny blue shack to buy hot, greasy pancakes filled with chopped vegetables and other intriguing bits and pieces. Yves brings out his special soy mixture and sprinkles it lavishly over our steaming slabs of dough. Further down vendors are selling oranges, hard-boiled eggs, cold chicken with rice, packages of dried white noodles (Yves, of course, buys an armload), and tiny jars of spiced pickles. The whistle blows, everyone crams back onto the train, guards whisk away the vendors like wastepaper, and we move on again into the bright new morning.

Our destination must be approaching. The loudspeaker is getting louder, women are coming through, sweeping floors (ours is an utter wasteland of discards but they don't seem to mind), removing Thermos flasks and spitoons, ordering the beds closed (Duffy sleeps on regardless).

Images are piling up again as we near the city: groves of delicate bamboo sway in the breeze; a soaring sandstorm way off to the east; flocks of dusty goats squeezing down the narrow lanes of a village of mud houses; a mule drawing a cart piled high with feathery desert scrub for kindling. Different kinds of faces here. More weathered, stronger—flickers of Ghenghis Khan and his conquering army of Mongol hordes.

Finally we arrive in Baotou and it's chaos once again. Everyone rushing to get out of the station before the crush. Duffy awakes and advises a relaxed approach. He drinks some of Barney's tea in a leisurely display of gentlemanly ease. The guards can't understand why we won't join the throng. . . .

Out into the main square. Crowds of people once again. High drab buildings decorated with red banners (but no posters of Mao). Street stores galore selling pickles, buns, cigarettes, maotai, and cookies. Street snack bars with white-hatted waiters serving rice gruel and dim sum breakfasts. More loudspeakers and marching music for a hundred railroad employees who do ritual exercises in front of the railroad offices. Huge volumes of steam from the locomotive that has pulled us from Beijing (they still build these great cast-iron creatures to run China's forty thousand miles of railroad); sidewalk displays of used Chinese

429

and Western magazines for sale; big billboards advocating one-child-only families (big fines for additional children plus official reprimands from local party comrades), also billboards of TVs, bikes, watches, radios (materialism is rife here and new bonus-incentive schemes for workers encourage "patriotic" consumerism). "Not too much, though, not too fast," one student told me in Beijing. "You must be careful. Official policy changes fast. You buy fancy things one week. Next week confiscated! People still remember the Red Guards." (All this was months before the Tiananmen Square debacle.)

A sudden glimpse of cracks in the social façade. People seem so placid and self-contained in the endless crowds of bicyclists pedaling to work. Then, one cyclist falters and brings down another behind and two more on either side. The flow is broken. Pent-up fury erupts instantly. Inscrutable faces turn furious and purple with rage. A hundred people suddenly shouting and cursing and blaming one another in utter confusion. A brief flurry of fists. Police and rail guards run and begin loud reprimands. No real damage to the bikes but a glimpse of hoarded anger. Frightening. Normalcy returns eventually, and the sea of cyclists waves on. Everyone seems calm again. Order has been restored.

Without strict control and imposed discipline one wonders what China might be—a nation of one billion creative dynamic live-wire capitalists or a place of utter social chaos? Maybe a bit of both. More recent events have proved the government's reluctance to take chances. "Democratic" freedom is anathema to totalitarian regimes.

Duffy has the last word as usual. "In China, nothing is what it seems. Especially nowadays." He smiles through black morning stubble and maotai eyes. Barney and Yves nod in agreement and wonder where to find more hot water for tea and noodles.

I can hardly wait for the next stage of our journey together, deep into Inner Mongolia.

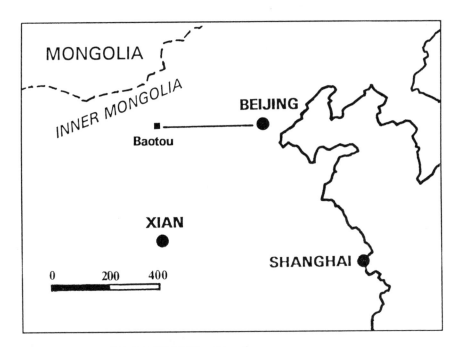

20. CHINA– INNER MONGOLIA

Yurts, Kangs, and Kashmir Goats

Silence in silver limbo.

I lay in the lee of a sandy hill. Spears of brittle grass rose from the still-warm earth and glowed in brilliant moonlight. I could see for miles across gently rolling plains—across the vast silvered silences below a canopy of black velvet, pinpricked by a billion stars.

A soft crunch and I turned. The man, silhouetted on the hillside, paused, spotted my movement and came down slowly. It was the commune secretary, an elderly individual of grace and almost constant humor, who had never stopped smiling since we arrived at this lonely herdsman's house in the heart of China's Inner Mongolian grasslands. He eased himself into the sand,

and we sat together without speaking for a long time, looking out into the glowing night.

Was I really here? The place—the whole experience—had an ethereal quality to it—the fulfillment of a fantasy. Somehow I had arrived in the heart of this mysterious, almost mythical, land that forms part of China's northern boundary for over eight hundred miles, a region the size of Texas (three times the size if you include Outer Mongolia to the north, now a separate nation within the USSR sphere of influence). From Hohhot, capital of Inner Mongolia, you can extend lines on a map to the north and west across deserts, mountain ranges, grassland plains, and steppes and never touch a major road, a city, or even a village for over two thousand miles!

Somehow, after a desert journey I'd gladly forget, I arrived at this lonely place in the middle of nowhere to spend time with the Mongolian descendents of the infamous Genghis Khan, one of those characters of history whose predeliction for cruel conquest during the fourteenth century filled my schoolboy lessons with bloodcurdling images. Somehow I'd been allowed in by the authorities after days of negotiation—the first Westerner to visit this "closed area" since the revolution of 1949. I'd come to see how people lived in these vast spaces. I'd come to meet the herdsmen, who endure torrid summers and the shrieking Siberian winds of winter when temperatures often sink to $-40°F$ or below, all for the sake of their precious (and very tough) Kashmir goats, whose silky underlying fleece produces the world-famous cashmere wool.

The commune secretary was still smiling as we sat looking across the endless horizons skimmed by moonglow.

At the top of the hill we returned to the world again. In a dip to our right a couple hundred white sheep and goats lay huddled together around a solitary tree (trees are as rare as people in this vast nowhereness). Ahead, the small three-room farmhouse was a flurry of noise, light, and activity. Figures scurried around inside the high-walled courtyard at the front of the house, hefting huge slabs of just-slaughtered sheep into the kitchen. Steam poured from two giant woks perched on furiously flaming coal stoves; the shy girl with brilliant red cheeks

432

and broad Mongolian face was obviously in charge and directed her helpers with Bernsteinlike bravado. (She only went shy outside the kitchen!) And from the living room came the now-familiar toasts of "ganbei!" as yet one more round of fiery maotai liquor—scorched a score of throats once again. And the scratching and yowling of strange stringed instruments—the morin khour, hugin, and erhu—and the wail of the bamboo flute accompanied yet another plaintive "long song," sending it soaring into the night through the bright candlelit windows.

On the raised platform, or *kang*, which stretched fifteen feet from wall to wall at the far end of the room, sat the motley members of our expedition—Ed Duffy, China trader, self-proclaimed "King of Cashmere" and raconteur extraordinaire, our interpreters Yves and Barney (very Anglicized versions of their unpronounceable Chinese names), Tony from the Dongsheng cashmere factory, and our silent driver—all humming a discordant harmony as Etu, the singer, pushed her sad notes higher and higher and the two-stringed hugin fiddle screeched its closing chords.

"Duffy-sing, Dawi-sing! Sing, sing!"

So once more Duffy and I launched into ribald, half-remembered choruses of old sixties party favorites plus the inevitable "Skip to m'Lou," which they loved best of all but could never quite make the words sound right ("Sip-u-mee-oo" was about as close as they got. Visiting anthropologists will one day ponder this odd fragment of dialect.) And they clapped and we clapped and the songs raced faster and faster and the candles trembled as twenty strident voices blasted out the inane lyrics into this night-to-end-all-nights in the middle of nothingness—lost in the great grasslands and loving every second of it.

Getting here in search of the Kashmir goat herdsmen had been a long and arduous process. The journey was planned with the precision of a Napoleonic campaign but invariably suffered from those interminable delays and frustrations that seem an integral part of travel in China, if you are determined, as I was, to resist standard tourist itineraries.

"Everything's just fine," we were told as we left the *China Flyer* train after the seventeen-hour night ride in "soft-sleeper" to

Baotou on the fringe of the grasslands. "You're off tomorrow," they said as we drove another one hundred miles across a Saharan wilderness of magnificent golden dunes to Dongsheng—and the first of our logistical roadblocks.

Someone in authority had realized that my route entered "closed areas" and suggested we make do with a visit to the special tourist "nomad camps" of traditional felt and canvas yurts (Disneyesque collections of herders' tents set on concrete plinths with all modern facilities!), a couple of camels, some wrestling, and maybe horse-racing if the weather's good. "Very good photos—very much color," we were told.

"Sorry," I insisted. "We've come to see the *real* Inner Mongolia. We want to stay with a real herdsman—yurts or no yurts!" It didn't seem a lot to ask, but to the Chinese authorities it was an outrageous proposition.

"These areas are closed. There has been a mistake. Have some tea."

In this country where "face" is a key factor of communication, no one likes to say "no" outright!

And so the meetings began, sixteen in all, and we became increasingly depressed. Finally, on the third day, as we waited for the ultimate "no" to be pronounced, in walked the local chief of security police and declared that we may go where we wished and that special passes would be issued immediately.

"You are very lucky," he told us as we toasted one another's endurance. "You are going somewhere that has never been opened to Westeners before. You will see many things. You will remember this journey."

How right he was.

Out, out, and even further out. Across eroded hills, over vast areas of dunes, salt flats, and high steppes where wild horses roamed the horizons, silhouetted against burning skies. Out where the road became a track, then a vague marking in the soft earth, and then nothing but an improvised line of sight across dry hardscrabble grasslands. Out across more than three hundred backside-flattening miles of empty country into the unknown, to find the herdsmen and a place to rest for a while. We were a happy and expectant bunch of explorers and quite unprepared for our next challenge.

It began innocently enough—brief buffetings of breezes from the north and the prattle of blown sand on the side of the Jeep. Then—almost imperceptibly—the sun began to take on halos, a series of strange golden rings in a gradually yellowing sky. Dust devils whirled up in the distance, first one, then four simultaneously, then a whole stretch of grasslands spinning skyward in a swirling column.

We all became quiet. The driver sat up straight and tightened his grip on the wheel. Then the sun disappeared. Just like that, it vanished in a strange beige mist and sand began blowing in through the open windows. "Uh-oh!" groaned Tony. "A blooty sandstorm." (Tony always had problems with his *d*s). In less than a minute visibility was down to yards, and a gale came howling straight across our path, blowing the sand horizontally. We closed all the windows. The heat became unbearable and fine dust still billowed through. Sweat streamed down our faces in brown rivulets. The track—hardly more than a path—kept disappearing, and telltale tiremarks ahead were quickly obliterated. At one point we almost ran straight into a dune, until we realized that the dune itself was actually moving across the track in front of us, driven on by the furious wind. The driver's face was as set as stone. Somehow we kept on moving. Six times we hit soft sand and labored out with four-wheel drive. No one talked —we all watched for signs of the route and willed on our silent driver.

"We must not stop," Tony broke the silence. "Neber" (Tony also had problems with his *v*s). But fate had other plans.

We stopped as abruptly as hitting a barn door. We had lost the track and slid into talcuum-soft sand. This time the superdrive failed, and we sank deeper.

"Out—push" said Tony, and we knew it was the only way.

The next few minutes are as imprinted on my mind as the "sand burns" were on my body. We heaved and gasped and heaved again in that mad maelstrom. The wind was blastfurnace hot and the sharp sand filled every pore. We were five deaf, blind, suffocating creatures, hardly human, struggling to push the heavy Jeep out before the newly drifting sand sealed

435

her even deeper. We were motivated by an increasingly real fear of being stuck and cut off by dunes without supplies in this howling wilderness.

Somehow we did it. Somehow we found the track and somehow we got out of that place. And just before we left I looked behind and saw, like ghostly shadow puppets, the faint silhouettes of two camels moving together through the fury ... I called to the others and we all turned. But they were gone.

And the party rolled on at the herdsman's house in the middle of nowhere. After the sandstorm, fate was kinder to us, and by evening we had found the perfect place to stay—this small brick house in a hollow with a family whose welcomes and kindnesses never ceased.

We had become celebrated guests of honor, a sheep had been killed for us in the courtyard (it is customary to watch the ritual but I invented some lame excuse and didn't), and, as we sprawled like Arabian potentates on the cushions and rugs spread across the kang, we could smell the meat—the whole animal—cooking in the adjoining kitchen.

And the dancing and the songs continued with no letup in pace or enthusiasm. I remember one Mongolian long song with the most beautiful words:

> I am a small flower hidden in the grass
> The spring winds let me breathe and grow high
> I live in the mountains and in the grassland
> The grassland is my mother
> I love Mongolia—I am Mongolia.

"In Mongolia," the pretty red-cheeked girl from the kitchen explained, "a person who cannot play the flute or the morin khour or sing the songs of this land is not alive—is not human —is not Mongolian! And," she added with a serious frown, "I am Mongolian, not Chinese. We are not Chinese!" She spat out the last word.

Then she whispered to her friend, who was also acting as our interpreter. "She wants to know if she can touch your beard.

436

She has never seen a West-man before. She has never seen a red beard!"

So the apple-cheeked girl stroked my beard with her plump fingers, blushed even more brightly, and scurried back into the kitchen to supervise the cooking. Her friend laughed, as did the others around the table. Then she leaned over and whispered: "They are very happy you are all here . . . they are very glad you come."

The night was full of moments like this. One song was so sad it left us all teary-eyed—even the singer; another was so loud and clap-happy that our palms blistered; a third, a rowdily erotic drinking song, transformed our placid driver into a raging romeo with a Mario Lanza voice and a lust for the pretty female duetist as big as his larynx.

Our herdsman-host at one point invited me to look at the old photographs of his family and relatives hanging in large frames on the wall next to a brightly painted red-and-green chest of drawers, one of the few pieces of furniture in the house. He led me outside into the moonlight to stand by the shrine to his ancestors, decorated with banners and ribbons and the remains of offerings. It stood like an altar just beyond the courtyard door, guarded by two silvered replicas of Genghis Khan's trident spear—the prime symbol of Mongolian identity and pride.

Then a great shout went up. It was 2:30 A.M. and the tiny house roared once again into frantic activity; people ran around with fresh bottles of maotai, gleaming plates, huge Mongolian meat knives, and baskets of fat white bread buns. "Sit-sit-sit!" we were told. "It's coming!"

And so—it came!

A mountain of meat emerged on a platter the size of a car hood; thigh-size chunks of juicy mutton piled up pyramid-fashion and covered with the sheep's fatty back (rear end pointing toward me as guest of honor!), topped by the whole head, eyeballs, horns—the lot—smiling through billows of steam and the whole vast display dripping deliciously. . . .

I cut the first slice with a ritual knife, and then it was a free-for-all as twenty ravenous revelers tore the exquisitely tender "finger mutton" from the bone and scooped moist meat into

437

INNER MONGOLIA
GRASSLANDS

mouths sore with songs and scorched from over seven hours of toastings.

And what a feast it was, flowing on and on into early dawn with that special camaraderie that comes from unexpected mutual enjoyment and excitement. At around 5:00 A.M. bodies collapsed one by one onto the kang; herdsmen, their wives, children, commune leaders, all of us, shoeless and serene, for two hours of deep sleep before breakfast.

Blurry-eyed, we awoke and washed in an enamel bowl in the courtyard. The sun was already warm and over the wall, I could see the goats beginning their never-ending search for grass across the hazy hills.

Bowls of mare-milk tea came to the table on the kang along with dishes of hard yellow millet, sweet yak butter (*souyou*), a golden pile of fried dough, and tooth-cracking cookies baked from yogurt and flour. Amid elaborate mixings of tea, millet, and souyou (stirred with the little finger), we slurped in unison, as was obviously the custom. Someone sprinkled the earthen floor of the room with water to keep the dust down and removed a couple of errant chickens wandering in from the courtyard. The women were busy as usual, cleaning, feeding a sick foal, checking the herd, milking the goats and horses (fermented mare's milk is used to make the potent *airag* drink of the herdsmen), and removing traces of the previous night's revelries. The men sat quietly, slurping endless bowls of tea, smoking ferocious little Mongolian cigarettes, and talking quietly to us about the old days in the grasslands.

We were curious about changes in the nomadic traditions of the herdsmen. Once the great grasslands were full of wandering groups of families with their herds of sheep and goats, living in ingenious round yurts made of layers of felt, canvas, and hides stretched over wood-lattice frames. They would select temporary camps, as many as ten different sites a year across the immense plains and ranges, moving their flocks, horses, and camels through sunny summer days and furious winter blizzards. The famous Kashmir goats were renowned for their endurance and the silky quality of their underlying fleece, which retained

440

warmth in conditions that would freeze a man to the marrow in minutes.

"Oh, we still have our yurts," our host told us. "Smaller ones though now. Normally we don't need them, the grasslands are better irrigated and most families build houses nowadays and stay in one place. Sometimes though, if the rain is late, like this year, we send the younger men off with the herd to new pastures, and they live in the small tents. But it's mostly communes now—there are around eight hundred families in our commune."

We looked out over the vast empty spaces beyond the courtyard.

"Ah!" He laughed. "You won't see many of them! We live a long way apart, we're quite independent, but for certain things we all come together. Particularly for weddings and the big festivals—we come together for the wrestling and the racing—and the maotai. There are over ten million people in Inner Mongolia, but you'll hardly see any. Strangers don't realize—they can't imagine—just how far these grasslands go. For hundreds of miles"—he stretched his arms as wide as he could and smiled gently to himself—"hundreds of miles..."

His smile was a smile we came to know well with these people. We called it the "Genghis Khan grin"—a proud knowingness of the immensity of their land, a smell of freedom in the wild unchecked winds, a sense of "possessing the whole earth," which must have given the great conqueror and his Mongol hordes the grand visions of world domination that they essentially achieved during the thirteenth and fourteenth centuries.

"We're just herdsmen now," said our host, but there was that flash in his eye that still sends shivers down the spines of the Han, China's primary racial group, who have been actively settling in these wild regions for decades to the point where they now form over eighty percent of the population.

I wondered about the two-humped Bactrian camels, once the main mode of transport in the grasslands.

"Many things are changing," they told us. "We still have our camels, but we let them wander for most of the year. We don't need them now to carry the fleece to the cities. They usually come home to birth and then leave again. We concentrate on our goats and sheep—these are our life."

Over the slow, easy days, we watched and became part of the steady rhythm of their lives. I sat cross-legged on the ground while the goats were combed for their precious white cashmere fleece, hardly more than four ounces per animal ("...takes at least twenty goats to make a good sweater"). I wandered with the younger herdsmen over the high windy hills and watched them use their pebble-throwing *yang-cha* sticks with unbelievable accuracy to keep their animals in check. I ate the hard *arul* cheese and drank airag for lunch in the bright midday sun.

And in the silences my mind would fall silent and become as vast as the spaces around me. It seemed that everything I saw was actually within me, within an all-enveloping mind—an eagle, alone and soaring on spiraling air, a flash of light on quartz crystals, a wisp of wind rattling the grasses, the crack of rocks splitting in the dry, hard heat. I had never sensed the power of silence so intensely: each object seemed wholly distinct and full of individual energy and yet totally a part of everything around me. And even my own body and spirit—for fleeting but seemingly infinite moments—became a part of the land in the vibrant wholeness of this magical place.

Eventually, we left, a lot more quietly and stilled in spirit than when we arrived. The herdsmen had allowed us to become part of their world for a brief period and to sense the slow, steady rhythms; the strong underpinnings of their lives. The ribbons on the ancestors' altar table waved in a warm breeze as we said our farewells, and the trident of Genghis Khan gleamed as bright as ever in the morning sun.

We headed off across the sandy hills; my mind was too full of feelings to talk, too full of excitement at what we had found, too full of anticipation for what was to come next. . . .

EPILOGUE
The Wildest Places of All

Time to fly.

The ground had held me too long.

I needed another landscape—a free-form topography of blue and white. I needed to float among the hammerheads, to ride the updrafts into a world beyond the grist and grind of the human merry-go-round—to leave the earth for a while and touch the wild places *inside* once again.

A friend had a plane, a tiny Piper Cherokee, forever tied down by a runway, too far out of town for casual jaunts. He dreamed of great journeys—an Atlantic crossing via Newfoundland and the Azores; a Pacific odyssey full of touchdowns on Robinson Crusoe Islands, a world circumnavigation with stops in all the forgotten places. But the plane just sat there, full of tantalizing possibilities, draped in dreams.

"America from Five Hundred Feet." What a splendid book idea excuse for this serendipitous photographic adventure. To bid farewell to the concrete calamities and the tawdry esthetics of the earthbound. To lift up, out, and off, leaping into infinities.

So we did.

I was proud of him. Beneath the careful man, clogged by schedules and mind-bound by meetings, I found the spirit of the boy, brimming with fantasies, clutching the cirrus tails, reaching out to touch new possibilities.

A small plane is pure magic. For what seems like forever, you're ticking off checklists, testing tires, tediously playing with dials and switches, deafened by the prattle and boom of the little engine, talking gibberish to robotlike voices in the tower, noting details about wind speed and air traffic and vectors and quirks of the ever-fickle weather. And then it's suddenly different. The runway skims by, the engine screaming in anticipation, the nose lifts, the seat springs groan and creak as your body weight doubles in that first thrust of flight, and—you're off. The ground drops away, becoming a rinky-dink, toy-town picture book of dollhouses and Matchbox cars and spongy trees and tiny white-spired churches.

The world is all yours. You can go anywhere, do anything. Turn left, turn right, fly in circles, climb, dive, do a somersault, loop a loop if you must, play peek-a-boo with clouds, chase a rainbow, tease a thunderhead, skim the spuming surf, kiss a mountaintop, make the long grasses wave like silky hair, roll your wings at a farmer in his field, bombard the cumulus galleons with their wind-ripped sails. Your spirit soars with the Cherokee; you feel light as duck down, free as a feather. And you remember, you know again, just how precious and perfect life and being alive can be. The high of the whole. The best high of all. Because it's true.

Look up and it's a pure Mediterrenean-blue dome, arching over to a golden haze. Look down and the patterns intermingle: the patchwork panels of fields, a random quilt of greens and golds and ochres; the pocket-comb geometrics and curlicues of

444

ploughed furrows; the silver-flashed streams; the Baroque tangles of woods and copses on humping hills; the sprinkle of villages along a tattered coastline ribboned with white surf. Gone are the gas stations and the hype lines of neon-decked motels and junk-food stands and auto showrooms and traffic lights and do-this do-that signs and billboards and all the gaudy excess of street-bound life.

This was a new world up here, fresh, bright, traffic free—and all mine! I wanted to shout down to farmers and tell them how beautiful their fields looked—bold abstract masterpieces of color and form that could grace the walls of any gallery. I saw lovely things: a single fishing boat with the shadow of a galleon, apexed in a flat pyramid of cut ocean; the fluid lines of submerged reefs, receding in filigreed layers from turquoise to the deepest of royal blues; moonscapes of gravel pits and quarries concealing pools of clear green water; the silty delicacy of estuaries edged by curled traceries of emerald marshes; Frankenthaler earth patterns of water absorption in fields of new wheat. It was an esthetic unfamiliar to me. A world of fresh beauty; juxtapositions of form, color, and texture I'd never imagined before.

Evening eased in slowly and seemed to last forever. As the sun slid down into its scarlet haze, we rose up to watch the shadows scamper across the rolling land. A modest line of trees following a winding country road cast quarter-mile-long shadows, purpling the furrows. Little hillocks produced mountain-sized echoes of themselves across the fields. Even a tiny white farm cluster of barns and outbuildings became a Versailles shadow, suggesting towers, turrets, and elegant cornices. Cows were giraffes, a tiny red truck became a triple-decker bus, a man heading for home across a bronze field was a stick-legged giant.

And when the night came, it came with grace in a slow canopy of velvety purple, sprinkled with stars. The west gave up its glow with reluctance and the night allowed a dignified retreat. An equitable ritual, well rehearsed over the eons. And we watched the gentleness of it all, floating easily in the evening air, not wanting to leave, reluctant to face the disordered scramble of earthly matters. So we flew on, abandoning ideas for a touchdown somewhere in the flatlands below us. Food and flight

445

plans, taxis, motels, and beds could all wait. The night invited us to stay and we accepted, watching it flow in, filling the lower places, rising up the flanks of the ranges, leaving little islets of light on the high tops for a while until they too were submerged in the purple tide as we floated on into the mysteries of the dark.

The tale of our odyssey across America from five hundred feet must be left to another time. It was a fascinating journey, a photographic record of esthetic experiences rarely matched by earthbound adventures. At the outset I had merely wanted to fly for a few hours, a few days, to get my world-wanderings in a fresh context and think of future directions for my life and travels. I had never expected to discover such new joys in the experience of flying itself—flying as an end rather than a means. My notebooks (rather shaggy things now, full of untidy scribblings, stained by spilled coffee and oil from a leaky engine pump) still tingle with a novice's sparkle-eyed euphoria:

—slow curling rivers—gentle essays in time—histories written clear on the earth: oxbows, old courses with the sinewy shadows of snakes; ancient lakes, now limpid marshlands with flurries of egrets rising to meet us

—spuming deltas with silt patterns like duck feathers; the thwack of midday sun on still water, gleaming like a new Porsche; forest-shaded curves where the bass lie cozy in the slow cool depths

—a range of snow-crusted peaks, seemingly another blending of cloud banks, then slowly taking on a sharper form of arêtes, ice ridges, and glacier-gouged ravines

—rising through gauzy morning mists, slipping off "the surly bonds of Earth," up into the purest blue that goes on forever.

—a swirl of silver-gold dunes, soft sensual curlings and rounded shadows—the pretty petticoats of shattered peaks

—the bare beige endlessness of sagebrush country, but also the strict patterning of the bushes, each occupying a precise and

446

evenly spaced territory, geometrics of logic rarely discernable on the ground

—faint radial scratchlines on a dry scorched land coalescing at a muddy brown waterhole in the middle of nowhere

—into canyons of cumulus, playing tag with the giant thunderheads, skimming the black tentacles of a storm column, feeling the life of this fleeting creature illuminated from within by its own lightning

—seeing our cruciform shadow, projected giant-size by the sun on the clouds, haloed in gold; suddenly from an insignificant speck we become manifest

—the unearthly solitude of flying above the clouds; it all belongs to me, utter limbo-land; the ultimate "I am"

—a sprinkling of ponds and little lakes, hardly visible at first across the dun Maine tundra, suddenly sparkling like scattered pearls, then neutered again as we fly on

—the gleam-sheened waterworld of the Atchafalaya bayous where the hard earth dissolves into droopy cypress swamps and blue-green blankets of reeds and fields of floating hyacinths

—jousting with the Arizona buttes, red-ochre remnants of ancient plateaus, pointing skinny fingers at the sky, chiseled reminders of time passing, skimming them with our wingtips

—close enough to see the flash of a vulture's eye—and then off again in wild trajectories, deeper into the wilderness, not wanting to leave this empty place; waiting to hear its secrets

—our shadow dancing over the swirl and switchbacking of the Utah wilderness; no roads, no tracks, no sign of human life for hours, a place left to play by itself, rejoicing in its sinewy contortions, raged up in tectonic fury, cracked open and flung apart by the elements, gashed and exposed—a warrior torso of a land, garlanded with ribbons of colored strata, crowned with shattered pinnacles and cooled by storms, roaring across its scoured belly and screaming through its broken teeth

—up here, floating, apart from it all, indivisible; a sense of greater perceptions—hierarchies of knowingness just beyond the next truth. Like the paradox of particle physics, never quite getting there, merely seeing deeper and deeper, space beyond space into the inner universe with its constellations of quarks (strange, charmed, and all those other multicolored entities), mesons, gluons, neutrinos, gravitons (and even antigravitons), matching the complexity and scale of the outer universe itself—an equilibrium of endlessness

—up here, floating, you see it all quite clearly. The clamor of experiences, the search for something forever out of reach, out of comprehension. Seeking the mind of God in the fragmentary illusions of everyday life, playing with *his* possibilities, cracking open the creaky walls of knowledge and flying out into pure beingness . . .

I wished it would all last forever. But it didn't, and finally we were back to the swelling hills of home, bosky with copses and stringy streams and things with associations, leaving all the wild places behind for a while.

But happy with a thought.

That the wildest places of all are deep within and there's no end to the exploration and enjoyment of their mysteries and magic.

And that is sufficient.

For the moment.

And finally, something I wrote a day or so after coming back home to Anne, the two cats and the lake. . . .

> Here
> Once again
> Smelling the grass above our lake
> (rippled now and then with turtle bobbings)
> and the burps of bullfrogs
> and the unraveling of silver clouds
> and the low pale light across the hills
> and the sun in the wings of dragonflies
> and the shaggy shadows of evening woods
> and the woolly-misted air

and the stalk-stiff herons, like meditating monks
and the bobbling butterflies
and the sound of beetles sucking sap in the fat leaves
and the wind, knobbly with raindrops
and all the warm familiarity of this piny place
glimmer-green and fusty with ancient wood rot
and Anne
boiling the kettle for a little tea-and-talk
between the books and books and books
and all the fresh expectations
of new perceptions
new journeys
new wild places
and another new today
tomorrow.

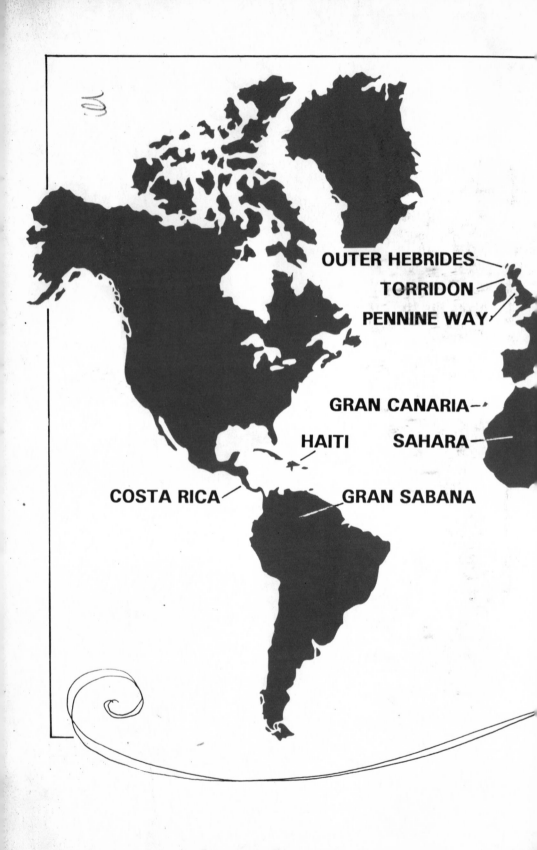